JEFFERSON

THOMAS JEFFERSON

Portrait by Rembrandt Peale

JEFFERSON

BY SAUL K. PADOVER

KONECKY&KONECKY

Konecky & Konecky
72 Ayers Point Rd.
Old Saybrook, CT 06475

Published by special arrangement with
Harcourt, Brace & Company

ISBN: 1-56852-417-X

Printed and bound in the USA

Acknowledgment

The author wishes to thank Harold D. Lasswell for reading a part of the manuscript and for many stimulating discussions on this and related subjects; William Cherin for some excellent suggestions; Isabel Ely Lord for checking the quotations with the sources; Ruth Cherin and Irina Raben for helping with the index.

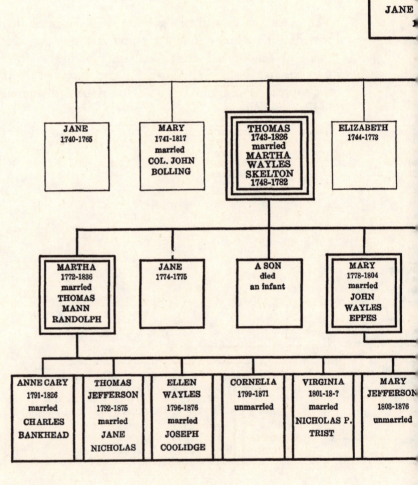

1
JANE

| JANE 1740-1765 | MARY 1741-1817 married COL. JOHN BOLLING | THOMAS 1743-1826 married MARTHA WAYLES SKELTON 1748-1782 | ELIZABETH 1744-1773 |

| MARTHA 1772-1836 married THOMAS MANN RANDOLPH | JANE 1774-1775 | A SON died an infant | MARY 1778-1804 married JOHN WAYLES EPPES |

| ANNE CARY 1791-1826 married CHARLES BANKHEAD | THOMAS JEFFERSON 1792-1875 married JANE NICHOLAS | ELLEN WAYLES 1796-1876 married JOSEPH COOLIDGE | CORNELIA 1799-1871 unmarried | VIRGINIA 1801-18-? married NICHOLAS P. TRIST | MARY JEFFERSON 1803-1876 unmarried |

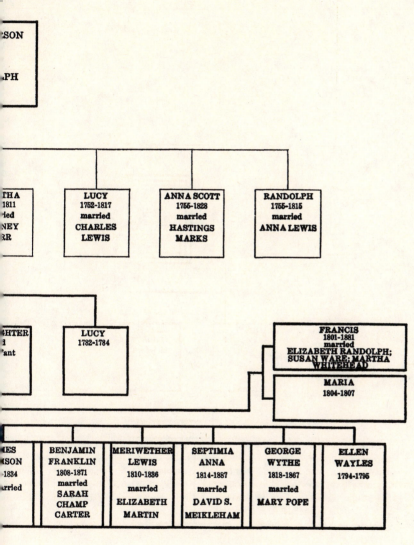

SON

PH

THA
1811
ried
NEY
RR

LUCY
1752-1817
married
CHARLES
LEWIS

ANNA SCOTT
1755-1828
married
HASTINGS
MARKS

RANDOLPH
1755-1815
married
ANNA LEWIS

HTER
ant

LUCY
1782-1784

FRANCIS
1801-1881
married
ELIZABETH RANDOLPH;
SUSAN WARE; MARTHA
WHITEHEAD

MARIA
1804-1807

ES
SON
1834
arried

BENJAMIN
FRANKLIN
1808-1871
married
SARAH
CHAMP
CARTER

MERIWETHER
LEWIS
1810-1836
married
ELIZABETH
MARTIN

SEPTIMIA
ANNA
1814-1887
married
DAVID S.
MEIKLEHAM

GEORGE
WYTHE
1818-1867
married
MARY POPE

ELLEN
WAYLES
1794-1795

Contents

I. Youth (*April 13, 1743-1759*) 3

II. Student (*1760-1767*) 8

III. Lawyer (*1767-1774*) 23

IV. Rebel (*1774-1776*) 42

V. Legislator (*1776-1779*) 66

VI. Governor (*1779-1781*) 84

VII. Philosopher (*1781-1783*) 104

VIII. Ambassador (*1784-1787*) 121

IX. Spectator (*1787-1789*) 152

X. Secretary of State (*1790-1793*) 169

XI. Vice-President (*1797-1801*) 231

XII. Candidate (*1800*) 264

XIII. President (*1801-1809*) 287

XIV. Sage (*1809-July 4, 1826*) 361

References 423

Bibliography 435

Index 449

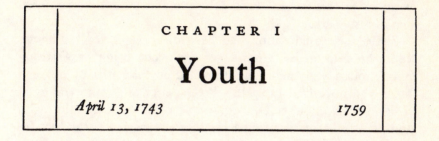

CHAPTER I

Youth

April 13, 1743   *1759*

WHEN Thomas Jefferson was seventy-seven years old he put down on paper, for the information of his family, a few factual and sparing notes about his life. With a warm respect for historical accuracy and a cool contempt for lineage, he wrote that he knew little about his ancestors:

The tradition in my father's family was that their ancestor came to this country from Wales, and from near the mountain of Snowdon, the highest in Gr[eat] Br[itain]. I noted once a case from Wales, in the law reports where a person of our name was either pl[aintiff] or def[endant] and one of the same name was Secretary to the Virginia company. These are the only instances in which I have met with the name in that country. . . . The first particular information I have of any ancestor was my grandfather. . . . He had three sons, Thomas who died young, Field who settled on the waters of Roanoke and left numerous descendants, and Peter my father, who settled on the lands I still own called Shadwell adjoining my present residence. He was born Feb. 29, 1707/08, and intermarried 1739, with Jane Randolph, of the age of 19. . . . They [the Randolph family] trace their pedigree far back in England and Scotland, to which let every one ascribe the faith & merit he chooses.

Peter Jefferson, Thomas's father, was one of the mighty men who broke the savage wilderness. He acquired land by surveying it, enduring hardships that killed weaker men. His physical strength was prodigious; he could "head up" (raise to an upright position) two 1,000-pound hogshead of tobacco at one time. Thomas Jefferson, who always cherished the memory of his Gibraltar-like parent, used to tell his children how when three strong slaves were trying vainly to tear down an old shed with a rope, his father seized the rope and pulled it apart with one mighty jerk.

"My father's education had been quite neglected," Thomas Jefferson tells in his *Autobiography;* "but being of a strong mind, sound judgment and eager after information, he read much and improved himself." Peter Jefferson was in the great American tradition, self-made and self-educated. Intellectually and physically he "improved himself" in the same way that his son, who was fortunate enough to inherit an estate, was to do all his life. By sheer strength of will Peter mastered the practical art of surveying and became deputy surveyor of Albemarle County. In 1751 Jefferson and Joshua Fry, a professor of mathematics in William and Mary College, compiled a "Map of Inhabited Parts of Virginia." By this time Peter Jefferson was the wealthiest and most respected squire in the county. He succeeded Fry as County Lieutenant and Burgess.

Wealth, which meant land and slaves, Thomas Jefferson's father acquired the hard way. He cleared fields, surveyed unbroken land, felled trees. Land was cheap in frontier Virginia. Once Peter's friend William Randolph of Tuckahoe, gave him 400 acres of land in exchange for "Henry Weatherbourne's biggest bowl of arrack punch." Weatherbourne's punch must have been good.

Social position Peter Jefferson achieved at thirty-one, by marrying into the Virginia aristocracy. He had met Jane, daughter of Isham Randolph, when she was seventeen. Having obtained from Jane Randolph the promise to marry him, Peter Jefferson rode into the dense forest and cleared 1,000 acres of land on the River Anna (Rivanna). After two years he had his farm cleared and a house built. Then he returned to Dungeness, on the north bank of the James, and claimed his bride.

Jane Randolph, Thomas Jefferson's mother, came from a rich family whose tree was ponderous with pedigrees. Of Jane Randolph Jefferson less is known than of most mothers of illustrious sons. Throughout his life Thomas Jefferson, who loved and admired his father, rarely mentioned his mother. It would seem that she was an amiable and cheerful lady who gave birth to ten children, many of whom died young.

It would be an exaggeration to say that Thomas Jefferson was not fond of his mother's family, but he did resent the Randolphs' claim to superiority of birth. As a boy he boasted of his father's humble origins and scoffed at his mother's aristocracy. On the frontier, where the necessities of life had to be produced by the hard labor of independent men and women, claims to nobility of birth seemed particularly ludicrous. This contempt for aristocrats and for those who claimed special dispensations persisted as one of the enduring emotions of Jane Randolph's son. He countered snobbery with hostility or with irony. Once he asked his London agent "to search the Herald's office for the arms of my family." If there were none, he wrote, he would buy new ones. "I would with your assistance become a purchaser, having Sterne's word for it that a coat of arms may be purchased as cheap as any other coat." Peter Jefferson might have appreciated the irony.

2

On April 2 (13, New Style) Jane Randolph Jefferson, at the age of twenty-three, gave birth to Thomas. He was her third child in three years, the other two being girls. The exact spot where Thomas Jefferson was born is not known, although a stone is supposed to mark the site. Shadwell, Thomas's birthplace, was a large wooden farm structure one and a half stories high with a red outside chimney; it was located in Albemarle County, about five miles east of Charlottesville.

The Jefferson family was hard-working, God-fearing, and affectionate. For all his taciturnity, Peter Jefferson was a tender and warmhearted man. His house was always open to friends and to the widely scattered neighbors who were in the habit of coming for advice and hospitality. Even the Indians, whose distrust for the white men was not without sufficient cause, found a friend in Peter Jefferson and stopped to visit Shadwell on their way to Williamsburg, the capital of the colony. In after years Thomas Jefferson, who inherited from his father his generosity and kindness, recalled how those visiting Indians made an indelible impression upon him as a youth:

So much in answer to your inquiries concerning Indians [Thomas Jefferson wrote to John Adams in 1812] a people with whom, in the early part of my life, I was very familiar, and acquired impressions of attachment and commiseration for them which have never been obliterated. Before the revolution, they were in the habit of coming often and in great numbers to the seat of government, where I was very much with them. I knew much of the great Outassetè, the warrior and orator of the Cherokees; he was always the guest of my father, on his journeys to and from Williamsburg. I was in his camp when he made his great farewell oration to his people the evening before his departure for England. The moon was in full splendor, and to her he seemed to address himself in his prayers for his own safety on the voyage, and that of his people during his absence; his sounding voice, distinct articulation, animated action, and the solemn silence of his people at their several fires, filled me with awe and veneration, although I did not understand a word he uttered.

When not working or entertaining, Peter Jefferson devoted his hours to thoughtful reading. The process of self-education was never-ending. In the library were well-worn sets of the *Spectator*, of Shakespeare, of Swift and Pope.

There was a surprising Puritan atmosphere in the household of Peter Jefferson, a strict Church of England man. He taught his son Thomas to say his prayers at a tender age and to read the Scriptures.

Peter applied himself to molding his only son, who came to resemble him in face and figure, in his own well-limned image. What made Peter stand out among his fellow men was the quality of hard and rigorously applied discipline, whether physical or mental, and that quality the father developed in the flexible spirit of young Thomas. Peter taught his freckled boy to read and write, to keep accounts, and to work systematically. "Never," Peter was in the habit of saying, "ask another to do for you what you can do for yourself."

The father, a successful farmer and frontiersman, also set his impressionable boy an example of vigorous physical out-of-doors life. Thomas, following his adored giant of a father, soon learned to ride, to shoot, to paddle a canoe on the Rivanna, and to hunt deer and turkey. His lean young body grew to marvelous health and endurance. That he was to enjoy extraordinary health for the rest of his eighty-odd years can be traced and credited to his father. Even before his death, Peter Jefferson remembered to enjoin his wife that in taking care of Tom's education she should not neglect the "exercise requisite for his bodie's development."

Tom did not ride and shoot and canoe only; he also studied diligently. His education consisted of the typical classical curriculum of the period. In his *Autobiography* he has compressed the story of his early education into six bare lines:

He [father] placed me at the English school at 5. years of age and at the Latin at 9. where I continued until his death. My teacher Mr. Douglas a clergyman from Scotland . . . with the rudiments of these [Latin and Greek] languages taught me the French, and on the death of my father I went to the revd Mr. Maury a correct classical scholar, with whom I continued two years.

For teaching Thomas Jefferson Latin, Greek, and French, the Reverend William Douglas was paid £16 sterling annually. This sum also covered room and board.

Tom mastered languages, both classical and modern, with great ease. As a boy it was Homer that he would read in his canoe trips down the Rivanna and Virgil that he brought with him when he stretched under an oak tree.

CHAPTER II

Student

1760   *1767*

THE DEATH of Peter Jefferson when Thomas was fourteen left the latter the sole youth in a family consisting of an infant boy and seven women, his mother and six sisters.[1] The level-headed Thomas knew how to absorb affection. The lanky boy who could read Greek and play the fiddle was not spoiled by his affectionate family. Years afterward he recalled that, upon his father's death, the "whole care & direction of myself was thrown on myself entirely, without a relation or friend qualified to advise or guide me." This, by the way, casts a curiously oblique reflection on his mother, whom, apparently, he did not judge "qualified" to advise him.

Thomas, relying upon himself, decided, in typical American fashion, that the best way to improve his mind and strengthen his character was to go away to college. To a Virginian of Thomas Jefferson's social position, college in those days meant William and Mary at Williamsburg.[2] We have Thomas's own letter, written to his guardian John Harvey in January, 1760, giving his reasons for wanting to go to college. The letter is one of the earliest preserved Jefferson pieces, penned before his seventeenth birthday:

[1] Thomas Jefferson had a younger brother named Randolph who was a child of two when their father died. Although Randolph Jefferson lived to be sixty (1755-1815), he seems not to have played an important role.

[2] Princeton, where James Madison studied, was also a favorite college.

8

Sir,—I was at Colo. Peter Randolph's about a Fortnight ago, & my Schooling falling into Discourse, he said he thought it would be to my Advantage to go to College, & was desirous I should go, as indeed I am myself for several Reasons. In the first place as long as I stay at the Mountains, the Loss of one-fourth of my Time is inevitable, by Company's coming here & detaining me from School. And likewise my Absence will in a great Measure put a Stop to so much Company, & by that Means lessen the Expences of the Estate in House-Keeping. And on the other Hand by going to the College I shall get a more universal Acquaintance, which may hereafter be serviceable to me; & I suppose I can pursue my Studies in the Greek & Latin as well there as here, & likewise learn something of the Mathematics. I shall be glad of your opinion, and remain, Sir, your most humble servant, Thomas Jefferson, Jr.

Here we have a combination of characteristic reasons: the dislike for wasted time, the desire for financial economy by curtailing hospitality (which for the next sixty-six years he was never to succeed in achieving), and finally the wish to enrich his mind. In these matters Jefferson at seventeen was Jefferson at seventy.

2

In December, 1759, Thomas bade good-by to his family at Shadwell and took the long road to Williamsburg. The distance was about 120 miles. Midway between Shadwell and Williamsburg there was a little place on the Pamunkey River called Hanover. Today Hanover is a metropolis of 75 people. It was probably not much bigger in 1760, although it boasted a courthouse and a tavern (Shelton's, made famous by Patrick Henry, who had married the tavern-keeper's daughter). At Hanover was the home of Colonel Nathan Dandridge, and there the young student from Shadwell stopped off for the Christmas holidays.

One of the guests at Hanover was a robust and infectiously gay former storekeeper with a ringing voice and an irrepressible gift of lively talk. He was not a bookish man, nor one possessed of polished manners, but he had a spontaneous liveliness and zest for pleasure that fascinated old and young, including the studious boy from Shadwell. The amusing stranger was twenty-three years old, and his name was Patrick Henry. "During the festivity of the season," Jefferson relates, "I met him in society every day, & we became well acquainted, altho I was much his junior. . . . His manners had something of coarseness in them. His passion was music, dancing, and pleasantry. He excelled in the last, and it attached every one to him."

3

The festivities over, "Long Tom," as his friends called him affectionately, left gay Hanover for an even gayer Williamsburg. Tom had made, as usual, an excellent impression upon both men and women. He was not handsome. Standing well over six feet, the boy from the woods of western Virginia was lean, bony, roughhewn, and broad-shouldered, but surprisingly slender. His neck was long and thin, and his face, like his fox hair, had a reddish tint, not unlike the soil of his native county. The cheeks were lean and the jaw square and firm, but the wide-winged nose was somewhat feminine and inquisitive. Quizzical hazel eyes, set deep, were flanked by bushy temples. Despite his lanky figure he danced gracefully, and his walk had the lightness of one seasoned in the forest. His voice, which he always kept on a low conversational level—the perpetual charmer—was soft like his eyes, and well modulated.

Williamsburg, sitting placidly on the tongue of land between the York and James rivers, was only a few miles from where the broad Chesapeake joins the Atlantic. The town was not large, but to the boy from Shadwell it was something of a metropolis. Named in honor of William III and made the capital of Virginia in the last year of the seventeenth century, Williamsburg, when young Jefferson got there, had about two hundred one-story houses and a population of around 1,000 whites and blacks. The capital of the royal colony had not yet achieved the dignity of sidewalks or the refinement of sewers. Grass grew in the half-dozen streets.

Despite its miniature size, the town was the political, social, and cultural center of the upper South. Life was gay and hospitable. The main stem was the Duke of Gloucester Street. Along this street were some fine houses, including those combinations of bar-hotel-restaurant known as taverns, a courthouse, and Bruton Parish Church, supposed now to be the oldest Episcopal church in the country. At the head of the Duke of Gloucester Street snuggled three or four buildings, collectively known as William and Mary College. At the end, and within view of the college, was the capitol. Off on the side stood the Governor's Palace. College, capitol, and palace formed a tight triangle, knit by social ties and enclosing an animated world, as Tom soon learned. It was a limited world, this short triangle, and "Long Tom" with his vigorous strides could walk from point to point in less time than it took him to mutter ecstatically half a dozen verses from Ossian.

4

The registers show that Thomas Jefferson entered William and Mary on March 25, 1760.

The college, to quote one of its historians, was then "rife with dissensions and discontent," probably because it mixed ruthless politics and an acrid theology. The Reverend Thomas Dawson was a case in point. For £200 sterling per annum, the Reverend Mr. Dawson united in his person the offices of president of the college, commissary, member of the Council, and rector of Bruton Church. His colleagues accused him of being a stooge for Fauquier, the genial Acting Governor of the colony, which was very likely. Also the Reverend Mr. Dawson was not infrequently drunk, a failing which he freely admitted to the college board. Governor Fauquier, however, neatly defended the president's drinking, on the ground that the intrigues of his long-faced and black-gowned faculty drove him to it.

The Reverend Thomas Dawson's faculty was full of Reverends. The Reverend Emanuel Jones was master of the Indian school (in 1754 eight of the seventy-five students at the college

were Indians). The Reverend Thomas Robinson was in charge
of the grammar school. The Reverend William Preston professed moral philosophy. The Reverend John Camm taught
theology. The Reverend Richard Graham preached natural
philosophy. But fortunately for Jefferson there was one professor—of natural philosophy and mathematics—who was not a
Reverend. This man, William Small, a Scot of great learning
and a friend of Erasmus Darwin, arrived at the college about
the same time that Jefferson came there as a student. Professor
and student were magnet and steel. Dr. Small found that the red-
headed boy had a thirst for learning equal to his own, and a
curiosity that knew no restraint. A warm friendship sprang up
between the two, despite the discrepancy of age and position.
Young Jefferson benefited immeasurably from the association
with the older man. To the eager boy from the American backwoods the European professor introduced the larger universe
of science and scholarship, and set a pattern of liberal thinking
stripped of orthodoxy. Dr. Small had a lasting influence on
Jefferson. Years later Jefferson said that Small "probably fixed
the destinies of my life." He described his teacher and friend
in glowing terms:

. . . a man profound in most of the useful branches of science,
with a happy talent of communication, correct and gentlemanly manners, & an enlarged & liberal mind. He, most happily for me, became
soon attached to me & made me his daily companion when not
engaged in the school; and from his conversation I got my first views
of the expansion of science & of the system of things in which we are
placed.

Dr. Small did more than merely bring his protégé into contact with the exciting world of ideas. What was almost as important, he introduced him to his select circle of friends. Perhaps the greatest man among these friends was the thirty-five-
year-old George Wythe, professor of law at the college and the
foremost jurist in Virginia. Wythe was a man of classic mold,
thoughtful, scrupulous, ethical, and above all a believer in a
republican form of government. Contemporaries called him
Aristides the Just. Young Jefferson spoke of him as "my faith-

STUDENT 13

ful and beloved Mentor." Fourteen years after meeting the boy
from Shadwell, Wythe was destined to sign his name to a document entitled "The Unanimous Declaration of the thirteen
united States of America," composed in moving prose by his
red-haired student and friend.[3]

Wythe and Small were so impressed by their soft-spoken and
brilliant young friend that they introduced him to a third man,
the biggest person in the town and in the whole colony, Francis
Fauquier, Acting Governor of Virginia. The two professors were
the Governor's "*amici omnium horarum*." When they inducted
the stripling of eighteen, they became an inseparable "*partie
quarree*." (These expressions are Jefferson's own.)

Governor Fauquier also added to the education of young
Jefferson. The Governor was both a man of the world and a
scholar. The son of a director of the Bank of England, Francis
Fauquier at the outbreak of the Seven Years' War published
*An Essay on Ways and Means of Raising Money for the Sup-
port of the Present War without Increasing the Public Debt.*
When he came to America he warned Pitt against England's
oppressive colonial policy, foreseeing resistance on the part of
the American colonies. London did not heed Fauquier, but Jefferson undoubtedly listened with growing interest to the Governor's conversation on the subject of colonial policy. For
Fauquier was an open-minded and openhearted eighteenth-
century gentleman, interested in new ideas and good talk. He
was also, it must be admitted, a bon vivant, devoted, among
other things, to cards. Half a century later, the great democrat
Jefferson recalled the gentlemanly royalist Governor Fauquier
as "the ablest man who ever filled that office."

Small, Wythe, and Jefferson, together with Dr. Smith, a
professor of mathematics who treated the young student "as a
father," frequently dined with the Governor and often listened
to chamber music at the Governor's Palace. The dinners were
a joy and a sweet memory ever after. They meant genial com-
panionship, fine food, worldly manners, and, above all, conversation that struck fire. Jefferson's young mind absorbed every-

[3] George Wythe's name headed the list of the Virginia signers of the
Declaration of Independence.

thing he saw and heard. It was as if fate had introduced three or four brilliant and experienced men for the express purpose of enriching the mind of a young man born to do great things.

In 1815 Jefferson wrote: "At these dinners I have heard more good sense, more rational and philosophical conversations, than in all my life besides. They were truly Attic societies. The Governor was musical also, and a good performer, and associated me with two or three other amateurs at his weekly concerts."

5

College was not all music and conversation. Jefferson also studied with intense absorption over long hours. He was robust enough to study fifteen hours a day and then, for exercise, run a mile out of Williamsburg and back. Often he rose at dawn and plunged into books, books, books, until two in the morning. William and Mary had never seen such a student. Everything interested him, nothing was alien to him. His mind seized with equal avidity upon Greek grammar and Newtonian physics. He mastered calculus with the same ease as Spanish. He learned to read Plato in Greek, Cicero in Latin, Montesquieu in French. To get to the roots of the English common law he studied Anglo-Saxon. To read Ossian ("this rude bard of the North [is] the greatest poet that has ever existed") he learned Gaelic. Apart from the classics—he preferred Greek thought to Roman —he read the English novelists Sterne, Fielding, Smollett. He also read Marmontel, Le Sage, and Cervantes—*Don Quixote* twice. Among the poets, his favorites were Shakespeare, Milton, Dryden, and Pope.

Already he displayed a vigorous empiricism even in the field of ethics. Wary of ideas beyond the range of experiment, he dropped the shutters of his mind on metaphysics and theology. But underlying his character and re-enforcing his whole mental texture was a conviction of the all-pervasiveness of a moral sense. He could not, to be sure, prove it, but he assumed it as an eternal principle. His whole life was to be oriented on the basis and in the direction of social morality and innate justice.

What he wrote to his nephew Peter Carr in 1787 he also believed as a student:

Man was destined for society. His morality therefore was to be formed to this object. He was endowed with a sense of right & wrong merely relative to this. This sense is as much a part of his nature, as the sense of hearing, seeing, feeling; it is the true foundation of morality, & not the Το Καλον, truth, &c., as fanciful writers have imagined. The moral sense, or conscience, is as much a part of man as his leg or arm. It is given to all human beings in a stronger or weaker degree, as force of members is given them in greater or less degree. It may be strengthened by exercise, as may any particular limb of the body. This sense is submitted indeed in some degree to the guidance of reason. . . . State a moral case to a ploughman & a professor. The former will decide it as well, & often better than the latter, because he has not been led astray by artificial rules.

Here was the basic faith of Jefferson—he had no other religion, even as a boy. This belief in innate morality was the foundation on which he was to build the structure of democratic government.

6

Withal he was a normal youth who loved exercise, riding, singing, dancing, and flirting with the girls. His love of life and of innocent gaiety was infectious, and everyone, men as well as women, was attracted to him. Sprightly animation and unrestrained kindliness lent a kind of beauty to that freckled, angular, plain face. For a time he affected a certain foppishness in dress. On social occasions he would put on a flowered waistcoat and silk stockings, and carry a laced hat under his arm. Such dress was an extravagance which pricked his conscience and when, in a burst of contrition, he asked his guardian to deduct the cost from his share of his father's property, he received the droll reply: "No, no; if you have sowed your wild oats in this manner, Tom, the estate can well afford to pay your expenses."

Although Jefferson was not actively addicted to humor, he enlivened gatherings with his spontaneous laughter as well as his fiddle. His hazel eyes would light up quizzically at something ludicrous or incongruous, but he rarely told funny stories. One of his favorite anecdotes was about Arthur Lee, who had a passion for contradiction. Lee once heard a man say that it was a very cloudy day and retorted: "It is cloudy, sir; but not very cloudy." Jefferson thought that was funny.

Society in Williamsburg was "fast." The young blades (and the old ones too) liked cockfighting, gambling, drinking, racing, and wenching. Young Jefferson participated in these activities sparingly. He never used tobacco, never played cards, never fought, and hardly ever drank. He did, however, play the swain as well as "at yᵉ billiard tables." His moral sense and distaste for loafing diminished the pleasure that a youth might find in dissipation. Sometimes he would refer to the gay college town as "Devilsburg." Once after a binge with other students he wrote from the melancholy depths of a hangover:

Last night, as merry as agreeable company and dancing with Belinda in the Apollo could make me. I never could have thought the succeeding sun would have seen me so wretched as I now am! . . . Affairs at W. and M. are in the greatest confusion. Walker, M'Clurg, and Wat Jones are expelled *pro tempore,* or, as Horrox softens it, rusticated for a month. Lewis Burwell, Warner Lewis, and one Thompson, have fled to escape flagellation.

Of course there never was any danger that the intellectually vital son of Peter Jefferson would succumb to the temptations of "Devilsburg" and become just another racing and gambling Virginia gentleman, like so many of his acquaintances. Still, Tom's company was admittedly "bad," and he himself had a passion for horses. Looking back upon his youth, Jefferson in later years often wondered what had kept him from becoming a wastrel; with characteristic modesty he concluded that what saved him was not any innate virtue but the examples of his great friends Small and Wythe (the third, Governor Fauquier, was himself an inveterate gambler), whom he incessantly strove to imitate. Almost half a century after sowing his tame oats in the gay capital he told his grandson Thomas Jefferson Randolph:

When I recollect . . . the various sorts of bad company with which I associated from time to time, I am astonished I did not turn off with some of them, & become as worthless to society as they were. . . . Under temptations & difficulties, I would ask myself what would Dr. Small, Mr. Wythe, Peyton Randolph do in this situation? . . . I am certain that this mode of deciding on my conduct, tended more to its correctness than any reasoning powers I possessed. . . . From the circumstances of my position, I was often thrown into the society of horse racers, card players, fox hunters, scientific & professional men, and of dignified men; and many a time have I asked myself . . . which of these kinds of reputation should I prefer? That of a horse jockey? a fox hunter? an orator? or the honest advocate of my country's rights?

This, however, was but the blossom of retrospect. In the early 1760's Jefferson was more deeply concerned with pretty faces than with colonial rights.

7

At the end of two years and one month Jefferson left college. In William and Mary's Book of the Bursar there is a notation by John Blair: "Jefferson tells me he left the College ab^t 25th April" (1762).

Leaving college meant no interruption in his studies, his routine, or his friendships. For Jefferson had decided to remain at Williamsburg and to study law. At the age of nineteen he entered the law office of his friend George Wythe, and despite his dislike for the law and its jargon, which he always ridiculed, he worked at it for five years.

That he studied thoroughly and read arduously is shown by his *Commonplace Book*, a notebook in which he jotted down and sometimes fully summarized the volumes he read and the ideas they stimulated in him.[4] He told Thomas Cooper in 1814:

[4] *The Commonplace Book of Thomas Jefferson: A Repertory of His Ideas on Government*, with an introduction and notes by Gilbert Chinard (1926). Out of the 905 entries in *The Commonplace Book*, no less than 550 were written when Jefferson was a student or a young lawyer. These entries deal with technical legal questions. The entries on feudal law, on political science, on Montesquieu and Beccaria, were written between 1774 and 1776, before the Declaration of Independence.

When I was a student of the law, now half a century ago, after getting through Coke Littleton, whose matter cannot be abridged, I was in the habit of abridging and common-placing what I read meriting it, and of sometimes mixing my own reflections on the subject. . . . They were written at a time of life when I was bold in the pursuit of knowledge, never fearing to follow truth and reason whatever results they led [to], and bearding every authority which stood in their way.

It was in the spring of 1764 that the young law student had his first real experience in patriotic inspiration. He was attending the session of the Virginia House of Burgesses when it was debating the Declaratory Act of the British Parliament to tax the American colonies. Suddenly up stood one of the delegates, an old friend of Tom's, and after offering a series of resolutions to the general effect that taxation without representation would "destroy British as well as American freedom," burst into a torrent of eloquence that electrified the assembly. "Caesar," thundered Patrick Henry, "had his Brutus, Charles the First his Cromwell—and George the Third—" The House of Burgesses echoed with the words "Treason!" "Treason!" But Henry finished his sentence—"may profit by their example. If *this* be treason, make the most of it." Upon Jefferson, who had no gift of eloquence, Henry's speech made a powerful impression. Although he was rather inclined to look down upon Henry as an uncouth and uneducated backwoodsman, he admitted that on this occasion the orator was "splendid." Patrick Henry, he said, "appeared to me to speak as Homer wrote."

It was at this time that the young law student adopted for his motto the words "Resistance to tyrants is obedience to God."

8

Hard studies and youthful pleasures went hand in hand. Feudal law, Anglo-Saxon tenets, *curia regis* procedure, all these did not make Tom a dull boy. Gaily he continued his dancing and fiddling and courting the belles. He was extremely susceptible to the fluttering and flirtatious beauties, and he was still at an age when a lad can be made blissful by a smile or miserable by a slight.

Inevitably he fell in love and was by turn happy and wretched, hopeful and dejected, as have been lovers since the beginning of time. The object of his sighs was Rebecca, daughter of Lewis Burwell, president of the Virginia Council. She was beautiful, impish, not very intellectual, and men were crazy about her. Tom carried her portrait—"my dear picture"—in his watch and no doubt looked at it worshipfully many times a day. When, during the Christmas holidays at Shadwell, rain ruined his watch and defaced the visage of his Rebecca—or Belinda, as he called her poetically—he was inconsolable. He wrote to his intimate friend John Page:

I would have cried bitterly, but I thought it beneath the dignity of a man. . . . my hearty prayers shall be, that all the health and happiness which Heaven can send may be the portion of the original. . . . although the picture be defaced, there is so lively an image of her imprinted in my mind, that I shall think of her too often, I fear, for my peace of mind; and too often, I am sure, to get through old Coke this winter.

The infatuated boy struck no responsive chord in Belinda. Tom probably realized that the girl was merely playing with his affections. On a flyleaf of a book Tom sighingly wrote:

Jane Nelson is a sweet girl,
Betsy Page is a neat girl,
Rebecca Burwell is the devil;
If not the devil she's one of his imps.

Tom was not a bold lover. Instead of offering his love to his Belinda, he mooned and moped and moaned, and, typical intellectual that he was, debated the problem in lengthy communications with his friend Page. He asked Page in a letter written from Shadwell in January, 1763:

How does R.B. do? Had I better stay here and do nothing, or go down and do less? . . . Inclination tells me to go, receive my sentence, and be no longer in suspense: but reason says, if you go, and your attempt proves unsuccessful, you will be ten times more wretched than ever.

The affair did not run smoothly at all. Tom was planning to go on an extended European tour that would last about three years. Would Belinda wait for him that long? Would he dare ask her to wait? And what if she refused? John Page, the future Governor of Virginia, told his moping friend to talk to the girl frankly and directly. Tom was frightened at such boldness:

. . . you advise me to go immediately and lay siege *in form*. . . . No, no, Page; whatever assurances I may give her in private of my esteem for her . . . they must be kept in private. . . . because I never can bear to remain in suspense so long a time. . . . if Belinda will not accept of my service, it shall never be offered to an-other. . . . that she will, she never gave me reason to hope.

He wanted Page to do the talking for him, for Belinda had a devastating effect upon his poise. When he met her he became tongue-tied with emotion. One evening—this was in October, 1763—he danced with her in the Apollo Room of the Raleigh tavern and excitement choked his speech. All he could manage, he admitted to Page, was "a few broken sentences, uttered in great disorder." Stammeringly he hinted to her about his plans, but did not have the courage to propose to her. "I asked no question which would admit of a categorical answer."

But in the midst of these youthful bitter-sweet love torments, he was already seeking philosophic consolation. If Rebecca would not have him, he would make the best of it. "Perfect happiness, I believe," concluded the philosopher of twenty, "was never intended by the Deity to be the lot of one of his creatures in this world." Thus Tom overcame his first love with his usual good sense. He was too balanced ever to be completely swept off his foundations by passion, and when Belinda announced that she would marry one Jacquelin Ambler, Jefferson's reaction was one of polite coolness. "I have been so abominably indolent," he wrote a friend a few months after his trembling-shy dance at the Apollo, "as not to have seen her since last October. . . . Well, the Lord bless her I say! . . . Many and great are the comforts of a single state." [5]

[5] A few years later young James Madison had an unhappy love affair and his friend Jefferson consoled him with mild cynicism: "the world still presents the same and many other resources of happiness."

CHAPTER III

Lawyer

WHEN Thomas Jefferson began to practice law at the age of twenty-four, he was brilliantly prepared and poorly equipped for his profession. It cannot be denied that he was not cut out to be a lawyer; a scholar, a scientist, an inventor, an architect, a botanist, yes—but not a lawyer. His mind was too inquisitive, too speculative, and, above all, too much given to ideas as such to be happy in the arid wastes of jurisprudence.

For all his great learning, moreover, the young man was handicapped by three shortcomings in the pursuit of his chosen profession: his distaste for rough-and-tumble fighting, his inability to speak in public effectively, and his ethics, which were scrupulous. A delightful conversationalist, he was a poor debater, preferring the play of ideas to the clash of wits. Decades later, Jefferson's grandson Randolph asked an old man who had known Jefferson as a lawyer what kind of an advocate his grandfather was in court. "Well, it is hard to tell," came the reply, "because he always took the right side."

The artist in Jefferson found legal language repugnant. A man with an innate sense of style, Jefferson was repelled by the dry, flatulent legal verbiage with its plethora of "whereases" and its underlying chicanery. He often jeered at "lawyerish." Once, in 1817, he sent his friend Joseph Cabell the draft of a bill for the establishment of elementary schools in Virginia, and added an ironic comment:

I should apologize, perhaps, for the style of this bill. I dislike the verbose and intricate style of the English statutes. . . . You, however, can easily correct this bill to the taste of my brother lawyers, by making every other word a "said" or "aforesaid," and saying every thing over two or three times, so as that nobody but we of the craft can untwist the diction, and find out what it means; and that, too, not so plainly but that we may conscientiously divide one-half on each side.

His antipathy for lawyers was pronounced, despite the many friends he had in the legal profession; undoubtedly he would have argued that lawyers like George Wythe and Peyton Randolph, being exceptional men, were exceptions. Jefferson said that the "lawyers' trade is to question everything, yield nothing, & talk by the hour." And in his celebrated pamphlet commonly called *The Rights of British America*, written on the eve of the American Revolution, he could not refrain from taking a sideswipe at his "brother lawyers." "Our ancestors . . . who emigrated hither," he wrote with hardly concealed mockery, "were laborers, not lawyers."

2

Nothing Jefferson undertook could be mediocre, and it is no surprise to learn that he became a successful lawyer. Although his opinion of the profession was not high, he seems to have enjoyed the practice of the law. It did not take him long to achieve a place among the leaders of the Virginia bar, and his erudition was put at the service of his peers. Famous clients— Burwells, Byrds, Lees, Nelsons, Pages, Randolphs—sought his services, and distinguished lawyers consulted him. Leaders of the bar like Wythe, Pendleton, Patrick Henry, and Robert Carter Nicholas paid young Jefferson the compliment of retaining him as associate counsel. He, in turn, retained Wythe and Pendleton when he needed assistance. The relationship among these lawyers was cordial. In a private memorandum Jefferson once made a note on George Wythe: "in these cases of G.W.'s I meant to charge nothing which was not voluntarily offered."

Jefferson's practice grew rapidly. In 1767 he was engaged in sixty-eight cases before the General Court. Four years later, in 1771, this rose to four hundred and thirty cases. His practice was so great that when Robert Carter Nicholas retired from the bar and offered his business to Jefferson, the latter was "under the necessity of declining it." The account book of the young lawyer shows that his law work was lucrative, despite the unfavorable economic conditions in the colony. In 1767 Jefferson's "total profits" amounted to £293 4s. This rose to £421 5s. in 1770. During the eight years of his practice he averaged the equivalent of about $3,000 a year, which was a good income in those days.[1]

3

Legal business did not occupy Jefferson exclusively. He still read voluminously and made meticulous observations on everything that fell within the range of his unquenchable curiosity. Between law cases and overseeing the plantation, he continued to lead the agreeable social life of an eligible bachelor, especially when visiting Williamsburg. "I was bred to the law," he once told John Bernard during his Presidency; "that gave me a view of the dark side of humanity. Then I read poetry to qualify it with a gaze upon its bright side."

He continued to enjoy the company of women. Their gaiety and their quick, sympathetic understanding found a responsive echo in his own nature, which had a pronounced feminine streak. He was steeped in tenderness—a tenderness that overflowed to

[1] It must be admitted that these were paper earnings. Due to a slump in the tobacco industry, cash was scarce and difficult to collect. Jefferson's account book shows that between 1767 and 1770 he earned, on paper, £1,489 9s.; of this, he collected only £474 19s.—or about one-third. He used to charge from 10s. to 21s. for drawing up a will or deed and £10 for appearing before the General Court. Compare this to Bellamy Partridge's father, who, a generation ago in New York State, charged $1 (the equivalent of 4s.) for a will (see Bellamy Partridge, *Country Lawyer*, McGraw-Hill, 1939). Compare this also to William Howard Taft—like Jefferson, a lawyer who became President—whose legal earnings in 1885, at the age of twenty-eight, amounted to $5,000 (see H. F. Pringle, *The Life and Times of William Howard Taft*, 2 vols., Farrar and Rinehart, 1939, Vol. I, p. 80).

everything in nature, to birds, to flowers, and to horses. He had a passion for all that grew and for all that was helpless. Sensitive women instinctively understood his need to give and to receive affection. To his friend Page he admitted in 1770: "I was always fond of philosophy, even in its drier forms; but from a ruby lip, it comes with charms irresistible. Such a feast of sentiment must exhilarate and lengthen life, at least as much as the feast of the sensualist shortens it." His admiring feminine friends helped to bring out in him those qualities of charm and persuasiveness that were to make him so irresistible a political figure.

4

In his third year as a lawyer Jefferson began to carry into effect a dream of his youth: to build a home for himself on the highest summit of his estate. In 1769 he commenced to level off the top of the hill known as Monticello (580 feet high) and to plant numerous varieties of fruit trees on the slope. He had never studied architecture, but he read all the books he could find on the subject, and presently he knew as much as there was to know. Several hundred of his architectural drawings are still in existence.

The home on Monticello grew like a tree, slowly, solidly, gracefully. Jefferson was the architect, the builder, the engineer, the construction foreman, the cabinetmaker, the landscape artist. All the materials except such things as hardware (excluding nails) and glass were made on the plantation. It was a quarter-century before the house on the hill was completely finished. A one-room red-brick little building on the south end of the terrace was ready for occupancy in the fall of 1769.

Within a few months after completion, the little red-brick structure (today mellowed with age and smothered with ivy) was occupied by its owner. Shadwell, Jefferson's birthplace and the residence of his family, burned to the ground early in 1770, and all the books, papers, and records were reduced to ashes. Only the fiddle seems to have escaped the flames. Nothing was left for the family but to move to Monticello, which was still

a-building. Jefferson's mother and sisters found quarters with
the overseer.

The fire destroyed Jefferson's most precious possession, his
books, a loss that would have been staggering to any but a
wealthy man. In a letter to Page, Jefferson estimated "the *cost*
of the books burned to have been £200 sterling." He could not
live or work without books. Within three years he possessed a
new library of 1,254 volumes, as is shown by an interesting
entry in his *Diary:*

August 4, 1773. My library

In the mahogany book case with glass doors	510 vols.
Walnut book case in N.W. corner of room	180 "
Walnut book case in N.E. corner of room	224 "
Shelves in N.W. corner of room	157 "
Shelves in N.E. corner of room	131 "
Lent out	42 "
Lying about	10 "

Note this does not include vols of Music, nor my books in Wil-
liamsburgh.

Collecting such a library—and it kept growing throughout
Jefferson's lifetime—was a costly process. It was expensive even
for a landowner like Jefferson, who had inherited 1,900 acres,
but had to support a family of thirty-four persons and eighty-
three slaves. The plantation, it should be remembered, was not
making money. Slavery was becoming unproductive; slaves ate
up what profits there were. Jefferson's cash crop, tobacco, probably brought him on an average no more than £200 or £300 a
year. The sale of tobacco, together with his earnings as a lawyer,
boosted his annual income to the equivalent of about $5,000.
He bought approximately four hundred books a year, and if the
average book cost only $3, it meant that Jefferson may have
spent as much as one-fourth of his income on books.[2]

[2] The cost of books may be computed from the following statement made
by Jefferson as President, in April, 1802: ". . . folios may be stated as cost-
ing one and a half guineas, quartos a guinea, octavos 12/—, twelvemos 4/—
in England, and in France three-fourths of those prices." There could have
been no great difference in price between 1770 and 1800.

5

He was getting on in the twenties and still a bachelor, dally-ing with the belles. But not for long. Sometime in the year 1770, when he was twenty-seven, he met and fell quietly in love with a beautiful brunette widow of twenty-one. Martha Wayles Skelton, the object of his love, combined in her slender person a number of irresistible qualities. She was well-born, beautiful, finely educated, warmhearted, a graceful dancer, a fine musician, full of high spirits, and wealthy.

Her father, John Wayles, was a rich Williamsburg lawyer whom Jefferson knew in a business and social way. "Mr. Wayles," Jefferson tells in his *Autobiography*, "was a lawyer of much practice, to which he was introduced more by his great industry, punctuality & practical readiness, than to eminence in the science of his profession. He was a most agreeable com-panion, full of pleasantry & good humor, and welcomed in every society." Wayles owned a dozen plantations and four hundred slaves. His home The Forest, on the edge of Williams-burg, was a center of gaiety and music. Jefferson was a frequent visitor there.

Martha did not discourage Jefferson's shy wooing, but for a long time apparently she played no favorites among the young swains who courted her. Jefferson did not give up hope. More than a year after he met Martha he confessed to a friend: "In every scheme of happiness she is placed in the foreground of the picture, as the principal figure. Take that away, and it is no picture for me." The lover's tone here is on a much lower key than it was eight years earlier in the Belinda affair. He was now a poised and thoughtful man, cautious in behavior and precise in observation.

Consider, for instance, his meticulous account book. Toward the end of 1771 Martha Skelton agreed to marry Jefferson, and he, despite his great happiness, did not neglect to jot down every single penny he spent on the wedding. This was neither parsimony nor a false sense of economy—Jefferson was the most generous of men—but a habit of accurate observation he had acquired and which he applied to personal matters as well as to scientific phenomena. The entries in his account book in connection with his marriage have a peculiar flavor:

1771, Dec. 24. Paid entertainment at the Fork Church ordinary 2/.

Dec. 25. Gave servant at Martin Key's, 7d 1/2. Gave Jupiter [his body slave] for ferriage at Goochland court house 2/.

Dec. 28. Paid ferriage and gave ferryman at the Hundred 4/.

Dec. 29. Gave mrs. Sk [soon to be Mrs. Jefferson] 4ms 10/. Gave Jupiter to pay ferriage at Westover 1/4 1/2.

Dec. 30. Inclosed to M. Debnam for marriage licence 40/.

1772, Jan. 1. Gave rev^d W. Coutts £5. borrowed of mr. Coutts 20/.

Jan. 2. Gave rev^d mr. Davies marriage fee £5. Gave mrs. Eppes [his sister-in-law] 1/3.

Jan. 3. Gave a fidler 10/.

Jan. 11. Paid carriage at Shirley 2/6.

Jan. 12. Paid John at Shirly for mending Phaeton 50/.

Jan. 13. Paid at Dr. Brown's for wax 1/. Paid at Galt's for watch-chrystal 2/6.

Jan. 18. Gave Ben at Forest 5/. Gave Jamey 10/. Gave Martin 2/3. Gave Betty Hemmins 5/. Gave Tom 5/. Gave Kikey 5/. Gave other servants 15/. Inclosed to James New for marriage license 40/.

Jan. 22. Gave mrs. J. 7/6. Paid smith at Tuckahoe 2/6.

The wedding took place at The Forest on New Year's Day, 1772, and was one of the festive occasions of the season. Friends and relatives came from far and near, and there was much dancing and jollity. The bridegroom paid £5 to each of the officiating clergymen (of the Church of England), 40s. for the marriage license, and 10s. to the fiddler. Apparently he was short of cash, for on the same day that he paid £5 to the Reverend Mr. Coutts he borrowed 20s. from him. The servants had to wait more than two weeks to receive presents of 5s. each.

The month of the wedding saw a record snowfall in Virginia. In places the colony was blanketed with snow three feet deep. Despite the storm, the newly-weds set out for Monticello, more than a hundred miles from Williamsburg. The two young people traveled in a two-horse chaise, which broke down on the way and had to be mended at a cost of 50s. It was not a comfortable honeymoon journey, but Mrs. Jefferson took it in good spirit. Jefferson's oldest daughter Martha was to relate years later:

They were finally obliged to quit the carriage, and proceed on horseback. Having stopped for a short time at Blenheim, where an overseer only resided, they left it at sunset to pursue their way through a mountain track rather than a road, in which the snow lay from eighteen inches to two feet deep, having eight miles to go before reaching Monticello.

Deep into the night and deeper through the snow their horses trudged up the steep path leading to the summit of the hill, where Jefferson's home was still in the skeletal stage, with only the one-room lodge prepared for occupancy. The night was cold and dreary, and Jefferson, with his usual consideration for others, would not disturb the servants. He stabled the horses himself and took his bride into their new "home." The bridegroom kindled a fire, and found a bottle of wine on the shelf; the two shared a toast and succumbed to laughter out of sheer happiness.

6

The young couple was exceedingly happy and exceedingly busy. Martha Jefferson, despite her youth, knew how to run a plantation and how to be a gay and loving companion at the same time. Her husband fully reciprocated her devotion. Their lives were rich and full. Presently children came—three died in infancy, a tremendous strain on the delicate health of Mrs. Jefferson; three others were to survive their mother. The house on the hill was still in the process of building, hundreds of acres were being cultivated, slaves had to be cared for, law and politics had to be attended to. There was much entertainment and good living. In the midst of it all Jefferson found time for reading and study.

A little over a year after her marriage, Martha Jefferson's

father died and left her one-third of a "handsome fortune," which, Jefferson tells, "doubled the ease of our circumstances." To be specific, Martha inherited from her parent 40,000 acres of land and one hundred and thirty-five slaves.[3] This put the Jeffersons in the class of the greatest landholders in Virginia and enabled them to buy luxuries, such as imported wines and liquors.[4] Jefferson's wine cellar became celebrated. Years later a Federalist epicure was to make the caustic comment: "I wish his French politics were as good as his French wines."

7

As yet Jefferson had no specific politics, except the general enlightened liberalism of a cultivated gentleman who was rich and tolerant. Few of his early letters show any great passion for social causes. His career was the reverse of that described in Lord Chesterfield's celebrated quip to his son: "He who is not a radical at sixteen has no heart; he who is a radical at sixty has no head." Jefferson was not a radical at sixteen, but was one at sixty; and he had both a heart and a head. No doubt, even at this early date he was stirred by injustice and indignant at persecution. Still, he lacked motivation for action, being serene in his philosophical beliefs and happy in his personal pursuits. It took years of growth, as well as revolutionary upheavals and a personal tragedy, to propel him onto the arena where men fight and sometimes die for causes.

As a young man Jefferson was incapable of expressing the sort of violent social indignation that James Madison, for example, revealed in his early twenties. The irony was that Madison, Jefferson's lifelong friend and devoted follower, grew increasingly placid and conservative with the years, while Jefferson became steadily more leftist as he grew older. In Janu-

---

[3] Most of this land, however, was sold. Jefferson retained a total of about 10,000 acres.

[4] Even before his wife's inheritance Jefferson kept a small stock of liquor in his cellar. His account book for 1772 shows that he had 3 gallons of rum, about 12 gallons of Madeira, and several bottles of port and beer. He drank wine with his meals, always in great moderation.

ary, 1774, Jefferson and Madison had not yet met, but both lived in the same environment and read more or less similar books and periodicals. On that date James Madison, a lad of twenty-two, wrote a letter which Jefferson could not have written at that age. Young Madison's letter to his friend William Bradford is memorable for the graphic pictures it gives of the climate of opinion in Virginia and of the mind of a man who was to become Jefferson's alter ego:

I have indeed as good an atmosphere at home as the climate will allow; but have nothing to brag of as to the state and liberty of my country. Poverty and luxury prevail among all sorts; pride, ignorance, and knavery among the priesthood, and vice and wickedness among the laity. This is bad enough, but it is not the worst I have to tell you. That diabolical, hell-conceived principle of persecution rages among some; and to their eternal infamy, the clergy can furnish their quota of imps for such business. This vexes me the worst of anything whatever. There are this time in the adjacent country not less than five or six well-meaning men in close jail for publishing their religious sentiments, which in the main are very orthodox. I have neither patience to hear, talk, or think of anything relative to this matter; for I have squabbled and scolded, abused and ridiculed, so long about it to little purpose, that I am without common patience. So I must beg you to pity me, and pray for liberty of conscience for all.

An educated eighteenth-century Virginia landholder could not escape politics altogether, no matter how detached his outlook or how philosophical his temperament. The times, moreover, were critical, and the colonies were growing restive under British rule. As a matter of course, the squire of Monticello, who had inherited his father's office of justice of the peace, entered politics. He had neither political ambitions nor a particular program, but it was usual for the squire to represent his county in the House of Burgesses. In 1769 Jefferson stood for that body, and was of course elected. His electioneering method was as simple as the dress of the neighbors whose votes he solicited. Colonel Peter Jefferson's young son visited the neighbors in the county and invited them to Shadwell for a bowl.

They came, had their drinks, and afterward quietly voted for the late Colonel's educated lawyer son.

Such elections took place as a matter of course, and were neither arduous nor costly. In 1771 Jefferson was re-elected, having spent the munificent sum of £4 19s. 3d.—the equivalent of about $25—on his "burgessing." The cakes which the prospective voters washed down with punch cost Jefferson 45 shillings. In the campaign of 1774 he spent only 24 shillings on "6 dozen cakes." Cakes and rum kept him in the Virginia legislature until the outbreak of the Revolution.

Jefferson was not at first a very conspicuous member of the House of Burgesses. This was partly due to the lack of any immediate program, and partly to the fact that he was extremely sensitive and easily hurt, and hesitated long before thrusting himself forward. In 1773, during his fifth year in the legislature, Pendleton asked young Jefferson to draft a reply to the Governor's address. It was a courtesy request, designed to give the young man a chance to distinguish himself. Either from excitement or from inexperience, Jefferson bungled the draft and it had to be rewritten. He was mortified. Later he admitted candidly: "Being a young man as well as a young member, it made on me an impression proportioned to the sensibility of that time of life." But he was learning. Great events were shaping, and presently Jefferson found himself deep in the political stream.

8

Reluctantly the American colonies were coming to grips with the royal government in London. As George the Third's Cabinet was becoming more arbitrary and violent, the Americans grew more stubborn in their resistance. Incident piled upon incident, and the colonial temper was slowly rising to incandescence. In 1772 an armed British revenue ship, the *Gaspee*, was burned in Narragansett Bay; the furious Parliament in London retaliated by passing an act making any violation of His Majesty's property punishable by death. The accused could also be transported to England for trial. Wide indignation greeted this threat to the liberties of the colonists.

Under the strain, Americans were beginning to recognize rising leaders, and to refurbish the arsenal of fact, reason, and law. The colonists split into Tories and Whigs, conservatives and radicals, according to their interests and their temperaments. Younger men were aggressive and defiant, older ones cautious and temporizing.

Throughout the American colonies battle lines were visibly forming and opinion was crystallizing. In 1773 a group of young members of the Virginia House of Burgesses took a long step in the direction of resistance to the mother country. With great political perspicacity the young Virginians forged a weapon of considerable striking power—the Committee of Correspondence, designed to act as a channel of communication, and ultimately perhaps of union, among the various colonies, North and South.[5] The shy legislator from Monticello was one of the organizers of the committee. How it happened he relates concisely in his *Autobiography:*

Not thinking our old & leading members up to the point of forwardness & zeal which the times required, Mr. Henry, R. H. Lee, Francis L. Lee, Mr. Carr & myself agreed to meet in the evening in a private room of the Raleigh to consult on the state of things. There may have been a member or two more whom I do not recollect.[6] We were all sensible that the most urgent of all measures was that of coming to an understanding with all the other colonies to consider the British claims as a common cause to all, & to produce a unity of action: and for this purpose that a committee of correspond-[en]ce in each colony would be the best instrument for intercommunication: and that their first measure would probably be to propose a meeting of deputies from every colony at some central place, who should be charged with the direction of the measures which should be taken by all. We therefore drew up the resolutions. . . . The

[5] A Committee of Correspondence had been organized in Massachusetts in 1770.
[6] The full committee consisted of Archibald Cary, Dabney Carr (Jefferson's brother-in-law), Dudley Digges, Benjamin Harrison, Patrick Henry, Jefferson, Francis L. Lee, Richard Henry Lee, Robert C. Nicholas, Edmund Pendleton, and Peyton Randolph, who was the chairman.

Gov[erno]r (then Ld. Dunmore) dissolved us, but the comm[itt]ee met the next day, prepared a circular letter to the Speakers of the other colonies.

After they established the committee the defiant Virginians left Williamsburg to spend the autumn and winter of 1773-74 at home, in peace. Participation in the Committee of Correspondence was Jefferson's first important political act.

9

It would be enlightening to know what Thomas Jefferson read and what he thought that winter in Monticello. The records are largely silent. He was not yet a famous man, and no one took the trouble to note down his conversation. Yet his thoughts must have been significant, for apparently he was quietly preparing himself for the great argument that was soon to shake the colonies. To all intents and purposes the squire of Monticello was still a loyal subject of George the Third, a landowner holding property under the protection of British laws, a gentleman educated in the English tradition. He was not a social rebel nor an open religious dissenter. Nor, seemingly, did he see anything objectionable in the institution of monarchy. His political readings on the eve of the American Revolution showed a definite trend. It is certain that about this time he read Lord Kames's *Historical Law Tracts* and his *History of Property*, Sir John Dalrymple's *Essay towards a General History of Feudal Property in Great Britain*, James Wilson's remarkable pamphlet, *Considerations on the Nature and Extent of the Legislative Authority of the British Parliament*, as well as Locke, Voltaire, Helvetius, and a number of constitutional historians. Evidently Jefferson, the philosophical lawyer, was studying the origins of property as well as those of society, and searching for principles underlying governments and constitutions.

One of the selections he made from Kames's *History of Property* is so characteristic that, as Professor Gilbert Chinard pointed out, Jefferson himself might have written it:

The perfection of human society, consists in that just degree of union among the individuals, which to each reserves freedom and independency, as far as is consistent with peace and good order. The bonds of society where every man shall be bound to dedicate the whole of his industry to the common interest would be of the strictest kind, but it would be unnatural and uncomfortable, because destructive of liberty and independency.

"Liberty" and "independency" were now the two guiding stars by which Jefferson steered his political career.

He had not talked much in public, but already his capacious mind was filled with a powerful arsenal of arguments in favor of certain "inherent" and "natural" rights to individual freedom and political independence. He had searched far and wide, in law, in history, in philosophy, and had found basic principles that would guide man to a free society. Once certain that he could support those political axioms with irrefutable historical arguments, he was ready to emerge from obscurity and to formulate ideas that men came to hold true and self-evident. Slowly the angular, soft-spoken landowner of Monticello swung into action.

10

The occasion came in the spring of 1774. A Northern city, which neither Jefferson nor most of his fellow legislators in Virginia had ever seen, supplied the spark. While the House of Burgesses was in session in Williamsburg, exciting news came from the North. As punishment for the action of a group of Massachusetts rebels who threw a cargo of tea overboard, the British Government ordered that the port of Boston be closed beginning with June 1, 1774. Instantly the radical wing of the Virginia House of Burgesses decided to support the Northern sister colony against the Crown. The legislators were lawyers well versed in history, and the claims of the British Parliament to enforce acts by arbitrary decree struck them as both illegal and dangerous.

The radical leadership of the House of Burgesses fell into the hands of Patrick Henry, the two Lees, and Jefferson. They had the support of George Mason and George Wythe, although the latter was inclined to be cautious. With Henry the inflammable orator and Jefferson the subtle logician, the radical group became a political power of major importance. Wise in political maneuver and experienced in parliamentary ways, the younger men did not make the mistake of alienating the conservatives. As Jefferson later explained: "We slackened our pace, that our less ardent colleagues might keep up with us; and they . . . quickened their gait somewhat . . . and thus consolidated the phalanx which breasted the power of Britain."

They knew what they wanted to do—"we must," Jefferson said, "boldly take an unequivocal stand in the line with Massachusetts." To stir up public opinion, the young radicals hit upon the propaganda stratagem of appointing a day of fasting and prayer. This would alarm the people and focus their attention on what was happening elsewhere in the colonies. Henry, the Lees, Jefferson, and a few other legislators met in private and cleverly prepared for the day of fasting. Jefferson relates:

. . . we cooked up a resolution . . . for appointing the 1st day of June, on which the Port bill was to commence, for a day of fasting, humiliation & prayer, to implore heaven to avert from us the evils of civil war, to inspire us with firmness in support of our rights, and to turn the hearts of the King & parliament to moderation & justice.

To give their resolution an air of dignity and an aura of respectability, they shrewdly selected Robert Carter Nicholas, a distinguished and religious gentleman, to move it. Nicholas accepted the honor, and the resolution passed unanimously. Then the group invited the co-operation of the clergy in all the counties in assembling the people on June 1. On that day, truly a revolutionary day, Virginia was stirred as she had not been in decades. "The people met generally," Jefferson recalls, "with anxiety & alarm in their countenances, and the effect of the day thro' the whole colony was like a shock of electricity, arousing every man & placing him erect & solidly on his centre."

II

Angry Governor Dunmore curtly dissolved the House of Burgesses. Undaunted, the Virginians met in the Apollo Room of the Raleigh tavern, about one hundred steps from the capitol. Under the chairmanship of Peyton Randolph, they reorganized, and agreed to propose to the Committees of Correspondence in the other colonies to meet annually in a united congress at some convenient place. They denounced the action of the British Government and, what was most significant, they declared that "an attack on any one colony should be considered as an attack on the whole." Then they called upon the counties to elect deputies to meet on August 1 in Williamsburg, to select representatives for the congress.

All over Virginia, during those hot July days, freemen were busy voting for delegates to represent them at the convention in Williamsburg. Albemarle County chose Jefferson. Hanover County voted for Patrick Henry. Fairfax County elected George Washington. On that August 1, 1774, Williamsburg was to see one of the most distinguished political gatherings in its history.

12

Before leaving Monticello for Williamsburg, Jefferson, the thirty-one-year-old delegate from Albemarle County, sorted his ideas and put them down on paper. He was moved by the conviction that since America was settled by freemen, it should be ruled by American freemen, and not by any foreign authority. He wrote fast, consulting no reference books but drawing upon the ample storehouse of his memory. In record time he had whipped into shape about sixty-five hundred words that were destined to ring throughout the colonies and Great Britain. Modestly he hoped that his paper, which he drew up tentatively, "with some uncertainties and inaccuracies," would serve as instructions to the delegates who would be chosen in Williamsburg for the Continental Congress. He made two copies.

Jefferson called his paper simply "Instructions." Ultimately it was printed under the title of *A Summary View of the Rights of British America,* and as such it is known to posterity. *A Summary View* is a landmark in American history, and a mirror of the mind of Thomas Jefferson in the summer of 1774. This pamphlet is the first link that bound Jefferson to the active destinies of his country. It is the matrix of the Declaration of Independence, two years older and five thousand words longer than the Declaration. In it the son of Peter Jefferson bluntly told the English King that he had no right to impose his will upon an America that was built by pioneers and not by peers. There are sentences in the *Summary* that scathe, others that purr, and throughout one senses a mind capable of indignant protest and of tactful appeal. This is the work of a master of English prose:

. . . his Majesty . . . is no more than the chief officer of the people, appointed by the laws, and circumscribed with definite powers, to assist in working the great machine of government, erected for their use, and consequently subject to their superintendence. . . .

To remind that our ancestors, before their emigration to America, were the free inhabitants of the British dominions in Europe, and possessed a right, which nature has given to all men, of departing from the country in which chance, not choice, had placed them, of going in quest of new habitations, and of there establishing new societies, under such laws and regulations as to them shall seem most likely to promote public happiness. That their Saxon ancestors had, under this universal law, in like manner, left their native wilds and woods in the north of Europe, had possessed themselves of the island of Britain. . . . Nor was ever any claim of superiority or dependence asserted over them. . . . no circumstance has occurred to distinguish . . . the British from the Saxon emigration. . . .

Single acts of tyranny may be ascribed to the accidental opinion of a day; but a series of oppressions begun at a distinguished period, and pursued unalterably through every change of ministers, too plainly prove a deliberate and systematical plan of reducing us to slavery. . . .

Can any one reason be assigned why 160,000 electors in the island of Great Britain should give law to four millions in the States of

America, every individual of whom is equal to every individual of them in virtue, in understanding, and in bodily strength? Were this to be admitted, instead of being a free people, as we have hitherto supposed, and mean to continue ourselves, we should suddenly be found the slaves not of one but of 160,000 tyrants. . . .

From the nature of things, every society must at all times possess within itself the sovereign powers of legislation. The feelings of human nature revolt against the supposition of a State so situated that it may not in any emergency provide against dangers which . . . threatened immediate ruin. . . .

America was not conquered by William the Norman, nor its lands surrendered to him or any of his successors. . . . Our ancestors . . . who migrated hither, were laborers, not lawyers. . . .

But can his majesty . . . put down all law under his feet? Can he erect a power superior to that which erected himself? He has done it indeed by force, but let him remember that force cannot give right.

. . . these are our grievances which we have thus laid before his majesty, with that freedom of language and sentiment which becomes a free people claiming their rights, as derived from the laws of nature, and not as the gift of their chief magistrate. Let those flatter who fear, it is not an American art. . . . They know . . . that kings are the servants, not the proprietors of the people.

Open your breast, sire, to liberal and expanded thought. Let not the name of George the third be a blot on the page of history. . . .

It is neither our wish nor our interest to separate from her [Great Britain]. We are willing, on our part, to sacrifice everything which reason can ask to the restoration of . . . tranquillity. . . . On their part, let them be ready to establish union on a generous plan. . . . But let them not think to exclude us from . . . other markets. . . . Still less let it be proposed that our properties within our own territories shall be taxed or regulated by any power on earth but our own.

The God who gave us life gave us liberty at the same time: the hand of force may destroy, but cannot disjoin them. This, sire, is our last, our determined resolution.

13

Jefferson never got to the convention at Williamsburg; on the way he was seized with a severe attack of dysentery and had to turn back home. A messenger carried two copies of his "Instructions" to Williamsburg, one copy to Patrick Henry and another to Peyton Randolph, the chairman of the assembly. The copy to Henry disappeared, Virginia's Demosthenes either losing it or throwing it away carelessly. "Whether Mr. Henry disapproved the ground taken," Jefferson tells, "or was too lazy to read it (for he was the laziest man in reading I ever knew) I never learned: but he communicated it to nobody." Randolph scrupulously presented his copy to the convention, where it was read with considerable astonishment and some trepidation. The majority thought it "too bold for the present state of things."

Later Jefferson candidly admitted that his paper was not sufficiently "tame" to be politically desirable. "The leap I proposed being too long, as yet, for the mass of our citizens," less revolutionary sentiments were preferred—"and, I believe, wisely preferred." The squire of Monticello had his convictions, but if public opinion was not ripe for his ideas, he could wait patiently for it to undergo a change, for truth sooner or later must prevail. Even as a revolutionist Jefferson was generally unrevolutionary, and always prudent. Leaders, he always held, should not run ahead of their followers. "Prudence required to keep front and rear together."

Jefferson's bold ideas were talked about in the convention, but someone else's "Instructions," mild as a "sucking dove," were adopted for the Virginia delegates. Jefferson's draft, however, was awarded the special honor of being printed in pamphlet form. The pamphlet fell upon the excitable political world like a bombshell. It soon reached London, where it was promptly seized upon by an eloquent Irishman named Edmund Burke, who used it as a club with which to beat the British Ministry. A Summary View ran rapidly through several editions, and caused the British Parliament to put the author's name on a bill of attainder for proscription.

CHAPTER IV

Rebel

1774   *1776*

THE LAWYERS and the planters and the orators of the thirteen separate colonies met in Philadelphia on the fourth of September, 1774, to talk over the situation created by the various unwelcome acts of the British Parliament. Jefferson was not among the delegates. He stayed at Monticello recuperating from his illness, knowing that Virginia was well represented by seven eminent sons. These were Richard Henry Lee; the dry, anticlerical John Bland; the massive Benjamin Harrison, whom John Adams (the crusty delegate from Massachusetts) depicted as "an indolent, luxurious, heavy gentleman"; the lean and eloquent Edmund Pendleton; the torrential Patrick Henry; the learned and aristocratic Peyton Randolph (who was elected president of the Congress); [1] and finally a big, rocklike man with a chilly exterior and a sensitive shyness—George Washington.

The delegates, representing views as diverse as the colonies they came from, were not yet ripe for union. They aired many problems and then adjourned until the following May. In England Lord Chatham praised their sagacity and moderation.

In the meantime Virginia was preparing to oppose the British Government by setting up independent administrative units,

[1] Young Jefferson felt warmly toward the middle-aged Randolph, of whom he said: "none was ever more beloved and respected by his friends. Somewhat cold and coy towards strangers, but of the sweetest affability when ripened into acquaintance. Of attic pleasantry in conversation, always good humored and conciliatory."

42

known as Committees of Safety. These committees in the various counties took over many of the functions of government, including the enlisting and arming of volunteers. Jefferson was chosen chairman of the Committee of Safety in his own Albemarle County.

2

In May, 1775, as prearranged, the Second Continental Congress assembled in the City of Brotherly Love. To the north, the Battle of Lexington had just been fought, and the consequences of this "accident" weighed heavily upon the minds of those who, like Jefferson, were as yet disinclined to surgery in the realm of politics. Jefferson had been playing revolutionist, but he had a horror of bloodshed and a gentleman's aversion to violence. The affair at Lexington disturbed him. "This accident," he groaned, "has cut off our last hope of reconciliation. . . . It is a lamentable circumstance, that the only mediatory power [the King] . . . should pursue the incendiary purpose of still blowing up the flames." To the Congress Virginia sent the same delegates as in the previous year, with one exception —Jefferson went as an alternate to Peyton Randolph, who was expected to become president of the assembly.

Jefferson was late for the Congress. It had already been in session one month when he left Williamsburg for Philadelphia. He traveled as quickly as possible in a light four-wheeled carriage, open at the sides but covered at the top to protect him from rain and sun. Like any good traveler, the practical Virginian carried spares—two extra horses. He rode fast, but the going was slow. The rivers were difficult to ford and the muddy roads were rutted. Jefferson took the short route to Fredericksburg and then swung eastward, crossing the Potomac to Annapolis at a narrow point somewhere near what is Washington today, paying a guide to take him over. Then he crossed the Chesapeake and drove straight north to Wilmington. Between Wilmington and Philadelphia the road was bad, and Jefferson again employed a guide.

Traveling, he looked about him with his usual curiosity,

making observations on flora, fauna, weather, and coinage. In Maryland he jotted down in his pocket account book the bewildering kinds of coins in circulation—pistareens, shillings, dollars, guineas, half-jos. It was financial disorder, disconcerting to a rational mind.

Ten days after leaving Williamsburg he arrived in Philadelphia. The distance was approximately three hundred miles, which means that Jefferson traveled about thirty miles a day. If we assume that he rode from morning to sunset—with two hours off for lunch—his average was hardly more than three miles an hour.

3

When Jefferson got to the big city, he took lodgings with a carpenter in a handsome house on Chestnut Street and went to the City Tavern to dine.

On the morrow—June 21—Jefferson entered the hall of the Congress, taking the seat of the distinguished Peyton Randolph, president of the assembly. The appearance of the now famous author of *A Summary View* created a little flurry. His reputation as a "fine writer," the possessor of a "masterly pen," had preceded him and aroused curiosity about his person.

He was something to look at, this angular, muscular, lean man, a long-legged horseman with tanned skin and brick-red hair. A tall poplar of a man, he stood out among the delegates —many of whom were short and some paunchy—with his virile youth and radiant exuberance. The youngest but one in an assembly of mature men, lawyers and businessmen, Jefferson's face shone with goodwill and intelligence. Neither aggressive nor oratorical, he easily attracted men and won their confidence. The testy little John Adams, a man of first-class intelligence, detected a like intelligence in the young delegate from Virginia and paid him the rare tribute of admiration and affection —"he was so prompt, frank, explicit and decisive upon committees and in conversation, not even Samuel Adams was more so," John Adams tells, "that he soon seized upon my heart."

Jefferson's reputation as the wielder of a smooth pen spread quickly, and within five days after taking his seat he was put on a committee to draw up a declaration of causes for taking up arms against Great Britain. The other member of the committee was John Dickinson, a conservative Philadelphia lawyer who favored conciliation and opposed revolution. He and Jefferson disagreed fundamentally—and amiably. Dickinson disliked Jefferson's draft, and Jefferson did not agree with Dickinson's. Jefferson good-naturedly yielded:

I prepared a draught of the Declaration. . . . It was too strong for Mr. Dickinson. He still retained the hope of reconciliation with the mother country, and was unwilling it should be lessened by offensive statements. He was so honest a man, & so able a one that he was greatly indulged even by those who could not feel his scruples. We therefore requested him to take the paper, and put it into a form he could approve. He did so. . . . We approved & reported it to Congress, who accepted it.

Dickinson's conciliatory draft, which the Congress reluctantly approved, retained four paragraphs written by Jefferson. Some of these Jeffersonian phrases are memorable, sparks that finally burst into the flame of the Declaration:

We . . . find nothing so dreadful as voluntary slavery. Honor, justice, and humanity, forbid us tamely to surrender that freedom which we received from our gallant ancestors, and which our innocent posterity have a right to receive from us. We cannot endure the infamy and guilt of resigning succeeding generations to the wretchedness which inevitably awaits them, if we basely entail hereditary bondage upon them.
Our cause is just. Our union is perfect—our internal resources are great. . . . [We are] resolved to die free men rather than to live slaves. . . .
We fight not for glory or for conquest. We exhibit to mankind the remarkable spectacle of a people attacked by unprovoked enemies, without any imputation, or even suspicion of offence. They boast of their privileges and civilization, and yet proffer no milder condition than servitude or death.

The fervent Jeffersonian phrases ended with a feeble Dickinsonian plea to Great Britain for "reconciliation on reasonable terms." But Congress disliked the idea of conciliation. Patrick

Henry's words were still fresh in the minds of the delegates—
"Gentlemen may cry peace, peace—but there is no peace. The
war is actually begun! . . . Our brethren are already in the
field! Why stand we idle here?"

A few of the delegates, John Dickinson for one, were des-
perately trying to avoid a final break with the mother country.
They were even opposed to the idea of a Congress, with its
implication of independence and union. Feeling ran high.
When John Dickinson rose and in defense of his draft said:
"There is but one word, Mr. President, in the paper which I
disapprove, & that is the word *Congress*," corpulent Benjamin Harrison could not refrain from snapping back: "There is
but one word in the paper, Mr. President, of which I approve,
and that is the word *Congress*."

4

Young Jefferson made no speeches, but he was openly identified with the leading advocates of resistance to Great Britain.
Despite his youth—he was only thirty-two—his popularity
seems to have been second only to that of the revered Benjamin
Franklin, who was old enough to be Jefferson's grandfather.

Several days after the unsuccessful Dickinson-Jefferson collaboration, the Congress appointed another committee to report on Lord North's conciliation proposal. Members were
chosen by ballot and, close behind Franklin, Jefferson led all
other candidates, including John Adams and Richard Henry
Lee. Once more Jefferson was asked by his colleagues to draft
a reply; once more he composed sonorous phrases defying King
and Parliament. At the end of July the Congress adopted the
young Virginian's resolution and adjourned.

5

In August Jefferson returned home as he came, by phaeton.
His feelings, strongly aroused by stimulating contact with dis-

tinguished fellow Americans from other colonies, were nevertheless mixed, and his thoughts disturbed. Despite his fiery
sentiments, he wanted neither separation from nor war with
England. He was, however, to the roots of his innermost being
a child of the American frontier, and the thought of any
arbitrary authority, particularly one exercised from a distance
of three thousand miles, touched his pride and anger to the
quick. The idea of a foreign Power claiming superiority over
indigenous Americans—the very word "colonial" had an invidious sound—galled the sensitive strain of the aristocratic Randolph in Jefferson. The son of Peter Jefferson, moreover, was
stubbornly proud of the fact that his father had cleared the
wilderness with his own hands, that his muscles had broken
the virgin land. Who was this German-descended princeling
in London, or his corrupt hirelings, to try arbitrary rule on
freeborn sons of freeborn pioneers? Again and again in Jefferson's early writings one hears the passionate echo of the
dead father who had personally conquered the wilderness. In
The Summary View we find it:

America was conquered, and her settlements made, and firmly
established, at the expense of individuals, and not of the British public.
Their own blood was spilt in acquiring lands for their settlements,
their own fortunes expended in making that settlement effectual;
for themselves they fought, for themselves they conquered, and for
themselves alone they have right to hold.

This, however, did not yet mean that Jefferson was ready to
fight for independence from Great Britain. America, he felt,
might still be satisfied to live under a "properly limited" British government. In August, 1775, he told his relative the pro-
British John Randolph:

I . . . would rather be in dependence on Great Britain, properly
limited, than on any nation on earth, or than on no nation. But I am
one of those, too, who, rather than submit to the rights of legislating
for us, assumed by the British Parliament, and which late experience
has shown they will so cruelly exercise, would lend my hand to sink
the whole Island in the ocean.

He was impatient for the conflict to be settled, one way or the other, for politics kept him from devoting himself to what he most loved: "domestic ease and tranquillity." So long as the political fire was smoldering he had little time for his home and extensive garden, for his wife and his adored three-year-old child Martha. He was so troubled that he even gave up his violin, but always he kept on hoping that he would soon withdraw himself "totally from the public stage." His genius for politics was so pronounced that in self-defense, fearing lest it absorb him, he always expressed distaste for the political life.

As the year 1775 was coming to an end and no solution was in sight, Jefferson's ordinarily calm temper was slowly beginning to boil. To John Randolph he wrote at the end of November in a tone of unusual truculence:

. . . there is not in the British empire a man who more cordially loves a union with Great Britain, than I do. But by the God that made me, I will cease to exist before I yield to a connection on such terms as the British Parliament propose; and in this, I think I speak the sentiments of America. We want neither inducement nor power, to declare and assert a separation. . . . One bloody campaign will probably decide, everlastingly, our future course; and I am sorry to find a bloody campaign is decided on. . . . we must drub him [General Howe] soundly, before the sceptred tyrant will know we are not mere brutes, to crouch under his hand, and kiss the rod with which he designs to scourge us.

6

That winter Jefferson spent at home in Monticello, alternately hopeful and despondent about a settlement with Great Britain. In this he reflected the general mood of the colonies, where opinion was not so much divided as uncrystallized. No less than five colonial legislatures, including those of Pennsylvania and New York, voted against independence. People wanted to have their cake and eat it too: they hoped to remain members of the British Empire and resented having to obey that empire.

Suddenly popular opinion crystallized. In January, 1776, while American officers at a mess presided over by General George Washington were toasting the health of the King of England, a fiery pamphlet fell upon America. It was forty-seven pages long, sold for 2s., and was entitled *Common Sense*. The author, it turned out, was an Englishman only one year in Philadelphia, a corsetmaker by trade, a journalist by profession, and a propagandist by inclination. His name was Thomas Paine. Within three months *Common Sense* sold 120,000 copies—in time it reached the best-seller heights with 500,000 copies.

Common Sense cried out boldly what many Americans had been feeling and not saying. Paine's words were clean and straight, like shot from a musket. A self-educated proletarian who had suffered much in England, Paine shared with many Americans contempt for monarchy and hatred for tyranny. His words burned themselves into the colonial American conscience:

> Society in every state is a blessing, but government even in its best state is but a necessary evil; in its worst state an intolerable one. . . . Government, like dress, is the badge of lost innocence; the palaces of kings are built upon the ruins of the bowers of paradise.

Common Sense delighted nonaristocratic, free Americans with its attack on kings as "crowned ruffians" and George the Third as the "Royal Brute." The pamphlet urged Americans to break with the corrupt tyranny of the British Empire and establish here a great haven of freedom.

> Ye that dare oppose not only the tyranny, but the tyrant, stand forth! Every spot of the old world is over-run with oppression. Freedom hath been hunted round the globe. Asia, and Africa, have long expelled her.—Europe regards her like a stranger, and England hath given her warning to depart. O! receive the fugitive, and prepare in time an asylum for mankind.

The pamphlet made converts by the thousands. Aristocrats like General Charles Lee were won over by its torrential eloquence, considering it a "masterly, irresistible performance." Cool heads like that of George Washington were swept along by the pamphlet; the General praised its "flaming arguments," its "sound doctrine," and its "unanswerable reasoning."

As for Jefferson, unlike many other patriots he continued to cherish a high regard for Thomas Paine. "No writer," Jefferson said in later years, "has exceeded Paine in ease and familiarity of style, in perspicacity of expression, happiness of elucidation, and in simple and unassuming language."

The powerful stuff of *Common Sense* went to the head of the American people.

7

Jefferson was in Monticello in January, 1776, when the irascible Lord Dunmore, the Royal Governor of Virginia, burned Norfolk and thereby drove the colony to armed revolt. Jefferson remained at home, staying away from the Congress in Philadelphia while his mother was ailing and the South was seething with revolution. In March the neighboring colony of North Carolina decided upon independence from Great Britain. In the same month Jefferson's mother died. Apparently he did not feel the loss keenly. There is a terse sentence in his pocket notebook: "March 31, 1776. My mother died about eight o'clock this morning in the 57th year of her age."

The political crisis was coming to a head. Critical news came from all over the country and jarred Jefferson out of his domestic ease and comfort. Early in May he hurried northward to Philadelphia, where he took lodgings in a three-story brick house on Market Street, between Seventh and Eighth. The house belonged to a newly married young German bricklayer named Graaf. Jefferson occupied the second floor, consisting of a parlor and bedroom, and paid 35s. (about $8.50 today) rent a week. "In that parlor I wrote habitually," he says.

On May 13 he took his seat in the Congress and was welcomed by those who were sharpening the scalpel with which to cut the umbilical cord that tied them to the mother country.

8

Jefferson was not the leader of the Virginia delegation in Congress, but he was probably its most learned member and certainly its best writer. At the age of thirty-two, to quote one of his earliest biographers, he was a gentleman "who could calculate an eclipse, survey an estate, tie an artery, plan an edifice, try a cause, break a horse, dance a minuet and play the violin." There were not many like him in the Congress.

Despite an abundance of other gifts, he lacked that of eloquence. On the floor of the Congress he was as silent as a conspirator; on paper he was a Demosthenes. John Adams recalled that "during the whole time I sat with him in Congress I never heard him utter three sentences together." But his reputation for learning was as solid as his diction was flawless. Everyone admired his "peculiar felicity of expression." When it came to drawing up resolutions or penning declarations, Jefferson was a natural choice.

On Friday, June 7, 1776, Jefferson's colleague Richard Henry Lee rose on the floor of Congress and introduced a startling resolution:

That these United Colonies are & of right ought to be free & independent states, that they are absolved from all allegiance to the British crown, and that all political connection between them & the state of Great Britain is & ought to be, totally dissolved.

The Congress burst into an uproarious torrent of debate, which continued passionately through Saturday and Monday and Tuesday. Arguments fell and scattered like hailstones, as Jefferson noted:

. . . That the people of the middle colonies . . . were not yet ripe for bidding adieu to British connection. . . .
. . . they had not yet accommodated their minds to a separation from the mother country. . . .
. . . such a secession would weaken us more than could be compensated by any foreign alliance. . . .

. . . foreign powers . . . would insist on terms proportionably more hard and prejudicial. . . .

. . . France & Spain had reason to be jealous of that rising power which would one day certainly strip them of all their American possessions.

Such were some of the arguments against independence uttered by men like James Wilson, Robert R. Livingston, Edward Rutledge, and John Dickinson.

On the other side were formidable debaters like John Adams, Richard Henry Lee, and George Wythe. They cried:

That the question was not whether, by a declaration of independence, we should make ourselves what we are not; but whether we should declare a fact which already exists. . . .

. . . as to the people or parliament of England, we had always been independent of them. . . .

. . . the people wait for us to lead the way . . . *they* are in favour of the measure. . . .

. . . it would be vain to wait either weeks or months for perfect unanimity, since it was impossible that all men should ever become of one sentiment on any question. . . .

. . . it was necessary for those colonies who had thrown themselves forward & hazarded all from the beginning, to come forward now also. . . .

. . . a declaration of Independence alone could render it consistent with European delicacy for European powers to treat with us. . . .

. . . it would be idle to lose time.

The end of the fierce debate was a sensible compromise. Since the Middle Colonies had "not yet matured for falling from the parent stem," as Jefferson phrased it with his customary felicity, it was decided to give them time to ripen. The final vote on Lee's resolution was therefore postponed until July 1. In the meantime a committee of five was appointed to work on a Declaration of Independence.

9

The committee consisted of Thomas Jefferson of Virginia, John Adams of Massachusetts, Dr. Benjamin Franklin of Pennsylvania, Roger Sherman of Connecticut, and Robert R. Livingston of New York—a shrewd selection of men representing the Southern, Northern, and Middle colonies. They were instructed to draw up a declaration giving reasons "which impelled us to this mighty resolution."

According to John Adams, he and Jefferson had a friendly disagreement as to who should do the writing. The tall Virginian is supposed to have insisted politely that the stocky little New Englander should have the honor of making the draft. Adams relates:

"I said, 'I will not. You should do it.' "

Jefferson: "Oh! no. Why will you not? You ought to do it."

Adams: "I will not."

Jefferson: "Why?"

Adams: "Reason enough."

Jefferson: "What can be your reasons?"

Adams: "Reason first—You are a Virginian, and a Virginian ought to appear at the head of this business. Reason second—I am obnoxious, suspected, and unpopular. You are very much otherwise. Reason third—You can write ten times better than I can."

Jefferson: "Well, if you are decided, I will do as well as I can."

Adams: "Very well. When you have drawn it up, we will have a meeting."

Adams's version appeared forty-seven years after the event, and was not entirely accurate. After referring to his notes, Jefferson denied that that is what had taken place: "Mr. Adams' memory has led him into unquestionable error." The truth seems to be that the committee met as a whole and unanimously insisted that Jefferson draw up the declaration. There never was any question of anyone else's doing the writing.

10

When Jefferson went to his parlor on the second floor of the bricklayer's house on Market Street to pen a draft, he did not feel that he was doing anything extraordinary nor did he suspect that he was toying with immortality. In his *Autobiography* he says laconically: "The committee for drawing the declaration of Independence desired me to do it. It was accordingly done."

Between June 11 and June 28 Jefferson sat at a little improvised desk in the stuffy parlor, his quill scratching tirelessly. For seventeen days he labored at the document, carving and polishing the words. He wrote fine, clear, meticulous script, revealing the neat precision of a scientific and poetic mind aware that each word counted, as indeed it did.

The inspiration behind his quill was not personal. He felt himself writing words that were, or should have been, common property. Only the composition was his; the sentiments belonged to mankind. He always insisted that the Declaration of Independence merely gave voice to what his compatriots felt. He was only the instrument, not the creator. Half a century after writing the Declaration he said: "Neither aiming at originality of principle or sentiment, nor yet copied from any particular and previous writing, it was intended to be an expression of the American mind."

11

But the words had wings and the phrases a haunting beauty.

When in the course of human events
it becomes necessary for one people
to dissolve the political bonds
which have connected them with another,
and to assume
among the powers of the earth,

the separate and equal station
to which the laws of nature
and of nature's God
entitle them,
a decent respect to the opinions of mankind requires
that they should declare the causes
which impel them to the separation.[2]

12

Thus far Jefferson was on familiar ground. Those who knew their Locke and their Milton—and what educated gentleman did not?—would not quarrel with the principle of voluntary dissolution of political bonds. Few lawyers in America at this time disbelieved in the theory of the social compact. It was the dominant doctrine of the middle class. Moreover, it was the experience of Americans on this new continent.

13

Jefferson's second sentence was dynamite.

We hold these truths
to be self-evident,
that all men are created equal,
that they are endowed by their Creator
with inherent and [3] unalienable rights,
that among these
are life, liberty, and the pursuit of Happiness.

The last three words are a declaration of faith, Jefferson's undying contribution to American life. The assertion that the pursuit of happiness was one of the objects for which governments exist was something new in the history of political doctrine. Ordinarily the triplex of political values included life,

[2] The ampersand so often used by Jefferson is changed to "and" in quotations from the Declaration of Independence.
[3] Congress struck out "inherent and" and substituted "certain."

liberty, and property. By substituting "the pursuit of happiness" for "property" Jefferson broke with the traditional concept and laid the foundation for a unique commonwealth of justice and freedom and security.

14

Having affirmed man's right to happiness, Jefferson then asserted the hardly less revolutionary doctrine of the right to self-government and to revolution.

> . . . that to secure these rights,
> governments are instituted among men,
> deriving their just powers
> from the consent of the governed;
> that whenever any form of government
> becomes destructive of these ends,
> it is the right of the people
> to alter or to abolish it,
> and to institute
> new government,
> laying its foundation on such principles,
> and organising its powers in such form,
> as to them shall seem most likely to effect
> their safety and happiness.

15

From these general principles Jefferson leaped to specific charges. With the cleverness of a subtle manipulator of public opinion, he personalized the enemy and exposed him to devastating attack. Instead of accusing the British nation, Jefferson singled out George the Third as the diabolus ex machina, and delivered him short, relentless jabs:

> . . . he has refused . . .
> . . . he has forbidden . . .
> . . . he has called together . . .
> . . . he has dissolved . . .

. . . he has endeavored . . .
. . . he has made . . .
. . . he has erected . . .
. . . he has kept . . .
. . . he has affected . . .
. . . he has combined . . .
. . . he has plundered . . .
. . . he has constrained . . .
. . . he has incited . . .

16

Then, without transition, Jefferson aimed a blow at the hapless George the Third that came close to being below the belt. The owner of more than two hundred slaves suddenly put the onus of slavery and the responsibility for its horrors upon the shoulders of the King of England.

He has waged cruel war
against human nature itself,
violating its most sacred rights
of life and liberty
in the persons of a distant people who never offended him,
captivating and carrying them into slavery in another hemisphere,
or to incur miserable death in their transportation thither.
This piratical warfare,
the opprobrium of *infidel* powers,
is the warfare
of the *Christian* king of Great Britain
determined to keep open a market
where MEN should be bought
and sold,
he has prostituted his negative
for suppressing every legislative attempt
to prohibit or to restrain
this execrable commerce.
and that this assemblage of horrors
might want no fact of distinguished die,
he is now exciting those very people
to rise in arms among us,

and to purchase
that liberty of which *he* has deprived them,
by murdering the people
on whom *he* also obtruded them:
thus paying off former crimes
committed against the *liberties*
of one people,
with crimes
which he urges them to commit
against the *lives* of another.[4]

17

After branding George the Third, Jefferson wrote about the English people, words that did not taste sweet.

They too have been deaf
to the voice of justice,
and of consanguinity,
and when occasions have been given them,
by the regular course of their laws,
of removing from their councils
the disturbers of our harmony,
they have
by their free election
re-established them in power.
At this very time too
they are permitting their chief magistrate
to send over
not only soldiers of our common blood
but Scotch and foreign mercenaries
to invade and destroy us.
These facts
have given the last stab
to agonizing affection,
and manly spirit bids us

[4] Congress struck out the whole passage, probably wisely, for it was not altogether fair to put the blame of slavery upon one man, be he king or planter. In any case, the Congress did not wish to alienate South Carolina and Georgia, which were in favor of continuing the importation of slaves. Some of the Northern States, likewise, made profits from the slave trade.

to renounce for ever
these unfeeling brethren.
We must endeavor
to forget our former love for them,
and hold them
as we hold the rest of mankind,
enemies in war,
in peace friends.
We might have been a free and a great people together;
but a communication of grandeur and of freedom,
it seems
is below their dignity.
Be it so
since they will have it.
The road to happiness and to glory
is open to us too,
we will tread it
apart from them,
and acquiesce in the necessity
which denounces our eternal separation.[5]

18

And he concluded:

We therefore,
the representatives of the United States of America
in General Congress assembled,
in the name and by the authority of
the good people of these states
reject and renounce
all allegiance and subjection
to the kings of Great Britain
and all others
who may hereafter claim by, through, or under them;

[5] Most of this passage was likewise struck out by Congress. The words sounded too bitter to people who up till yesterday still considered themselves Englishmen and had a "lingering affection" for the mother country. Moreover, the reference to "Scotch and foreign mercenaries" was too invidious in a country where almost 90 per cent of the population was Anglo-Scotch.

we utterly dissolve
all political connection
which may heretofore have subsisted
between us
and the people or parliament
of Great Britain;
and finally we do assert and declare
these colonies to be free
and independent states,
and that
as free and independent states,
they have full power
to levy war,
conclude peace,
contract alliances,
establish commerce,
and do all other acts
and things
which independent states may of right do,
And for the support
of this declaration,
we mutually pledge to each other
our lives,
our fortunes,
and our sacred honour.[6]

[6] From this point on Congress changed Jefferson's draft to read: ", appealing to the Supreme Judge of the world for the rectitude of our intentions, do, in the Name and by the Authority of the good People of these Colonies, solemnly publish and declare, that these United Colonies are, and of Right ought to be Free and Independent States; that they are Absolved from all allegiance to the British Crown, and that all political connection between them and the State of Great Britain, is and ought to be totally dissolved; and that as Free and Independent states, they have full Power to levy War, conclude Peace, contract Alliances, establish Commerce, and to do all other acts and things which Independent States may of right do.

"And for the support of this Declaration, with a firm reliance on the protection of divine Providence, we mutually pledge each other our Lives, our Fortunes, and our sacred Honor." It will be seen that Congress added many capital letters here, as they did throughout.

19

Entries in Jefferson's pocket account book during the time
he was sculpturing the words of the Declaration of Independence:

June 11. Paid £1.18.2 for Window shutter rings. . . .
June 18. Paid for a nest of trunks, 7/6. . . .
June 19. Paid Greentree for wine, 6/
June 20. Paid Aitkin for lining a map, 5/.
June 22. Paid Sparhawk for pair spiers, 25/. . . .
June 23. Paid Graaf 2 weeks lodging &c., £3.10.
June 25. Paid for 2 pr stockings for Bob, 15/. Paid for a straw
hat, 1/. . . .
June 28. Paid mrs. Lovemor washing in full, 39/9.

20

When Jefferson finished the draft, he presented it separately
to Franklin and Adams, the two men whose judgment he most
respected. They made a few slight corrections. "Their alterations," Jefferson says, "were two or three only, and merely
verbal." Then Jefferson meticulously rewrote the whole draft,
including the Franklin-Adams insertions, and presented it to
the whole committee. They approved unanimously, and on
June 28 "A Declaration by the Representatives of the United
States of America, in General Congress Assembled" [7] was
thrown into the lap of the Congress.

The sharp-witted lawyers of the Congress fell upon Jefferson's creation with a zest that cut the sensitive author to the
quick. For three days they flayed the paper with scalpels, slicing off words and phrases as if they were offensive tissue. Out
of more than eighteen hundred words the members of the Congress expunged four hundred and sixty, or about one-fourth of
the whole. They altered about two dozen words and made two

[7] This was Jefferson's original title. On July 19 an act of Congress changed
it to "The Unanimous Declaration of the thirteen united States of America."

insertions in the peroration—references to a "supreme judge" and a "divine providence." Jefferson had neglected the Deity here, though he had mentioned Him twice before.

The debate was an agonizing ordeal for Jefferson. He sat still and silent, "a passive auditor," he said, suffering more than his dignity permitted him to show. Burden of the defense lay with the chunky, hard-hitting John Adams, who, in the words of the grateful Jefferson, was "fighting fearlessly for every word." Every word under attack was a ruthless depredation upon the author's creation, and made him wince. Despite his pride, he could not altogether control his emotions. Finally the seventy-year-old Franklin took pity on the sensitive author. The great Doctor leaned over, and with the humorous wisdom for which he was famous, he spoke words of comfort to the unhappy Virginian. Jefferson tells the delightful story:

I was sitting by Dr. Franklin who perceived that I was not insensible to these mutilations.

"I have made it a rule," said he, "whenever in my power, to avoid becoming the draughtsman of papers to be reviewed by a public body. I took my lesson from an incident which I will relate to you.

"When I was a journeyman printer, one of my companions, an apprentice Hatter, having served out his time, was about to open shop for himself, his first concern was to have a handsome sign-board with a proper inscription. He composed it in these words, 'John Thompson, *Hatter, makes and sells hats for ready money,*' with a figure of a hat subjoined: but he thought he would submit it to his friends for their amendments. The first he showed it to thought the word 'Hatter' tautologous, because followed by the words 'makes hats,' which shew he was a Hatter. It was struck out. The next observed that the word 'makes' might as well be omitted, because his customers would not care who made the hats. If good & to their mind, they would buy by whomsoever made. He struck it out.

"A third said he thought the words '*for ready money*' were useless as it was not the custom of the place to sell on credit. Every one who purchased expected to pay. They were parted with, and the inscription now stood, 'John Thompson sells hats.' '*sells hats*' says his next friend? 'Why nobody will expect you to give them away. What then is the use of that word? It was stricken out, and '*hats*' followed it—the rather as there was one painted on the board. So the inscription was reduced ultimately to 'John Thompson' with the figure of a hat subjoined."

21

The hacking which the Declaration underwent did not, miraculously enough, spoil the force of its arguments or the cadence of its phrases. Many felt as did Richard Henry Lee, who told the pleased Jefferson: "The *Thing* is in its nature so good, that no Cookery can spoil the Dish for the palates of Freemen." Years later Woodrow Wilson was to call it a "whip for tyrants." [8]

On Monday, July 1, "the Thing" was put to a vote. After nine hours of acrimonious debate all the colonies except Pennsylvania and South Carolina (and partly Delaware) voted in its favor. On the following day the recalcitrant colonies changed their vote, and there was no dissenting voice.

The Declaration of Independence was approved on July 2. On July 3 the Congress took up Richard Henry Lee's original resolution of June 7 and debated the crucial point that "these United Colonies are & of right ought to be free and independent states." On that day Jefferson noted that the temperature was 76° Fahrenheit—not a hot afternoon for Philadelphia in July. On that same day Jefferson spent one hundred and three

[8] Another President who paid tribute to the Declaration of Independence was Abraham Lincoln. On February 22, 1861, Lincoln, on the way to Washington for his inauguration, stopped at Philadelphia and made the following comment on Jefferson's great prose poem:

"I have never had a feeling, politically, that did not spring from the sentiments embodied in the Declaration of Independence. . . . I have often inquired of myself what great principle it was that kept this Confederacy so long together. It was not the mere matter of separation of the colonies from the motherland, but that sentiment in the Declaration of Independence which gave liberty not alone to the people of this country, but hope to all the world, for all future time. It was that which gave promise that in due time the weights would be lifted from the shoulders of all men, and that all should have an equal chance. This is the sentiment embodied in the Declaration of Independence. . . . I would rather be assassinated on the spot than surrender it." *Abraham Lincoln, Complete Works*, ed. by J. G. Nicolay and John Hay, 2 vols., Century, 1920, Vol. 1, p. 691.

shillings. He bought a thermometer for "£3.15" and "7 pr. women's gloves" for 27 shillings; "1/6" he gave "in charity."

On July 4 the Congress debated all day—a comparatively cool one. Jefferson said nothing; he quietly took notes. He was not so absorbed, however, as to neglect to record the temperature in his notebook. He took at least four readings on his new $19 thermometer. While the statesmen of the newly born nation were arguing heatedly, Jefferson coolly recorded: "July 4th, 6 A.M., 68°; 9 A.M., 72¼°; 1 P.M., 76°; 9 P.M., 73½°." In the evening the debate was closed, and all the members present except John Dickinson signed the Declaration of Independence.[9]

To inform the citizens that the nation was born, the Declaration of Independence was read in the public square (Independence Square) in Philadelphia. Copies were made and published in all the hamlets and settlements throughout the thirteen colonies that had suddenly been declared States.

22

To write lofty phrases about liberty and marshal telling arguments against tyranny was one thing; to carry out those ideas, especially by force of arms, was another. Having declared independence, the Congress now faced the seemingly hopeless task of waging war against a powerful enemy. The young nation was ill prepared to fight; its political organization was in embryo and its military personnel without much experience. Colonists who had devoted their lives to the peaceful pursuits of farming and trade had neither the ready machinery nor the mental equipment for the sanguinary business of war. To peace-loving intellectuals like Jefferson the outlook was discouraging. "God knows," he groaned, "how this will end." And he begged Richard Henry Lee, who was in Virginia, to come to Philadelphia and help with the mounting work: "for God's sake, for your country's sake, & for my sake, come."

Jefferson was put on so many committees that he was too

[9] Many were not present and signed later.

hard-driven to find time for himself. His never-stilled yearning for the peace of the quiet countryside and his desire to leave politics came back in force. He was also worrying about the delicate health of Mrs. Jefferson, and yearning for his family. Every day he was away from his wife was a strain on his emotions. The burden grew too great, and when the Virginia Convention re-elected him to the Congress that summer, he wrote to its president, Edmund Pendleton, begging to be excused:

I am sorry the situation of my domestic affairs, renders it indispensably necessary that I should solicit the substitution of some other person here in my room. The delicacy of the House will not require me to enter minutely into the private causes which render this necessary. I trust they will be satisfied I would not urge it again, were it not unavoidable.

But men of ability were not so readily released. Pendleton, for whom Jefferson had great respect and affection, replied with a touch of severity:

I hope you'l get cured of y^r wish to retire so early in life, from the memory of man, & exercise y^r talents for the nurture of our new Constitution, which will require all the Attention of its Friends to prune exuberance and cherish the plant.

Jefferson waited until the Articles of Confederation were reported in the Congress and then resigned. Early in September he left Philadelphia and hurried home. There was work to do in Virginia.

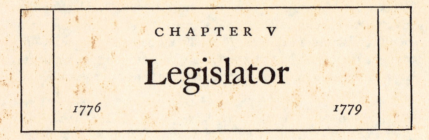

CHAPTER V

Legislator

1776   *1779*

A FTER Jefferson had been home about a month, happy
with his three young daughters and active in his fields,
word reached him that the Congress in Philadelphia
had appointed him and the great Doctor Franklin commissioners to negotiate treaties with the France of Louis Sixteenth. He declined the honor. Not only was his young wife
ailing, and he would not dream of leaving her for a prolonged
stay abroad, but there was urgent work to do in Virginia. "The
laboring oar was really at home," he said.

For Jefferson had quietly matured a plan to bring democracy
to his home State. Without heat or rhetoric, he had come to
the conclusion that a democratic (he used the word "republican") society, as he conceived it, could not be built upon a
monarchical foundation. It was not enough to cast out the king;
it was necessary also to destroy the king's institutions. To Jefferson's logical mind it was unreasonable to reject monarchy—
in the person of the British King—and at the same time retain
the trappings of monarchy. And despite her declared and stout
independence, Virginia was still a royalist State in everything
but name.

That revolutions do not stop halfway, that if you throw
away the crown, the appurtenances of the crown—throne, scep-
ter, symbolism, and all—must follow—this did not escape keen
observers of the political scene. The American planters who
thought that they could break with the British Crown and re-

tain the social system of the monarchy were in for an awakening. Men like Jefferson, determined men to whom words like "liberty" and "equality" had a positive meaning, were ready to go all the way in eradicating royalism and eliminating the props which held it up.

Keen lawyers and good scholars these republicans were, and they felt that the first thing to undergo a revolutionary cleansing was the legal system. No one knew better than Lawyer Jefferson that in any civilized society the whole complex of social relationships is held together, like intricate basketry, in a legal code. Change the law and you change the social system; alter the social system and the law must be adjusted. Property relationships and personal status were anchored in a body of laws that perpetuated ownership and sanctioned privilege in the hands of a tight little ruling class. That Jefferson, by inheritance and marriage and position, was a member of the controlling class did not alter the situation nor affect his intransigent attitude. He saw no contradiction in owning thousands of acres of slave-tilled land and at the same time believing in equality. To him the concept of democracy did not rest upon an equality of property but upon one of opportunity. The purpose of the law was to protect man not in special privilege, but in his various social freedoms—freedom of conscience, of speech, of assembly, of enterprise. Any code that perpetuated privilege and froze personal status was a bad code. Any law that granted citizens equal opportunities and protected them in all their "inherent" liberties was a good law.

The Virginia code, derived from the British Crown and elaborated by a class-conscious aristocracy, was ready for the ax. It was no longer acceptable to free farmers who had snapped the royal chains. The code, Jefferson said, had "many very vicious points" that called for liquidation:

When I left Congress, in [17]76. it was in the persuasion that our whole code must be reviewed, adapted to our republican form of government; and, now that we had no negatives of Councils, Governors, & Kings to restrain us from doing right, that it should be corrected in all it's parts, with a single eye to reason, & the good of those for whose government it was framed.

Socially, and even economically, Virginia was run by an aristocracy of birth, and this the son of the pioneer Peter Jefferson considered a menace to society and a danger to freedom. In his quietly unyielding way Jefferson held fast to his human faith, that men had inalienable rights to life, liberty, and the pursuit of happiness. Liberty could not coexist with privileged aristocracy, nor happiness be found where excess wealth was permitted to be concentrated in a few hands.

Virginia was stippled with magnificent manors, some of them as large as 50,000 acres. Black men, permanently enslaved, worked those acres and created the wealth which enabled the aristocracy to live in princely splendor. The Virginia baronies were held by a few families in entail. By the law of primogeniture the estates passed from heir to heir, and could be neither broken up nor divided. The result was as Jefferson described it:

The transmission of this property from generation to generation in the same name raised up a distinct set of families who, being privileged by law in the perpetuation of their wealth, were thus formed into a Patrician order, distinguished by the splendor and luxury of their establishments.

This permanent aristocracy was a constant threat to self-government by free men and for free men. To establish and perpetuate free government, which was Jefferson's ideal, it was necessary to blast away the foundations of the aristocracy. He explained:

To annul this privilege, and instead of an aristocracy of wealth, of more harm and danger, than benefit, to society, to make an opening for the aristocracy of virtue and talent, which nature has wisely provided for the direction of the interests of society, & scattered with equal hand through all it's conditions, was deemed essential to a well ordered republic.

2

Early in October, 1776, Jefferson, his head full of reform, was in Williamsburg for the autumn session of the Virginia House of Delegates. As soon as the various committees were organized and the House got down to business, Jefferson sprang his revolution upon Virginia. It was to be, he hoped, a peaceful revolution, a revolution by law. "No violence was necessary, no deprivation of natural right," he says.

This was Jefferson's first major political effort, and his strategy is worth observing. He preferred the background to the glare of footlights. He was the organizer behind the scenes, the indefatigable planner in small committees. He talked and persuaded. Without a political party, he knew how to instil his ideas into others so subtly that they came to feel themselves the originators. Singularly sweet-natured and devoid of aggressiveness, the thirty-three-year-old delegate from Monticello was followed by men who did not always know they were doing so. That was how it came about that the party of Patrick Henry, a popular leader without a program, supported some of the bills of Jefferson, who had only a program.

Jefferson's strength came also from another source. He had a genius for friendship and a shy warmth, and men of quality rarely failed to be attracted to him. As he was now preparing to transform Virginia by law and facing the hardest fight of his career, he was able to depend upon the loyalty and affection of three men, each one a host in himself. Without these devoted friends his bills might have been beaten, for the House of Delegates was sharply divided on basic social issues.

First in importance was Jefferson's friend and teacher George Wythe. Jefferson always spoke of him in terms close to adoration:

His virtue was of the purest tint; his integrity inflexible, and his justice exact; of warm patriotism, and, devoted as he was to liberty, and the natural and equal rights of man, he might truly be called the Cato of his country, without the avarice of the Roman; for a more disinterested person never lived. Temperance and regularity in all his habits gave him general good health, and his unaffected modesty and suavity of manners endeared him to every one. He was of easy elocution, his language chaste, methodical in the arrangement of his matter, learned and logical in the use of it, and of great urbanity in debate; not quick of apprehension, but with a little time, profound in penetration, and sound in conclusion. In his philosophy he was firm, and neither troubling, nor perhaps trusting, any one with his religious creed, he left the world to the conclusion, that that religion must be good which could produce a life of such exemplary virtue. . . . Such was George Wythe, the honor of his own, and the model of future times.

The second of Jefferson's "strenuous coadjutors in debate" was George Mason, one of the stanchest democrats in America. His fame should be greater than it is. Jefferson described him as

. . . a man of the first order of wisdom among those who acted on the theatre of the revolution, of expansive mind, profound judgment, cogent in argument, learned in the lore of our former constitution, and earnest for the republican change on democratic principles. His elocution was neither flowing nor smooth, but his language was strong, his manner most impressive, and strengthened by a dash of biting cynicism when provocation made it seasonable.

Finally there was a mousy little man in his middle twenties, of great legal learning and dry humor, with an inexhaustible capacity for work. His name was James Madison, a man whose homely features did not betray his powerful intelligence. Madison succumbed to the charm of the already distinguished delegate from Monticello, and for the next fifty years remained his closest friend and collaborator. Jefferson rewarded his friend with a lifelong affection, and with the Presidency of the United States. The friendship between the tall, sparkling Jefferson and the slight, dry, legalistic Madison is one of the longest on record. Jefferson later described Madison:

. . . he acquired a habit of self-possession which placed at ready command the rich resources of his luminous and discriminating mind, & of his extensive information, and rendered him the first of every assembly afterwards of which he became a member. Never wandering from his subject into vain declamation, but pursuing it closely in language pure, classical, and copious, soothing always the feelings of his adversaries by civilities and softness of expression, he rose to the eminent station which he held in the great National convention of 1787. . . . With these consummate powers were united a pure and spotless virtue which no calumny has ever attempted to sully.

3

Jefferson stormed the trenches of the old oligarchy with carefully aimed bills, each designed to transform the royal colony into a democratic commonwealth. The "Spirit of Levelling," Virginians called it. The Spirit, urged by the relentless Jefferson, took years to achieve the leveling, but it was finally accomplished by four factors: the abolition of entail, the overthrow of primogeniture, free public education, and the disestablishment of the Church.

The first bill had an innocent title: "to enable tenants in taille to convey their lands in fee-simple." Its intent, however, was not innocent in the eyes of the oligarchy. The bill was a blow at entail, permitting an owner to leave his landed property to whomever he liked. To the defense of the status quo and of the aristocratic institutions came one of the ablest lawyers of the day, Edmund Pendleton, who gave Jefferson the fight of his life. It was a battle of titans, subtle and calm, with all the amenities of cultured behavior but deadly nonetheless. Jefferson, hard-pressed, paid Pendleton the tribute of honest admiration:

. . . he was cool, smooth, and persuasive; his language flowing, chaste & embellished, his conceptions quick, acute and full of resource; never vanquished: for if he lost the main battle, he returned upon you, and regained so much of it as to make it a drawn one, by dexterous manoeuvres. . . . You never knew when you were clear of him, but were harassed by his perseverance until the patience was worn out. . . . Add to this that he was one of the most virtuous & benevolent of men, the kindest friend, the most amiable & pleasant of companions.

Pendleton knew all the tricks. Jefferson tells how when he once introduced a bill proposing a Court of Chancery and providing for trial by jury, Pendleton defeated it by slipping in four innocent-seeming words: "*if either party chuse.*" Since no plaintiff would dare say to his judge, "Sir, I distrust you, give me a jury," the consequence was that juries were rarely seen in the Court of Chancery.

Now Pendleton tried a similar maneuver to defeat Jefferson's entail bill. As a compromise, he proposed that the owners of entailed property be allowed to leave it to their heirs in fee simple "if they chose to do so." It almost worked. But Jefferson caught it in time, and the bill abolishing entail passed by a narrow margin.

4

No sooner had Jefferson won his first important legislative victory with the passing of the entail bill than he introduced a motion for the revision of the whole legal code. The motion was adopted, and a committee of five "Revisors" was appointed to carry on the work. The composition of the committee was a victory for Jefferson, for he himself was made chairman and two of his friends, Wythe and Mason, were members. On the other side were Pendleton and Thomas L. Lee. Virginia's Justinians met at Fredericksburg in January, 1777, to agree upon a plan of operation. As soon as they assembled they found, probably much to their own amusement, their traditional roles reversed. Pendleton, the conservative lawyer, argued in favor of a new and complete legal system; Jefferson, the radical former lawyer, favored merely an alteration of the existing code.

The reasons for Jefferson's seeming conservatism were as subtle as Pendleton's reasons for his apparent radicalism. Both were men of farseeing adroitness, inclined to take the long view. Jefferson easily saw through Pendleton's purpose. He realized that a completely new code, with untried principles and unaccustomed concepts, would not only take too much time, but would be at the mercy of those who would be in charge of interpreting it, that is, the judges. And judges, Jefferson knew, were a conservative tribe, leaning heavily to the side of property, precedent, and class. Much better, Jefferson thought, to leave the old legal notions intact, so as to make sure that the precedent-bound judges would tread in the beaten path and not be tempted to stray too far in the jungle of their own prejudices. In this instance, reform was wiser than revolution. Jefferson argued:

> . . . that to compose a new Institute like those of Justinian and Bracton, or that of Blackstone . . . would be an arduous undertaking, of vast research, of great consideration & judgment; and when reduced to a text, every word of that text, from the imperfection of human language, and it's incompetence to express distinctly every shade of idea, would become a subject of question & chicanery until settled by repeated adjudications; and this would involve us for ages in litigation, and render property uncertain until, like the statutes of old, every word had been tried and settled by numerous decisions, and by new volumes of reports & commentaries.

Mason and Wythe concurred with the chairman. When it came to a division of the work, Mason and Lee excused themselves as not being lawyers. The burden, therefore, fell on Jefferson, helped by Wythe and Pendleton. Jefferson took over the common law and the statutes to the year 1607, Wythe the laws from 1607 to 1776, and Pendleton the laws of colonial Virginia.

5

For two years Jefferson worked on the legal code. It was a tremendous job, exacting, as Madison said, "perhaps the most severe of his public labours." But it was a task to Jefferson's taste, for it enabled him to bring into play all those faculties with which he was endowed: disciplined thinking, immense learning, and limpid diction.

> In the execution of my part I thought it material not to vary the diction of the antient statutes by modernizing it, nor to give rise to new questions by new expressions. The text of these statutes had been so fully explained and defined by numerous adjudications, as scarcely ever now to produce a question in our courts. I thought it would be useful also, in all new draughts, to reform the style of the later British statutes, and of our own acts of Assembly; which from their verbosity, their endless tautologies, their involutions of case within case, and parenthesis within parenthesis, and their multiplied efforts at certainty by *saids* and *aforesaids*, by *ors* and by *ands*, to

make them more plain, do really render more perplexed and incomprehensible, not only to common readers, but to the lawyers themselves.

After two years of pruning the dead twigs of the old laws and streamlining the new statutes, Jefferson met the other two Revisors at Williamsburg early in 1779. They compared their work critically, "sentence by sentence, scrutinizing and amending," until they agreed upon the whole. Then they returned home and made clean copies. The whole revised code was refined into one hundred and twenty-six bills, so concisely drawn that they were printed in a mere ninety folio pages.

6

The revised code was more than "a Model of technical precision, and perspicuous brevity," as James Madison called it. It contained the principles of the new democracy. One of the bills, drawn by Jefferson, provided for the abolition of primogeniture in order to make real estate descendible to all the heirs. This was another blow at the upper classes, and Pendleton protested. Since his protest was unsupported by the other Revisors, Pendleton suggested a compromise on the basis of the ancient Hebrew principle of giving the elder son a double portion. But Jefferson, determined to eradicate every fiber of inequality, set his face like flint against any compromise. He told his colleague dryly that "if the eldest son could eat twice as much, or do double work, it might be a natural evidence of his right to a double portion; but being on a par in his powers & wants, with his brothers and sisters, he should be on a par also in the partition of the patrimony."

Another long stride in the direction of Jefferson's ideal of an enlightened commonwealth of free men was made by his three education bills: "for the more general diffusion of knowledge," "for the amending the constitution of the College of William and Mary," and "for establishing a public library." Underlying these bills was the democratic-revolutionary assumption that it was the duty of the State to supply free education to the poor. Such public schools were to teach reading, writing, and arithmetic, as well as acquaint the young students "with Graecian, Roman, English, and American history." The preamble to the first bill is a classic statement of the reasons for education in a democracy:

Whereas it appeareth that however certain forms of government are better calculated than others to protect individuals in the free exercise of their natural rights, and are at the same time themselves better guarded against degeneracy, yet experience hath shewn, that even under the best forms, those entrusted with power have, in time, and by slow operations, perverted it into tyranny; and it is believed that the most effectual means of preventing this, would be to illuminate, as far as practicable, the minds of the people at large. . . .

And whereas it is generally true that the people will be happiest whose laws are best, and are best administered, and that laws will be wisely formed, and honestly administered, in proportion as those who form and administer them are wise and honest; whence it becomes expedient . . . that those persons, whom nature hath endowed with genius and virtue, should be rendered by liberal education worthy to receive . . . the sacred deposit of the rights and liberties of their fellow citizens, and that they should be called to that charge without regard to wealth, birth or other accidental condition or circumstance; but the indigence of the greater number disabling them from so educating, at their own expence, those of their children whom nature hath fitly formed and disposed to become useful instruments for the public, it is better that such should be sought for and educated at the common expence of all, than that the happiness of all should be confided to the weak or wicked.

In brief, Jefferson boldly asserted four basic principles: that a democracy cannot long exist without enlightenment; that it cannot function without wise and honest officials; that talent and virtue, needed in a free society, should be educated regardless of "wealth, birth or other accidental condition"; and finally, that children of the poor must be thus educated at the "common expence." This document is hardly less important than the Declaration of Independence as a milestone in the evolution of the democratic doctrine.

Jefferson was keenly conscious of the basic importance of education for democracy. To George Wythe he wrote:

I think by far the most important bill in our whole code, is that for the diffusion of knowledge among the people. No other sure foundation can be devised, for the preservation of freedom and happiness. . . . Preach, my dear Sir, a crusade against ignorance; establish and improve the law for educating the common people. . . . the tax which will be paid for this purpose, is not more than the thousandth part of what will be paid to kings, priests and nobles, who will rise up among us if we leave the people in ignorance.

7

Of all the bills, however, the greatest sensation—one that was to shake Virginia to the depths of its conscience—was to be caused by the one proposing religious freedom. In back of that bill lay Jefferson's whole intellectual development. The course of his thinking and reading inevitably led to a crystallized attitude toward religion, that climactic point at which men feel most strongly, argue most heatedly, and fight most fiercely. This pitch of human emotions had in the past resulted in cruelty and persecution, precisely because it was subject neither to the voice of reason nor to the call of mercy. To Jefferson, who believed in reason with passionate conviction, it was axiomatic that religion, or rather the institution of the Church, was the enemy of freedom and the ally of obscurantism.

Jefferson's critical attitude did not extend to the ethical teachings of religion, which he fully accepted, but to its political alignments and aspects, which he thoroughly rejected. Religion was a menace to a free society when it was either an instrument of the State, as was the case with Lutheranism in Prussia, or when it used the State for its sanguinary purposes, as was the case in Inquisition-ridden Spain. There was sufficient historical evidence to prove that the partnership of Church and State had always led, and perforce must lead, to tyranny and oppression. "In every country and in every age," Jefferson said, "the priest has been hostile to liberty. He is always in alliance with the despot, abetting his abuses in return for protection of his own." So long as the Church was woven in the same fabric as the State, a self-governing commonwealth based upon justice and freedom was a fool's illusion.

In few things was Jefferson more consistent than in his advocacy of religious liberty, or more resolute than in his hatred of religious tyranny. He went farther than those who merely believed in toleration. Mere toleration was a lazy man's creed; it meant indifference toward the political problems involved in the religious question. Toleration, therefore, was not enough. What Jefferson wanted, and ultimately achieved, was liberty—liberty, fully protected by the law, to believe or not to believe whatever a man saw fit; liberty of the genuine Protestant variety, for a man and his conscience to care for his soul in his own fashion.

The problem of religion and all its sociopolitical implications had troubled Jefferson for a long time. A few months after writing the Declaration of Independence, in October, 1776, he had jotted down a few searching "Notes on Religion":

How far does the duty of toleration extend? . . .

No man complains of his neighbor for ill management of his affairs, for an error in sowing his land, or marrying his daughter, for consuming his substance in taverns, pulling down building &tc. in all these he has liberty: but if he does not frequent the church, or there conform to ceremonies, there is an immediate uproar.

The care of every man's soul belongs to himself. But what if he neglect the care of it? Well what if he neglect the care of his health or estate, which more nearly relate to the state. Will the magistrate make a law that he shall not be poor or sick? Laws provide against injury from others; but not from ourselves. God himself will not save men against their wills. . . .

If the magistrate command me to bring my commodity to a publick store house I bring it because he can indemnify me if he erred & I thereby lose it; but what indemnification can he give one for the k[ing]dom of heaven?

I cannot give up my guidance to the magistrates, bec[ause] he knows no more of the way to heaven than I do, & is less concerned to direct me right than I am to go right.

The battle for religious liberty was unending. All the entrenched forces of religious institutions and vested clerical interests had to be challenged if a free self-governing society were to exist. To Jefferson it was a struggle between science and superstition, a conflict between reason and dogmatism. He knew that the beliefs of a lifetime die hard, and that it takes tireless hammering to open up cracks for the light of reason to enter. And this gentle planter, who shrank from violence, never flinched. There was no margin for compromise. In his *Notes on Virginia* Jefferson raked the whole problem with subdued passion. The arguments are still mint-fresh:

The rights of conscience we never submitted, we could not submit. We are answerable for them to our God. The legitimate powers of government extend to such acts only as are injurious to others. But it does me no injury for my neighbor to say there are twenty gods, or no god. It neither picks my pocket nor breaks my leg. . . . Constraint may make him worse by making him a hypocrite, but it will never make him a truer man. . . .

Reason and free inquiry are the only effectual agents against error. . . . Had not the Roman government permitted free inquiry, christianity could never have been introduced. Had not free inquiry been indulged at the aera of the reformation, the corruptions of christianity could not have been purged away. If it be restrained now, the present corruptions will be protected, new ones encouraged.

Was the government to prescribe to us our medicine and diet, our bodies would be in such keeping as our souls are now. Thus in France the emetic was once forbidden as a medicine, and the potato as an article of food. Government is just as infallible, too, when it fixes systems in physics. Galileo was sent to the inquisition for affirming that the earth was a sphere; the government had declared it to be as flat as a trencher, and Galileo was obliged to abjure his error. This error however at length prevailed, the earth became a globe. . . . the Newtonian principle of gravitation is now more firmly established, on the basis of reason, than it would be were the government . . . to make it an article of necessary faith. . . . It is error alone which needs the support of government. Truth can stand by itself.

Subject opinion to coercion: whom will you make your inquisitors? Fallible men; men governed by bad passions, by private as well as public reasons. And why subject it to coercion? To produce uniformity. But is uniformity of opinion desirable? No more than of face and stature. Introduce the bed of Procrustes then, and as there is danger that the large men may beat the small, make us all of a size, by lopping the former and stretching the latter. . . .

Is uniformity attainable? Millions of innocent men, women, and children, since the introduction of Christianity have been burnt, tortured, fined, imprisoned: yet we have not advanced one inch towards uniformity.

What has been the effect of coercion? To make one half the world fools, and the other half hypocrites. To support roguery and error all over the earth. . . .

Let us . . . get rid, while we may, of those tyrannical laws. It is true we are as yet secured against them by the spirit of the times. I doubt whether the people of this country would suffer an execution for heresy, or a three years imprisonment for not comprehending the mysteries of the trinity. But is the spirit of the people an infallible, a permanent reliance? Is it government? . . . Besides, the spirit of the times may alter, will alter. Our rulers will become corrupt, our people careless. A single zealot may commence persecuter, and better men be his victims. It can never be too often repeated, that the time for fixing every essential right on a legal basis is while our rulers are honest, and ourselves united.

8

Such were some of the ideas in Jefferson's mind when he drafted his Bill for Establishing Religious Freedom. The bill, together with the rest of the revised code, was submitted by Jefferson and Wythe to the House of Delegates in June, 1779. It stunned the majority of the House and enraged the oligarchic interests in the State. The whole code was subjected to bitter attack—"the endless quibbles, chicaneries, perversions, vexations and delays of lawyers and demi-lawyers," as Jefferson described the procedure, resulted in a momentary shelving of the code.

But Jefferson and his followers, particularly James Madison, convinced that they were on the side of reason and progress, never relinquished the battle. Victory was in their hearts, and they could afford to be patient. They did not have to wait long.

Within six years virtually the whole code was passed, largely as a result of Madison's "unwearied exertions," as Jefferson gratefully acknowledged.

The Bill for Establishing Religious Freedom and severing the Church from the State, passed with but minor changes, opened a new era of freedom and toleration in American history. Since Virginia was far the most populous,[1] and probably the most influential, State in the Union, Jefferson's bill set a model for the rest of the country. Jefferson himself was prouder of that bill than of all the high offices he was to hold, including the Presidency. Before he died, he asked that it be engraved on his tombstone that he was its author. The Preamble is a ringing declaration of free faith as against coercive religion. Every argument in favor of religious liberty is stated with limpid and inclusive precision:

Well aware ~~that the opinions and belief of men depend not on their own will, but follow involuntarily the evidence proposed to their minds;~~ [2]

that Almighty God hath created the mind free, ~~and manifested his supreme will that free it shall remain by making it altogether insusceptible of restraint;~~

that all attempts to influence it by temporal punishments, or burthens, or by civil incapacitations, tend only to beget habits of hypocrisy and meanness, and are a departure from the plan of the holy author of our religion, who . . . chose not to propagate it by coercions . . . as was in his Almighty power to do, ~~but to exalt its influence on reason alone;~~

that the impious presumption of legislators and rulers, civil as well as ecclesiastical, who, being themselves but fallible and uninspired men, have assumed dominion over the faith of others . . . hath es-

[1] The population of Virginia was almost twice as large as that of Pennsylvania, her closest rival. According to the Census of 1790, the population of the thirteen States ranked as follows: Virginia, 747,610; Pennsylvania, 434,373; North Carolina, 393,751; Massachusetts, 378,787; New York, 340,120; Maryland, 319,728; South Carolina, 249,073; Connecticut, 237,946; New Jersey, 184,139; New Hampshire, 141,885; Georgia, 82,548; Rhode Island, 68,825; Delaware, 59,096. A large proportion of the population in the South was Negro. Around 1780, for example, the combined white population of Georgia (27,000), South Carolina (93,000), and North Carolina (183,000) did not equal that of Massachusetts.

[2] The words crossed out were struck by the legislature.

tablished and maintained false religions over the greatest part of the world and through all time:

That to compel a man to furnish contributions of money for the propagation of opinions which he disbelieves and abhors, is sinful and tyrannical . . .

that our civil rights have no dependance on our religious opinions, any more than our opinions in physics or geometry;

and therefore the proscribing any citizen as unworthy [of] the public confidence by laying upon him an incapacity of being called to offices of trust and emolument, unless he profess or renounce this or that religious opinion, is depriving him injudiciously of those privileges and advantages to which . . . he has a natural right;

that it tends also to corrupt the principles of that very religion it is meant to encourage by bribing, with a monopoly of worldly honors and emoluments, those who will externally profess and conform to it. . . .

that the opinions of men are not the object of civil government nor under its jurisdiction;

that to suffer the civil magistrate to intrude his powers into the field of opinion . . . is a dangerous fal[l]acy, which at once destroys all religious liberty. . . .

that it is time enough for the rightful purposes of civil government for its officers to interfere when principles break out into overt acts against peace and good order;

and finally, that truth is great and will prevail if left to herself; that she is the proper and sufficient antagonist to error. . . .

errors ceasing to be dangerous when it is permitted freely to contradict them.

Then follows the short, almost staccato resolution, fashioned into law, that freed men's minds from the tyranny of "fallible and uninspired" men.

We the General Assembly of Virginia do enact that no man shall be compelled to frequent or support any religious worship, place, or ministry whatsoever, nor shall be enforced, restrained, molested, or burthened in his body or goods, or shall otherwise suffer, on account of his religious opinions or belief; but that all men shall be free to profess, and by argument to maintain, their opinions in matters of religion, and that the same shall in no wise diminish, enlarge, or affect their civil capacities.

It would be impossible to improve upon the language of this law, to state it in fewer or better words. And with his usual skepticism of all governments and laws, and his fear that times might change for the worse, as times had in the past, Jefferson ended his bill with a warning to posterity that to repeal or restrict it in the future would be "an infringement of natural right."

The bill was designed to protect all citizens, regardless of race or creed, in their freedom of conscience. It aimed, Jefferson explained, "to comprehend, within the mantle of it's protection, the Jew and the Gentile, the Christian and Mahometan, the Hindoo, and infidel of every denomination."

9

Thus it took nine years of struggle for Jefferson and his followers to transform Virginia into a democratic commonwealth. In the course of the battle even Patrick Henry was turned into an enemy. It was a bloodless revolution, carefully planned and calmly executed by the young philosopher-planter who had a vision of free men in a free land. He led his forces with cool brilliance, subtle and unrelenting. "I considered 4 of these bills, passed or reported," he tells almost casually, "as forming a system by which every fibre would be eradicated of antient or future aristocracy; and a foundation laid for a government truly republican." [3]

The process of "leveling" begun by Jefferson could not be halted, and the ultimate result was as Jefferson had foreseen and planned: a breaking-up of the power and the estates of the aristocracy. Two generations later the Virginia-born Henry Clay, son of poor and humble parents, was to sit by the waters

[3] The repeal of entail prevented the "accumulation and perpetuation of wealth." The abolition of primogeniture removed feudal distinctions which made "one member of every family rich, and all the rest poor." The establishment of religious freedom relieved the poor people from taxation in support of the "religion of the rich." Finally, the bill for a general education helped the poor to learn to maintain their rights, and enabled them "to exercise with intelligence their parts in self-government," Jefferson explained.

of the Potomac and bewail Jefferson's democratic handiwork. In 1833 Clay exclaimed:

In whose hands now are the once proud seats of Westover, Cerles, Maycocks, Shirly, and others on the James and in lower Virginia? They have passed into other and stranger hands. Some of the descendants of illustrious parentage have gone to the far West, while others lingering behind . . . behold themselves excluded from their fathers' houses, now in the hands of those who were once their fathers' overseers, or sinking into decay.

Bitterness was generated by Jefferson's reforms. The squire of Monticello was accused of being a traitor to his kind, of stirring up class against class, of destroying the sacred foundations of society. Gradually he was becoming an object of animosity, for not only did he lead the democratic forces successfully, he also supplied them with arguments, which are in the long run the deadliest kind of ammunition. But the common people of Virginia, and ultimately of all America, had at last a champion in Tom Jefferson. To him they rallied, for he knew how to articulate the groping aspirations of humble folk in language that haunted the imagination.

CHAPTER VI

Governor

IN THE spring of 1779, when Jefferson had completed revising the code, the governorship of Virginia fell vacant. Patrick Henry had served three years as governor and was disqualified by the constitution for re-election.

The one hundred and thirty-odd planters and tobacco farmers who made up the legislature looked to three candidates to carry the burden of heading a defenseless State in wartime. These three were John Page, Jefferson's friend from Williamsburg student days; General Thomas Nelson, a signer of the Declaration of Independence whom John Adams described as "a fat man . . . alert and lively for his weight"; and finally Jefferson, who was thirty-six years old and was hoping to find leisure from politics in order the better "to indulge my fondness for philosophical studies."

Jefferson's chances to devote himself to theoretical pursuits, whether philosophical or scientific, were not strong. Already, despite his comparative youth, he loomed large in the public eye. The democratic forces looked upon him as the natural leader in the struggle for political liberty and social reform, and Jefferson had enough vanity and too much sense of duty to fail those who depended upon him. His State-wide prestige, burgeoning into branches outside the borders of Virginia, was reflected in the House of Delegates, where next to Patrick Henry the author of the Declaration of Independence was the most commanding figure.

The contest for the governorship was not sharply competitive, for Jefferson accepted the candidacy more from a desire to please his supporters (he was not unsusceptible to flattery) than from a yearning for the emoluments and the burdens of office. He was, moreover, in the delicate position of having to run against Page, his boyhood friend whom he had always considered as a brother. "It had given me much pain," he told Page, "that the zeal of our respective friends ever have placed you and me in the situation of competitors. I was comforted, however . . . that it was their competition, not ours." Page amiably assured his friend that he felt the same way about it.

On the first ballot Jefferson led with 55 votes, against 36 for Page and 32 for Nelson. On the second ballot, with Nelson dropping out, Jefferson won a clear though not impressive majority—67 votes against 61 for Page. Thus he had reached the first major stage in his political career. He may have reflected, with a quiet sense of pride, that within a dozen years of his student days he was to sit in the chair occupied with so much distinction by his friend Fauquier, the Royal Governor of Virginia.

There is no doubt that Jefferson was pleased with the "appointment," as it was called. He was still young enough to be thrilled by high public office. Disillusionment and a hardening of the political arteries (but never cynicism) were to come with the harsh blows of experience. This time was not yet. Jefferson could not have known that the cup of the governorship contained wormwood dregs. When the House of Delegates selected a committee of three to notify the young man that he was "appointed" to be "Governor or Chief Magistrate of this Commonwealth," he received the notification with gracious tact. If he had had the gift of prophecy he would have looked dubiously at the committee as Greeks bearing gifts. To the Assembly he spoke a few well-chosen words which in any word-lavish democracy might serve as a model for acceptance speeches:

In a virtuous and free State no rewards can be so pleasing to sensible minds, as those which include the approbation of our fellow-citizens. My great pain is, lest my poor endeavors shall fall short of the kind expectations of my country. So far as impartiality, assiduous attention, and sincere affection to the great American cause, shall enable me to fulfil the duties of my appointment, so far as I may with confidence undertake; for all beyond, I must rely on the wise counsels of the General assembly.

It was a hopeful beginning, and enlightened opinion in the State rejoiced at the new regime, which, incidentally, started a new era in a new capital, Richmond. From his headquarters up at New Windsor, General Washington sent the Governor his "sincere congratulations upon your appointment." Young Madison, a rising leader in the State, was happy to see in the new Governor a realization of the ancient dream of philosophers being kings and vice versa. For he considered Jefferson the most learned man of his time. Later he said of Jefferson: "It may be said of him as has been said of others that he was a 'walking Library,' and what can be said of but few such prodegies [sic], that the Genius of Philosophy ever walked hand in hand with him." St. George Tucker, a learned lawyer to become a distinguished judge, also exulted in the new Chief Magistrate. "I wish," he wrote, "his excellency's activity may be equal to the abilities he possesses in so eminent a degree. In that case we may boast of having the greatest man of the continent at the helm." And Joseph Jones, a member of the Continental Congress and a major general in the Virginia militia, told his nephew, twenty-one-year-old James Monroe, to cultivate the new Governor: . . . "he is in my opinion as proper a man as can be put into the office, having the requisites of ability, firmness and diligence. You will do well to cultivate his friendship." That is what Virginia thought of her rising star.

2

It was a bad time for a philosopher to be king. The war with Britain—the American Revolution—was now in its fourth year, and still no end was in sight. Hitherto the fighting had taken place in the North. But unfortunately for Jefferson, at about the time he became Governor both the international outlook and the British strategy underwent a change. The France of Louis Sixteenth, who had made an alliance with the United States in 1778, at last threw her forces into the conflict and thus potentially tipped the scales in favor of the young American States. The British then changed their tactics and shifted the war to the South, which, because of its open coastline and sparsity of settlement, was vulnerable to attack. Virginia, the heart of the South, was to bear the brunt of the new assault.

Despite her potential wealth and resources, Virginia had no defensive forces. The State slopes like a pyramid from the Alleghenies to the west and sinks flat into the Chesapeake Bay and the Atlantic Ocean to the east. At least four great navigable rivers cut deep into the State from the ocean side, all open to hostile ships and armies. Vessels of more than one hundred tons could sail as far inland as Richmond. To defend this vulnerable and wide-open coastline, Virginia possessed a mighty flotilla of four little vessels (with a total of five dozen guns) and three armed boats. Nowhere was there a fortification strong enough to resist a stout British frigate. What military forces there were consisted of poorly armed, untrained, undisciplined militia. In short, from a military standpoint Governor Jefferson's State was what a later generation of Americans would call a pushover.

Economically the State was no better off. Three years of war had laid a heavy burden on Virginia, which had been generous in her supplies to General Washington's Army in the North. There was an absence of specie, and paper money was hardly worth the stuff on which it was printed.[1] The State, whose administrative machinery was by no means a model of efficiency, in desperation did what States have been doing since time immemorial: it imposed more and more taxes. But the people were simply too poor and too disorganized to pay. Of sixty-odd counties, in the spring of 1780 less than half paid their taxes and nine did not even return any assessments. The accounts, moreover, were not kept satisfactorily. Army commissaries and recruiting officers lived by "sheer plunder."

Spirits sank as low as Virginia's tidewater region, and pessi-

---

[1] Currency depreciated so that a physician received £300 for a call, a chicken cost about £10, and a quart of brandy brought about £24.

mism reigned everywhere. Madison, writing from Philadelphia, where he was a member of the Congress, complained to
Jefferson, who was grappling with a hopeless job in Richmond:
. . . "the public treasury empty; public credit exhausted . . .
Congress complaining. . . ." From his retirement in the Blue
Ridge, former Governor Patrick Henry, whose resentful followers in the legislature were out to knife the young Governor,
wrote Jefferson a letter nut-full of despondency:

I have had many anxieties from our commonwealth, principally
occasioned by the depreciation of our money. . . . I have feared
that our body politic was dangerously sick. God grant it may not
be unto death. But I cannot forbear thinking, the present increase
of prices is in great part owing to a kind of habit, which is now of
four or five years' growth, which is fostered by a mistaken avarice
. . . But tell me, do you remember any instance where tyranny
was destroyed and freedom established on its ruins, among a people
possessing so small a share of virtue and public spirit? I recollect
none, and this, more than the British arms, makes me fearful of
final success.

3

The problems that the young Governor faced in a war-
exhausted State that was threatened with invasion were both
novel and unprecedented. Peace-loving, compromising, devoted
to orderly and constitutional procedure, Jefferson was psycho-
logically unprepared to cope with the violent reality of war.
Moreover, he did not seem to realize the gravity of the situation. When the legislature proposed drastic retrenchment and
a reduction in the military establishment of the State, the Governor tacitly approved, and Virginia found herself less protected than ever. Perhaps his inveterate optimism made him
feel that Virginia would somehow escape the scourge of invasion.

The Governor worked hard, as he always did, and grappled
with numerous details that would have irked a less patient
man. Though constitutionally limited in his powers, he was
burdened with dozens of responsibilities. He had to supply
Washington's army in the North and Gates's troops in the

South. He had to keep in touch with the various commanders in the field—Steuben, Nelson, Greene, Muhlenberg, Lafayette —for Virginia was a key State and her chief a vital figure. He had to take care of British and Hessian prisoners of war, which he did with rare humanity.[2] He had to think of shoes and of uniforms, of victuals and of arms, in response to the appeals of the harassed generals. (General Washington wrote him: "It [is] essentially necessary that every measure should be taken to procure supplies of Cloathing for them [the troops], especially of Shoes, Stockings and linen.") Finally, having formally taken possession of an enormous territory extending to the Mississippi in the West and the Great Lakes in the North, the Governor had to defend his vast State against Indians, who were being incited by the British. A letter to General George Rogers Clark, written on Christmas Day, 1780, shows one of the peace-loving Governor's troubles:

. . . we have reason to believe that a very extensive combination of British & indian savages is preparing to invest our western frontier to prevent the cruel murders and devastations which attend the latter species of war, and at the same time to prevent it producing a powerful diversion of our force from the southern quarter . . . it becomes necessary that we aim the first stroke in the western coun-

[2] Jefferson's humanitarian action in this respect was well known. After Burgoyne's army surrendered at Saratoga in October, 1777, a number of the prisoners of war were sent down to Albemarle County. At the protest of the population that the prisoners were consuming too much food, Governor Henry signed an order that they be removed. Jefferson promptly intervened with a beautiful letter to the Governor:

"But is an enemy so execrable, that, though in captivity, his wishes and comforts are to be disregarded and even crossed? I think not. It is for the benefit of mankind to mitigate the horrors of war as much as possible. The practice, therefore, of modern nations, of treating captive enemies with politeness and generosity, is not only delightful in contemplation, but really interesting to all the world—friends, foes, and neutrals."

The intervention saved the prisoners. Jefferson and his wife treated the British and German officers with gracious hospitality, lending them books and making them as comfortable as possible. The officers were warm in their gratitude. To one British gentleman who thanked him, Jefferson replied: "The great cause which divides our countries is not to be decided by individual animosities. The harmony of private societies can not weaken national efforts. To contribute by neighborly intercourse and attention to make others happy, is the shortest and surest way of being happy ourselves."

try and throw the enemy under embarrassments of a defensive war rather than labor under them ourselves.

4

The Governor's chief headache, however, was the ancient sinews of war, money. And of money Virginia had none. Nor could Jefferson, for all his ingenuity, find a proper substitute for money. Confiscation of supplies was neither constitutionally permissible nor physically possible, since the democratic State was poor and exhausted. Jefferson himself virtually denuded his own estate of horses and wagons for the army, and so did other patriotic farmers. But not only were these voluntary supplies insufficient, they also crippled the productivity of the farms. In the meantime the British were invading North Carolina and threatening to crush the country in a pincer movement. All eyes, and all desperate appeals, were directed toward centrally situated Virginia, which loomed big and was presumably rich.

General Washington, worried for the safety of his native State and discouraged by the poverty of his troops, kept on writing at least twice a month to his fellow Virginian in Richmond, asking for urgent help, complaining, pleading. These letters throw a glaring and almost embarrassing light on the plight of the great Commander in Chief, struggling with tight-lipped determination against defeatism and despair.

The burden of Washington's complaint—not against Jefferson, but against the whole American system of waging the war —was lack of men and lack of vital supplies. Chief trouble was that the independent citizens of the young democracy could not be recruited and forced into uniform like so many Prussians or Hessians. The American yeomen had to be cajoled and attracted by bounties, and then they took up arms under contract, usually for short periods of time. As soon as their time was up—and often before that—they simply left everything and went home. These "deserters" (some were technically deserters and others were not) drove General Washington to fury. It was a stinging humiliation for a courageous officer to command troops on whom he could not depend for a campaign.

General Washington kept on pleading for periods of enlistment of at least eighteen months' duration. If he could be sure of having an army for over a year, he could plan a campaign and try for victory. But what was the use of attempting anything when his soldiers melted away like snow in the sun? "Short inlistments," he wrote to Jefferson bitterly, "have subjected Us to such distresses, to such enormous expences, have so intimately hazarded our liberties that I never reflect upon them, but with a degree of horror." Short levies, he told Jefferson, had protracted the war and threatened the whole American cause with collapse. He poured his heavy heart out to the sympathetic young Governor:

. . . to this we may ascribe near all our other misfortunes and present embarrassments, and to this the loss of our liberties and Independence, if the fatal event should take place. This system of politics has brought us very low indeed, and had we not been held up by providence and a powerful Ally, we must have submitted before this to the Yoke of bondage. A perseverance in the system may yet effect it. I beg Your Excellency to pardon this digression, which the misfortunes we have suffered and the difficulties that now surround us have led me as it were to make involuntarily.

The Governor, almost as hard-pressed as the General, could give him little more than sympathy. Their letters asking for help crossed each other. Jefferson wrote to Washington in the summer of 1780:

North Carolina is without arms. We do not abound. Those we have, are freely imparted to them, but such is the state of their resources, that they have not been able to move a single musket from this State to theirs. All the wagons we can collect have been furnished to the Marquis de Kalb. . . . I have written to Congress to hasten supplies of arms and military stores for the Southern States, and particularly to aid us with cartridge-paper and boxes, the want of which . . . renders our stores useless. The want of money cramps every effort. This will be supplied by the most unpalatable of all substitutes, force. . . .

Virginia could probably have furnished men to the Northern and Southern armies, but it had no guns, no powder, no wagons, no medical supplies. To General Edward Stevens in Gates's army Jefferson wrote: "What is to be done for wagons, I do not know. We have not now one shilling in the treasury to purchase them."

In August, General Washington wrote to Jefferson in a tone of near-despair: "I have the mortification to inform Your Excellency that for several days past the Army has been almost intirely destitute of meat, on some days without a mouthful." The soldiers were living off the impoverished countryside. "Those failures and these wants on our part," the General concluded bitterly, "blast almost every hope of successful operations in any case, and the latter produce a most licentious spirit in the soldiery. An Army should be well fed, well cloathed and paid and then You may exact and expect almost any thing from it . . . but with respect to Our Army it does not operate in any one of those instances."

Washington's forebodings came true, for at about the time he wrote that letter the Continental Army was humiliatingly defeated at Camden and the Virginia militia covered itself with a resounding lack of glory. Everyone was in despair except Jefferson, whose natural optimism nothing could long repress. To General Stevens, the brave officer who was humiliated by the behavior of his Virginia men at Camden (they were farm boys, unused to cannon, so they ran away at the first burst), Governor Jefferson wrote a letter of encouragement. He condoled with the General on what had happened and told him to forget the past: "we are to look forward and prepare for the future. . . . Another Body of 2000 Militia are ordered to you. . . . We shall exert every Nerve to assist you in every way in our power being as we are without any Money in yᵉ Treasury."

5

Money was not all the Governor lacked. The State had no troops for land defense, no fortresses at the wide mouth of the rivers, and no armed ships to protect hundreds of miles of coast. There was one gun for every five militiamen, one militiaman to every square mile of territory to be defended, little powder, and no containers for cartridges. If the enemy came to Virginia, he could just walk in.

The enemy came, and presented Jefferson with a shocking New Year's gift. On December 30, 1780, a fleet of twenty-seven boats was sighted at the mouth of Chesapeake Bay, off the Virginia capes. Governor Jefferson, in Richmond, was immediately informed and he sent General Nelson down the river "to call on the Militia in that quarter."

Anxious days followed. In Richmond no one knew the origin or destination of the hostile fleet at the capes, since the Governor's intelligence service was virtually nonexistent. It took him three days to learn that the enemy fleet was sailing up the James River, that it carried several hundred armed British troops, and that it was commanded by an American turncoat, General Benedict Arnold. Distressed, Jefferson ordered out the militia and consulted with General Steuben, who commanded in Virginia. The legislature went home. The Governor was left to face the British music.

Not until Benedict Arnold was close to Richmond did Jefferson realize that the State capital was the enemy objective. Richmond had no defenses. Quickly Jefferson ordered that the public stores be removed. Men worked all night. At one o'clock in the morning of January 6 the Governor hurried from the capital to get his wife and young children, who were at Tuckahoe, out of reach of danger. He took them eight miles farther up the river, left them with some friends, and hurried back to Manchester, across the river from Richmond. He had been on horseback for thirty-six hours, and now his horse fell exhausted within sight of the besieged capital. Jefferson swung the saddle on his back and walked to a farmhouse, where he obtained a colt. When he got to Manchester he could see, from across the river, that the British had already taken Richmond. As he watched, fire burst from the capital. Arnold and his men were burning public buildings and large stores of food and tobacco. Then they left the way they came.

Two days after the invasion Jefferson "resumed his residence" in Richmond and proceeded to investigate the damage. The losses turned out to be not as severe as the blows to the Governor's reputation and to the State's prestige. Among the losses, according to Governor Jefferson's report, were:

The papers and books of the Council. . . . The papers of the Auditors. . . . Five brass field-pieces, four pounders. . . . About one hundred and fifty arms. . . . About one hundred and fifty in a wagon. . . . About five tons of powder, and some made ammunition. . . . Some small proportion of the linens, cloths, etc., in the public store . . . one hundred and twenty sides of leather. Some of the tools in the artificers' shops. Foundry, magazine, four artificers' shops, public store, quarter masters' store, one artificer's shop, three wagons.

Only nine buildings were burned by Arnold's expedition, but there was enough smoke to blacken the reputation of the Governor.

6

The following months were the darkest that the American cause had yet experienced. The British had an iron grip on the seacoast and seemed to be slowly choking the breath of life out of the American defenders. Virginia lived under the constant threat of destruction. When the British commander, Lord Cornwallis, came to Virginia in the spring of 1781, the State seemed lost. Cornwallis cut into Virginia like a knife into an apple. Despondency was universal. Even Jefferson, whose temper was usually serene, gave way to discouragement. He appealed to General Washington to save his native State from what seemed to be certain destruction:

Were it possible . . . to justify in your Excellency a determina‧ tion to lend us your personal aid, it is evident from the universal voice, that the presence of their beloved Countryman . . . to whose person they have still flattered themselves they retained some right, and have ever looked up as their dernier resort in distress . . . would restore full confidence of salvation [to our citizens]. . . . I have undertaken to hint this matter to your Excellency not only on my own sense of its importance to us but at the solicitations of many members of weight in our Legislature.

Jefferson concluded the letter with the information that he was happy that his term as Governor was up. The governorship of an invaded State was not an office for a pacifist. As an after-thought he added: "still as an individual I should feel the comfortable effects of your presence."

7

For strategic reasons General Washington could not leave the North. He hoped, however, that American pressure upon the British in New York would reduce them to the "necessity of recalling part of their force from the Southward" and thus perhaps save Virginia. In the meantime Lord Cornwallis penetrated into Virginia as far west as the River Anna (Rivanna), about fifty miles from Charlottesville and Jefferson's home.

Jefferson and the legislature fled. When the British got to Richmond, the Virginia government was in Charlottesville. Then Cornwallis conceived the clever idea of capturing Governor and legislature. Such a coup would have been a grave blow to the already low American morale. Cornwallis detached one of his officers, the "hunting leopard" Colonel Tarleton, and a troop of cavalry with instructions to dash swiftly to Charlottesville to capture the Virginia legislature and then to near-by Monticello to seize the Governor.

Tarleton and his troops got to the tiny town of Louisa,[3] within about forty-five miles of Charlottesville, before a single American realized what was afoot. Fortunately, there was one such American; his name was Captain John Jouett. Stopping at the Cuckoo Tavern in Louisa to spend the night, he looked out of the window and saw the white-coated troopers galloping westward. Between Louisa and the Blue Ridge Mountains there was only one town of any importance—Charlottesville. It took no gift of divination on the part of Captain Jouett to guess

[3] In 1940 the population of Louisa was 300.

whither the British were heading. It was eleven o'clock at night, but the Captain quickly swung on his horse and galloped toward Monticello to warn the Governor. His horse, Prince Charley, was considered the "best and fleetest horse in seven counties." Jouett, wearing a bright red coat and a plumed hat, was racing Tarleton over mountain paths known only to a few native Virginians. Fortunately Prince Charley held out, and the moon was full enough to light the way. At four-thirty in the morning, after having ridden five and one-half hours over wild mountain paths, Jouett reached Monticello.

Awakened by the clattering of hoofs, Jefferson came out on the east portico to see what was doing. The scarlet-coated officer, his plume askew, rode up to the steps, dismounted, and delivered the news to His Excellency. Jefferson invited Jouett into the house, treated him to a glass of his best Madeira, and sent him down the road to Charlottesville to wake up the legislators who were sleeping at the Swan Tavern. The Governor woke his family and guests, among whom were the Speakers of the two houses and several members of the legislature. The gentlemen breakfasted leisurely and departed for Charlottesville, where they called a quorum and adjourned to Staunton, some thirty-five miles further west. Jefferson sent his wife, who was ill, and his children in a carriage down the mountain and remained behind, arranging his papers and putting things in order. His favorite horse, saddled and newly shod, was waiting for him at a designated spot on the road.

A few miles from Charlottesville, Colonel Tarleton detached a small troop under Captain McLeod to ride up the hill to Monticello, seize Jefferson, and hold the place as a lookout point. Monticello commanded a view of about a dozen counties. While Jefferson was packing his papers and the servants were storing valuables in the cellar, a man rode up hastily with the news that the British were coming up the mountain. The Governor hurried to the spot where his horse was waiting. Before mounting, Jefferson looked at Charlottesville through a telescope. The town seemed quiet, and the Governor, who disliked unnecessary haste, concluded that the report of British occupation was exaggerated. He walked back to the house, but on the way he decided to take another look, and saw that the streets of Charlottesville were overrun with dragoons. Quietly Jefferson retraced his steps and got on the horse.

Five minutes later McLeod's troopers, brilliant in their white coats, surrounded Monticello. They took over the estate like harmless guests. Tarleton had given McLeod "strict orders . . . to suffer nothing to be injured," and the British behaved like gentlemen. They remained in Monticello for eighteen hours and then they left after having, in the words of Jefferson, "preserved everything with sacred care." They behaved with similar circumspection in Charlottesville, where Colonel Tarleton succeeded in capturing seven members of the legislature. For the rest, Jefferson tells, Tarleton "did little injury to the inhabitants." But it was an unhappy experience.

8

Tarleton's swift incursion set the temper of the refugee legislature, meeting at Staunton, on edge. Weary from their flight and full of anxiety for the future, the members of the legislature looked for a scapegoat and found one. Who was to blame for their plight? The Governor. Who was responsible for the defenselessness of the State? The Chief Magistrate. Fury gathered about Jefferson's carroty head. What the State needed in the crisis, cried a large number of the legislators, was a dictator, not a democrat. The followers of Patrick Henry were vociferous in their demand for the appointment of a dictator, and they went so far as to suggest openly that the Governor be put out of the way.

The so-called Dictator party argued that events showed that a democratic government was no good in wartime—hence by implication no good at any time. They insisted that the constitution be suspended and one man (preferably Patrick Henry or some general) be given absolute powers. The very suggestion was outrageous to Jefferson, whose belief in democratic forms and democratic principles amounted to a personal religion. He could not let the enemies of democracy get away with the argument that self-government was worthless in a crisis. If it was of no value in a crisis, then it had no worth at any time. For the test of an institution is its workability under the greatest point of tension. If it cracks under pressure, then it is obviously weak and not viable. The "Dictator party" was determined to smash the already tottering State government, which would, of course, prove that it did not work. Then a dictator would step in and "save" the State. Later Jefferson wrote:

The very thought alone was treason against the people; was treason against mankind in general; as rivetting forever the chains which bow down their necks, by giving to their oppressors a proof, which they would have trumpeted through the universe, of the imbecility of republican government, in times of pressing danger. . . . Those who assume the right of giving away the reins of government in any case, must be sure that the herd, whom they hand on to the rods and hatchet of the dictator, will lay their necks on the block when he shall nod to them. . . . What a cruel moment was this for creating such an embarrassment, for putting to the proof the attachment of our countrymen to republican government!

Jefferson's friends and followers united for a decisive struggle on the floor of the House. The vote for a dictator was taken in secret, and was barely defeated. "A few votes only" decided the issue in favor of democracy.

9

The "Dictator party," whom the handsome Colonel Theodorick Bland not without some exaggeration characterized as "enemies to America, or fools, or knaves, or all three," aimed a new dagger at the Governor. On June 12, 1781, just as Jefferson's term was coming to a close, a stocky and impulsive young member of the legislature named George Nicholas made his debut in the House of Delegates by asking that Governor Jefferson's conduct be officially investigated. Jefferson's friends were in no position to protest, since it would have exposed them to the charge of being afraid to face the truth. The legislature voted unanimously "That at the next session of the Assembly an inquiry be made into the conduct of the Executive of this State for the last twelve months."

Although there was nothing else the legislature could do, as Jefferson realized, it was nevertheless an unprecedented insult. He had entered office under the warm rays of popular approval, a hero to the common people, and now, two years later, he was leaving under a black cloud. After years of sacrifice in the public service, at great personal cost, he now faced public disgrace. Sick in his soul, Jefferson retired to his home and asked George Nicholas, who was his neighbor and later his devoted friend, for a list of particular charges that would be made against him in the autumn, so that he could defend himself. Nicholas complied and Jefferson answered every point meticulously. The charges dealt mainly with Arnold's and Cornwallis's invasions of Virginia and Jefferson's behavior in those crises.

5th Objection.—That we had not look-outs.

Answer.—There had been no cause to order look-outs more than has been ever existing. This is only in fact asking why we do not always keep look-outs.

6th Objection.—That we had not heavy artillery on travelling carriages.

Answer.—The gentlemen who acted as members of the Board of War a twelve-month can answer this question, by giving the character of the artificers whom, during that time, they could never get to mount the heavy artillery. . . . We have even been unable to get those heavy cannon moved from Cumberland by the whole energy of government. . . .

7th Objection.—That there was not a body of militia thrown into Portsmouth, the Great Bridge, and Suffolk.

Answer.—In . . . 1780, we asked the favor of General Nelson, to call together the county lieutenants of the lower counties, and concert the general measures which should be taken for instant opposition, on any invasion . . . and the county lieutenants were ordered to obey his call; he did so the first moment. . . . We asked the favor of General Nelson to go down, which he did, with full powers to call together the militia of any counties he thought proper, to call on the keepers of any public arms or stores, and to adopt for the instant such measures as exigencies required. . . .

Objection.—As to the calling out a few militia, and that late.

Answer.—It is denied that they were few or late. Four thousand and seven hundred men (the number required by Baron Steuben) were called out the moment an invasion was known to have taken place.

The other questions and answers were of a similar nature.

10

When autumn came, Jefferson's neighbors in Albemarle County unanimously elected him to the legislature in order that he be given a decent chance to defend his official character. The men of Albemarle never lost confidence in their Tom. This sign of trust somewhat assuaged Jefferson's pain, but he vowed to resign from the legislature and leave politics forever as soon as he had vindicated himself.

Upon his arrival in Richmond, the mortified former Governor found, to his surprise, that the legislature was not merely friendly but apologetic. As a mark of genuine esteem, and perhaps because of a bad conscience, the House of Delegates honored him by naming him to important committees and by selecting him member of the Congress in Philadelphia, a position which Jefferson turned down. In the meantime, a committee of five was going through Nicholas's charges and Jefferson's replies.

In the middle of December the committee was ready with its report. Jefferson rose and said quietly that he was ready to answer all charges. He read the same replies that he had made to George Nicholas, who, curiously enough, was not present. No one on the floor either asked any questions or raised any objections. Then Colonel John Banister, chairman of the committee of five, brought his report to the House. His findings were clear and sharp: "no information being offered on the subject matter of the said inquiry, except that some rumors prevailed," the committee concluded that "said rumors were groundless." Immediately after, the House of Burgesses unanimously adopted a resolution of thanks to the former Governor for his upright conduct and thus vindicated him handsomely:

Resolved, That the sincere thanks of the General Assembly be given to our former Governor, Thomas Jefferson, Esq. for his impartial, upright, and attentive administration of the powers of the Executive, whilst in office; popular rumors gaining some degree of credence, by more pointed accusations, rendered it necessary to make an inquiry into his conduct and delayed that retribution of public gratitude so emminently [sic] merited; but that conduct having become the object of scrutiny, tenfold value is added to the approbation founded on a cool and deliberate discussion, the Assembly wish therefore, in the strongest manner, to declare the high opinion which they entertain of Mr. Jefferson's ability, rectitude, and integrity, as chief magistrate of this Commonwealth, and mean, by thus publicly avowing their opinion, to obviate all future and remove all former unmerited censure.

In the legislature and all over the State Jefferson's friends and followers celebrated his vindication. His Albemarle constituents and neighbors received him jubilantly upon his return home. But the whole experience rankled. Jefferson was only thirty-eight, and not yet toughened for the barbs of political life. A thick-skinned politician would have taken the affair as merely a passing, albeit a somewhat unpleasant, incident which turned out right. A scheming politician would have made capital out of his thorough vindication by the legislature. But Jefferson was hypersensitive. "I find," he once told Francis Hopkinson, "the pain of a little censure, even when it is unfounded, is more acute than the pleasure of much praise." He could not forget that he had stood *accused* before his peers—he, the most well-meaning and most honest of men. Never again, he told his friends with an undercurrent of bitterness, would he return to public life. Domestic animals were less ungrateful and cultivated fields were more responsive than men. Why waste time on human beings? That was the low-watermark period in Jefferson's life, when his philosophy deserted him.

He sulked for months, nay, for more than a year. His friends, even so devoted a one as James Madison, became annoyed. Such a petty reaction, though understandable under the circumstances, was not worthy of a man of Jefferson's caliber. In a letter to Edmund Randolph young Madison expressed his irritation in unwontedly sharp language:

Great as my partiality is to Mr. Jefferson, the mode in which he seems to be determined to revenge the wrong received from his country does not appear to me to be dictated either by philosophy or patriotism. It argues, indeed, a keen sensibility and strong consciousness of rectitude. But the sensibility ought to be as great towards the relentings as the misdoings of the Legislature.

Another one of Jefferson's disciples,[4] the twenty-three-year-old James Monroe, informed the former Governor that public opinion was condemning him for his selfish behavior in withdrawing from public life. In a long reply Jefferson admitted that, after all his years of sacrifice in the public service, the legislature's investigation of his conduct had given him an awful shock. Only death could heal the wound that was inflicted upon his spirit:

Before I ventured to declare to my countrymen my determination to retire from public employment, I examined well my heart to know whether it were thoroughly cured of every principle of political ambition, whether no lurking particle remained which might leave me uneasy when reduced within the limits of mere private life. I became satisfied that every fibre of that passion was thoroughly eradicated. . . . I considered that I had been thirteen years engaged in public service, that during that time I had so totally abandoned all attention to my private affairs as to permit them to run into great disorder and ruin, that I had now a family advanced to years which require my attention & instruction . . . that by a

4 "Disciple" is not too strong a word to apply to such followers of Jefferson as Monroe and Madison. In the earliest letter that Monroe wrote to Jefferson, on September 9, 1780, he admitted, in quaint phraseology, that he owed everything to Jefferson and vowed him eternal fidelity: "Your kindness & attention to me in this & a variety of other instances has really put me under such obligations to you that I fear I shall hardly ever had it in my power to repay them. But believe me in whatever situation of life ye chance of fortune may place me, no circumstance can happen wch. will give me such pleasure or make me so happy, at present or during my progress thro' life, as to have it in my power to convince you of ye proper impressions they have made on me. . . . had I not form'd a connection with you I sho'd most certainly have retir'd from society. . . . In this situation you became acquainted with me & undertook ye direction of my studies & believe me I feel that whatever I am at present in ye opinion of others or whatever I may be in future has greatly arisen from y'r friendship. My plan of life is now fix'd."

constant sacrifice of time, labour, parental & friendly duties, I had been so far from gaining the affection of my countrymen, which was the only reward I ever asked or could have felt, that I had even lost the small estimation I had before possessed.

That however I might have comforted myself under the disapprobation of the well-meaning but uninformed people yet that of their representatives was a shock on which I had not calculated: that this indeed had been followed by an exculpatory declaration. But in the meantime I had been suspected . . . in the eyes of the world, without the least hint then or afterwards being made public which might restrain them from supposing that I stood arraigned for treason of the heart and not merely weakness of the mind; and I felt that these injuries, for such they have been since acknowledged had inflicted a wound on my spirit which will only be cured by the all-healing grave.

Then he added with a touch of passion that one would rather be dead than admit the right of the State to command the services of its citizens:

It were contrary to feeling & indeed ridiculous to suppose that a man had less right in himself than one of his neighbors. . . . This would be slavery & not that liberty which the bill of rights has made inviolable. . . . Nothing could so completely divest us of that liberty as the establishment of the opinion that the state has a *perpetual* right to the services of all it's members. This to men of certain ways of thinking would be to annihilate the blessings of existence; to contradict the giver of life who gave it for happiness & not for wretchedness; and certainly to such it were better that they had never been born.

This, however, was not immutable doctrine with Jefferson. He wrote that way because he had been hurt.

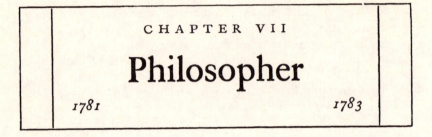

CHAPTER VII

Philosopher

1781   *1783*

JEFFERSON was certain, at the age of thirty-eight, that never again would public life ensnare him. He had no need, he felt, for politics as a creative expression. For a man of varied interests there were more fruitful pursuits to follow. In the natural sciences he would find truth and in the civic arts serenity. Affection and emotional security he had in full in the bosom of his family. Come peace, there was little else a thoughtful man could ask for. "I had folded myself in the arms of retirement," he said.

His country, he was sure, no longer had urgent need of his services, and he could practice the arts of peace with a clear conscience, particularly so since the military situation had changed in favor of the American cause. For almost simultaneously with Jefferson's retirement from the governorship, in the summer of 1781 the French fleet arrived at last and began to break the British stranglehold on America. It was high time. In September, 1781, Jefferson was happy to hear that the French Admiral de Grasse had battered the British fleet in the Chesapeake. Six weeks later came the electrifying news of Lord Cornwallis's surrender with his entire army to General Washington at Yorktown. British power was broken and American independence virtually assured. The years of pain and struggle were coming to a happy end. "The play is over," exulted young Lafayette. Jefferson, at Monticello, was quietly thankful that it was.

The former Governor could now devote himself to the kind

of life he craved, the life of a cultivated grand seigneur who was at the same time a scientist and a large-scale farmer who was also a philosopher. Days would be devoted to planting and to planning, and evenings given up to conversation when the opportunity offered, to poetry when the mood was there, and to music whenever possible. Music was one of his passions. "If there is a gratification which I envy," he once wrote to an Italian friend ". . . it is music. This is the favorite passion of my soul, & fortune has cast my lot in a country where it is in a state of deplorable barbarism." He had long hoped to import half a dozen skilled Italian artisans who would ply their trade during the day and form a small orchestra in their leisure hours. Since he was not rich enough to support a band outright, by obtaining musical craftsmen he would combine his "passion for music" with "that economy which we are obliged to observe." In passing it should be remarked that Jefferson's admiration for Italians was so great that he preferred Italian and other Mediterranean immigrants to those of any other country.[1]

His home, Monticello, a half-domed, Italian-styled structure perched in proud isolation amid shrubs and flowers on the crest of the hill, had windows facing every point of the compass. From Monticello the circular horizon could be seen in unobstructed splendor. The windows in the house were open to every breeze that blew from the misty pastel-blue of the Blue Ridge and the darkling green of the surrounding hills. The house was not simply light and airy, but as spacious as ingenuity could make it and as comfortable as imagination could conceive it. "Mr. Jefferson," a French aristocratic visitor remarked, "is the

[1] Jefferson wrote to Richard Henry Lee in 1778: "Emigrants too from the Mediterranean would be of much more value to our country particularly than from the more Northern countries. They bring with them a skill in agriculture & other arts better adapted to our climate. I believe that had our country been peopled thence we should now have been further advanced in rearing the several things our country is capable of producing. . . . Our own country wants nothing but skilful labourers to raise with success wine, oil & silk. From the Levant & Archipelago we might hope to have introduced together with the people many useful plants, esculant [sic], medicinal & for manufacture and arts." He made arrangements with his Tuscan-born friend Dr. Philip Mazzei, who became his neighbor in 1773, "in procuring emigrants which I own is with me almost as great an object as trade."

first American who has consulted the fine arts to know how he should shelter himself from the weather." This visitor, the Marquis de Chastellux, spent four delightful days in Monticello in the spring of 1782. The observant Frenchman was impressed by the genius and charm of his American host:

Let me describe you a man, not yet forty, tall, and with a mild and pleasing countenance, but whose mind and understanding are ample substitutes for every exterior grace. An American, who without ever having quitted his own country, is at once a musician, skilled in drawing, a geometrician, an astronomer, a natural philosopher, legislator, and statesman. . . . A mild and amiable wife, charming children, of whose education he himself takes charge. . . .

I found his first appearance serious, nay even cold; but before I had been two hours with him we were as intimate as if we had passed our whole lives together; walking, books, but above all, a conversation always varied and interesting.

Worldly and sophisticated guests were not so common in Monticello that Jefferson would neglect a single hour in entertaining them. The democrat from Virginia and the aristocrat from France "clicked" immediately. In the eighteenth century there was a community of interests and ideas among cultivated gentlemen who, regardless of origins or political affiliation, were inclined to see the world through the common spectacles of rationalism and enlightenment. Jefferson and De Chastellux spent hours in eager and exciting conversation, and this made the four days, the Marquis tells, "pass away like so many minutes."

One evening when the family had retired, Jefferson suddenly removed his mask of worldly detachment and the Frenchman saw the eager face of a boy lighted up by the excitement of poetry.

I recollect with pleasure that as we were conversing one evening over a bowl of punch, after Mrs. Jefferson had retired, our conversation turned on the poems of Ossian. It was a spark of electricity which passed rapidly from one to the other; we recollected the passages in those sublime poems, which particularly struck us. . . . In our enthusiasm the book was sent for, and placed near the bowl, where, by their mutual aid, the night far advanced imperceptibly upon us.

De Chastellux's conclusion about his host was that, like another Bacon, he had made all knowledge his field in which to roam:[2]

. . . it seemed as if from his youth he had placed his mind, as he has done his house, on an elevated situation, from which he might contemplate the universe.[3]

2

At about the same time another Frenchman, the Marquis de Barbé-Marbois, secretary of the French Legation in Philadelphia, asked Jefferson to supply him with some data on the State of Virginia. There was no *World Almanac* in those days, no governmental reports, no census data, and when relevant information was needed it had to be obtained by guess and by God. The French Government was anxious to know something concrete about its American ally, and the Legation in Philadelphia was making inquiries in the various States. The result as to Virginia was an early American masterpiece.

Gathering and compiling information about his native State was a task entirely to Jefferson's taste. His notebooks were filled with precise observations on natural phenomena, and his mind was stocked with a vast store of scientific information. All he needed to do was to marshal his stuff on paper. But he did more: he presented his data not as dry facts, but as muscle reinforcing a point of view. He worked over and polished his *Notes on Virginia* for months. The "notes" were really sculptured essays on a variety of subjects, ranging from paleontology to history, from zoology to theology, from anthropology to economics, from geography to botany. He consulted no reference book but his own eyes and his memory.

[2] In that year (1782) William and Mary College honored Jefferson with an honorary doctor's degree. He was later to receive degrees from Yale (1786), Harvard (1787), Brown (1787), and Princeton (1791), but he despised such things as empty snobbishness.
[3] F. J. de Chastellux, *Travels in North-America in 1780-81-82*, tr. by J. Kent, New York, 1827, pp. 227-28.

The *Notes on Virginia* remained in manuscript for about two years, until Jefferson got to Paris. Then he had two hundred copies struck off at a cost of 1,254 francs. Copies were distributed among a circle of carefully chosen friends, with the request that they be kept absolutely confidential. Jefferson, whose sense for trends in public opinion was always acute, realized that many of his social and religious comments were dynamite, and he was not inclined to have his character exposed to a clerical auto-da-fé in his native country. Always he had a distaste for martyrdom, especially of the fruitless variety. He knew that the rage of the zealots, like the bite of a snake, would do him no good. The inscription on the flyleaf of the *Notes on Virginia* which he presented to Lafayette shows his characteristic caution. It ends:

Unwilling to expose these sheets to the public eye the writer begs the favor of the Marquis to put them into the hands of no person on whose care and fidelity he cannot rely to guard them against publication.

3

After more than a century and a half, the *Notes on Virginia* is still relevant and fresh. It is the work of an embattled liberal and a philosophic scholar. The *Notes* may not have contained much statistical data on the State, but the book told a good deal about the mind and opinions of one of Virginia's great sons. Here is a fresh well of democratic thought, seasoned by warm conviction and flavored with humanist dogma. On Indians:

Before we condemn the Indians of this continent as wanting genius, we must consider that letters have not yet been introduced among them. Were we to compare them in their present state with the Europeans North of the Alps, when the Roman arms and arts first crossed those mountains, the comparison would be unequal, because, at that time, those parts of Europe were swarming with numbers. . . . Yet I may safely ask, how many good poets, how many able mathematicians, how many great inventors in arts or sciences, had Europe, north of the Alps, then produced? And it was sixteen centuries after this before a Newton could be formed.

On free government among Indians:

Their only controls are their manners, and that moral sense of right and wrong, which, like the sense of tasting and feeling in every man, makes a part of his nature. An offence against these is punished by contempt, by exclusion from society. . . . Imperfect as this species of coercion may seem, crimes are very rare among them; insomuch that were it made a question, whether no law, as among the savage Americans, or too much law, as among the civilized Europeans, submits man to the greatest evil, one who has seen both conditions of existence would pronounce it to the last; and that the sheep are happier of themselves, than under care of the wolves.

On "fifth-column" tactics:

The time to guard against corruption and tyranny, is before they shall have gotten hold of us. It is better to keep the wolf out of the fold, than to trust to drawing his teeth and claws after he shall have entered.

On an educated democracy:

In every government on earth is some trace of human weakness, some germ of corruption and degeneracy, which cunning will discover, and wickedness insensibly open, cultivate and improve. Every government degenerates when trusted to the rulers of the people alone. The people themselves therefore are its only safe depositories. And to render even them safe, their minds must be improved to a certain degree. . . . And amendment of our constitution must here come in aid of the public education. The influence over government must be shared among all the people. If every individual . . . participates of the ultimate authority, the government will be safe.

On the horrors and evils of slavery:

And with what execrations should the statesman be loaded, who permitting one half the citizens thus to trample on the rights of the other, transforms those into despots, and these into enemies, destroys the morals of the one part, and the amor patriae of the other. For if a slave can have a country in this world, it must be any other in preference to that in which he is born to live and labour for another. . . .

On avoiding the evils of war:

Never was so much false arithmetic employed on any subject, as that which has been employed to persuade nations that it is their interest to go to war. Were the money which it has cost to gain, at the close of a long war, a little town, or a little territory, the right to cut wood here, or to catch fish there, expended in improving what they already possess, in making roads, opening rivers, building ports, improving the arts and finding employment for their idle poor, it would render them much stronger, much wealthier and happier. This I hope will be our wisdom.

And perhaps, to remove as much as possible the occasions of making war, it might be better for us to abandon the ocean altogether, that being the element whereon we shall be principally exposed to jostle with other nations: to leave to others to bring what we shall want, and to carry what we can spare. This would make us invulnerable to Europe, by offering none of our property to their prize, and would turn all our citizens to the cultivation of the earth; and, I repeat it again, cultivators of the earth are the most virtuous and independent citizens. It might be time enough to seek employment for them at sea, when the land no longer offers it. But the actual habits of our country-men attach them to commerce. They will exercise it for themselves. Wars then must sometimes be our lot; and all the wise can do, will be to avoid that half of them which would be produced by our own follies and our own acts of injustice; and to make for the other half the best preparations we can.

4

The retired philosopher at Monticello was not destined to enjoy his retirement. Tragedy befell him, and tore him from his comfortable nest. His fragile and beautiful wife Martha had given birth to five children in ten years. Three of those children were dead. In May, 1782, at the age of thirty-three and a half, the delicate and ailing Martha gave birth to a sixth child.[4] This last childbirth was too much for Mrs. Jefferson. Her life was visibly ebbing, and Jefferson was in a state of wordless terror at the prospect of her passing. She was the great love of his life,

---

[4] This child, a girl, died two years later.

and he dared not think of what existence would be without her. For four months he never left her bedside, nursing her with almost desperate tenderness.

Edward Bacon, the manager of the Jefferson plantation, is authority for the statement that the dying Martha exacted a promise from her husband never to give their children a step-mother: "Mr. Jefferson promised her solemnly that he would never be married again." In view of their passionate and un-clouded love, the story is not unlikely.

One noonday in September, Jefferson's "state of dreadful sus-pense," as he described it, came to an end. He had watched the last spark of life slowly flickering out, and he was dazed into insensibility. His sister Mrs. Carr led him out of the room. Moments later Martha expired. Jefferson had seen her die for four months, but he was unprepared for the shock. He fell in a frighteningly long faint. For three weeks he kept to his room, a silent being, tortured with sorrow. Night and day he walked incessantly up and down his room, alone with his wild thoughts, as if he had lost his reason. When he went out at last, it was to mount his horse and ride into the mountains, aimlessly ram-bling along unfrequented paths, a solitary man weeping for his beloved. Occasionally his ten-year-old daughter accompanied him and was a silent witness "to many a violent burst of grief." For six months he was alone with his sorrow, never communi-cating with, never writing to, anyone.

On the white marble tombstone of his wife who was "torn from him by death" Jefferson inscribed a verse of such tender-ness that, to shelter his emotions from the public gaze, he had it chiseled in Greek:

> If in the melancholy shades below,
> The flames of friends and lovers cease to glow,
> Yet mine shall sacred last; mine undecay'd
> Burn on through death and animate my shade.[5]

[5] These lines are from the *Iliad*, in Pope's translation.

5

Life made its inexorable demands. Gradually the flames of grief died down, and Jefferson began to take himself in hand. A father of three orphaned girls, he could not go on torturing himself to madness. Martha, the eldest child, was ten, Mary four, Lucy an infant; they all needed care. Jefferson took his children to Ampthill, residence of Archibald Cary, and had them inoculated for smallpox. He was the children's "chief nurse."

Jefferson remained for a while at Ampthill, not knowing what to do with himself. Martha's death had shattered his plans for retirement. Monticello was too intimately associated with ten years of "unchequered happiness," as he said, for him to be able to live there now alone. A decision as to his future was finally made by his friends, who had never given up the hope of enticing him back into politics, where they felt he naturally belonged.

In Philadelphia the Congress was then making arrangements for peace with England. This gave Jefferson's friends an idea. Someone in the Congress, possibly James Madison, suggested that Jefferson be appointed Minister Plenipotentiary to negotiate the peace. The proposal was unanimously approved. News of the appointment reached Jefferson in November and, to the delight of his friends, he did not turn it down. A trip to Europe, which he had never seen but whose culture he had always admired, he felt would stimulate him to new life. He would, moreover, be acting on behalf of his country. He explained his reasons on November 26, 1782, in a letter to his French friend De Chastellux. This is one of the first letters he wrote after the tragedy of his wife's death:

[Your letter] found me a little emerging from the stupor of mind which had rendered me as dead to the world as was she whose loss occasioned it. Your letter recalled to my memory that there were persons still living of much value to me. If you should have thought me remiss . . . you will I am sure ascribe it to it's true cause, the state of dreadful suspense in which I have been kept all the summer & the catastrophe which closed it.

Before that event my scheme of life had been determined. I had folded myself in the arms of retirement, and rested all prospects of future happiness on domestic & literary objects. A single event wiped out all my plans and left me a blank which I had not the spirits to fill up. In this state of mind an appointment from Congress found me, requiring me to cross the Atlantic. . . . I accepted the appointment.

6

Reluctantly Jefferson tore himself away from his two youngest children, whom he left with their aunt Mrs. Francis Eppes, and took the third girl, Martha, with him to Philadelphia. There he left her in a private school. He was to sail for Europe from Baltimore on the French frigate *Romulus,* but bad luck was with him. The *Romulus* was blocked in the ice, and sailing was delayed indefinitely. Jefferson waited in Philadelphia for the ice to break. The old year went and the new year came, and still the ship was ice-blocked. In the meantime the waiting Plenipotentiary was getting his diplomatic bearings and recovering his political finesse. He wrote a fine letter to General Washington:

I cannot leave the continent without separating myself for a moment from the general gratitude of my country to offer my individual tribute to your Exc[ellenc]y for all you have suffered & all you have effected for us. Were I to indulge myself in . . . warm effusions . . . they would wear an appearance of adulation very foreign to my nature; for such is become the prostitution of language that sincerity has no longer distinct terms in which to express her own truths. Should you give me occasion, during the short mission on which I go, to render you any service beyond the water, I shall for a proof of my gratitude appeal from language to the zeal with which I shall embrace it.

The shy General was pleased with the letter of admiration from his fellow Virginian. Chilly in exterior, Washington was grateful for words of kindness and appreciation. He replied with considerable warmth that he felt himself flattered by the favorable sentiments which Jefferson was pleased to entertain of his services for "our common country," using that peculiarly stilted style which yet managed to be nut-full of meaning:

To merit the approbation of good and virtuous Men is the height of my ambition, and will be a full compensation for all my toils and Sufferings in the long and painful Contest [in which] we have been engaged. It gave me great pleasure to hear that the call upon you from Congress to pass the Atlantic in the Character of one of their Ministers for Negotiating Peace had been repeated. . . . You will please to accept my grateful thanks for your obliging offer of Services during your stay in France. To hear from you frequently will be an honor and very great satisfaction.

At the end of January, 1783, word came to Philadelphia that the *Romulus* might break from its icy grip and set sail. Jefferson and his secretary, Major Franks, hurried south to catch the boat. It was a terrible journey of five days. Ferry service across the various arms of the Chesapeake was wretched. The two travelers waited in miserable inns, cold and unhappy, for the chance to cross icy waters. At the end of the trip Jefferson had reached the limit of his endurance. From Baltimore the exasperated Plenipotentiary wrote to James Madison:

. . . we lost two days in the most execrable situation in point of accommodation & society which can be conceived. In short braving all weather & plunging thro' thick and thin we arrived here last night being the fifth from Philadelphia.

In Baltimore Jefferson's troubles were not over. The frigate lay twelve miles offshore and had to be reached by boat. Heavy ice floes made the passage perilous. Nevertheless, the impatient Jefferson attempted it and almost came to grief:

. . . we got about half way with tolerable ease, but the influx of the tide then happening the ice closed on us on every side & became impenetrable to our little vessel, so that we could get neither backwards nor forwards. We were finally relieved . . . by a sloop which forced it's way down & put us on board the Romulus, where we were obliged to remain all night.

But the *Romulus* did not sail. Its captain, the Chevalier de Villebrun, was informed that a small British fleet of seven ships (totaling 268 guns) was lurking at the capes of the Chesapeake to intercept the French ship with the American envoy. Jefferson, with dry modesty, considered this "a most amazing force for such an object." The British fleet forced Jefferson to return to Baltimore and wait. He waited, fretting and irritable. He could neither return to Philadelphia in comfort nor resign his position in honor. Like the frigate *Romulus*, the Plenipotentiary was himself caught in a jam—a Minister who could not go to his post, a father who could not rejoin his family.

Patience began to desert the philosopher. Perhaps his country did not need him after all? Perhaps peace would be ably negotiated without him? In a letter to Robert R. Livingston, the Secretary of Foreign Affairs, Jefferson suggested that he should resign, since the negotiations in Europe were in such competent hands as those of John Adams. Livingston, however, would not release him. "Congress seems anxious to avail themselves of your abilities," he replied. There was nothing to do but wait.

It was all in vain. While Jefferson was fretting, news came from Europe that a provisional treaty of peace had been agreed upon. Jefferson returned to Philadelphia and waited for further instructions from the Congress. By the middle of March, news of the peace treaty was confirmed and Jefferson asked the Congress to release him. It took that body two more weeks before it finally resolved to inform "the Hon. Thomas Jefferson . . . that Congress consider the object of his appointment so far advanced as to render it unnecessary for him to pursue his voyage."

For three and a half months of trouble and vexation, Jefferson was given polite thanks. The Congress thanked him for his "readiness . . . in undertaking a service." He returned to Monticello somber and uncommunicative. The joy of life had gone out of the house on the hill. There was little to do, and no incitement to do it. This was Jefferson's fortieth birthday. For the first time in his life he was aimless.

7

When autumn came Jefferson shook off his lethargy. Gradually, haltingly, he began to return to his normal occupations. He was like a man who had taken a beating, had been on his knees up to the count of nine, and then rose grimly to continue the fight. In beginning a new life at the age of forty, the tragedy-chastened Jefferson was aided by the Virginia Assembly, which seems to have had an uncanny sense for picking men of brains and distinction. As soon as it was known that Jefferson was available again, the legislature chose him as delegate to the Congress, to take his seat in November. Among the other Virginia delegates was Jefferson's protégé James Monroe, a young man of twenty-five.

The Congress was sitting in Annapolis, and there Jefferson joined it in the middle of December. Immediately he plunged into activity with a zest that pleased his friends and inspired his colleagues. Still disliking public speeches and despising long-winded talk, he did not participate in debates. He worked quietly, with concentrated energy, sitting on every important committee, drawing up reports, and soothing exasperated tempers. His mastery of the assuaging word and the flattering phrase was remarkable; his conciliatory temper was pervasive. In no time, the quiet delegate from Monticello was regarded as the most influential member of the Congress. Men loved him for his graciousness and trusted him for his unassertive devotion to work. "Take things always by their smooth handle" was one of his guiding mottos.

To the Congress, with its talking lawyers and squabbling partisans, the lean, carrot-haired Virginian who had given up the legal profession was a novelty and a godsend. The Congress, being what there was of the government of the poorly united States, faced tasks of enormous complexity. There was a natural tendency to talk a lot and to pass the well-known buck. Responsibility was diffused, authority undefined, and precedent nonexistent. Thus constituted, the Congress was called upon to solve problems of money and finance, commerce and debt, public lands and foreign policy. There was need for executive talent and for decisive action. Jefferson brought to the Congress not merely a genius for compromise but also a knack for solving problems by action.

He was a magnet for work. In the six months that he was in the Congress he headed most of the important committees and drafted no less than thirty-one essential state papers. Some of these papers have become foundation stones of the American republic. Among these reports was Jefferson's classic paper proposing the dollar unit and the present coinage of the United States.

He labored tirelessly, drawing inspiration from his own renewed interest in life. His colleagues did not particularly inspire him. For most of his fellow delegates he had no respect, although he was far too courteous socially and too adroit politically to show his true feelings. His prejudice against the one hundred and fifty members of the Annapolis Congress was not diminished by the fact that they were lawyers, and many were voluble lawyers. Some of them were afflicted, Jefferson said privately, with a "morbid rage of debate." Himself imbued with the scientific spirit, Jefferson was annoyed by those who pretended that it was possible to arrive at truth by means of a "copious flow of words," but as a tactful gentleman he masked his disapproval in courteous silence. Being a philosopher, he was, he said, "willing to listen." But argumentative and professional talkers had a way of getting under his skin.

His comments on a talky Congress are not without relevance:

Our body was little numerous, but very contentious. Day after day was wasted on the most unimportant questions. [A member] was one of those afflicted with the morbid rage of debate, of an ardent mind, prompt imagination, and copious flow of words, he heard with impatience any logic which was not his own. Sitting near me on some occasion of a trifling but wordy debate, [he] asked me how I could sit in silence hearing so much false reasoning which a word should refute? I observed to him that to refute was easy, but to silence impossible. That in measures brought forward by myself, I took the laboring oar, as was incumbent on me; but that in general I was willing to listen. . . .

I served with General Washington in the legislature of Virginia before the revolution, and, during it, with Dr. Franklin in Congress. I never heard either of them speak ten minutes at a time, nor to any but the main point which was to decide the question. They laid their shoulders to the great points, knowing that the little ones would follow of themselves. If the present Congress errs in too much talking, how can it be otherwise in a body to which the people send 150. lawyers, whose trade it is to question everything, yield nothing, & talk by the hour? That 150. lawyers should do business together ought not to be expected.

8

At Annapolis Jefferson's leisure hours were spent in reading, riding, and correspondence with his little daughter Martha, whose education he supervised with the same scrupulous care that he gave to affairs of state. His treatment of the twelve-year-old Martha was a delicate blend of gentlemanly courtesy, thoughtful pedagogy, and parental love. He shaped Martha's education so that she would become at the same time a lady of refinement and an educated member of society. And always he imbued her with his own moral ideas and social ideals. His letters to her make delightful reading:

. . . the following is what I should approve:
From 8 to 10, practice music.
From 10 to 1, dance one day and draw another.
From 1 to 2, draw on the day you dance, and write a letter the next day.
From 3 to 4, read French.
From 4 to 5, exercise yourself in music.
From 5 till bed-time, read English, write, etc.

The father set his daughter an ideal of goodness and accomplishment:

I have placed my happiness on seeing you good and accomplished; and no distress this world can now bring on me would equal that of your disappointing my hopes. If you love me, then strive to be good under every situation and to all living creatures.

On another occasion he wrote her:

I hope you will have good sense enough to disregard those foolish predictions that the world is to be at an end soon. The Almighty has never made known to any body at what time he created it; nor will he tell any body when he will put an end to it, if he ever means to do it. As to preparations for that event, the best way is for you always to be prepared for it. The only way to be so is, never to say or do a bad thing.

A few days later he gave his little daughter an earnest lecture on dress:

I omitted in that letter to advise you on the subject of dress, which I know you are a little apt to neglect. I do not wish you to be gaily clothed at this time of life, but that your wear should be fine of its kind. But above all things and at all times let your clothes be neat, whole, and properly put on. Do not fancy you must wear them till the dirt is visible to the eye. You will be the last one who is sensible to this. Some ladies think they may, under the privileges of the *déshabillé*, be loose and negligent of their dress in the morning. But be you, from the moment you rise till you go to bed, as cleanly and properly dressed as at the hours of dinner or tea. . . . Nothing is so disgusting to our sex as a want of cleanliness and delicacy in yours. I hope, therefore, the moment you rise from bed, your first work will be to dress yourself in such style, as that you may be seen by any gentleman without his being able to discover a pin amiss, or any other circumstance of neatness wanting.

He did not neglect the more bookish aspects of his child's education. Once he reminded her to "take care that you never spell a word wrong." Another time he wrote:

I am anxious to know what books you read, what tunes you play, and to receive specimens of your drawings. . . . I have much at heart your learning to draw, and should be uneasy at your losing this opportunity.

In a letter to his French friend Marbois, Jefferson explained his plan of education for Martha. The letter contains a rare flash of humor:

I had left with her [Martha] a *Gil Blas* and *Don Quichotte* which are among the best books of their class as far as I am acquainted with them. The plan of reading which I have formed for her is considerably different from [that] which I think would be most proper for her sex in any other country than America. I am obliged in it to extend my views beyond herself, and consider her as possibly at the head of a little family of her own. The chance that in marriage she will draw a blockhead I calculate at about fourteen to one. . . . With the poets and prose writers I shall therefore combine a certain extent of reading in the graver sciences.

CHAPTER VIII

Ambassador

1784   *1787*

IN MAY, 1784, Congress once more appointed Jefferson to a
foreign post. He was made Minister Plenipotentiary, with
instructions to collaborate with John Adams and Benjamin
Franklin in negotiating treaties of commerce with European
nations. There was a touch of irony in the choice of a Virginia
landowner who believed that "Those who labour in the earth
are the chosen people of God" to help in the growth of trade.
But Jefferson the agriculturalist was a practical man. In a letter
to George Washington in 1784 he explained ruefully:

All the world is becoming commercial. . . . Our citizens have
had too full a taste of the comforts furnished by the arts & manufactures to be debarred the use of them. We must then in our defence endeavour to share as large a portion as we can of this modern source of wealth & power.

Jefferson went to Philadelphia to fetch his daughter Martha
and then set out with her for the North in quest of a passage
to Europe. They spent eighteen leisurely June days covering
the distance from New York to Boston. It was not time wasted.
New England was unknown territory to Jefferson, and he made
careful observations. "I made a point of informing myself of
the state of the commerce," he tells. He also observed customs,
manners, and architecture.

They sailed from Boston on July 5 on the ship *Ceres*. The
crossing was short and pleasant, taking only nineteen days from
Boston to Cowes. Jefferson had never been on the ocean, and

now he enjoyed the sun and was happy at escaping the scourge of seasickness. His young daughter described the trip in a letter to friends in Philadelphia: "We had a lovely passage in a beautiful new ship, that had made but one passage before. There were only six passengers, all of whom Papa knew, and a fine sunshine all the way, with a sea which was as calm as a river."

But the English Channel was not friendly. Indifferent to the rank of voyagers, the Channel behaved with its customary rudeness. Martha did not feel well. "It rained violently all the way," she complained, "and the sea was exceedingly rough."

The French countryside came as a delightful surprise, and compensated the American visitors for the roughness of the Channel. It was early August, and Western France, even under Louis XVI, was a flourishing garden. The fertility of the country delighted Jefferson's practiced eye, reminding him of his own Virginia. From Le Havre to Paris he traveled at snail's pace, for three full days relishing the lush fields and the neat farms redolent of loam and life. This was a country, he wrote to Monroe, "than which nothing can be more fertile, better cultivated & more elegantly improved."

But in the midst of fertility there was misery, and now Jefferson learned the first paradox of cast-ridden yet highly cultivated Europe. He came from a country where extremes of wealth and poverty were as yet happily unknown. In his own young State there were no slums and no professional beggars. He was therefore disturbed at making the acquaintance of that peculiar form of human wretchedness which has to resort to beggary for survival. Wherever the Jefferson phaeton stopped, mendicants surrounded it, pleading for alms. Martha wrote to a friend:

We should have had a very delightful voyage to Paris . . . through the most beautiful country I ever saw in my life— it is a perfect garden—if the singularity of our carriage (a phaeton) had not attracted the attention of all we met; and whenever we stopped we were surrounded by beggars—one day I counted no less than nine where we stopped to change horses.[1]

[1] This situation obtained not only in Normandy but also in Lorraine. In April, 1788, Jefferson, traveling through Northeastern France, observed: "The roads through Lorraine are strung with beggars."

2

Paris has fascinated Americans since Americans began to cross the Atlantic. Jefferson was no exception. He had never seen a city larger than Philadelphia, with its population of about 25,000, and now he found himself in the biggest metropolis in Christendom. The impact of Paris upon the sensitive planter from Virginia was stunning.

The French capital had everything to offer to a man of Jefferson's tastes and habits, although he never learned to like either congested streets or the proximity of teeming proletarians. Paris, with its beautiful, shifting pastel clouds, with its boulevards and bridges and parks and palaces and river quays, was an artist's dream and a gentleman's paradise. The city had a population of about 600,000, some getting fat on capon and others, many others, living miserably and half-starving. About one-fifth of the population was unemployed, their sullen and hungry faces seen everywhere along the thirteen hundred streets of the city. But over and above the restive masses of the poor, who were soon to blow up the whole mess, there was a stratum of superrefinement, of exquisite living, of precious manners. The city also had colleges (twenty-four) and hospitals (twenty-nine) and institutions of art and of learning. Men of culture and of taste met frequently and talked lofty ideas and read serious books; worldly men and women met, gossiped, flirted, and seduced. It was an exciting and stimulating world into which Jefferson entered.

His first step in Paris was to call upon Dr. Franklin, who lived at Passy. His second was to take an apartment. He found a place on the cul-de-sac Têtebout (now rue Taitbout), near the present Boulevard Haussmann. Later he moved to a house at the corner of the Grande Route des Champs Elysées and the rue Neuve de Berry, where he remained for the rest of his stay in Paris. It was the usual elegant house of an eighteenth-century gentleman, with a large garden, a court, and outbuildings for horses and carriages.

The establishment, if the truth be told, cost more than Jefferson could afford. He felt, however, that his position required that he live and entertain as befitted his station. His rent nearly absorbed his salary. Congress paid him only £1,800 a year, and nothing for expenses. He appealed to his young friend Congressman Monroe to get Congress to increase his funds. "I live here about as well as we did at Annapolis," he wrote to Monroe. "I keep a hired carriage & two horses. A riding horse I cannot afford to keep. . . . Yet it absorbs the whole allowance." He spent 28,000 livres on furniture, carriage, clothes, for which he had to borrow money. Congress paid him less than it did Dr. Franklin, and he certainly could not live on less. "I ask nothing for my time: but I think my expences should be paid in a stile equal to that of those with whom I am classed." His debts were mounting, and while he was serving his country he saw no way of meeting them except by an increase in salary. "The outfit has cost me near a thousand guineas; for which I am in debt, and which, were I to stay here seven years, I could never make good by savings out of my salary: for be assured we are the lowest & most obscure of the whole diplomatic tribe."

But though he was rarely ever to be free from the incubus of debt, nothing could ever long quench his optimism or weaken his resilience. He borrowed money here and there— some from John Adams at The Hague—drew funds from his estate in Virginia, and continued to live well and entertain with his usual generosity.

3

Jefferson placed Martha in an aristocratic convent, the Abbaye Royale de Panthémont, "the best and most genteel school in Paris." The school was recommended to Jefferson by a "lady friend" of Lafayette's.

The young French hero of the American Revolution was one of Jefferson's most loyal supporters. It was Lafayette who gave his American friend the golden key to French society. Anyone recommended and received by the Marquis de Lafayette, who was himself connected with the highest French families, was sure to find an opening almost everywhere in Paris. Through Lafayette, Jefferson met an ever increasing number of upper-class Frenchmen and Frenchwomen. Jefferson's home on the Grande Route des Champs Elysées became a center of sophisticated men and women. There was good food, and fine talk. He dined out regularly, and was a visitor to the better salons. He led the life of an unmarried gentleman, and it would be an exaggeration to say that he did not enjoy it.

Among his friends was Baron Grimm, Catherine the Great's personal representative in Paris, a witty talker and a professional gossip, a man about town who knew everybody in town. In twentieth-century America Grimm would have been a successful gossip columnist. There was the great Count George Louis Leclerc Buffon, the naturalist, with whom Jefferson argued for hours about the length of American deer horns. Jefferson was right, but Buffon was not convinced until his American friend sent him four-foot specimens after his return to Virginia. There was Madame d'Houdetôt, who had a salon where Jefferson was a welcome visitor. He found her society "one of the most agreeable." Another delightful French friend was the lame and jesting Baron de Grignon, an authority on painting and the stage. Jefferson thought him "the most agreeable person in French society" and his "persiflage was the keenest and most provoking I ever knew."

Still another acquaintance was the ambitious, nervous social climber Madame Necker, domineering wife of a Swiss banker who was soon to play a fateful role in the events that were shaping. Jefferson considered her a "very sincere and excellent woman," but she annoyed him by her jitters. She had what Virginians called the "budge," that is, she could not sit still. During dinner she would upset everybody by jumping up several times in nervous excitement. But she was a clever woman, nonetheless. There was Jean François Marmontel, the writer, whom Jefferson found to be a man of culture and of wit. The two men saw each other regularly. "He dined with me every Thursday for a long time, and I think told some of the most agreeable stories I ever heard in my life."

It was, indeed, an agreeable circle in which Jefferson moved. His private opinions of France's political system he kept to himself and to a few intimates in America. To his French hosts and visitors he was the essence of graciousness. John Adams's wife Abigail, who visited there, was so charmed with Jefferson that she described him as one of the "choice ones of the earth." Most of those who knew him shared that opinion. After one of Jefferson's receptions Mrs. Adams wrote:

Well, my dear niece, I have returned from Mr. Jefferson's. When I got there I found pretty large company. It consisted of the Marquis and Madame de Lafayette; the Count and Countess de ————; a French count who had been a general in America, but whose name I forget; Commodore Jones; Mr. Jarvis, an American gentleman lately arrived . . . a Mr. Bowdoin, an American also; I ask the Chevalier de la Luzerne's pardon—I had like to have forgotten him.

The place teemed with gentlemen and aristocrats, but that did not necessarily mean that the atmosphere was pretentious or stuffy. Many of the visitors were witty, some were serious. Among them all, particularly those who had served as officers in the American Revolution, the author of the Declaration of Independence enjoyed great prestige. To them, Jefferson was more than just a gentleman with courtly manners; he was a patriot who had been tested in the hard field of politics. The young aristocrats looked up to him, respected his judgment and admired his character. In his quiet way the gracious Virginian, who always took things by their "smooth handle," thus exercised a discreet, yet pervasive, influence on the Frenchmen who gathered about him. It is a pity that the Virginia democrat had little, if any, contact among the leaders of the nonaristocratic classes who were soon to leap into the arena of sanguinary politics. He might have been able to imbue them with some of his own matured ideas on the subject of a balanced, genuinely representative democracy.

4

Though Jefferson enjoyed life in Paris socially, he suffered climatically. In Paris, as everyone who had lived there knows, it rains about three hundred days in the year.[2] Dampness, Parisian or other, is never conducive to good health, and Jefferson's tough, lanky constitution was no proof against Parisian rains. Though his health had been well-nigh perfect in the high clear climate of his native Virginia, it gave way before the humidity of Paris. The first winter he spent largely indoors, in great discomfort. "I have had a very bad winter," he confided to Monroe, "having been confined the greatest part of it. . . . The air is extremely damp, and the waters very unwholesome."

He recovered in the spring, and began his routine of rising early and riding or walking a few miles daily. By the time his forty-second birthday came around he was able to walk seven or eight miles every day. On one of these walks he stumbled, fell, and broke his right wrist. It was set badly, and never quite recovered its suppleness or strength. Jefferson learned to write very well with his left hand. Years later, when he was an old man, he fell again and broke his left wrist. Thenceforth writing was to be an ordeal for him.

Mornings he would read, study, and write. By one o'clock he was ready for his vigorous hike. Later in the afternoon he would go browsing through the streets, shops, and stalls. Those were happy, adventurous hours. Everything was exciting and stimulating—a graceful fountain here, an imposing arch there, a bit of skillful engineering elsewhere. He found almost child-like joy in novel inventions, for which he had a never-quenched curiosity. A new oil-burning lamp with wick and cylinder delighted him. Another recent invention pleased him no end:

[2] When this writer lived there in 1936-37, he found that it rained part of the time nearly every day. Jefferson had a similar experience. On Feb. 8, 1805, he wrote to Volney: "During a residence of between six and seven years in Paris, I never, but once, saw the sun shine through a whole day, without being obscured by a cloud in any part of it."

of "phosphoric matches" he exclaimed in a letter to a friend in America: "They are a beautiful discovery and very useful. . . . The convenience of lighting a candle without getting out of bed, of sealing letters without calling a servant, of kindling a fire without flint, steel, punk, &c. are of value."

There was progress and invention everywhere.[3] Jefferson, like the equally inventive Dr. Franklin, even looked forward to the time when men would fly in machines, like birds. But above all, it was books that fascinated the Virginian. Only the true lover of books can savor the full pleasure of book-hunting on the stalls and in the shops of Paris. Jefferson could not live without books. He roamed through the bookstores, browsed through the shops, touched rare and strange books with the suppressed thrill of the reverent bibliophile. "While in Paris," he wrote, "I devoted every afternoon I was disengaged . . . in examining all the principal bookstores, turning over every book with my own hand, and putting by everything which related to America, and indeed whatever was rare and valuable in every science." The shopkeepers found the tall, smiling *Améri-cain* a windfall of a customer.

5

But Jefferson was also critical of France, an attitude that was not lessened by his loneliness for his country and his children. He was not too proud to plead with his friends on the other side of the Atlantic to write him all the little gossip and to send him all the "small facts" from home. A letter mailed

---

[3] Jefferson was, of course, a strong believer in progress. During the campaign year 1800 he wrote:

"Progress is either physical or intellectual. If we can bring it about that men are on the average an inch taller in the next generation than in this; if they are an inch larger round the chest; if their brain is an ounce or two heavier, and their life a year or two longer,—that is progress. If fifty years hence the average man shall invariably argue from two ascertained premises where he now jumps to a conclusion from a single supposed revelation,— that is progress! I expect it to be made here, under our democratic stimulants, on a great scale, until every man is potentially an athlete in body and an Aristotle in mind."

in Virginia took six weeks to reach Paris, forty-two long and anxious days. Often there was no news from America, and Jefferson groaned that the "dearth of American information places us as to our own country in the silence of the grave." His was a double loneliness, that of a patriot away from his country, and that of a father separated from his children. He passed many a day in the solitude of a sensitive man without a family, yearning for home or even for news from home. Often he was sick of politics and of the so-called higher things. He wanted all those little earthy things that one gets from living with one's family and one's friends. His state of mind is revealed in a touching letter written to James Currie in September, 1785, one year after he came to Paris:

Of political correspondents I can find enough, but I can persuade nobody to believe that the small facts which they see passing daily under their eyes are precious to me at this distance; much more interesting to the heart than events of higher rank. Fancy to yourself a being who is withdrawn from his connections of blood, of marriage, of friendship, of acquaintance in all their gradations, who for years should hear nothing of what has passed among them, who returns again to see them and finds the one-half dead.[4] This strikes him like a pestilence sweeping off the half of mankind. Events which had they come to him one by one and in detail he would have weathered as other people do, when presented to his mind all at once are overwhelming. Continue then to give me facts, little facts, such as you think every one imagines beneath notice, and your letters will be the most precious to me. They will place me in imagination in my own country, and they will place me where I am happiest.

He saw Martha at the convent as often as possible and did all he could to encourage her in her studies. Once she complained of her inability to master Latin—"*Titus Livius* puts me out of my wits." Jefferson chided her gently: "I do not like your saying that you are unable to read the ancient print of your Livy. . . . We are always equal to what we undertake with resolution." And he added a magnificent sentence—like a cry of defiance in his diplomatic exile: "It is a part of the Amer-

---

[4] A few months earlier Jefferson received the news from Virginia that his youngest child, Lucy, had died.

ican character to consider nothing as desperate, to surmount every difficulty by resolution and contrivance." After three years in the nuns' school, young Martha suggested to her father that she would like to become a Catholic and remain at the Abbaye. Jefferson quietly took Martha out of the convent. Father and daughter never spoke of the matter afterward.

He wanted to have his other little daughter, Mary, whom everybody called Polly, join him in Paris. She was staying in Virginia with relatives and was too young or too thoughtless to write to her father. His yearning for her was one long pain. For more than a year after he came to Paris, he received no word from the child. Finally, he could bear it no longer and wrote Polly, who was seven, a long letter pleading with her to join him in Paris and holding out to her all manner of inducements:

My dear Polly,—I have not received a letter from you since I came to France. If you knew how much I love you and what pleasure the receipt of your letters gave me at Philadelphia, you would have written to me, or at least have told your aunt what to write. . . . I wish so much to see you, that I have desired your uncle and aunt to send you to me. I know, my dear Polly, how sorry you will be, and ought to be, to leave them and your cousins; but your sister and myself cannot live without you, and after a while we will carry you back again to see your friends in Virginia. In the meantime you shall be taught here to play on the harpsichord, to draw, to dance, to read and talk French, and such other things as will make you more worthy of the love of your friends. . . .

. . . When you come here you shall have as many dolls and playthings as you want for yourself, or to send to your cousins whenever you shall have opportunities. I hope you are a very good girl, that you love your uncle and aunt very much, and are very thankful to them for all their goodness to you; that you never suffer yourself to be angry with any body, that you give your playthings to those who want them, that you do whatever any body desires of you that is right, that you never tell stories, never beg for any thing, mind your books and your work when your aunt tells you, never play but when she permits you, nor go where she forbids you; remember, too, as a constant charge, not to go out without your bonnet, because it will make you very ugly, and then we shall not love you so much. If you always practice these lessons we shall continue to love you as we do now, and it is impossible to love you any more.

But little Polly had a mind of her own; she was as spirited and firm-willed as her father. The child replied:

Dear Papa—I long to see you, and hope that you and sister Patsy are well; give my love to her and tell her that I long to see her, and hope that you and she will come very soon to see us. I hope that you will send me a doll. I am very sorry that you have sent for me. I don't want to go to France, I had rather stay with Aunt Eppes. . . .

> Your most happy and dutiful daughter,
>> Polly Jefferson.

The little girl told the great man who was her father that she was quite happy in Virginia, thank you—and why don't you come to see me? To further pressing invitations from her father, she replied:

Dear Papa—I should be very happy to see you, but I can not go to France, and hope that you and sister Patsy are well.
> Mary Jefferson

Dear Papa—I want to see you and sister Patsy, but you must come to Uncle Eppes's house.
> Polly Jefferson

She did not come to Europe until July, 1787.

6

Jefferson's official duties were not heavy, though they were sometimes irksome. At first he was only a Minister Plenipotentiary, whose object was to arrange treaties of commerce. The actual envoy was Benjamin Franklin, a man whose popularity was as great as his wit was renowned. In the spring of 1785, however, Franklin retired and was succeeded by Jefferson. It was then that Jefferson made the bon mot that convinced Frenchmen that he was worthy of occupying the place which Dr. Franklin had so long graced. When France's Foreign Minister, the Count de Vergennes, said to the Virginian, "It is you who replace Monsieur Franklin?" Jefferson replied quickly, "No one can replace him, sir: I am only his successor." [5]

It was well for the young American republic that its first two envoys to France were men as suave and as brilliant as Franklin and Jefferson. For Frenchmen had no high opinion of the American character, having had too many unpleasant experiences with American businessmen whose commercial behavior did not bear the test of either law or ethics. American States defaulted their debts and American merchants were sharp traders. As a result, the young American republic was widely disliked, and it took all the wit of a Franklin and the adroitness of a Jefferson to prevent disagreeable incidents between the two countries.

Jefferson was humiliated by the commercial and financial behavior of his countrymen, who made his position as Minister uncomfortable. The reputation of Americans in Europe was not flattering. He wrote with quiet bitterness: "Among many good qualities which my countrymen possess some of a different character, unhappily mix themselves. The most remarkable are indolence, extravagance, & infidelity to their engagements."

But he could not escape the merchants. His chief activities as a diplomat, in fact, were devoted to commerce and trade. In this he was "powerfully aided by all the influence" and energies of Lafayette, who likewise was no businessman. [6] He tells in his *Autobiography:*

My duties at Paris were confined to a few objects; the receipt of our whale-oils, salted fish, and salted meats on favorable terms, the admission of our rice on equal terms with that of Piedmont,

[5] When John Adams, who was envoy at The Hague, heard of Jefferson's appointment, he was delighted. "He is an old friend." Adams wrote, "with whom I have often had occasion to labor at many a knotty problem, and in whose abilities and steadiness I always found great cause to confide."

[6] Lafayette was enthusiastic about Jefferson. "I am more and more pleased with Mr. Jefferson," he wrote to General Washington; "his abilities, his virtues, his temper, everything about him, commands respect and attracts affection; he enjoys universal regard, and transacts the affairs of America to perfection. It is the happiest choice that could be made."

Egypt & the Levant, a mitigation of the monopolies of our tobacco by the Farmers-general, and a free admission of our productions into their islands; were the principal commercial objects which required attention.

Jefferson realized that there was a need for commerce, but the more he saw of businessmen, the less he cared for trade. His experiences in Paris further confirmed his planter's bias against business, and he hoped that his country would not succumb to the temptations of a commercial economy, with its attendant evils of greed and the extremes of wealth and poverty. He had neither understanding for the profit motive nor any craving for wealth. His idea of a balanced and happy state was a commonwealth where the population was devoted to farming.

For city workers Jefferson had sympathy but no strong affection. He believed that they should be paid a just wage to maintain them and their families in decent comfort. "It may be reasonably allowed," he had noted in his *Commonplace Book*, "that a labouring man ought to earn at least twice as much as will maintain himself in ordinary food and cloathing; that he may be enabled to breed up children, pay rent for a small dwelling, find himself the necessary utensils etc." But he distrusted the poor city-dwellers. Jefferson knew that crowded and dirty slums were not ideal breeding-places for good citizens. What did a homeless and landless man know about liberty? Only a man who possessed his own acres and worked in the open air could be really free and could appreciate the blessings of life. In 1785 he wrote candidly to a friend:

You ask what I think on the expediency of encouraging our states to be commercial? Were I to indulge on my own theory, I should wish them to practise neither commerce nor navigation, but to stand with respect to Europe precisely on the footing of China. We should thus avoid wars, and all our citizens would be husbandmen. Whenever indeed our numbers should so increase as that our produce would overstock the markets of those nations who should come to seek it, the farmers must either employ the surplus of their time in manufactures, or the surplus of our hands must be employed in manufactures, or in navigation. But that day would, I think, be distant, and we should long keep our workmen in Europe, while Europe should be drawing rough materials & even subsistence from America.

His diplomatic experiences in Paris, as well as his knowledge of history, made him dread the prospect of a growing American commerce that involved shipping, international competition for markets, and thus, inescapably, war. Why, he demanded, could not his countrymen stay at home and cultivate the vast and rich acres that stretched between the Atlantic and the Mississippi, crying for farmers to bring them to abundant life? To John Jay, he wrote vehemently on the desirability of an agricultural economy:

We have now lands enough to employ an infinite number of people in their cultivation. Cultivators of the earth are the most valuable citizens. They are the most vigorous, the most independent, the most virtuous, & they are tied to their country & wedded to its liberty and interests by the most lasting bonds. As long therefore as they can find employment in this line, I would not convert them into mariners, artisans or anything else. But our citizens will find employment in this line till their numbers, & of course their productions, become too great for the demand both internal & foreign. This is not the case as yet, & probably will not be for a considerable time. . . . I consider the class of artificers as the panders of vice & the instruments by which the liberties of a country are generally over-turned.

7

The years that Jefferson spent in France were years of growth and of a deepening maturity. France taught him the horrors of bad government and the miseries of inequality. The more he saw of France, the more he resisted what charm she had. Conditions there only strengthened his love for his own country. What he saw in Europe confirmed his conviction, so fully justified by history, that the future belonged to America. In a revealing letter to Monroe he burst out:

I sincerely wish you may find it convenient to come here. The pleasure of the trip will be less than you expect but the utility greater. It will make you adore your own country, it's soil, it's climate, it's equality, liberty, laws, people & manners. My God! how little do my country men know what precious blessings they are in possession of, and which no other people on earth enjoy. I confess I had no idea of it myself. While we shall see multiplied instances of Europeans going to live in America, I will venture to say no man now living will ever see an instance of an American removing to settle in Europe & continuing there.

Bourbon France taught Jefferson a vivid lesson. Here was perhaps the most fertile country in Europe; here was one of the most intelligent and likable people on the Continent ("polite, self-denying, feeling, hospitable, good-humoured"); here were skills and arts and crafts unexcelled anywhere in the world. And yet the nation was unhappy, and large sections of the population lived in a state of semistarvation. Why? The answer was no mystery to Jefferson. "I do love this *people* with all my heart," he confessed to Abigail Adams, "and think that with a better religion, a better form of Government . . . their condition & Country would be most enviable."

Not being a mystic, Jefferson knew that the prevailing misery was man-made and therefore ameliorable. It was sometimes like a nightmare, living in a world as wretched and ill-contrived as this, and nobody doing anything about it. In a letter to Mrs. Trist, Jefferson gave vent to his feelings on the subject:

Indeed, it is difficult to conceive how so good a people, with so good a King, so well-disposed rulers in general, so genial a climate, so fertile a soil, should be rendered so ineffectual for producing human happiness by one single curse,—that of a bad form of government. But it is a fact, in spite of the mildness of their governors, the people are ground to powder by the vices of the form of government. Of twenty millions of people supposed to be in France, I am of opinion there are nineteen millions more wretched, more accursed in every circumstance of human existence than the most conspicuously wretched individual of the whole United States.

When Jefferson spoke of the French people "ground to powder" by their political system, he knew from firsthand observation whereof he spoke. On his long daily hikes through the country he would stop and talk to peasants and laborers, and he heard tales of woe that wrung his heart with pity. One day he took a walk to Fontainebleau, and on the way met a workingwoman who talked freely about her wretched existence. That conversation gave the sensitive American Minister a shocking insight into the dark, smoldering depths of prerevolutionary France. Jefferson shared his observations with his friends in America. In a letter to the Reverend James Madison he relates:

As soon as I had got clear of the town I fell in with a poor woman walking at the same rate with myself & going the same course. Wishing to know the condition of the laboring poor I entered into conversation with her. . . . [I] proceeded to enquiries into her vocation, condition & circumstances. She told me she was a day labourer, at 8 sous or 4d sterling the day; that she had two children to maintain, & to pay a rent of 30 livres for her house, (which would consume the hire of 75 days) that often she could get no emploiment, and of course was without bread. As we had walked together near a mile . . . I gave her, on parting, 24 sous. She burst into tears of . . . gratitude.

The weeping woman gave Jefferson "furiously to think," as the French say.

This . . . led me into a train of reflections on that unequal division of property which occasions the numberless instances of wretchedness which I had observed in this country & . . . all over Europe. The property of this country is absolutely concentrated in a very few hands. . . . These employ the flower of the country as servants (some . . . having as many as 200 domestics). . . . the most numerous of all classes, that is, the poor . . . cannot find work. I asked myself what could be the reason that so many should be permitted to beg who are willing to work, in a country where there is a very considerable proportion of uncultivated lands . . . ? I am conscious that an equal division of property is impracticable. But the consequences of this enormous inequality producing so much misery to the bulk of mankind, legislators cannot invent too many devices for subdividing property. . . . The earth is given as a common stock for man to labour & live on. . . . But it is not too soon to provide by every possible means that as few as possible shall be without a little portion of land. The small land holders are the most precious part of the state.

8

No, France the famous, the beautiful, the core of European civilization, did not impress the "savage of the mountains of America," as Jefferson styled himself ironically. Everywhere and always he was driven by some inner compulsion to make comparisons between Europe and America, usually to the disadvantage of Europe. If he had been asked to state his objections to Europe in one brief sentence, he probably would have replied: Misery at the bottom and mischief at the top. "Europe," he concluded bluntly, "was hell."

Emotionally and mentally he rejected the whole social and political system on which European society was based. A rebellious, egalitarian, aggressive Americanism broke through his observations. This sort of cast-ridden and poverty-stricken world, even though it received him with cordiality and deference, was not for him, and still less for his countrymen on the other side of the Atlantic! One year after his arrival in France, in a letter to his Italian friend Bellini he summarized his impressions with severe disillusionment:

Behold me at length on the vaunted scene of Europe! It is not necessary for your information, that I should enter into details concerning it. But you are, perhaps, curious to know how this new scene has struck a savage of the mountains of America. Not advantageously, I assure you.

I find the general fate of humanity here most deplorable. The truth of Voltaire's observation, offers itself perpetually, that every man here must be either the hammer or the anvil. It is a true picture of that country to which they say we shall pass hereafter, and where we are to see God and his angels in splendor, and crowds of the damned trampled under their feet.

While the great mass of the people are thus suffering under physical and moral oppression, I have endeavored to examine more nearly the condition of the great, to appreciate the true value of

the circumstances in their situation, which dazzle the bulk of spectators, and, especially, to compare it with that degree of happiness
which is enjoyed in America, by every class of people. Intrigues of
love occupy the younger and those of ambition, the elder part of
the great. Conjugal love having no existence among them, domestic
happiness, of which that is the basis, is utterly unknown. In lieu of
this, are substituted pursuits which nourish and invigorate all our
bad passions, and which offer only moments of ecstacy, amidst days
and months of restlessness and torment. Much, very much inferior,
this, to the tranquil, permanent felicity with which domestic society
in America blesses most of its inhabitants.

Was there nothing good in Europe! Yes, there was. Jefferson wryly admitted that France's strawberries, cherries, plums,
gooseberries, and pears were better than those in America. The
grapes were likewise superior. So were the manners of Frenchmen, their arts, and their architecture. Jefferson envied
Frenchmen their temperance, recalling the heavy drinking
among the gentry of his own country. He also envied Europe
its arts, especially music, for which he always craved.

In the pleasure of the table, they are far before us, because, with
good taste they unite temperance. They do not terminate the most
sociable meals by transforming themselves into brutes. I have never
yet seen a man drunk in France, even among the lowest of the people. Were I to proceed to tell you how much I enjoy their architecture, sculpture, painting, music, I should want words. It is in
these arts they shine. The last of them, particularly, is an enjoyment,
the deprivation of which with us, cannot be calculated. I am almost
ready to say, it is the only thing which from my heart I envy them,
and which, in spite of all the authority of the Decalogue, I do covet.

He hoped that no American would ever come to Europe to
live or to study. Europe would only be a bad influence on any
American student: . . . "an American, coming to Europe for
education, loses in his knowledge, in his morals, in his health,
in his habits, and in his happiness." Europeans should come
to America to learn what real happiness was.

Such were the feelings of Thomas Jefferson, Minister, while
living in the greatest city in Christendom, the pearl of European civilization.

9

In March, 1786, Jefferson had occasion to confirm his impressions of European civilization by a visit to England. Minister Adams had invited him to join him in London to help in the negotiation of a treaty with the visiting Minister from Tripoli. Jefferson accepted the invitation eagerly.

He stayed in England for seven weeks, by turns skeptical and appreciative. He saw the sights, visited places of interest, met personages. Together with Minister Adams, he was duly presented at the court of George the Third. It was not a happy experience. His Majesty had an understandable prejudice against "rebels," and he also may have read the Declaration of Independence, in which he was mercilessly castigated as a tyrant. When the two Americans were introduced to him, His Majesty promptly turned his back upon them—the insult being intended for Jefferson more than for Adams. The author of the Declaration of Independence took the cutting hint that he was not welcome in Britain. "It was impossible," he tells with a touch of bitterness, "for anything to be more ungracious, than their [the King's and Queen's] notice of Mr. Adams & myself. I saw at once that the ulcerations in the narrow mind of that mulish being left nothing to be expected on the subject of my attendance."

Some of the English Ministers took their cue from the monarch and were likewise rude to Jefferson. Deciding that it was a waste of time to court politicians, he devoted himself to visiting places in and near London. Except for gardens and machines, the land of his ancestors did not greatly impress him. On his return to Paris he wrote John Page:

I traversed that country much, and own both town & country fell short of my expectations. Comparing it with this, I have found a much greater proportion of barrens, a soil in other parts not naturally so good as this, not better cultivated, but better manured, & therefore more productive. . . . The labouring people are poorer [here] than in England. They pay about one half of their produce

in rent, the English in general about one third. The gardening in
that country is the article in which it surpasses all the earth. I mean
their pleasure gardening. This indeed went far beyond my ideas.
The city of London, tho' handsomer than Paris, is not so handsome
as Philadelphia. Their architecture is in the most wretched stile I
ever saw, not meaning to except America where it is bad. . . . The
mechanical arts in London are carried to a wonderful perfection.

Jefferson spent 2 shillings to see the house where Shakespeare was born, as well as his tomb, and having thus paid his
respect to the arts, he was free to devote his attention to practical matters. Technological improvements set him on edge
with excitement, and when he saw a gristmill run by steam
he could hardly contain himself. He watched one steam-driven
mill (it consumed 100 bushels of coal daily) turning eight
pairs of grindstones, and in a flash realized the "extensive consequences," the revolutionary implications, of steam as a motive power. "I have little doubt," he said prophetically, "but
that it will be applied generally to machines so as to supercede
[sic] the use of water ponds and of course to lay open all the
streams to navigation." The "famous Boulton," owner of the
London steam mills, explained to the amazed Jefferson that a
peck and a half of coal performed exactly as much grinding
work in a day as a horse. A brave new world was opening up
in his mind's eye.

10

Some time after Jefferson returned from England, he fell
in love. The affair was brief and apparently not successful.
Maria Cecilia Cosway was a miniature-painter. Her husband,
Richard Cosway, was likewise a miniature-painter. They were
an English couple who had lived on the Continent for some
time, and Jefferson probably met Mrs. Cosway in one of the
Paris salons.

Not very much is known of the Jefferson-Cosway relationship, nor even that anything serious took place between them.
But whatever happened, there is reason to believe that Jefferson was smitten hard. He had repressed his emotions since his

wife's death, and now Mrs. Cosway caused a brief and, for him, somewhat violent flare-up. When Mrs. Cosway left Paris, Jefferson was overcome with emotion, and he poured himself out in a long, prolix, Wertherian, unsubtle epistle. As a love letter, it may perhaps not rank with those of Abélard and Héloïse, but as a psychological document it is invaluable. The letter to Mrs. Cosway reveals the conflict between the man of sentiment and the man of intellect. In the case of Jefferson, sentiment was rarely a victor.

My Dear Madam,—Having performed the last sad office of handing you into your carriage . . . and seen the wheels get actually into motion, I turned on my heel & walked, more dead than alive, to the opposite door. . . . I was carried home. Seated by my fireside, solitary & sad, the following dialogue took place between my Head & my Heart:

Head. Well, friend, you seem to be in a pretty trim.

Heart. I am indeed the most wretched of all earthly beings. Overwhelmed with grief, every fibre of my frame distended beyond its natural powers to bear, I would willingly meet whatever catastrophe should leave me no more to feel or to fear.

Head. These are the eternal consequences of your warmth and precipitation. . . .

Heart. Oh, my friend! this is no moment to upbraid my foibles. I am rent into fragments by the force of my grief!

The letter continued in this vein. In one passage Jefferson confessed, "my mind broods . . . constantly over your departure," but he never came out flatly and said that he loved her. A later paragraph, however, was as near to an epistolary confession of love as Jefferson ever committed to paper:

But that you may not be discouraged from a correspondence which begins so formidably, I will promise you on my honour that my future letters shall be of a reasonable length. . . . But on your part, no curtailing. If your letters are as long as the bible, they will appear short to me. Only let them be brimful of affection. I shall read them with the dispositions with which Arlequin, in *Les deux billets,* spelt the words *"je t'aime,"* and wished that the whole alphabet had entered into their composition.

Mrs. Cosway who, one suspects, had encouraged the flirta-
tion in Paris, for some reason did not continue it. Her reply
to Jefferson's eighteen-page outpouring consisted of four lines.
It was all up. Your four lines, he wrote her in effect, show
that you at least still think of me—"little indeed, but better a
little than none." Even that little soon ceased.

II

In the third year of Jefferson's residence in Paris, he decided
to see something of the other parts of France and Europe. He
did not go for fun but for enlightenment. His object was to
learn what Europe had to offer in the way of arts, crafts, and
agriculture, and then to give America the cream of his observations.

Systematic man that he was, he worked out a careful plan
that tourists, himself and others, should follow when traveling
in Europe. Under "General Observations," he jotted down:

On arriving at a town, the first thing is to buy the plan of the
town, and the book noting its curiosities. Walk round the ramparts
when there are any, go the top of a steeple to have a view of the
town and its environs.

When you are doubting whether a thing is worth the trouble of
going to see, recollect that you will never again be so near it, that
you may repent the not having seen it, but can never repent having
seen it. But there is an opposite extreme too, that is, the seeing too
much.

For American tourists in Europe, Jefferson made a number
of recommendations, which he followed himself. The first object to look for, he said, was agriculture and everything that
related to it, including animals and plants that might be transported to America. The second object was mechanical arts, such
as forges, quarries, boats, and particularly bridges. Thirdly,
manufactures. Jefferson recommended that the traveler give
these only a superficial view—"circumstances rendering it impossible that America should become a manufacturing country
during the time of any man now living, it would be a waste of

attention to examine these minutely." Gardens, on the other hand, he said were "peculiarly worth the attention of an American, because it is the country of all others where the noblest gardens may be made without expense."

Architecture was worth special attention, because a rapidly growing America needed new edifices. "As we double our numbers every twenty years, we must double our houses." Architecture was, therefore, a most important art for America. Moreover, Jefferson concluded sensibly, "it is desirable to introduce taste into an art which shows so much." On the other hand, he did not think that the American tourist should bother with painting and sculpture. The arts, he said, were "too expensive" for a country as comparatively poor as the United States. "It would be useless, therefore, and preposterous, for us to make ourselves connoisseurs in those arts. They are worth seeing, but not studying."

Politics and administration he recommended particularly. Politics, he said, should be studied by the American traveler in order to see its "influence on the happiness of the people." He advised:

Take every possible occasion for entering into the houses of the laborers, and especially at the moments of their repast; see what they eat, how they are clothed, whether they are obliged to work too hard; whether the government or their landlord takes from them an unjust proportion of their labor; on what footing stands the property they call their own, their personal liberty, &c., &c.

He also urged American travelers in Europe to visit the royal courts in order to learn how extravagant, wasteful, and vicious they were. Americans, Jefferson advised, should go to see courts the way people go to the zoo—to observe the queer animals. He wrote:

Courts. To be seen as you would see the tower of London or menagerie of Versailles, with their lions, tigers, hyenas, and other beasts of prey, standing in the same relation to their fellows. A slight acquaintance with them will suffice to show you that, under the most imposing exterior, they are the weakest and worst part of mankind. Their manners, could you ape them, would not make you beloved

in your own country, nor would they improve it could you introduce them there to the exclusion of that honest simplicity now prevailing in America.

Jefferson left Paris in March, 1787, and for three months
he toured southern France and northern Italy. It was an experience as memorable as it was valuable, particularly since he
traveled with notebook in hand, looking for plants, forges,
bridges, machines, gardens, chimneys, sidewalks, pumps, and
everything that was ingenious or practical. He did not miss
much, and much of what he saw and put down on paper was
to bear practical fruit in America. His *Memoranda* of the tour
cover fifty-four printed pages, or approximately twenty-one
thousand words. "I have not visited all the manufactures at
this place," he wrote from Lyon to his secretary William Short,
"because the knowledge of them would be useless, and would
extrude from the memory other things more worth retaining.
Architecture, painting, sculpture, agriculture, the condition of
the laboring poor fill all my moments."

On the subject of the "laboring poor," he observed keenly
that the women did all the heavy work in the fields—"an unequivocal sign of extreme poverty." From Jefferson's memoranda:

Dauphiné. . . . Nature never formed a country of more savage
aspect, than that on both sides the Rhone. A huge torrent, rushes
like an arrow between high precipices, often of massive rock, at other
times of loose stone, with but little earth. Yet has the hand of man
subdued this savage scene, by planting corn where there is a little
fertility, trees where there is still less, and vines where there is none.
. . . The high mountains . . . are now covered with snow. The
almond is in general bloom, and the willow putting out its leaf.
. . . The soil is white, tinged a little, sometimes, with yellow,
sometimes with red, stony, poor, and laid up in terraces. Those parts
of the hills only, which look to the sun at mid-day, or the earlier
hours of the afternoon, produce wines of the first quality.
. . . They sell of the first quality and last vintage, at one hundred
and fifty livres the piece. . . . Transportation to Paris is sixty livres,
and the bottle four sous. . . .
There are few chateaux in this province. The people, too, are

mostly gathered into villages. There are, however, some scattering farm houses. These are made either of mud, or of round stone and mud. . . . Day laborers receive sixteen or eighteen sous the day, and feed themselves. . . . They rarely eat meat; a single hog salted, being the year's stock for a family. But they have plenty of cheese, eggs, potatoes and other vegetables, and walnut oil with their salad. . . . they have few cattle. I have seen neither hares nor partridges since I left Paris, nor wild fowl on any of the rivers.

Languedoc: They are now pruning the olive. A very good tree produces sixty pounds of olives, which yield fifteen pounds of oil: the best quality sells at twelve sous the pound, retail, and ten sous, wholesale. . . . After the vernal equinox, they are often six or eight months without rain. Many separate farm houses, numbers of people in rags, and abundance of beggars.

At Nîmes Jefferson was powerfully impressed by the remains of Roman grandeur. No student of history and architecture could remain indifferent to the majestic ruins of ancient Rome. And Jefferson, like the historian Edward Gibbon a few years earlier, succumbed to the moldering beauty of the ruins that were once Rome. It was a moving experience. ("For me, the city of Rome is actually existing in all the splendor of its empire.") He wrote from Nîmes to his Parisian friend Madame de Tessé:

Here I am, Madam, gazing whole hours at the Maison quarree,[7] like a lover at his mistress. The stocking weavers and silk spinners around it consider me as a hypochondriac Englishman, about to write with a pistol the last chapter of his history. This is the second time I have been in love since I left Paris. The first was with a Diana at the Chateau de Laye-Epinaye in Beaujolais, a delicious morsel of sculpture, by M. S. Slodtz. This, you will say, was in rule, to fall in love with a female beauty; but with a house! it is out of all precedent.

The south of France at the end of March was like Southern California in the spring, fresh with new life under a dazzling blue sky. Jefferson had never seen a semitropical region, and he was enchanted. His notes and letters sang with joy. "I am

[7] He made sketches of this building which he later used as a model in his design of the State Capitol in Richmond, Virginia.

now in the land of corn, vine, oil, and sunshine," he wrote to William Short. "What more can man ask of Heaven? If I should happen to die at Paris I would beg of you to send me here and have me exposed to the sun, I am sure it would bring me to life again."

To Lafayette in Paris Jefferson wrote that his journey was one "continued rapture." He invited the young General, now busy (at the Assembly of Notables recently convened at Versailles) preparing himself to become a statesman, to join him and learn something about his own country:

I think you have not made this journey. It is a pleasure you have to come, and an improvement to be added to the many you have already made. It will be a great comfort to you, to know, from your own inspection, the condition of all the provinces of your own country, and it will be interesting to them at some future day, to be known to you. This is, perhaps, the only moment of your life in which you can acquire that knowledge. And to do it most effectually, you must be absolutely incognito, you must ferret the people out of their hovels as I have done, look into their kettles, eat their bread, loll on their beds under pretence of resting yourself, but in fact, to find if they are soft. You will feel a sublime pleasure in the course of this investigation, and a sublimer one hereafter, when you shall be able to apply your knowledge to the softening of their beds, or the throwing a morsel of meat into their kettle of vegetables.

This kind of advice—to come in contact with the common people and to take the trouble to discover their condition in order to ameliorate it—was entirely American. It must have sounded eccentric to a Frenchman, particularly one of the aristocracy.

Jefferson certainly wasted little time on the journey. He was an indefatigable questioner. "In the course of my journey," he tells, "[I] have sought their [informed persons'] acquaintance with as much industry as I have avoided that of others who would have made me waste my time." When he reached Marseille he was asking everybody about rice, a superior variety of which he was hoping to plant in America. He got no satisfactory answer, so he decided to find out in northern Italy.

Jefferson spent his forty-fourth birthday on muleback, crossing the Maritime Alps into Italy. From his *Memoranda:*

In crossing Mount Brois, we lose the olive tree after getting to a certain height, and find it again on the other side. . . . From the foot of the mountain to Coni, the road follows a branch of the Po, the plains of which begin narrow, and widen at length into a general plain country, bounded on one side by the Alps. They are good, dark colored, sometimes tinged with red, and in pasture, corn, mulberries, and some almonds. . . . A great deal of golden willow all along the rivers, on the whole of this passage through the Alps. . . .

We cross the Po, in swinging batteaux. Two are placed side by side, and kept together by a plank floor, common to both, and lying on the gunwales. . . . About one hundred and fifty yards up the river, is a fixed stake, and a rope tied to it, the other end of which is made fast to one side of the batteaux, so as to throw them oblique to the current. . . . To support the rope in its whole length, there are two intermediate canoes, about fifty yards apart, in the heads of which are short masts. To the top of these, the rope is lashed.

It took him four days to reach Turin from Nice. In the Piedmontese capital Jefferson tasted a new wine, the "red wine of Nebiule," which he found "as sweet as the silky Madeira, as astringent on the palate as Bourdeaux, and as brisk as Champagne." He also heard the song of the nightingale for the first time that year. He was still pursuing rice in Piedmont, but did not find it until he reached Vercelli two days later. "From Vercelli to Novara the fields are all in rice, and now mostly under water." Here he made the discovery he was looking for, that the superiority of European rice to American (Carolinian) was inherent in the species, and not, as he thought, due to a better cleaning machine used in Italy.

April 23d. *Casino,* five miles from Milan. I examined another rice-beater of six pestles. They are eight feet nine inches long. Their ends, instead of being a truncated cone, have nine teeth of iron, bound closely together. Each tooth is a double pyramid, joined at the base. When put together, they stand with the upper ends placed in contact, so as to form them into one great cone, and the lower ends diverging. The upper are socketed into the end of the pestle.

. . . They say here, that pestles armed with these teeth, clean the rice faster, and break it less.

Knowing how the machine worked did not solve the problem of the inferiority of American rice. Jefferson decided to take with him some of the Piedmontese rice and grow it in America. But to his surprise he was told that he could take rice out of the country only at the cost of his life. There was a death penalty attached to the exportation of rice from Piedmont. Jefferson considered that sort of regulation so arbitrary that he had no scruples about breaking the law. He filled his coat pockets full of rice and then, to make doubly sure that he would get his precious species out of Piedmont, he hired a muleteer to smuggle two sacks of rice across the Apennines to Genoa.

Absorbed in his pursuit of rice and other agricultural improvements in northern Italy, he found little time for historical or artistic observations. He spent three weeks in the country, going only as far as Genoa. It is significant that he did not take the trouble to visit either Venice or Florence or Rome, although he could have done so without much difficulty. It must be said, however, that he would have been the first to admit that a steam wheel excited him more than a Titian and that he would travel farther to see a new machine than an old Michelangelo. Nevertheless, one is surprised that he did not go to Florence. He would have found the sketches of Leonardo to his taste and would certainly have been excited by the Florentine's engineering genius. In a letter to his friend and former teacher George Wythe, Jefferson wrote that he had no time to visit other Italian cities. He confessed that he was interested in other things more than in classical or medieval culture:

I scarcely got into classical ground. . . . In architecture, painting, sculpture, I found much amusement: but more than all in their agriculture, many objects of which might be adopted with us to great advantage. I am persuaded there are many parts of our lower country where the olive tree might be raised, which is assuredly the richest gift of heaven. I can scarcely except bread. I see this tree supporting thousands among the Alps where there is not soil enough to make bread for a single family. The caper too might be cultivated with us. The fig we do raise. I do not speak of the vine, because it is the parent of misery. Those who cultivate it are always poor, and he would employ himself with us in the culture of the corn, cotton, &c. can procure, in exchange much more wine, & better than he could raise by its direct culture.

From Genoa Jefferson sailed back to Marseille; for two miserable days on sea he was "mortally sick." Afterward he took it easy. He rented a barge on the tree-lined canal of Languedoc, dismounted his glass-doored carriage from its wheels, and had himself towed up toward Toulouse. He sat in the carriage reading, writing, or looking out of the window. Occasionally he would follow the barge on foot along the beautiful bank of the canal. It was an enchanting journey, as Jefferson wrote to his daughter Martha:

I write you, my dear Patsey, from the canal of Languedoc, on which I am at present sailing, as I have been for a week past, cloudless skies above, limpid waters below, and on each hand a row of nightingales in full chorus. This delightful bird had given me a rich treat before, at the fountain of Vaucluse.

Early in June he was back in Paris.

12

The following year Jefferson took another trip, this time to the Low Countries and western Germany. On March 3, 1788, he left Paris by carriage and four days later arrived at The Hague, where he shook hands with John Adams, who was American Minister there, and talked over some diplomatic business.

From The Hague he went to Amsterdam, then to Utrecht and Nimwegen and points east. Like Peter the Great a century earlier, Jefferson was impressed by the mechanical arts of the ingenious Dutch, and he spent considerable time making sketches. He sketched joists of houses, window sills, brick arches, flagstaffs on the masts of vessels, dining-tables with removable leaves, wind sawmills, wheelbarrows. Farther east, in the Rhineland, Jefferson made sketches of gates, oil and vinegar cruets, castle ruins, marks of porcelain manufacturers, curtain bedsteads with iron rods, geometric mountain paths, flues of stoves, moldboards, topography of vineyards, and hooks for holding up vines.

What he did not sketch he described in detail. Everything interested him. He saw and described a machine for drawing empty boats over a dam at Amsterdam. He admired a bridge across a canal "formed by two scows, which open each to the opposite shore and let boats pass." Another bridge he admired was one set on a swivel, which turned so as to permit boats to pass. A hexagonal lantern over a street door also struck him as a fine idea.

When he crossed the Rhine from prosperous Holland into Germany, Jefferson was surprised by the poverty of the Germans. The reason was obvious. "The soil and climate are the same," he noted; "the governments alone differ." The Dutch had a comparatively free and comparatively responsible government. The Germans did not. "With the poverty, the fear also of slaves is visible in the faces of the Prussian subjects." The country was poorly cultivated. "Universal and equal poverty overspeads the whole." German farmhouses, Jefferson observed, were made of "mud, the better sort of brick," covered with thatch.

In Westphalia Jefferson looked over the famous hogs—"tall, gaunt, and with heavy lop ears"—from which fine pork and ham were made. Like the Americans, Jefferson observed, the Westphalians smoked their bacon. Cologne impressed him as a city with plenty of commerce and plenty of poverty. Trade was in the hands of a handful of Protestants, who were being discriminated against by the Government, "which is Catholic, and excessively intolerant." In the region of Coblentz Jefferson studied the wines, especially Moselle. In Coblentz itself, in the Elector's palace, Jefferson first saw an invention which was to become a household institution in later America—central heating. He noticed that the big rooms in the palace were well heated "by warm air conveyed from an oven below, through tubes which open into the rooms."

Between Frankfort-on-the-Main and Hanau in Hesse-Cassel Jefferson again observed the devastating effects of a tyrannical government. Frankfort, an independent and self-governing free city, was rich and active; Hanau was a ghost town. "In Frankfort all is life, bustle, and motion; in Hanau the silence and quiet of the mansions of the dead. Nobody is seen moving in the streets; every door is shut; no sound of the saw, the hammer, or other utensil of industry. The drum and fife is all that is heard." Such was one of the "effects of tyranny."

From Frankfort Jefferson went to Mainz, then to Mannheim and Heidelberg, where he admired the wines and the aviaries. The return journey led through Carlsruhe, Strassburg, Nancy, and Château Thierry. Everywhere he paid minute attention to the cultivation of the grape.

In the latter part of April, after a journey of about seven weeks, he was back at his post in Paris.

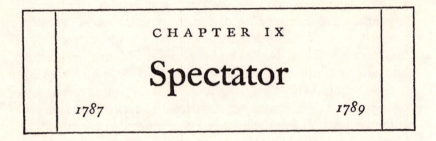

CHAPTER IX

Spectator

1787   *1789*

JEFFERSON's return from his southern tour in 1787 coincided with two events of world importance. At Versailles, the Assembly of Notables, invited by the bewildered and bedeviled Louis XVI to advise him on the sorry state of the nation, was squabbling furiously but at the same time was preparing French public opinion for a new world. At Philadelphia at about the same time, fifty-five Americans, most of them lawyers and many of them personally known to Jefferson, gathered to shape a Constitution for the young American Republic. Indirectly and obliquely, Jefferson shared in both of these epochal events.

Jefferson was vitally interested in both the American convention and the French assembly, but distance prevented him from personal participation in the one and diplomatic rules kept him from direct intervention in the other. There was nothing, however, to keep him from giving advice.

With his usual political adroitness, Jefferson employed the indirect method of influencing events through men. He had friends in key positions and he used them to achieve his ideal, which was the establishment of commonwealths where men could lead free lives uncrushed by any kind of tyranny, governmental or ecclesiastic. Among the Notables at Versailles, Jefferson's key figure was his friend the enthusiastic Lafayette. Like General Washington, Jefferson was very fond of the young Marquis, though he by no means overlooked his shortcomings. Lafayette's greatest weakness, Jefferson observed, was "a canine appetite for popularity and fame." That, however, did not prevent him from being effective under certain conditions.

Jefferson's uncanny insight into political drifts is well illustrated by his advice to Lafayette against imitating the United States. Every society must follow its own patterns, based upon its background and culture, and Jefferson was convinced that it would be a tragedy for France—a monarchy for over a thousand years—to plunge precipitously into an antiroyalist revolution. France was not mentally ready for such a sharp cleavage with her past. Jefferson urged upon Lafayette the need for gradual reforms, the slow and systematic seizure of position after position, rather than impetuous revolution. He told Lafayette, who was a leading figure in the nascent French revolution, to keep "the good model of your neighboring country before your eyes" and then to "get on, step by step, towards a good constitution."

This advice came from a man who hated monarchs with savage hatred. To him they were enemies of everything he considered desirable—liberty, justice, peace, toleration. He hoped that youthful America would "besiege the throne of heaven with eternal prayers, to extirpate from creation this class of human lions, tigers, and mammoths called Kings; from whom, let him perish who does not say, 'good Lord deliver us.'" Nevertheless, the author of the Declaration of Independence, who had lashed George III as a sanguinary despot, advised the French that there was nothing to be gained from overthrowing the absolutist Louis XVI by force. It was cheaper to buy off the French King, for whom Jefferson had no exaggerated admiration,[1] than to fight him. "If every advance is to be purchased by filling the royal coffers with gold, it will be

[1] Jefferson to Madison, June 20, 1787: "The King loves business, economy, order, & justice, and wishes sincerely the good of his people; but he is irascible, rude, very limited in his understanding, and religious, bordering only on bigotry. He has no mistress, loves his queen, and is too much governed by her." (Part of this letter, as with a number of others, is in cipher, here decoded.) On the life and character of this monarch see Saul K. Padover, *The Life and Death of Louis XVI* (Appleton-Century, 1939).

gold well employed." But there was not much chance that even excellent advice could halt the relentless march of the revolution.

2

While across the Atlantic at Philadelphia a group of men were hammering out a new Constitution for the young American republic, Jefferson, though physically absent, was not silent. He corresponded on vital matters not only with such luminaries of the Constitutional Convention as George Wythe and James Madison, but also with other influential Americans.

In his correspondence Jefferson systematically argued in favor of republican institutions, clarified democratic ideas, refuted the assumptions of aristocrats and monarchists. He set himself up, as Voltaire had done on another occasion half a century earlier, as a one-man agency of enlightenment and democratic opinion. Lacking a press of his own and not being in a position to make speeches for his cause, Jefferson wrote letters. And what letters they were! Today, more than a century and a half after they were written, these letters are mint-fresh and, mutatis mutandis, as contemporary as this morning's headlines. Of democratic government in America, he wrote to David Hartley:

I have no fear, but that the result of our experiment will be, that men may be trusted to govern themselves without a master. Could the contrary of this be proved, I should conclude, either that there is no God, or that he is a malevolent being.

On the subject of rumors that some individuals in America were advocating a monarchy, Jefferson wrote to Benjamin Hawkins:

And above all things I am astonished at some people's considering a kingly government as a refuge. Advise such to read the fable of the frogs who solicited Jupiter for a king. If that does not put them to rights, send them to Europe to see something of the trappings of monarchy. . . . No race of kings has ever presented above one man of common sense in twenty generations. The best they can do is to leave things to their ministers. . . . If the king ever meddles it is to do harm.

To Dr. David Ramsay, the Pennsylvania historian, Jefferson expressed himself in a similar vein, pointing out that although democratic government had its faults, they were remediable, while absolutist government was hopeless:

I rely, too, on the good sense of the people for remedy, whereas the evils of monarchical government are beyond remedy. If any of our countrymen wish for a King, give them Aesop's fable of the frogs who asked a King; if this does not cure them, send them to Europe. They will go back good republicans.

To Governor Edward Rutledge of South Carolina he wrote in the same bitter-contemptuous tone of European despotisms:

. . . and we think ours a bad government. The only condition on earth to be compared to ours, in my opinion, is that of the Indian, where they have still less law than we.[2] The European, are governments of kites over pigeons. The best schools for republicanism are London, Versailles, Madrid, Vienna, Berlin, &tc.

The cruel misgovernment of the European absolutisms, as well as the revolutionary fever that obtained in Paris, drove the ordinarily cautious Jefferson to an advocacy of the principle of rebellion. The blood of patriots and tyrants, he said, must refresh the tree of liberty, regardless of whether it is planted in Europe or America. His letter to Colonel William S. Smith, John Adams's son-in-law, is probably the most extreme statement on the subject of revolution ever penned by a responsible American:

God forbid we should ever be 20 years without such a rebellion. The people cannot be all, & always, well informed. The part which is wrong will be discontented in proportion to the importance of

[2] Jefferson expressed a similar sentiment in the 1787 edition of his *Notes on Virginia*, where he revised one passage on the Indians to read: . . . "were it made a question, whether no law, as among the savage Americans, or too much law, as among the civilized Europeans, submits man to the greatest evil, one who has seen both conditions of existence would pronounce it to be the last; and that the sheep are happier of themselves, than under care of the wolves."

the facts they misconceive. If they remain quiet under such misconceptions it is a lethargy, the forerunner of death to the public liberty. We have had 13. States independent for 11. years. There has been one rebellion. That comes to one rebellion in a century & a half for each state. What country before ever existed a century & a half without a rebellion? & what country can preserve it's liberties if its rulers are not warned from time to time that this people preserve the spirit of resistance? Let them take arms. The remedy is to set them right as to facts, pardon & pacify them. What signify a few lives lost in a century or two? The tree of liberty must be refreshed from time to time with the blood of patriots & tyrants. It is it's natural manure.

3

But the man whom Jefferson influenced most was James Madison, one of Virginia's seven remarkable delegates to the Constitutional Convention at Philadelphia.[3] For years Jefferson had been molding the younger Madison, treating him virtually as a son. Jefferson's admiration for the always black-clad and dry-humored little Madison was exceeded only by his affection for him. This confidence was fully justified, particularly during the crucial struggle at the Constitutional Convention when the insignificant-looking Madison emerged as one of the great political minds of his time.

After sixteen weeks of strenuous work and inevitable compromise while Jefferson was writing letters from Paris, the convention finished its work at Philadelphia. On September 17, 1787, the draft was signed "By unanimous consent of the States present." It now faced the severe test of public debate in popularly elected conventions in the thirteen States. Nine States were necessary for ratification. Success or failure of the Constitution would depend upon the quality of its defenders and champions in the various state legislatures.

Sometime in November Jefferson knew the provisions of the Constitution, at least in outline. His first reaction was not favor-

[3] The quality of Virginia's delegates may be judged from the fact that they included, besides Madison, such men as George Mason, Edmund Randolph, George Wythe, and George Washington.

able, but he waited for more details before stating his objections. In the latter part of December he apparently had a copy of the Constitution before him. It was probably Madison who sent it to him, for it was to Madison that he wrote one of his most statesmanlike letters, embodying in incisive detail his criticism of the instrument. It should be stressed that when the Constitution first emerged from the laboratory at Philadelphia it did so without a Bill of Rights. That is what shocked Jefferson.

In his letter to Madison, Jefferson explained that there were a number of things he liked about the Constitution. He approved the division of the government into legislative, judiciary, and executive branches. He liked the provision that gave the legislature the power to levy taxes, which preserved "inviolate the fundamental principle that the people are not to be taxed but by representatives chosen immediately by themselves." He was "captivated by the compromise" that gave the big States and the little States the same representation in the Senate. He liked the idea of the veto power for the President. All that was excellent, as far as it went. But it did not go far enough to satisfy a man who believed that human liberties were at least as important as property rights. The original draft of the Constitution did not emphasize human rights. To Jefferson a Constitution that did not specifically guarantee civil liberties was hardly worth the effort it took to engross it on parchment.

I will add what I do not like. First the omission of a bill of rights providing clearly, & without the aid of sophisms for freedom of religion, freedom of the press, protection against standing armies, restriction against monopolies, the eternal & unremitting force of the habeas corpus laws, and trials by jury in all matters of fact triable by the laws of the land & not by the laws of nations.

He then went on to elaborate the meaning and the significance of a Bill of Rights that should be perpetually riveted to the Constitution, and not be dependent upon the shifting bias of judges or the whims of public opinion. The people themselves had to be eternally protected against the Government.

Let me add that a bill of rights is what the people are entitled to against every government on earth, general or particular, & what no just government should refuse, or rest on inferences.[4]

Another thing about the Constitution that aroused Jefferson's fears was that it put no time limit to office, particularly the presidential office. Experience, contemporary and historical, showed that officeholders who were not limited in their tenure tended to hang onto their positions by fair means or foul. Political power, Jefferson knew, offered irresistible temptations to those who had once tasted it. A wise Constitution must put an iron limit to office in order to minimize temptation. Moreover, Jefferson dreaded the possibility of the intervention of foreign Powers in American elections in order to achieve their own ends. Such was the tragic example of contemporary Poland, which because she had an elective Chief Executive was the constant prey of her powerful neighbors. To avoid these dangers, Jefferson favored—though he later somewhat modified his position—a President elected for one term and ineligible forever after.

The second feature I dislike, and greatly dislike, is the abandonment in every instance of the necessity of rotation in office, and most particularly in the case of the President. Experience concurs with reason in concluding that the first magistrate will always be re-elected if the Constitution permits it. He is then an officer for life. This once observed, it becomes of so much consequence to certain nations to have a friend or a foe at the head of our affairs that they will interfere with money & with arms. A Galloman or an Angloman will be supported by the nation he befriends. If once elected, and at a second or third election outvoted by one or two votes, he will pretend false votes, foul play, hold possession of the reigns of government, be supported by the States voting for him . . . and they will be aided by one nation in Europe, while the majority are aided by another. The election of a President of America, some years hence will be much more interesting to certain nations of Europe than ever the election of a King of Poland was.

Reflect on all the instances in history, antient & modern, of elective monarchies, and say if they do not give foundation for my fears.

[4] After long agitation the Bill of Rights (the first ten amendments to the Constitution) was finally adopted by Congress on Dec. 15, 1789.

The Roman emperors, the popes, while they were of any importance, the German emperors till they became hereditary. in practice, the Kings of Poland, the Deys of the Ottoman dependancies. It may be said that if elections are to be attended with these disorders, the seldomer they are renewed the better. But experience shews that the only way to prevent disorder is to render them uninteresting by frequent changes.

Another point that Jefferson raised as to the Constitution was the question of how much power the Government should have. Here he faced the seemingly insoluble dilemma of every democrat—that of liberty versus order. He knew that while strong governments have always been the enemies of the people, weak governments have never been able to protect them. Powerful governments, moreover, by their very exercise of ruthless power have encouraged frequent insurrections. The solution, Jefferson argued, lay in a balanced democracy where public opinion should be free and enlightened and where the majority should prevail. And in no case should the Government be given too much power on any trumped-up excuse, such as the fear of insurrections.

I own, I am not a friend to a very energetic government. It is always oppressive. The late rebellion in Massachusetts has given more alarm than I think it should have done.[5] Calculate that one rebellion in 13 States in the course of 11 years, is but one for each state in a century & a half. No country should be so long without one. Nor will any degree of power in the hands of government prevent insurrections. . . . France, with all it's despotism, and two or three hundred thousand men always in arms has had three insurrections in the three years I have been here in every one of which greater numbers were engaged than in Massachusetts & a great deal more blood was spilt. In Turkey, which Montesquieu supposes more despotic, insurrections are the events of every day. In England, where the hand of power is lighter than here [France],

[5] In 1786 a group of Massachusetts farmers, led by Daniel Shays, a former army captain, tried to stop the county courts by force from issuing further judgments for debt. The farmers were trying to find relief from the crushing burden of debt, pending the next election. Poorly armed, they were easily defeated and hunted down by the middle classes. Merchants and other townfolk pretended to be frightened by "Shays' Rebellion," but the so-called "rebellion" did not upset Jefferson very much.

but heavier than with us they happen every half dozen years. . . .

Compare again the ferocious depredations of their insurgents with the order, the moderation & the almost self extinguishment of ours.—After all, it is my principle that the will of the majority should always prevail. . . . Above all things I hope the education of the common people will be attended to; convinced that on their good sense we may rely with the most security for the preservation of a due degree of liberty.

In America not everybody agreed with Jefferson that there was danger that the Constitution granted the Government too much power. For example, William Plumer, the Baptist preacher who was subsequently to become Speaker of the House of Representatives (1791-97) and Senator from New Hampshire (1802-07), thought diffe ntly. "The constitution," Plumer wrote, "is opposed here by many, because they think it a grant of too much power. My fears are all the other way. In my opinion, the executive is not strong enough."

The people for whom Jefferson argued, and to whose uncoerced judgment he was willing to entrust the free commonwealth of his dreams, were farmers, not industrial workers. With the tragic example of wretched European slum-dwellers before his eyes, Jefferson found it difficult to imagine the poor of the cities in the guise of self-respecting and self-reliant citizens. He undoubtedly felt that, at least in countries like America, men had the choice of leaving the filthy, crowded slums to live on the land. If they preferred dirt and congestion to clear air and open space, then there was something wrong with them. Not only could such people not be trusted with self-government, but they were a direct menace to it. "The mobs of great cities," Jefferson wrote, "add just so much to the support of pure government, as sores do to the strength of the human body." He was haunted by the dread of a landless big-city proletariat:

I think our governments will remain virtuous for many centuries; as long as they are chiefly agricultural; and this will be as long as there shall be vacant lands in any part of America. When they get piled upon one another in large cities, as in Europe, they will become corrupt as in Europe.

Jefferson's final reaction to the Constitution, especially after a Bill of Rights was attached to it, was enthusiastic. He regarded it as "unquestionably the wisest ever yet presented to men."

4

In the meantime monarchical France was rapidly disintegrating, and Jefferson was an open-eyed witness to the fascinating and yet frightening spectacle that was unfolding before him. A sensitive political barometer, he watched events with hope and fear, sharing in the ardent democratic hopes of his friends and at the same time dreading the incalculable consequences of violence.[6]

Revolutions, Jefferson knew, are gradual in growth. They take years to develop. Minds must be ready for the change and public opinion prepared to accept new ideas. Certain striking events elsewhere, such as the American Revolution, for example, act both as stimuli and as examples. The more thinking portion of the population begins to ask critical questions and to make political demands. Gradually the queries and the demands filter down to the common people, and then the whole fermented mass breaks through ancient bonds and casts off its shackles. What seems to be sudden and unexpected violence is thus actually an evolutionary and understandable process.

In a letter to Dr. Richard Price, written half a year before the storming of the Bastille, Jefferson thus explained the process that led to the revolution that was then in ovo:

. . . the American war seems first to have awakened the thinking part of this nation in general from the sleep of despotism in which they were sunk. The officers too who had been to America, were mostly young men, less shackled by habit and prejudice, and

[6] The excesses of the French Revolution, particularly when Napoleon, whom Jefferson loathed, took over power, ultimately tempered Jefferson's enthusiasm. In 1807 he confessed to a French correspondent: "A vast deal of human misery has already flowed from this revolution, accompanied by some good, but what will be its permanent effect on the happiness of mankind those who come after us will decide."

more ready to assent to the dictates of common sense and common right. They came back impressed with these. The press, notwithstanding its shackles, began to disseminate them; conversation, too, assumed new freedom; politics became the theme of all societies, male and female, and a very extensive and zealous party was formed, which may be called the Patriotic party, who, sensible of the abusive government under which they lived, longed for the occasions of reforming it. This party comprehended all the honesty of the kingdom, sufficiently at its leisure to think; the men of letters, the easy bourgeois, the young nobility, partly from reflection, partly from mode; for those sentiments became a matter of mode, and as such united most of the young women of the party.

And three months later, in March, 1789, he prophetically told his French friend Madame de Bréhan: "A great political revolution will take place in your country." The only mistake he made was when he added "and that without bloodshed." Louis XVI, Jefferson was sure, would be helpless, "disarmed by force of public opinion and want of money." That was true enough, but what Jefferson did not foresee was that the very weakness of the King was an invitation to violence on the part of his opponents.

5

The revolutionary fever rose quickly in France in the spring of 1789. There had been a bitter winter, with floods and hailstorms destroying about half the harvest. The price of bread had risen catastrophically. There was grave unemployment in the cities. In Lyon, for example, 20,000 out of nearly 60,000 workers had no employment; in Paris, one-fifth of the people, about 120,000, were without work. There was not only widespread undernourishment but a haunting dread of actual starvation.

In that situation Louis XVI assembled the Estates General at Versailles. It was the desperate act of a bewildered monarch who was a despot in law, a weakling in practice. He had inherited absolute power over a nation of 20,000,000 people, and he unwittingly paved a hell for them with the noblest intentions. Now, by the spring of 1789, after incredible bungling, confusion, and debt-piling, the monarch had to save the state from bankruptcy by the (to him) humiliating process of consulting with the representatives of the people. And Jefferson, watching this extraordinary spectacle, concluded sardonically that, as he told George Washington, "there is not a crowned head in Europe, whose talents or merits would entitle him to be elected a vestryman, by the people of any parish in America."

Among the members of the Estates General, particularly among the liberals, Jefferson had many friends. In fact, while they were preparing to clip the wings of absolutism from the French monarchy, many of the Deputies met in Jefferson's house. He thus knew intimately what was going on. In his *Autobiography* Jefferson tells: "I was in circumstances peculiarly favorable for a knowledge of the truth. Possessing the confidence and intimacy of the leading Patriots, & more than all of the Marquis [La]Fayette, their head and Atlas, who had no secrets from me, I learned with correctness the views & proceedings of that party." Gouverneur Morris, the clever American conservative and financial speculator who was then visiting Paris, informed General Washington that Jefferson was "very much in the confidence of the patriotic party here, and consequently well informed of their views and intentions." Naturally Jefferson was too prudent to violate openly his diplomatic position by giving counsel against the King, but there was nothing to prevent him from entertaining his friends at his own home. If those friends happened to be active in revolutionary politics, it was surely not the fault of His Excellency the American Minister.

Light on Jefferson's attitude at this critical period is thrown by Gouverneur Morris's *Diary*. Jefferson had a prejudice against Morris, whose open scorn for democrats and revolutionists was exceeded only by his arrogance of manner. The imperious Morris had no love for the democratic Jefferson either.

Wednesday [June] 3d, [1789]. . . . Go to M^r. Jefferson's. Some political Conversation. He seems to be out of Hope of any-

thing being done to Purpose by the States General. This comes
from having sanguine Expectation of a downright republican Form
of Government. The literary People here, observing the Abuses of
their monarchical Form, imagine that every Thing must go the
better in Proportion as it recedes from the present Establishments
and in their Closets they make Men exactly suited to their Systems. . . .

　　Friday [*June*] *12th.* . . . Mʳ. Jefferson has been to Versailles.
The Tiers [third estate] have called on the Nobles and Clergy
to join them and proceed to Business, which has thrown the former
into a Rage. He considers the Affairs of this Country as being in
a very critical Situation. They are so, but the Royal Authority has
yet great Weight, and, if brought to the Aid of the privileged Orders may yet prevent their Destruction. However, he and I differ
in our Systems of Politics. He, with all the Leaders of Liberty here,
is desirous of annihilating Distinctions of Order. . . .

　　Saturday [*July*] *4th.* . . . Go . . . to Mʳ. Jefferson's to Dinner. A large Party of Americans, and among them Monsʳ. & Madame de La Fayette. Some political Conversation with him after
Dinner in which I urge him to preserve if possible some constitutional Authority to the Body of Nobles as the only Means of preserving any Liberty for the People. The Current is setting so strong
against the Noblesse that I apprehend their Destruction, in which
will I fear be involved Consequences most pernicious, tho little
attended to in the present Moment. . . .

　　Thursday [*September*] *17th.* . . . go to Mʳ. Jefferson's.
. . . the Duc de la Rochefoucault comes in from the States General and at half past four La Fayette, when we sit down to Dinner. He tells us that some of his Troops under his Command are
about to march To Morrow to Versailles to urge the Decisions of
the States General. This is a rare Situation for which they must
thank themselves.

Jefferson was not the extremist that Gouverneur Morris
made him out to be. In truth, he constantly urged moderation
upon the hotheads. His repeated advice to his friends at the
Estates General was to avoid violence, to compromise with the
King, and to buy him off with financial concessions in return
for political liberties. He reminded Lafayette a quarter-century
later:

Possibly you may remember . . . I urged yourself and the patriots of my acquaintance, to enter then into a compact with the king, securing freedom of religion, freedom of the press, trial by jury, *habeas corpus*, and a national legislature, all of which it was known he would then yield, to go home, and let these work on the amelioration of the condition of the people, until they should have rendered them capable of more. . . . You thought otherwise.

6

Events galloped with dramatic swiftness. On June 17 the third estate, representing the common people, seceded from the Estates General and declared itself the sole National Assembly. Three days later the commoners, meeting at an indoor tennis court at Versailles, swore to stick together until the King had granted France a constitution. Paris and Versailles seethed with excitement. On July 14 a crowd of wrathful Parisians, having seized arms, stormed the massive-stoned Bastille and killed its governor. That night Louis XVI, at Versailles, was informed of the turmoil in Paris. "It's a riot!" the King cried. "No, Sire," he was told, "it's a revolution."

The revolution was spreading like fire and in the heat the other two estates—nobility and clergy—melted into the National Assembly. And the Assembly, sensing its strength and excited with its historic destiny, began to demand from the King a share in the government of France. That is where the fierce struggle began.

A curious incident occurred nearly a week after the fall of the Bastille, showing the prevailing excitement as well as the respect in which Jefferson was held. On July 20, 1789, Champion de Cicé, Archbishop of Bordeaux, having been appointed by the National Assembly chairman of its Constitutional Committee, wrote a letter to the American Minister, who was considered to be a specialist in such things, asking him to help in drafting a constitution for France. The letter, probably to Jefferson's consternation, read:

The Committee instructed by the Assembly to draw up a project of Constitution being anxious not to neglect anything in order to bring to perfection so important an undertaking wishes to have an interview with you and thus to make use to the profit of France of the lights of your reason and experience. We hope, Sir, that you will have that kindness. There are no foreigners . . . [for us] where the happiness of man is at stake. In this hope we have the honor to beg you to grant us an interview, next Wednesday.

Fearing that such an invitation would compromise his diplomatic position, Jefferson quickly replied—in somewhat stilted French—excusing himself on the ground that as a stranger he could not participate, and giving the committee his "most sincere and most ardent wishes" for perfect success.

The conflict over the constitution split the ranks of the Assembly, and the abler members decided to talk over the situation in a calm atmosphere. Lafayette knew where to go. He wrote to Jefferson asking him for permission to bring over six or eight members of the Assembly for dinner. Jefferson assured him of their welcome. The next day they came, eight of the leading men of the Assembly—Lafayette, Duport, Barnave, Alexander La Meth, Blacon, Mounier, Maubourg, and Dagout.

After dinner the tablecloth was removed, wine was set on the table, and Lafayette took the chair. From four o'clock in the afternoon until ten at night the discussion went on, while Jefferson sat by, a sympathetic and silent listener. In his *Autobiography* Jefferson pays tribute to the patriotism and eloquence of his visitors, many of whom were destined to lose their heads under the knife of the guillotine:

I was a silent witness to a coolness and candor of argument unusual in the conflicts of political opinion; to a logical reasoning, and chaste eloquence, disfigured by no gaudy tinsel of rhetoric or declamation, and truly worthy of being placed in parallel with the finest dialogues of antiquity, as handed to us by Xenophon, by Plato and Cicero.

On the next day, in order to avoid the embarrassment of diplomatic complications, Jefferson informed Montmorin, the

French Foreign Minister, of the dinner party at his house. To his surprise, he was told by Montmorin that he already knew of the meeting. The Foreign Minister added that he earnestly wished that he, Jefferson, would make it a habit of being present at such conferences, so that he would serve as an influence "in moderating the warmer spirits."

That was Jefferson's last connection with the French Revolution.

7

The time had come when Jefferson felt that he had had enough of Europe. His daughters were growing up and he felt that they needed the "society and care of their friends" in America. There was no future for them in Europe. Nor for him, for that matter. Despite the excitement of the French Revolution, Jefferson liked living abroad less and less. "Europe," he wrote to John Adams in May, 1789, "would be a prison to me were it ten times as big."

A few days before that letter was written, on April 30, 1789, George Washington, standing erect on a balcony overlooking Wall Street, New York City, was sworn in as first President of the United States. John Adams was his Vice-President.

For over a year Jefferson had been asking Congress for leave, hoping to spend a few months in America and then return "to my prison." Now, after Washington's inauguration, he made an urgent plea to the Chief Executive for permission to visit America. "I am excessively anxious to receive the permission without delay, that I may be able to get back before the winter sets in. Nothing can be so dreadful to me as to be shivering at sea for two or three months in a winter passage." President Washington promptly complied, and at the end of August Jefferson received the good news. He left Paris in the latter part of September, believing that he would return to his post within a few months. A great number of admiring and devoted friends gathered to bid the popular Minister farewell. Most of them he was never to see again.

In his *Autobiography*, written thirty years later, Jefferson paid touching tribute to the country where he had spent five years rich in friendships and ripe with experience:

And here I cannot leave this great and good country without expressing my sense of it's preeminence of character among the nations of the earth. A more benevolent people, I have never known, nor greater warmth & devotedness in their select friendships. Their kindness and accommodation to strangers is unparalleled, and the hospitality of Paris beyond anything I had conceived to be practicable in a large city.[7] Their eminence too in science, the communicative dispositions of their scientific men, the politeness of the general manners, the ease and vivacity of their conversation, give a charm to their society to be found nowhere else. . . . So ask the travelled inhabitant of any nation, In what country on earth would you rather live?—Certainly in my own, where are all my friends, my relations, and the earliest & sweetest affections and recollections of my life. Which would be your second choice? France.

8

The Jeffersons, father and pretty daughters, sailed from Le Havre to Cowes on October 8. In England Jefferson's voluminous baggage, including plants and shepherd dogs, was exempted from customs examination by special order of Prime Minister Pitt. Contrary winds kept the Jeffersons from sailing for two weeks, which time they spent sightseeing, especially on the Isle of Wight. On October 22, 1789, the Jeffersons sailed from Yarmouth, and after a smooth passage of one month they set foot on American soil at Norfolk. Never again was Jefferson to leave his native country.

[7] In this respect Paris certainly underwent a drastic change after the days when Jefferson lived there. Whatever virtues twentieth-century Parisians may have, hospitality is decidedly not one of them.

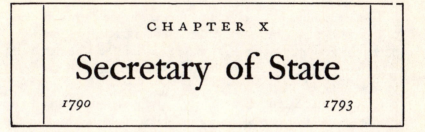

CHAPTER X

Secretary of State

1790   *1793*

WHEN Jefferson arrived at Norfolk on November 23, 1789, he opened a newspaper and, to his surprise, read that he had been nominated to the newly created post of Secretary of State. He hoped that it was not true, for his plans were to return to Paris for a few months and then to retire from politics for good—"to sink into the bosom of my family and friends, and devote myself to studies more congenial to my mind," he tells in his *Autobiography*.

Politics, however, kept on pursuing him. On their way to Monticello the Jeffersons stopped off at Eppington, the residence of their relatives the Eppeses, and there an express courier brought Jefferson a letter from President Washington offering him the Secretaryship of State. It was with "real regret" that Jefferson read:

Dear Sir, In the selection of characters to fill the important offices of Government, in the United States, I was naturally led to contemplate the talents and dispositions which I knew you to possess and entertain for the service of your country; and without being able to consult your inclination, or to derive any knowledge of your intention from your letters, either to myself or to any other of your friends, I was determined, as well by motives of private regard, as a conviction of public propriety, to nominate you for the Department of State, which, under its present organization, involves many of the most interesting objects of the executive authority. But, grateful as your acceptance of this commission would

169

be to me, I am at the same time desirous to accommodate your wishes, and I have therefore forborne to nominate your successor at the court of Versailles, until I should be informed of your determination.

The scrupulous Washington emphasized that he had no wish to interfere with Jefferson's choice, but he tactfully hinted that he would very much appreciate having him in his Cabinet. With seeming casualness the wise President remarked that the office of Secretary of State "involves many of the most interesting objects of the executive authority." Jefferson understood the hint, namely, that the Secretary of State would be, next to the President, the highest and most important active officer in the new government.[1]

It was a flattering offer and Jefferson was not insensible to it. That General Washington, for whom he had a solid admiration if not blind worship, should select him from so many other men of talent who were available was a compliment which Jefferson warmly appreciated. Still, accepting another responsible political job meant more years of sacrifice, of mounting debt, of separation from his family. Yet he could not categorically turn down a man like General Washington. "It was impossible to give a flat refusal to such a nomination," he told a friend.

On his way to Monticello Jefferson pondered the offer, and after several days of soul-searching he informed the President that, while he preferred to return to his Paris post for a time, he would accept the Secretaryship of State if he, Washington, believed that it was best for the public welfare. "It is not for an individual to choose his post," Jefferson said.

His letter to Washington depicted his attitude with that blend of tact and good politics in which he was a master:

[1] After the organization of the government under the new Constitution, Congress abolished the old office of Secretary of Foreign Affairs and created in its place the Secretaryship of State. The duties of the Secretary of State were not to be confined to foreign affairs but were to include also domestic affairs. Thus Jefferson, as first Secretary of State, combined in himself some of the functions that are entrusted today to the Secretary of State, the Secretary of the Interior, the Secretary of Agriculture, the Secretary of Commerce, the Secretary of the Navy, and other diverse duties that are comprehended in the word "State."

I . . . am truly flattered by your nomination of me to the very dignified office of Secretary of State for which permit me here to return you my very humble thanks. Could any circumstance seduce me to overlook the disproportion between its duties and my talents it would be the encouragement of your choice. But when I contemplate the extent of that office, embracing as it does the principal mass of domestic administration, together with the foreign, I can not be insensible to my inequality to it; and I should enter on it with gloomy forebodings from the criticisms and censures of a public, just indeed in their intentions, but sometimes misinformed and misled, and always too respectable to be neglected. I can not but foresee the possibility that this may end disagreeably for me, who, having no motive to public service but the public satisfaction, would certainly retire the moment that satisfaction should appear to languish.

On the other hand, I feel a degree of familiarity with the duties of my present office, as far, at least, as I am capable of understanding its duties. The ground I have already passed over enables me to see my way into that which is before me. The change of government, too, taking place in the country where it is exercised, seems to open a possibility of procuring from the new rulers some new advantages in commerce, which may be agreeable to our countrymen. So that as far as my fears, my hopes, or my inclination might enter into this question, I confess they would not lead me to prefer a change.

But it is not for an individual to choose his post. You are to marshal us as may be best for the public good. . . . If you think it better to transfer me to another post, my inclination must be no obstacle . . . be so good as only to signify to me by another line your ultimate wish, and I shall conform to it accordingly. If it should be to remain at New York, my chief comfort will be to work under your eye, my only shelter the authority of your name, and the wisdom of measures to be dictated by you and implicitly executed by me.

2

Having thus left the decision in the hands of President Washington, Jefferson, his mind relieved, continued on his way to Monticello. It was a slow journey, the Jeffersons stopping on the way to visit many friends. Two days before Christmas they finally reached the outskirts of their estate. Jefferson had not been home for more than five years.

Never before had there been such jubilation as now took place when the master and his two attractive daughters arrived home. The Negroes had learned of the approach of the Jeffersons when they reached Shadwell, four miles from Monticello, and they streamed down the mountain in a frenzy of jubilant excitement. When the carriage appeared, the slaves surrounded it with unrestrained emotion. Nothing, not even the entreaties of the master, could stop them from unhitching the four horses and pushing and dragging the heavy vehicle up the steep mountain to the house. They sang and cried with joy. And when Jefferson, himself deeply moved, stepped out of the carriage, his slaves fell upon him in an orgy of worship. "When the door of the carriage was opened," Martha relates, "they received him in their arms and bore him to the house, crowding around and kissing his hands and feet—some blubbering and crying—others laughing. It seemed impossible to satisfy their anxiety to touch and kiss the very earth which bore him." [2]

3

Monticello had one important and welcome visitor after Christmas. It was James Madison, recently come from New York, where he was a member of Congress. Madison, it seems, had promised President Washington that he would personally find out how Jefferson felt about accepting the Secretaryship of

[2] Of course Jefferson's slaves were proud to serve a master who was a famous man as well as an aristocrat. For it must be remembered that strong feelings of class distinction prevailed among slaves. Robert Anderson, *From Slavery to Affluence* (Hemingsford, Neb., 1927, p. 29), writes: "There was a social distinction with the slaves. The house and personal servants were on a higher social plane than the field slaves, while the colored persons who would associate with the 'po' white trash' were practically outcasts, and held in very great contempt. The slaves belonging to the lower class of white folks, were not considered on the same level as those belonging to the 'quality folks,' and the slaves of these families were always proud of, and bragged of their connection with the better families." For interesting examples of slave behavior see the excellent book by Frazier, *The Negro Family in the United States*, University of Chicago Press, 1939.

State. Possibly Madison was also to use some gentle persuasion. The two friends discussed the matter in detail, and Madison was able to set Jefferson's mind at rest on a number of points. One of them concerned the burden of the office, involving both domestic and foreign affairs—it would not be as great as Jefferson feared. After this conversation, Madison wrote to President Washington hinting that Jefferson was receptive: "All whom I have heard speak on the subject are remarkably solicitous for his acceptance, and I flatter myself that they will not, in the final event, be disappointed."

That was a green light to the President. Once again Washington repeated his offer, this time stressing the importance of the position. The success of the Government depended upon able men, and he, the President, could think of no one better fitted to fill the post than Jefferson:

> I consider the successful administration of the general government, as an object of almost infinite consequence to the present and future happiness of the citizens of the United States. I consider the office of secretary for the department of state very important on many accounts, and I know of no person, who in my judgment could better execute the duties of it than yourself. Its duties will probably be not quite so arduous and complicated in their execution as you may have been led at the first moment to imagine. . . . But, in order that you may be better prepared to make your ultimate decision on good grounds, I think it necessary to add one fact, which is this . . . your late appointment has given very extensive and very great satisfaction to the public. My original opinion and wish may be collected from my nomination.

Not only did General Washington urge him to accept, but there was also pressure from other quarters. Madison wrote him from New York that "a universal anxiety is expressed for your acceptance." The "general good" required that the ablest men serve the young republic, and Jefferson was recognized by both friend and foe as one of the commanding figures in America. So great were the urgings for him to accept the Cabinet post that he felt he could not refuse without "the danger of giving disgust, and I value no office enough for that." In the middle of

February he finally informed the President that he would leave for New York as soon as possible to take up his new duties.

There had been no false modesty about his hesitation to accept a distinguished position under George Washington. The truth was that Jefferson could hardly afford to leave Monticello at this time. On and off, he had been away from his estate for about ten years, and in the absence of the master the land had deteriorated. The estate comprised 10,000 acres and two hundred slaves, but its productivity had gone down dangerously. It required both the owner's presence and money to make the estate productive, and Jefferson had no money. His salary of $3,500 as Secretary of State ($500 more than that of the other members of the Cabinet) would be just enough to support him personally. There would be little if anything left for the estate. A few days before Jefferson left for New York, he made an appeal to private bankers for a loan of $2,000. "I am only a farmer," he wrote, "and have no resource but the productions of the farms." He offered his personal bond on his land for the loan, at 6 per cent interest.

A week before Jefferson left Monticello his daughter Martha, a tall girl of seventeen, was married to her brilliant second cousin Thomas Mann Randolph of Tuckahoe. The "high-toned" Randolph and the distinguished Martha, whom John Randolph had once called "the noblest woman in Virginia," made a fine pair. Jefferson was delighted with his son-in-law, whom he described as "a young gentleman of genius, science and honorable mind." [3]

4

Once again Jefferson tore himself away from his family and went North in the service of his country. He had no illusions about the struggle that lay ahead, for from the moment of his arrival in the United States he had sensed a deep undercurrent of political tension in the country. Events in France were having their repercussions in America. The French Revolution, Jef-

[3] In Jefferson's absence, his son-in-law Randolph farmed the estate.

ferson knew, was but "the first chapter" of the history of European liberty, and American conservatives feared the effects of the spread of French liberal ideas. Class cleavages were deepening. Among Jefferson's social equals there were many who favored some kind of monarchy to serve as a bulwark against the rising tide of freedom. Jefferson, whose political sensitivity was acute, felt that a sharp conflict between the conservatives and the liberals—by whatever name they went—was bound to take place. "The Gentlemen who opposed it [the Constitution]," he wrote to William Short in Paris only a few days after his arrival in America, "retain a good deal of malevolence towards the new Government."

Jefferson was convinced that the revolution in France, with its exciting promises of freedom and equality, would be the acid test of the young and struggling American republic. The new Government, which he was now going to serve under President Washington, would be swayed by the fury of the French Revolution like a sapling in a storm. Men's principles would stand or fall by their attitude toward revolutionary France. Jefferson was sure that the tide of the revolution was irresistible and that it would sweep away the tyrants in all parts of the civilized world. In the meantime the struggle would be bitter; in Europe it would probably claim "its millions of human victims." There need be no such violence in America, but whatever happened, he was ready for the war for freedom.

In that mood he went North, traveling by way of Richmond, Alexandria, and Philadelphia. When he arrived at Alexandria on March 10, the mayor and the citizens gave him a public reception. Jefferson seized the occasion to preach democracy to the people. In his letter of thanks for the reception, he reminded the citizens that the country owed its commercial prosperity to France, and added a homily:

Convinced that the republican is the only form of government which is not eternally at open or secret war with the rights of mankind, my prayers & efforts shall be cordially distributed to the support of that we have so happily established. It is indeed an animating thought that, while we are securing the rights of ourselves & our prosperity, we are pointing out the way to struggling nations

who wish, like us, to emerge from their tyrannies also. Heaven help
their struggles, and lead them, as it has done us, triumphantly thro'
them.

He always believed that preaching such "useful truths" was
an effective means of educating the people for democracy.

A heavy snowstorm slowed his progress to about two or three
miles a day, and it took him about a week to reach Philadelphia.
Almost his first act was to visit the "venerable and beloved"
Franklin, who was sick in bed. Both friends were excited by the
meeting. The eighty-four-year-old Franklin, who had only one
month to live, was eager to know what was going on in France
and how his friends were faring. Despite age and illness, he had
been anxiously following the course of the revolution. "Ah,"
he had exclaimed upon hearing the news from Paris and Versailles, "they served their apprenticeship in America, and now
they mean to set up for themselves."

Jefferson was able to satisfy the old sage's curiosity about his
French friends: "He went over all in succession, with a rapidity
and animation almost too much for his strength." Then he gave
Jefferson a confidential paper to keep. Jefferson later returned
it inadvertently to Franklin's heir.

5

Jefferson arrived in New York on March 21; after being
cordially received by the President, he rented a small house on
Maiden Lane. He immediately went to work on matters that
had been accumulating for months. Foreign and domestic problems were pressing for attention, and the new Secretary of State
had little precedent to guide him and even less assistance to
ease the burden of work. The Department of State consisted
of three copying clerks at $500 a year and two at $800.[4] There
was no money for new appointments. In terms of sheer work it
looked as if Jefferson would have to devote every ounce of
strength and every minute of time to the job. But he felt that

[4] In 1941 the Department of State employed 5,700 persons, among them being
engineers, lawyers, economists, historians, stenographers, and cryptographers.

at least he could be useful, particularly as regards revolutionary France, around which a host of enemies was already crystallizing. He wrote wistfully to Lafayette:

Behold me, my dear friend, elected Secretary of State, instead of returning to the far more agreeable position which placed me in the daily participation of your friendship. . . .

I have been here then ten days harnessed in my new geer [sic]. Wherever I am, or ever shall be, I shall be sincere in my friendship to you and to your nation. I think, with others, that nations are to be governed according to their own interests, but I am convinced that it is their interest, in the long run, to be grateful, faithful to their engagements even in the worst of circumstances, and honorable and generous always. If I had not known that the head of our government was in these sentiments, and that his national & private ethics were the same, I would never have been where I am.

He wrote this letter more to reassure himself than to cheer Lafayette. For the New York atmosphere, both in the Government and in society, was so rabidly antidemocratic that Jefferson, recently arrived from a France that was in fever with democratic ideas, was scared for the future of the American republic. He was frankly unprepared for the bitter antidemocratic feeling that prevailed in New York. The situation was not only politically disturbing but also personally embarrassing, for on many occasions when he dined out the eminent Secretary of State found himself the only democrat among the guests.

Here I found a state of things which, of all I had ever contemplated, I the least expected. I had left France in the first year of its revolution, in the fervor of natural rights, and zeal for reformation. My conscientious devotion to these rights could not be heightened, but it had been aroused and excited by daily exercise. The President received me cordially, and my Colleagues & the circle of principal citizens, apparently, with welcome. The courtesies of dinner parties given me as a stranger newly arrived among them, placed me at once in their familiar society. But I cannot describe the wonder and mortification with which the table conversations filled me. Politics were the chief topic, and a preference of kingly, over republican, government, was evidently the favorite sentiment. An apostate I could not be; nor yet a hypocrite; and I found myself, for the most part, the only advocate on the republican side of the question.

Possibly Jefferson exaggerated the extent and the power of the antidemocratic (he called it "monarchist") sentiment in New York and elsewhere, but there is no doubt that it existed, particularly among the upper classes. There were too many antiliberal straws flying in the wind to make any friend of democracy feel sanguine.

Take, for example, the incident that had occurred in the United States Senate on May 1, 1789. On that day Vice-President John Adams, speaking of the address by President Washington, referred to it as "His most *gracious speech.*" A little matter, perhaps. But it happened that such an expression was customarily applied to kings. Some of the Senators were shocked, and one of them, William Maclay of Pennsylvania, rose and protested:

Mr. President, we have lately had a hard struggle for our liberty against kingly authority. The minds of men are still heated: everything related to that species of government is odious to the people. The words prefixed to the President's speech are the same that are usually placed before the speech of his Britannic Majesty. I know they will give offense. I consider them as improper. I therefore move that they be struck out.

Vice-President Adams, whose vanity was not an inconspicuous element in his admirable character, replied pettishly that he was one of the first to fight against Britain, and that *"if he could have thought of this* [democratic protest against monarchical form], *he never would have drawn his sword."* (Italics Maclay's)

Other eminent and powerful men in the Government were no less hostile to democracy. Fisher Ames, a member of Congress from Massachusetts and a friend of Alexander Hamilton, considered democracy to be like death, a dismal passport to a more wretched hereafter. Common people, like slaves, should be ruled, he felt. Another enemy of democracy was Gouverneur Morris, who helped to frame the Constitution (without the Bill of Rights). He believed in a Senate appointed by the President for life from the ranks of the rich and the aristocratic. Oliver Wolcott, Comptroller of the Treasury, was convinced that the republican Government must and would fail. John Jay, the Chief Justice of the Supreme Court, was skeptical as to the people's ability to govern themselves. George Cabot, Senator from Massachusetts, said bluntly that "Democracy in its natural operation is the government of the worst."

The republic was not yet stable enough and its institutions were not sufficiently rooted in the affections of the people to make the latter resist a determined onslaught on the part of the antidemocratic forces. These, to be sure, were not organized for such an attack, but Jefferson feared that a crisis might crystallize general feeling into compact organization.

If the word had been current at that time, Jefferson would have been known as the "Red" Secretary of State in the aristocratic circles of New York. For his ideas were not hidden under a bushel and he had no desire to conceal his sympathies. Antidemocratic sentiment running high, Jefferson, despite his unfailing courtesy, could not avoid getting into arguments. Madison tells that at one dinner party somebody argued against an elective executive and in favor of a hereditary ruler. Jefferson, recalling Louis XVI and George III and a long line of similar incompetents, smiled, and made the devastating remark that he had heard of a "University somewhere in which the Professorship of Mathematics was hereditary." That killed that argument.

6

Such were the gusts of doctrine that blew at the time when the Constitution was planted. And the men who were called upon to water and to tend the delicate constitutional plant were a remarkable group.

At the time Jefferson took up his duties as Secretary of State he found in Washington's Cabinet three other members. They were no strangers to him. The thirty-three-year-old Alexander Hamilton was Secretary of the Treasury; the forty-year-old General Henry Knox was in charge of the War Department;

the forty-three-year-old Edmund Randolph, a fellow Virginian, was Attorney General.

Jefferson was no stranger to them either. His appearance at this time has been described by the Senator from Pennsylvania, William Maclay, who as chairman of the Senate Committee on Foreign Affairs had a good opportunity of observing the new Secretary of State. Senator Maclay's pen portrait, while it is not altogether complimentary, has the merit of being contemporary and graphic.

Jefferson is a slender man; has rather the air of stiffness in his manner; his clothes seem too small for him; he sits in a lounging manner, on one hip commonly, and with one of his shoulders elevated much above the other; his face has a sunny aspect; his whole figure has a loose, shackling air. He had a rambling, vacant look, and nothing of that firm, collected deportment which I expected would dignify the presence of a secretary or minister. I looked for gravity, but a laxity of manner seemed shed about him. He spoke almost without ceasing . . . he scattered information wherever he went, and even some brilliant sentiments sparkled from him.

The Secretary of State was, except for height, in striking contrast to the President. President Washington, at this time fifty-eight, was not quite as tall and lean as Jefferson, but straighter and stronger. In 1763, when Washington was under thirty, he thus described himself in a letter to a London tailor: "a Gentleman who wares well made-Cloaths of the following size: to wit, 6 feet high and proportionably made; if any thing rather slender than thick for a person of that highth with pretty long Arms and thighs."

Washington was in marked contrast to Jefferson in his human relations. Where Jefferson invited affection, Washington did not encourage it. Both men were kindhearted, but where the one was ebullient in the presence of his friends, the other was excruciatingly shy. Washington's shyness gave the impression of coldness. Those who did not know him well considered him a cold, calculating man without a heart. In 1785 Jefferson sent the famous French sculptor Houdon to America to do a bust of General Washington. The bust was successfully executed, but keen observers were struck by the lack of warmth in the face.

"He has," Madame de Staël observed after looking at the head, "the coldest features that I have ever seen. . . . One would be tempted to think that Washington could not be warmly interested in anything and that even fame left him cold."

The seeming iceberg, however, was capable of volcanic eruptions. The General did not often lose his temper, but when he did it was something to remember. His wrath was then "most tremendous," and few people cared to brave it. But a combination of iron will and prudence made him keep his temper in leash.

Jefferson knew a great man when he saw one, and he came to know Washington intimately. What most impressed him was the General's balanced judgment and his unswerving sense of justice. He considered Washington's granitelike character by and large "perfect." Jefferson knew that, while not an out-and-out democrat, Washington was not a monarchist, or a reactionary either. The General was entrusted with the job of being Chief Executive of a democratic republic, and no force would make him swerve from his path of duty. "He was neither an Angloman, a monarchist, nor a separatist. He sincerely wished the people to have as much self-government as they were competent to exercise themselves." Such was Jefferson's judgment in later years.

Jefferson's analysis of Washington's character, written some fifteen years after the General died, is not only a great tribute but a model of good writing.

I think I knew General Washington intimately and thoroughly. . . . His mind was great and powerful, without being of the very first order; his penetration strong, though not so acute as that of a Newton, Bacon, or Locke; and as far as he saw, no judgment was ever sounder. It was slow in operation, being little aided by invention or imagination, but sure in conclusion . . . hearing all suggestions, he selected whatever was best; and certainly no General ever planned his battles more judiciously. . . . He was incapable of fear, meeting personal dangers with the calmest unconcern.

Perhaps the strongest feature in his character was prudence, never acting until every circumstance, every consideration, was maturely weighed. . . . His integrity was most pure, his justice the most inflexible I have ever known, no motives of interest or consanguinity, of friendship or hatred, being able to bias his decision. He was, indeed, in every sense of the words, a wise, a good, and a great man. His temper was naturally high toned; but reflection and resolution had obtained a firm and habitual ascendency over it. If ever, however, it broke its bonds, he was most tremendous in his wrath.

In his expenses he was honorable, but exact; liberal in contributions to whatever promised utility; but frowning and unyielding on all visionary projects and all unworthy calls on his charity. His heart was not warm in its affections; but he exactly calculated every man's value, and gave him a solid esteem proportioned to it.

His person, you know, was fine, his stature exactly what one would wish, his deportment easy, erect and noble; the best horseman of his age, and the most graceful figure that could be seen on horseback.

Although in the circle of his friends, where he might be unreserved with safety, he took a free share in conversation, his colloquial talents were not above mediocrity, possessing neither copiousness of ideas, nor fluency of words. In public, when called on for a sudden opinion, he was unready, short and embarrassed. Yet he wrote readily, rather diffusely, in an easy and correct style. This he had acquired by conversation with the world, for his education was merely reading, writing and common arithmetic, to which he added surveying at a later day. His time was employed in action chiefly, reading little, and that only in agriculture and English history. . . . His correspondence . . . with his agricultural proceedings, occupied most of his leisure hours within doors.

On the whole, his character was, in its mass, perfect, in nothing bad, in few points indifferent; and it may truly be said, that never did nature and fortune combine more perfectly to make a man great, and to place him in . . . an everlasting remembrance.

The Secretary of State obviously admired his chief. Despite differences in temper and education, the disagreement between the two men was not deep. Where they differed was in the imponderable realm of faith. Washington was a practical administrator, not heavily burdened with imagination or carried away by flights of vision. Jefferson, on the other hand, had a lively fancy, a warm heart, and an irrepressible faith in mankind. Washington was a craftsman with the materials that were at hand. Jefferson had a vision and a hope for the future. He believed, with all the faith that was in him, that man, being capable of progress, was rising ever higher. He summarized the essential difference between himself and Washington in these words: "I had more confidence than he had in the natural integrity and discretion of the people, and in the safety and extent to which they might trust themselves with a control over their government."

7

The man with whom the Secretary of State clashed almost immediately upon entering his duties was his next in rank in the Cabinet, Secretary of the Treasury Alexander Hamilton.

The conflict between these two has a touch of the epic quality. Their sharply divergent points of view, and the key positions they occupied in the formative years of the republic, lift their struggle from the level of politics to the realm of principles.

Hamilton, absurdly young for his position, was not the kind of man whom Jefferson could either like or understand. For one thing, the Secretary of the Treasury was too brilliant and too facile—the volatile type described by the Scotch-Irish as a "skite." For another, he was obviously a climber and obviously a careerist. Jefferson distrusted the volatility in Hamilton and despised his careerism.

Hamilton's ancestry and background were such that even a liberal aristocrat could look down upon them, especially under the stimulus of political heat. The Secretary of the Treasury, having been born in 1757 on the British island of Nevis in the West Indies, was thus not even a native American. Moreover, his birth was illegitimate. His father was a Scot.[5] What his mother was is not certain. We know little more about her than that her name was Rachel and the name of her husband (not Alexander's father) was Levine.

[5] Blunt-spoken John Adams once referred to Hamilton as "the bastard brat of a Scotch pedlar."

Nor is very much known about Hamilton's youth. He came to America to make his career at the age of fifteen. That was in 1772, a critical time when the colonies were at the crossroads. After attending King's College (now Columbia) in New York, Hamilton became a political writer on the liberal side, that is, against the British crown. His brilliance attracted attention, then as always. When the war broke out he joined the militia. In March, 1777, General Washington appointed him aide-de-camp with the rank of lieutenant-colonel. Henceforth his rise was rapid, and his fame spread. In 1780 he achieved the ultimate of success by marrying into one of the bluest of New York's blue-blooded families. His wife was Elizabeth, daughter of General Philip Schuyler. The Schuylers were rich and aristocratic, and inevitably powerful. For an immigrant boy without family, that marriage was no insignificant achievement.

Hamilton's political principles underwent a change after his successful career in the army and his fashionable marriage. He became steadily more conservative, and made himself the cogent spokesman of the upper classes. So effective was he that even Jefferson paid reluctant tribute to his enemy. He once referred to Hamilton as a "colossus" and "an host within himself."

It is no discredit to Hamilton to say that in his case self-interest coincided with natural inclination. A man of his powerful intelligence undoubtedly realized on which side of his bread the butter lay. Well-born men who inherited thousands of acres of land—like, for example, the squire of Monticello—had little to lose by taking the radical side; but to men who had to make their way in the world, the popular side was bound to be thorny. Tom Paine had discovered that. Hamilton, moreover, lacked faith in human character.

Even so, he carried his hostility for the common people too far. To him the people were a "great beast." At the Federal Convention he said: "Take mankind in general, they are vicious." For the poor and the lowly he had a withering contempt. Men, he was convinced, were governed by crude self-interest or blind passion. Most men, he was sure, were incapable of taking care of themselves. At the Federal Convention he said:

Take mankind as they are, and what are they governed by? Their passions. . . . One great error is that we suppose mankind more honest than they are. Our prevailing passions are ambition and interest; and it will ever be the duty of a wise government to avail itself of those passions, in order to make them subservient to the public good. . . . All communities divide themselves into the few and the many. The first are the rich and well-born; the other the mass of the people . . . turbulent and changing, they seldom judge or determine right. Give, therefore, to the first class a distinct, permanent share in the government.

Hamilton, unlike Jefferson, was not interested in liberty; he was concerned with property. His aim was the creation of an aristocratic government in which only the wealthy should rule. In his outlook he was thus essentially a British Tory. The idea of a democracy filled him with horror. Republican government, even when severely limited as to suffrage, he regarded, in the words of Gouverneur Morris, as "radically defective."

Hamilton's dark view of human nature may have had a dose of truth in it, but it was a dangerous outlook upon which to build a government. The assumption that man is both selfish and stupid inevitably leads to political tyranny, for it gives ambitious and reckless individuals the excuse and the rationale for their depredations upon the rights of the majority. The Hamiltonian outlook meant the perpetuation of political power in the hands of a few, which in turn must lead to stagnation and ultimately perhaps to revolution.

Paradoxical as it may sound, Hamilton, the conservative, did not see that the consequences of a class system are ultimate unrest, not stability. For experience has shown that in a world where ideas can spread on the wings of the printed word, men cannot be kept permanently chained to their status or deprived of hope for betterment. Jefferson, the radical, realized that the price of rigid conservatism was perpetual upheaval and instability. He knew that the way to get social stability was to distribute political power as widely as possible. That is what Jefferson meant by democracy. Without such a spread of power—and, of course, also of responsibilities—government was not stable and the people not contented.

The Boston historian Henry Adams, whose love for democracy was decidedly not a grand passion and whose admiration for Jefferson was less than lukewarm,[6] has described the difference between Jefferson and Hamilton in these words:

Mr. Jefferson meant that the American system should be a democracy, and he would rather have let the world perish than that his principle . . . should fail. Mr. Hamilton considered democracy a fatal course, and meant to stop its progress.

Jefferson had a word for the bouncing young Hamilton. It was "monarchist." Hamilton, he said, was "not only a monarchist, but for a monarchy bottomed on corruption." At that time "monarchist" had the connotation and the force of the word "Fascist" today. To Jefferson everything that was politically evil and morally objectionable was comprehended in the label "monarchist." Those who hate and fear Fascism today will readily understand Jefferson's animus for everything that even smacked of "monarchism."

Jefferson may not have been able to conceal a certain contempt that he felt for an upstart who made himself the spokesman of the rich.[7] It is probable that, with his Southern agrarian and aristocratic background, he never quite considered Hamilton, who represented the commercial-financial interests of the Northern cities, to be an American. He spoke of him as a British snob. One of Jefferson's nineteenth-century biographers, James Parton, writes that "Hamilton was singularly incapable of Americanization." Jefferson did not express himself quite that bluntly, but he often hinted as much.

While in the Cabinet, the two men did maintain social contact, but there was a deep current of antipathy between them. They did not spare each other's views or feelings. Jefferson relates that he once invited Vice-President Adams and Secretary Hamilton to dinner. Over the mellow wine the men—three of the four most important men in the country—fell into political

[6] "It is always safe to abuse Jefferson and much easier than to defend him." —Henry Adams to Henry Cabot Lodge, June 7, 1876.

[7] Henry Adams, himself a snob of rather monumental proportions, shared this view of Hamilton. "I dislike Hamilton," he wrote to Henry Cabot Lodge on May 15, 1876, "because I always feel the adventurer in him."

conversation. They argued the merits of the British constitution, and Adams was saying that if some of its abuses were corrected, it would be the "most perfect constitution of government ever devised by the wit of man." Hamilton disagreed. He insisted that even with the existing defects, the British was the "most perfect government which ever existed." To Jefferson such views were nonsense, and even dangerous nonsense. There was, he knew, precious little self-government or equality in Britain. England was an oligarchy, a country ruled by the rich and the well-born for the benefit of the rich and the well-born. Laborers were wretchedly exploited. Most of the good land was held in the hands of a few landlords. Parliament was corrupt, elected by notoriously crooked methods. Press and opinion were not free.[8] Despite all that, the Vice-President of the United States and the Secretary of the Treasury both considered the British to be a nearly perfect government! What chance, Jefferson wondered uneasily, did the young American democracy have when such men were at the helm?

After delivering himself on the perfection of the British Government, Hamilton looked around the room and asked Jefferson whose were the portraits that hung on the wall. The Secre-

[8] Jefferson thus described the British government: . . . "her King is a cypher; his only function being to name the oligarchy which is to govern her. The parliament is, by corruption, the mere instrument of the will of the administration. The real power and property in the government is in the great aristocratical families of the nation. The nest of office being too small for all of them to cuddle into at once, the contest is eternal, which shall crowd the other out. For this purpose, they are divided into two parties, the Ins and the Outs, so equal in weight that a small matter turns the balance. To keep themselves in, when they are in, every stratagem must be practised, every artifice used which may flatter the pride, the passions or power of the nation. Justice, honor, faith must yield to the necessity of keeping themselves in place. The question whether a measure is moral is never asked; but whether it will nourish the avarice of their merchants, or the piratical spirit of their navy, or produce any other effect which may strengthen them in their places. . . .

"This is the true character of the English government in practice, however different its theory; and it presents the singular phenomenon of a nation, the individuals of which are as faithful to their private engagements and duties, as honorable, as worthy, as those of any nation on earth, and whose government is yet the most unprincipled at this day known."—Jefferson to Langdon, 1810.

tary of State replied that they were Bacon, Newton, and Locke. "I told him they were my trinity of the three greatest men the world had ever produced." Hamilton thought for a time and then said: "The greatest man that ever lived, was Julius Caesar." That, Jefferson thought, was the measure of the man.

The Secretary of State and the Secretary of the Treasury were sometimes able to collaborate, especially when they met at dinner. One such occasion had far-reaching consequences. The young republic had not yet solved the problem of where to locate the capital. In days when men were more attached to their home State than to their country, and when transportation was slow and difficult, the location of the national capital was a matter of vital importance. When Jefferson arrived in New York to take up his duties, Congress was wrangling bitterly over the problem. Congressmen from the South moved for a reconsideration of the "Federal Town" bill, whereby the capital would be located on the "easterly bank of the Potomac." Congressmen from the North defeated the bill. In May, 1790, a compromise was reached whereby Philadelphia was made the temporary capital for a period of ten years. Feeling, particularly on the part of the Southerners, was intense. There were mutterings of secession.

At about the same time Hamilton had introduced his Assumption Bill, which provided that the Federal Government assume the war debts of the various States. The bill was necessary to save the credit of the Union, but the Southern members had defeated it. That in turn created angry sectional feeling in the North. Jefferson, although no financier and reluctant to agree with Hamilton, realized that the Assumption Bill was needed to "save us from the greatest of all calamities, the total extinction of our credit in Europe." Moreover, there was too much sectional prejudice in Congress. For the good of the republic it must be dissipated; otherwise Jefferson feared "a dissolution of our union at this incipient stage." Why not arrange a horse trade?

The Secretary of State invited Hamilton and two Virginia Congressmen, Lee [9] and White, [10] for dinner. At the meal a bar-

[9] Richard Bland Lee (1761-1827).
[10] Alexander White (1738-1804).

gain was struck. Hamilton promised that he would get the Northern members of Congress to vote for the bill establishing the national capital somewhere on the Potomac. The Virginians gave their word to switch their votes on assumption. Both sides carried out their pledges. Hamilton got his bill passed, and the South got the Federal capital on its border on the Potomac, "not exceeding 10 miles square."

Thus the credit of the United States and the city of Washington, D. C., were born at the same time.

8

Jefferson was not happy in New York. On and off, he had been in public life for twenty years, and still he had not become accustomed to political conflict. A man who craved affection and courted approval, he did not thrive in an atmosphere of suspicion and opposition. It was conviction, not inclination, that made Jefferson fight the Secretary of the Treasury and all that he stood for. The strain of the struggle was so great that Jefferson's health suffered. He had severe headaches—a symptom of nervous tension. There were many hours of unhappiness and even moments of doubt. Why was he wasting his time with politics, when he could be happy cultivating his lands and living with his family? To a man who asked him for a job, Jefferson replied bitterly:

The happiest moments of my life have been the few which I have past at home in the bosom of my family. Emploiment any where else is burning the candle of life in perfect waste for the individual himself. I have no complaint against any body. . . . I only say that public emploiment contributes neither to advantage nor to happiness. It is but honorable exile from ones family & affairs.

The more hostile the environment was in New York, the more poignantly Jefferson missed his two children in Virginia. His letters to the two girls blended extreme tenderness with persuasive hortation. He wrote them regularly once a week, hoping, with no great success, that they would emulate his example. To Martha, a bride of but a few weeks, he wrote:

I am anxious to hear from you of your health, your occupations. . . . Do not neglect your music. It will be a companion which will sweeten many hours of life to you. I assure you mine here is triste enough. Having had yourself and dear Poll to live with me so long, to exercise my affections and cheer me in the intervals of business, I feel heavily the separation from you.

He had a special tenderness for little Polly (Maria), who resembled her mother, whom she had lost at the age of four, in her fragility and beauty. Polly was not a systematic letter-writer, and her long silences drove her father into black depths of anxiety. Jefferson wrote to the twelve-year-old girl.

Where are you, my dear Maria? how are you occupied? Write me a letter by the first post, and answer me all these questions. Tell me whether you see the sun rise every day? how many pages you read every day in Don Quixote? how far you are advanced in him? whether you repeat a grammar lesson every day; what else you read? how many hours a day you sew? whether you have an opportunity of continuing your music? whether you know how to make a pudding yet, to cut out a beefsteak, to sow spinach? or to set a hen? Be good, my dear, as I have always found you . . . take more pleasure in giving what is best to another than in having it yourself, and then all the world will love you, and I more than all the world.

The child replied with a gravity worthy of her loving and hortatory father:

I have not been able to read in Don Quixote every day, as I have been travelling ever since I saw you last, and the dictionary is too large to go in the pocket of the chariot, nor have I yet had an opportunity of continuing my music. I am now reading Robertson's America. I thank you for the advice you were so good as to give me, and will try to follow it. Adieu, my dear papa. I am your affectionate daughter,

Maria Jefferson.

After this there was a long silence from Polly and her father had to plead with her again:

I have written you, my dear Maria, four letters since I have been here, and I have received from you only two. You owe me two, then, and the present will make three. This is a kind of debt I will not give up. You may ask how I will help myself. By petitioning your aunt, as soon as you receive a letter, to make you go without your dinner till you have answered it. How goes on the Spanish? How many chickens have you raised this summer? Send me a list of the books I have promised you at different times. Tell me what sort of weather you have had, what sort of crops are likely to be made, how your uncle and aunt and the family do, and you do yourself.

She replied, studious and grave:

I hope you will excuse my not writing to you before, though I have none for myself. I am very sorry to hear that you have been sick, but flatter myself that it is over. . . . The books that you have promised me are Anacharsis and Gibbon's Roman Empire. If you are coming in September, I hope you will not forget your promise of buying new jacks for the piano-forte that is at Monticello.

In September, five months after assuming his duties as Secretary of State, Jefferson went home to Virginia to recover in the midst of his family from the strain of office. On the way he stopped for a two-day visit with the Washingtons at Mount Vernon. His traveling companion was the faithful James Madison, member of Congress, where he was the intellectual leader of the as yet unorganized democrats.

9

During the two-month stay at Monticello, Jefferson recovered his health and his buoyancy. In November he returned to his post, again accompanied by Madison. This time the journey was shorter by at least ninety miles, for the Government had moved from New York to Philadelphia.

The Secretary of State rented a house in Philadelphia and settled down to frugal, bachelor housekeeping. His finances were not in flourishing condition, and he was compelled to watch his expenditure. In the first quarter of 1791 his living expenses exceeded his salary by more than $100 a month. On a salary of a little less than $300 a month, Jefferson spent around $38 for rent, about $32 on his stable (for he could not live without horses), and approximately $44 on groceries and food. Service, including laundry, cost him approximately $29 and firewood about $24 a month. Coffee and tea, like wines, were expensive items in the budget. Coffee cost $3.20 a pound, and Jefferson, ever the precisionist, figured out that every time he served a cup of coffee with sugar the "dish is worth 2 cents." Tea was a little less expensive, only $2 a pound. Jefferson noted in his account book: "March 8 Tea out, the pound has lasted exactly 7 weeks, used 6 times a week; this is 8/21 or .4 of an oz. a time for a single person." After this experiment Jefferson figured that a cup of tea cost only 1.6 cents, as compared to 2 cents for coffee. Henceforth he served only tea. He also served wine and French cooking. Some patriots resented such un-American goings-on in the house of the author of the Declaration of Independence. Patrick Henry, Jefferson's old crony and later political enemy, denounced him on the stump as a recreant to roast beef, a man who had "abjured his native victuals."

He had not abjured his native principles, however. As Secretary of State, he attended to his specific duties and at the same time did not relinquish his jealous watch over democratic ideas and republican institutions. The former involved long hours of work on state papers and communications; the latter dragged him into more and more bitter conflict with Hamilton and the Federalists.

Among the Secretary of State's activities was one that gave him considerable satisfaction and brought lasting results. When Jefferson took over the office, there was scarcely any foreign service. The United States had a few diplomatic representatives and a handful of consuls abroad,[11] but the service was without plan or system. Jefferson pioneered in the organization of the American diplomatic service by infusing it with purpose and direction. In a circular letter, which the Secretary of State sent

[11] In 1941 the Department of State had on its rolls 20 Embassies, 33 Legations, 49 consulate generals, 172 consulates, 13 vice-consulates, and 24 consular agencies—scattered throughout the civilized world.

out to all consuls in 1790, he laid down the duties for their guidance:

I must beg the favor of you to communicate to me, every six months, a report of the vessels of the United States which enter at the ports of your district, specifying the name and burthen of each vessel, of what description she is, the names of the masters and owners and number of seamen . . . her cargo . . . the port to which she is bound . . . the whole arranged in a table under different columns. . . .

That you give to me, from time to time, information of all military preparations and other indications of war which may take place in your ports. . . .

The consuls and vice-consuls of the United States are free to wear the uniform of their navy if they choose to do so. This is a deep blue coat with red facings . . . yellow buttons with a foul anchor, and black cockades and small swords.

Be pleased to observe that the vice-consul of one district is not at all subordinate to the consul of another. They are equally independent of each other. . . .

It will be best not to fatigue the government in which you reside . . . with applications in unimportant cases. Husband their good dispositions for occasions of some moment, and let all representations to them be concluded in the most temperate and friendly terms, never indulging in any case whatever a single expression that may irritate.

Matters were not shaping altogether to Jefferson's liking. Under Hamilton's aggressive leadership, financiers, speculators —"stock-jobbers," as Jefferson called them—were getting a grip upon the Federal Government. Hamilton's financial policies— his Excise Bill, his Bank Bill, his Assumption Bill—were taking effect. The country was beginning to enjoy what even Jefferson admitted was "unparalleled prosperity." Mills and factories were springing up, particularly in the North. Merchants were making money; financiers were flourishing. Nevertheless, Jefferson was uneasy.

He was uneasy as he watched the democratic republic, which he had envisioned as a commonwealth inhabited by men who tilled the fields, become "corrupt" and gradually fall into the hands of merchants and speculators. The incipient American capitalism, particularly of the Massachusetts and New York variety, filled Jefferson with dismay. The men of business were not interested in liberty or equality. They were interested in profits. What they wanted was the help of the Government in making money. That implied the control of the state. It also meant a reluctance to share political power with others, particularly with those who did not enjoy the blessings of property. And though the country was still overwhelmingly rural, the business interests, led by Hamilton, were getting what they wanted.

Secretary of the Treasury Hamilton was riding the waves. He was successful, he was powerful, and he was idolized by what a later generation called the "special interests." His work in the fields of finance and economics brought him into close contact not merely with businessmen but also with influential members of Congress. Inevitably he became the head of a powerful group, although it was not a "party" in the modern sense. These men, sharing common aims, furthered each other's interests: . . . "all the business is done in dark cabals," complained Senator Maclay, a Republican who was not in sympathy with the Hamiltonians. "Mr. Hamilton is all-powerful, and fails in nothing he attempts."

Success increased Hamilton's power and power swelled his bumptiousness. More and more the Secretary of the Treasury took on the airs of a Prime Minister, not hesitating to tell others over whom he had no jurisdiction what to do. He intervened in other departments. He meddled in matters that were not strictly his concern. As his contempt for democracy grew, so did his disregard for the Secretary of State. At Cabinet meetings the aggressive Secretary of the Treasury spoke his mind with vehemence and stated his opinions with dogmatism, while the Secretary of State, always soft-spoken, confined himself to quiet, unaggressive arguments.

The worst of it was that in the field of finance Jefferson was no match for Hamilton. The Secretary of State, with his lack of sympathy for business and the business point of view, naturally developed no skills in that field. And it was precisely in matters financial and fiscal that Hamilton was a specialist. It is not surprising, therefore, that President Washington, whose viewpoint was neither strictly agrarian nor entirely commercial and who strove to steer a middle course between the two, accepted the financial ideas of his gifted Secretary of the Treasury. Jefferson could offer no acceptable alternative. And Jefferson was not happy as he viewed the shape of things present and to come.

10

The dissensions behind the impressive façade of the Washington Administration were bound to reach the ears of the public. Both sides, the Southern-agrarian group led by Jefferson and the Northern-commercial interests headed by Hamilton, were playing for the highest stake in civilized society—political power. Victory would go to the side that had, not the heaviest artillery, but the most public support. It was therefore to be expected that the press, such as it was, would be used as the big cannon and the pamphlets as the small arms in this war for political domination.

Although there was no such wide and systematic use of the press then as there is now, nevertheless newspapers were employed to trumpet the views of their backers and to castigate those of their opponents. The press was partisan in its politics, unrestrained in its utterances, abusive in its tone, and altogether venal. Hamilton's mouthpiece was the *Gazette of the United States*, a sheet 17 by 21 inches, with a circulation not exceeding 1,400. This is not, to be sure, an impressive number, but the readers of the *Gazette* were influential and its views were those of the Government.

The editor of this Philadelphia newspaper was John Fenno, son of a Boston leather-dresser. Fenno was often in trouble. He was saved from bankruptcy by Alexander Hamilton, the Secretary of the Treasury, and he was caned by Benjamin Franklin Bache, the editor of the Philadelphia *General Advertiser* (later the *Aurora*). There is a connection between these two seemingly discrepant events. For Fenno hated republicanism and democracy, and the Philadelphia *Aurora* supported both. Editor Fenno did not hide his monarchical sympathies under the proverbial bushel. He wanted to see the United States Government transformed into a monarchy, and he hoped that his newspaper would become the gazette of the royal court. His sheet, in fact, gave itself the airs of a royal gazette. In his pretentious manner he imitated the pomposity of the royal court of Great Britain: "We are informed that the President, His Excellency, the Vice-President, His Excellency, the Governor of this State, and many other personages will be present—"

The voice of Fenno was the voice of Hamilton. Like the Secretary of the Treasury, the editor of the *Gazette of the United States* professed contempt for democracy. "Take away thrones and crowns from among men and there will soon be an end of all dominion and justice," wrote Fenno. He argued that in the past democracy had "immediately changed into anarchy." As for his patron Hamilton, the editor lauded him in the hushed terms of a courtier speaking of His Majesty. "He"—Fenno referred to the Secretary of the Treasury—"is the highest jewel in Columbia's crown."

The voice of Fenno was also, but more indirectly, the voice of John Adams. The Vice-President spoke bluntly of his lack of confidence in a democratic form of government. He preferred the power and the trappings of monarchy. "Democracy," wrote the Vice-President of the United States, "never has been and never can be so desirable as aristocracy or monarchy; but while it lasts, is more bloody than either. . . . Remember, democracy never lasts long. It soon wastes, exhausts and murders itself."

It was indeed time for the democratic voice of America to make itself heard. It was, as Jefferson well knew, potentially a million-throated voice. All it needed was leadership and a chance to express itself.

The patient Secretary of State was fed up with all these vocal democracy-haters. He saw no reason why the enemies of republicanism should have a monopoly of the printed word. Early in 1791, at the advice of James Madison and Henry Lee, Jefferson offered a job as translating clerk in the Department of State to one Philip Morin Freneau, poet, journalist, and ardent democrat. Freneau was an old college mate of Madison's. "The salary indeed," the Secretary of State wrote him, "is very low, being but two hundred and fifty dollars a year; but also, it gives so little to do, as not to interfere with any other calling the person may choose."

There was no secret as to what the "other calling" referred to. What Jefferson was offering Freneau was a sinecure in order to enable him to publish a newspaper in which the democratic ideal, of both the American and the French varieties, would be championed. Freneau at first refused the offer, but Jefferson and Madison persisted. In a letter to Madison, the Secretary of State frankly explained what he was expecting of and how he could help the poet-journalist:

I am sincerely sorry that Freneau has declined coming here. Though the printing business be sufficiently full here, yet I think he would have set out on such advantageous ground as to have been sure of success. His own genius in the first place is so superior to that of his competitors. I should have given him the perusal of all my letters of foreign intelligence and all foreign newspapers; the publication of all proclamations and other public notices within my department and the printing of the laws, which, added to his salary, would have been a considerable aid. Besides this, Fenno's being the only weekly or semi-weekly newspaper and under general condemnation for its toryism and its incessant efforts to overturn the government, Freneau would have found that ground as good as unoccupied.

It took nearly half a year of persuasion before Freneau agreed to take the job and do battle with Fenno. In the summer of 1791 he came to Philadelphia and in October began to publish the *National Gazette,* one of the earliest organs of American democracy. Freneau issued his newspaper every Monday and Thursday. In it the "Poet of the Revolution" took up the cudgels in defense of American republicanism and the French Revolution.

II

The press war increased in virulence and ferocity, and few gentlemen cared to claim the credit of authorship. A broadside attack on the Republicans, signed Publicola, was ascribed to John

Adams, who denied it. A pamphlet assault on the Federalists, signed Agricola, was believed to have been written by Jefferson, who disavowed it. Adams doubted Jefferson's denial, and Jefferson did not believe Adams's disclaimer. The Secretary of State told the Vice-President: "I never did in my life, either by myself or by any other, have a sentence of mine inserted in a newspaper without putting my name to it; & I believe I never shall."

It was true that Jefferson did not write anonymously for the public prints. But it was equally true that he encouraged his friends and followers to do so. Averse to squabbling, he preferred to have others do the rough fighting, while he quietly worked out the plans. "For my part," he told his son-in-law Randolph in the summer of 1791, "I am determined to let them write and wrangle as they please without intermeddling in word or deed."

It was a fair division of labor. Jefferson liked to think and to plan; his followers enjoyed acting upon his suggestions. But among those who were not enthusiastic about the person or the ideas of Jefferson, such a division of work was neither well understood nor warmly appreciated. For an eighteenth-century gentleman, particularly one in the Anglo-Saxon tradition, Jefferson's behavior seemed too subtle. Men used to the eloquent roars of a Patrick Henry or the blunt realism of an Alexander Hamilton did not know what to make of the adroit indirections of the publicity-shy Jefferson. Moreover, the notion of a political strategist behind the scenes, a leader who never appeared in person on the field of conflict, was still a novelty in America, a land which had had no Richelieus or Mazarins in its uncrowded history. Not knowing into what category to put such a man, Jefferson's exasperated opponents were inclined to label him a hypocrite. To his political enemies, Jefferson began to loom as a dangerous and slippery customer.

He did, indeed, confound them. In the summer of 1791, after having made arrangements to put Freneau behind the journalistic battery that was aimed at Hamilton, Jefferson discovered that there were some interesting botanical specimens up the Hudson Valley in New York. He and Madison then took a leisurely trip to New York State. But they did not go to pick flowers. They went to light fires. The fires were intended to burn some of Hamilton's political friends in New York State at the next presidential election, which was only a little more than a year off.

New York State was split between two factions, one led by Alexander Hamilton and the other by George Clinton. Hamilton, through his marriage, had the backing of the aristocratic families in New York State; Clinton, through Aaron Burr, had the support of the Sons of St. Tammany society in New York City. The Hamiltonians enjoyed Federal patronage; the Clintonians hoped to. It was an ideal situation in which the botanical gentlemen from Virginia could exercise their political talents.

Jefferson and Madison came to an understanding with Clinton and Burr. The result of this agreement was that in the presidential election of 1792, Virginia and North Carolina threw their support to George Clinton, as against John Adams, for Vice-President.[12] It was an auspicious beginning, for it laid the foundations of a new political party. Since 1792, the South and Tammany Hall, regardless of differences and despite occasional separations, have been the two mainstays of the Democratic party.

Satisfied with having quietly laid foundation stones for his alliance with New York, Jefferson extended his botanical excursion farther north. He said little about the political fauna and much about the botanical flora of New York State. Up in the region of Lake George he admired the sugar maple, the silver fir, the white pine, the decumbent juniper, the wild honeysuckle, the velvet aspen, the downy shrub-willow, and the abundance of wild berries.

12

The little fires that Jefferson lighted in New York were to break into flame within a few years, but the big newspaper cannon which he planted in Philadelphia hurled its shells im-

[12] Adams was elected with 77 electoral votes, as against 50 for Clinton. But this was only a beginning of the Virginia-New York political alliance.

mediately. Jefferson and his Republican friends, considering Hamilton an enemy of the republic, set out to eliminate him from power and to destroy his prestige. Jefferson did not make the mistake of underestimating his opponent. Possibly he overestimated him.

Editor Freneau used exactly the right technique in his war on Hamilton. Instead of arguing with the Secretary of the Treasury, or trying to refute his ideas, Freneau ridiculed him. Instead of attacking him as a worthy opponent, the poet-editor made Hamilton appear odious. Freneau was a master of mockery. His barbs soon got into the skin of the Secretary of the Treasury. Freneau's *National Gazette* sneered at Hamilton and his friends as flunkeys of monarchy. With straight-faced irony Freneau printed a program on how to set up a kingly government in the United States. The program was, of course, supposed to have been that of the Hamiltonians. This, the *National Gazette* mocked, was the way one should go about transforming the United States into a monarchy:

1. Get rid of constitutional shackles.
2. Confer rank and titles.
3. Persevere in indoctrinating the people with the notion of titles.
4. Harp upon the dangers of mob rule.
5. Always talk about a perpetual public debt.
6. Interest legislators in speculation and speculators in legislation.
7. Establish a bank of enrichment of those who are to inherit the kingdom.
8. Arrogate all political power to the Federal Government under the slogan of "national welfare."
9. Secure a rich manufacturing class by making laws in its interest.
10. Create a standing army.
11. Follow the English model.

Mix up all these ingredients and you have a full-blown kingdom, complete with king, court, and titled gentry. The common people of America understood this kind of propaganda. So did

Hamilton, who not only realized its danger to himself but also was personally wounded by the barbs of Freneau.

Hamilton's editor Fenno replied in defense of his patron. But as a dialectician and a stylist, the Boston schoolteacher was no match for the New York poet. The editor of the *Gazette of the United States* showed the weakness of his position by resorting to name-calling. He applied to Freneau a series of adjectives that were more colorful than stinging. To Hamilton's Fenno, Jefferson's Freneau was "wretch," "spaniel," "parasite," "blackguard," "grumbletonian," "crash brain," "Bedlamite," "jackal of mobocracy." The clever Freneau reprinted the epithets without comment, as a mute and ironic rejoinder. Occasionally, however, the poet replied with jeering verse:

Since the day I attempted to print a gazette
This Shylock-Ap Shenkin does nothing but fret;
Now preaching and screeching, then nibbling and scribbling
Remarking and barking and Whining and pining
    And still in a pet
From morning till night with my humble gazette.

The circulation of the "humble gazette" was rising, and people were laughing. It was no laughing matter to Hamilton. His ideas, as well as his person, were being ridiculed, and he could not afford to ignore the challenge. He was, he said, "unequivocally convinced" that Jefferson was behind Freneau. The Secretary of State and his lieutenant Madison, the leader of the Virginians in Congress, were "hostile to me and my administration," Hamilton wrote angrily. They were out, he felt, to destroy him. And since anger is a wretched counselor, the high-tempered Secretary of the Treasury committed a serious mistake. Stung by the needles of the *National Gazette*, he published an anonymous attack on Freneau.

Hamilton's article, printed under the pseudonymous signature "An American," caused a furore. It accused Freneau of being the tool of Jefferson, of being paid from government funds, and even of an ignorance of the French language, which he was supposed to translate. Then the article turned its attention to Jefferson and raked him for all his political sins—of omission as well as commission. It accused the Secretary of State of being an enemy of the Government, of advocating "national disunion, national insignificance, public disorder, and discredit."

Jefferson, true to his method, did not answer. Freneau did. He went before the mayor of Philadelphia and swore truthfully that Jefferson had never hired him to edit a newspaper, had never paid him to do so, had never written a line for it. His own conduct, Freneau said, was "free, unfettered and uninfluenced." That was true, if for no other reason than that Freneau, sharing the political views of Jefferson, did not have to be told what to print.

Hamilton, still writing as "An American," refused to accept Freneau's oath, saying in effect that the "pensioned tool" was as much a liar as his boss Jefferson. Ultimately Hamilton, unable to find proof that Jefferson had really established Freneau's newspaper, had to retract his charges. That did his prestige no good.

Despite Jefferson's conspicuous silence, the war was definitely on. A few weeks after his first assault, Hamilton renewed the battle with a series of six articles signed "Catullus." [13] He repeated his former charges and added new accusations. "Catullus" flayed the Secretary of State as an enemy of the Constitution, a treacherous business adviser, and a hypocrite.

How long it is since that gentleman's real character may have been divined, or whether this is only the first time, that the secret has been disclosed [so reads one of the "Catullus" passages], I am not sufficiently acquainted with the history of his political life to determine; but there is always a "first time" when characters studious of artful disguises are unveiled; when the visor of stoicism is plucked from the brow of the epicurean; when the plain garb of quaker simplicity is stripped from the concealed voluptuary.

That "Catullus" was Hamilton soon became an open secret and a public sensation. Violent attacks by a member of the Cabinet upon a colleague were not usual events that could be dis-

---

[13] They were all published in Fenno's *Gazette of the United States*. The first article appeared on Sept. 15, 1791, the second on Sept. 19, the third on Sept. 29, the fourth on Oct. 17, the fifth on Nov. 24, and the sixth on Dec. 26.

regarded. The person who was most mortified by these printed recriminations was the two antagonists' chief, President Washington. A man of moderation and prudence, the President could not understand such passionate outbursts as were printed in the warring gazettes. He was fed up with politics anyhow, and now his two lieutenants were at daggers' points. The President was afraid that such a feud might rend the republic in two.

Washington, a man of sixty and with failing health, wanted to retire. Only a few weeks before the journalistic war started, the President had called in wise little James Madison and talked to him about a successor. Washington wanted to know whether the Secretary of State would consider the Presidency. Madison, knowing his friend's mind, said that he doubted it. ". . . with respect to Mr. Jefferson," Madison told the President, "his extreme repugnance to public life, & anxiety to exchange it for his farm & his philosophy made it doubtful . . . whether it would be possible to obtain his own consent; and if obtained, whether local prejudices in the Northern States . . . would not be a bar to his appointment."

The President had not been in "any wise satisfied" with Madison's opinion. He did not want to run again in 1792, and hoped to find a successor who had a chance of being elected and who could be trusted to carry on. But there was no one in America of sufficient political stature to replace Washington at a time when the country was threatened with disunity. Both Jefferson and Hamilton realized this and pleaded with Washington to be a candidate for a second term. The precarious unity of the republic hung upon the thread of the life of one man.[14]

[14] On May 23, 1792, Jefferson appealed to Washington in these eloquent words: "The confidence of the whole union is centred in you. Your being at the helm, will be more than an answer to every argument which can be used to alarm & lead the people in any quarter into violence and secession. North & South will hang together, if they have you to hang on; and, if the first correction of a numerous representation should fail in it's effect, your presence will give time for trying others not inconsistent with the union & peace of the states.

"I am perfectly aware of the oppression under which your present office lays your mind, & of the ardor with which you pant for retirement to domestic life. But there is sometimes an eminence of character on which society have such peculiar claims as to controul the predelection [sic] of the individual for a particular walk of happiness, & restrain him to that alone arising from

An inflexible sense of duty had made Washington agree to sacrifice his deepest inclinations and run for a second time in order to keep the Union intact. But now the two ablest members of his Cabinet were at open war and threatened the republic with that very disunity which they had pleaded with him to avert by becoming a candidate. The President's patience was not inexhaustible, and in "a plague o' both your houses" state of mind, he made a sharp appeal to both men for moderation. To Hamilton the President wrote:

I would fain hope that liberal allowances will be made for the political opinions of each other; and, instead of those wounding suspicions, and irritating charges, with which some of our gazettes are so strongly impregnated, and which cannot fail, if persevered in, of pushing matters to extremity, and thereby tearing the machine asunder, that there may be mutual forbearances and temporizing yieldings *on all sides.*

His letter to Jefferson was longer and less severe, but it was pointed nevertheless. The President appealed to his Secretary of State to avoid destroying the whole republic by a conflict of extreme opinions. To both men he repeated the phrase that was apparently uppermost in his mind—he asked that "there may be liberal allowances, mutual forbearances, and temporizing yieldings on all sides." Part of his truly statesmanlike letter to Jefferson reads:

How unfortunate, and how much is it to be regretted then, that, while we are encompassed on all sides with avowed enemies and insidious friends, internal dessensions should be harrowing and tearing our vitals. The last, to me, is the most serious, the most alarming, and the most afflicting of the two; and without more charity for the opinions and acts of one another in governmental matters, or some more infallible criterion by which the truth of speculative opinions, before they have undergone the test of experience, are to be forejudged, than has yet fallen to the lot of fallibility, I believe it

the present & future benedictions of mankind. This seems to be your condition, & the law imposed on you by providence in forming your character, & fashioning the events on which it was to operate; and it is to motives like these, & not to personal anxieties of mine or others who have no right call on you for sacrifices, that I appeal from your former determination, & urge a revisal of it, on the ground of change in the aspect of things."

will be difficult, if not impracticable, to manage the reins of government, or to keep the parts of it together; for if, instead of laying our shoulders to the machine after measures are decided on, one pulls this way and another that, before the utility of the thing is fairly tried, it must inevitably be torn asunder; and in my opinion the fairest prospect of happiness and prosperity, that ever was presented to man, will be lost, perhaps, *for ever*.

My earnest wish and my fondest hope, therefore, is, that instead of wounding suspicions and irritating charges, there may be liberal allowances, mutual forbearances, and temporizing yieldings *on all sides*. Under the exercise of these, matters will go on smoothly, and, if possible, more prosperously. Without them everything must rub; the wheels of government will clog; our enemies will triumph, and, by throwing their weight into the disaffected scale, may accomplish the ruin of the goodly fabric we have been erecting.

Washington concluded his oblique rebuke by assuring his Secretary of State, whom he knew to be as sensitive as himself, that he was not casting reflections upon "any particular person or character." He was merely giving advice in "general terms."

Jefferson was in Virginia when the letter reached him. He knew the cautious President well enough to realize that the "advice" was a rebuke. Stung by the implied criticism, Jefferson in a letter of nearly three thousand words made a vigorous defense of his position. It was a fighting letter, not unmixed with a flavor of bitterness. He criticized Hamilton sharply for his policies, accused him of corrupting Congress, and positively denied having instigated or influenced Freneau in his attacks on the Secretary of the Treasury. Selections from Jefferson's long letter follow. On the subject of Hamilton's pet Assumption Bill, he wrote resentfully:

I was duped . . . by the Secretary of the Treasury and made a tool for forwarding his schemes, not then sufficiently understood by me; and of all the errors of my political life, this has occasioned me the deepest regret.

He accused Hamilton of a systematic plan to corrupt Congress and thereby to destroy freedom:

That I have utterly, in my private conversations, disapproved of the system of the Secretary of the Treasury, I ackolege [sic] and avow: and this was not merely a speculative difference. His system flowed from principles adverse to liberty, & was calculated to undermine and demolish the republic, by creating an influence of his department over the members of the legislature. I saw this influence actually produced . . . the very persons . . . having swallowed his bait were laying themselves out to profit by his plans. . . . These were no longer the votes then of the representatives of the people, but of deserters from the rights & interests of the people. . . .

Thus the object of these plans taken together is . . . to establish means for corrupting a sufficient corps in that legislature to divide the honest votes & preponderate, by their own, the scale which suited, & to have the corps under the command of the Secretary of the Treasury for the purpose of subverting step by step the principles of the constitution, which he has so often declared to be a thing of nothing which must be changed.

He charged Hamilton with interfering in his own department and with twisting his foreign policy into a dangerous direction:

Has abstinence from the department committed to me been equally observed by him? To say nothing of other interferences equally known, in the case of the two nations with which we have the most intimate connections, France and England, my system was to give some satisfactory distinctions to the former, of little cost to us, in return for the solid advantages yielded us by them; & to have met the English with some restrictions which might induce them to abate their severities against our commerce. I have always supposed this coincided with your sentiments. Yet the Secretary of the Treasury, by his cabals with members of the legislature, & by high-toned declamations on other occasions, has forced down his own system, which was exactly the reverse. He undertook, of his own authority, the conferences with the ministers of those two nations.

He defended himself against Hamilton's charge that he had been hostile to the Constitution:

The . . . charge is most false. No man in the U. S. I suppose, approved of every tit[t]le in the constitution: no one, I believe approved more of it than I did: and more of it was certainly disproved by my accuser than by me, and of it's parts most vitally republican. Of this the few letters I wrote on the subject (not half a dozen, I believe) will be a proof; & for my own satisfaction & justification,

I must tax you with the reading of them when I return to where they are. You will there see that my objection to the constitution was that it wanted a bill of rights securing freedom of religion, freedom of the press, freedom from standing armies, trial by jury, & a constant Habeas corpus act. Colo Hamilton's was that it wanted a king and house of lords. The sense of America has approved my objection & added the bill of rights, not the king and lords.

On the question of his giving Freneau a post in the Department of State, Jefferson wrote bitterly:

I have never enquired what number of sons, relations & friends of Senators, representatives, printers or other useful partisans Colo Hamilton has provided for among the hundred clerks of his department, the thousand excisemen . . . at his nod, and spread over the Union; nor could ever have imagined that the man who has the shuffling of millions backwards & forwards from paper into money & money into paper, from Europe to America, & America to Europe, the dealing out of Treasury-secrets among his friends in what time & measure he pleases, and who never slips an occasion of making friends with his means, that such an one I say would have brought forward a charge against me for having appointed the poet Freneau translating clerk to my office, with a salary of 250. dollars a year.

He emphatically denied that he had ever, in any way, influenced Freneau or written for his paper:

But as to any other direction or indication of my wish how his press should be conducted, what sort of intelligence he should give, what essays encourage, I can protest in the presence of heaven, that I never did by myself or any other, directly or indirectly, say a syllable, nor attempt any kind of influence. I can further protest, in the same awful presence, that I never did by myself or any other, directly or indirectly, write, dictate or procure any one sentence or sentiment to be inserted *in his, or any other gazette,* to which my name was not affixed, or that of my office.

He admitted frankly that he was a supporter of Freneau, whose ideas he shared and whose genius he appreciated:

I took for granted from Freneau's character, which had been marked as that of a good whig, that he would give free place to pieces written against . . . aristocratical & monarchical principles. . . .

And I can safely declare that my expectations looked only to the chastisement of the aristocratical & monarchical writers, & not to any criticisms on the proceedings of government: Colo Hamilton can see no motive for any appointment but that of making a convenient partizan. But you Sir, who have received from me recommendations of a Rittenhouse, Barlow, Paine, will believe that talents & science are sufficient motives with me in appointments to which they are fitted: & that Freneau, as a man of genius, might find a preference in my eye to be a translating clerk, & make good title to the little aids I could give him as the editor of a gazette, by procuring subscriptions to his paper, as I did some, before it appeared [about a dozen], and as I have with pleasure done for the labours of other men of genius.

I hold it to be one of the distinguishing excellences of elective over hereditary successions, that the talents, which nature has provided in sufficient proportion, should be selected by the society for the government of their affairs, rather than that this should be transmitted through the loins of knaves & fools passing from the debauches of the table to those of the bed.

He then made a vigorous defense of the freedom of the press, both Freneau's and Fenno's:

As to the merits or demerits of his [Freneau's] paper, they certainly concern me not. He & Fenno are rivals for the public favor. The one courts them by flattery, the other by censure, & I believe it will be admitted that the one has been as servile, as the other severe. But is not the dignity, & even decency of government committed, when one of it's principal ministers enlists himself as an anonymous writer or paragraphist for either the one or the other of them?—No government ought to be without censors: & where the press is free, no one ever will. If virtuous, it need not fear the fair operation of attack & defence. Nature has given to man no other means of sifting out the truth either in religion, law, or politics. I think it is honourable to the government neither to know, nor notice, it's sycophants or censors, as it would be undignified & criminal to pamper the former & persecute the latter.

He concluded by announcing his desire to retire from office at the end of this Administration, and he warned the President that as a private citizen he would consider himself free to make a public defense of his character against the slanders of Hamilton. He had too high a regard for his reputation among the

American people to permit it to be smeared by a man like the Secretary of the Treasury:

> When I came into this office, it was with a resolution to retire from it as soon as I could with decency. . . . I look to that period with the longing of a wave-worn mariner, who has at length the land in view, & shall count the days & hours which still lie between me and it. . . .

> If my own justification, or the interests of the republic shall require it, I reserve to myself the right of then [as a private citizen] appealing to my country, subscribing my name to whatever I write, & using with freedom & truth the facts & names necessary to place the cause and it's just form before that tribunal. . . .

> I will not suffer my retirement to be clouded by the slanders of a man whose history, from the moment at which history can stoop to notice him, is a tissue of machinations against the liberty of the country which has not only received and given him bread, but heaped its honors on his head.—Still however I repeat the hope that it will not be necessary to make such an appeal. Though little known to the people of America, I believe, that as far as I am known, it is not as an enemy to the republic, nor an intriguer against it, nor a waster of it's revenue, nor prostitutor of it to the purposes of corruption.

13

Three weeks after the letter was dispatched, on September 30, Jefferson followed it with a visit to Mount Vernon. He spent the night at the President's cool house on the Potomac. In the morning before breakfast, the two Virginians had a long, frank talk. Jefferson recorded the conversation in his *Anas,* his confidential and somewhat indiscreet political diary.

The President expressed his wish that the Secretary of State would reconsider his decision to retire. He flattered his guest with the statement that he "could not see where he should find another character" to take Jefferson's place. Of course he sympathized with the Secretary of State's desire to leave his post, since he too found the burdens of office onerous. "Nobody disliked more the ceremonies of his office, and he had not the least taste or gratification in the execution of it's functions."

But the call of duty, Washington told his guest, was stronger than personal desires. The President realized, he said, "that he was the only man in the U.S. who possessed the confid[en]ce of the whole." Therefore, he could not avoid making the "sacrifice of a longer continuance." Would not the Secretary of State do the same?

This brought the conversation around to the subject that was uppermost in the President's mind, his deep concern over the conflict between Jefferson and Hamilton. Washington said that he was pained that the political difference between the two men had gone so far as to become a "personal difference" and he wished that he could be "the mediator." Without defending or criticizing either of the two men, the President said that both of them were needed in the Cabinet, to balance each other—"he thought it important to preserve the check of my opinions in the administration in order to keep things in their proper channel & prevent them from going too far."

It was a shrewd appeal, but Jefferson said that he was disturbed by Hamilton's monarchistic machinations. The President denied that there was any monarchist movement in the country; and even if there were, it did not amount to much—"he did not believe there were ten men in the U.S. whose opinions were worth attention who entertained such a thought."

Jefferson countered that "there were many more than he imagined." He argued that "tho' the people were sound, there were a numerous sect who had monarchy in contempl[atio]n. That the Secy of the Treasury was one of these." He quoted Hamilton as having said that "this Constitution was a shilly shally thing of mere milk & water, which could not last, & was only good as a step to something better." There was, Jefferson said, a powerful group in Congress that had benefited from Hamilton's financial policies and was, therefore, "ready to do what he should direct."

The President frankly admitted that such a group did exist in the legislature, but he doubted whether it could be "avoided in any government." Jefferson refused to accept this point of view. "I told him there was great difference between the little accidental schemes of self interest which would take place in every body of men & influence their votes, and a regular system for forming a corps of interested persons who should be steadily at the orders of the Treasury."

The President admitted that Hamilton's financial system had many critics, but he was willing to leave it to the test of time. So far, Washington said, Hamilton's policies had been successful—"he had seen our affairs desperate & our credit lost, and that this was in a sudden & extraordinary degree raised to the highest pitch." Jefferson did not argue the subject, and the President reverted to "another exhortation to me not to decide too positively on retirement." Then they were called to breakfast.

That same day Jefferson left Mount Vernon for Philadelphia. As soon as he arrived in the capital, he carried out his promise to Washington and forwarded to him copies of his letters on the subject of the Constitution, written during the struggle for its adoption. The letters disproved Hamilton's charge that Jefferson had been hostile to the Constitution. But that only made it worse, since it proved Hamilton's accusation false and thereby further widened the breach between the two men. The President made another effort to bring them together. He wrote to Jefferson a letter of warm esteem and made a touching plea for conciliation:

I did not require the evidence of the extracts, which you inclosed to me, to convince me of your attachment to the constitution of the United States, or of your disposition to promote the general welfare of this country; but I regret, deeply regret, the difference in opinions, which have arisen and divided you and another principal officer of the government; and wish devoutly there could be an accommodation of them by mutual yieldings. . . . I will frankly and solemnly declare, that I believe the views of both of you to be pure and well-meant, and that experience only will decide, with respect to the salubrity of the measures, which are the subjects of dispute. . . . I am persuaded there is no discordance in your views. I have a great, a sincere esteem and regard for you both, and ardently wish that some line could be marked out by which both you could walk.

The President was a gentle optimist when he wrote that there was "no discordance" between Jefferson's views and those of Hamilton. Much as Jefferson admired the President's character and appreciated his confidence, he saw no possibility of compromise between himself and the Secretary of the Treasury. Hamilton kept on saying that "there was no stability, no security in any kind of government but a monarchy," and he was deliberately creating a privileged class of financiers and rentiers. Members of Congress and of the Administration, encouraged by Hamilton, were being tempted to make money in stocks and in speculation. That put an end to their independence. Such behavior on the part of representatives of the people shocked Jefferson. When he was approached with a proposition to make money in a financial enterprise, he replied:

When I first entered on the stage of public life (now twenty-four years ago), I came to a resolution never to engage while in public office in any kind of enterprise for the improvement of my fortune, nor to wear any other character than of a farmer. I have never departed from it in a single instance; and I have in multiplied instances found myself happy in being able to decide and to act as a public servant, clear of all interest, in the multiform questions that have arisen, wherein I have seen others embarrassed and biased by having got themselves into a more interested situation. Thus I have thought myself richer in contentment than I should have been with any increase of fortune.

Jefferson saw no stability and no security in any other government but a democratic republic, where speculators and financiers did not rule. There was thus no common line on which both he and Hamilton could walk.

The Secretary of State was determined to leave his post so that he could be free to oppose Hamilton's antidemocratic policies. But for the time being the appeals of the President that he remain in office prevailed. James Madison likewise urged him to stay on for a while longer. The shrewd Congressman from Virginia had long argued with Jefferson about the danger of retiring under fire. He reasoned with his friend that his "exit from public life" must not be made until he could do so with "justifying circumstances which all good citizens will respect,

& to which your friends can appeal." Madison was to all intents and purposes Jefferson's public relations counsel, and he was thinking of the future.

14

In the autumn of 1792, in an atmosphere of political bitterness so intense that old friends crossed the street in order to avoid speaking to each other, George Washington reluctantly stood for re-election. He received the unanimous vote of the Electoral College. The election was significant for a number of reasons, not the least of them being the emergence of Jefferson's own party, the Republican, as a political power of national importance.

In a sense, the campaign of 1792 was a projection of the Jefferson-Hamilton conflict onto the national arena. Everywhere the Republicans put up a stiff fight against Hamilton's Federalist party. Both sides agreed upon Washington for President, but there was a severe struggle for the Vice-Presidency. In the end John Adams, the Federalist candidate, defeated George Clinton, Jefferson's choice, with 77 electoral votes against 50. The defeat of the Jeffersonians was not as serious as this would indicate, for they won a majority in Congress and were able to elect as Speaker of the House a man who was sympathetic to their views.[15] What was equally significant, as foreshadowing things to come, was that most of the South had voted for Jefferson's Northern candidate for Vice-President.[16]

15

For the successful candidate there was no joy in the election. Washington's second Administration started in an atmosphere

[15] The urbane Frederick Augustus Conrad Muhlenberg of Pennsylvania, a former Federalist who finally lined up behind Jefferson.

[16] George Clinton got Virginia's 21 electoral votes, North Carolina's 12, and Georgia's 4. Only two Southern States voted for John Adams—Maryland (6) and South Carolina (7). Kentucky, admitted to the Union that very year, gave its 4 votes to Jefferson (who was not a candidate).

black with dissensions and rent by hatreds. Fires of animosity, the hatred of section against section and class against class, burned throughout the Union.

The touchstone was the French Revolution. As the revolution in France spiraled (up or down, depending upon one's point of view) from protest to revolt and from revolt to massacre, Americans, shaken or thrilled by the events, passionately took sides. Feelings mounted to fever heat, for in the days when there was no baseball or cinema, politics was about the only catharsis that most men had to relieve pent-up emotions.

The French Revolution divided the United States according to class lines. Folk in the upper income brackets, particularly those engaged in commerce or industry, were inclined to regard the French revolutionists much in the same way that like-minded people regarded Bolshevists in a later day. In fact, the word "Jacobin" (it was applied in profusion to Jefferson) was used with the same purpose and effect as "Red" in recent years. Men who were not well-born or well-to-do tended to welcome the French Revolution as a force for the liberation of mankind from the yoke of tyranny and oppression.

This split in public opinion was mirrored in the Government, especially since Jefferson was a stanch friend of France, of French culture as well as politics. Around Jefferson, then, the hatreds swirled, for alone among the members of Washington's Cabinet he stood out, like a defying boulder, in defense of the newly created French Republic. President Washington, while he tried to maintain a temperate middle course in foreign policy, was alienated by the lengths to which the French revolutionists were going. In September, 1792, they had massacred more than eleven hundred human beings in the jails of Paris. This played into the hands of the enemies of the revolution in America.

In aristocratic Philadelphia ladies and gentlemen nourished a virulent hatred for revolutionary France and all its supporters, including the "Jacobin" Secretary of State. Jefferson was cut dead socially. Only three families would receive him in their homes. Former friends and acquaintances crossed the street when they saw his tall figure approaching.

Personal slights were insignificant compared to the national stakes involved. For the United States, depending as it did upon shipping for its exports and imports, faced a crucial test in foreign policy. The country had had a profitable commercial alliance with France since 1778; at the same time Britain, which controlled the seas, was unfriendly to America. Jefferson's policy was to continue the alliance with France, regardless of the upheavals in Paris. The influential Hamilton, however, had always been in favor of co-operation with England, even to the point of subservience; and now, when France was in the hands of the revolutionists, the Secretary of the Treasury impressed upon President Washington the desirability of a pro-British policy. Hamilton said that he saw no "solid ground of difference" between the rulers of England and the businessmen of the United States.

Jefferson had no objections to doing business with England, but to him the problem had political, rather than economic, implications. To be sure, he disliked the British ruling class and he knew that the latter had only contempt for America. But the matter went deeper than mere antipathy. A pro-British orientation on the part of the United States meant, in the first place, deserting the struggling French Republic at a period when it was surrounded by a hostile world. It meant, furthermore, an alliance with Europe's most vigorously antidemocratic ruling group, which, by controlling the seas and sea-borne commerce, was in a position to dictate, or at least influence, internal politics in America. That may have appealed to Hamilton, who admired everything British, but the very prospect was a nightmare to Jefferson.

But deeper than Jefferson's dread of British influence was his conviction that upon the success or failure of the French Republic depended the continued existence of American democracy. For Jefferson took a world view of politics. Unlike many of his parochial-minded contemporaries, he felt keenly that he lived in a revolutionary age and that the civilized world, especially the one lying on the edges of the Atlantic Ocean, was a unity. Waves that washed one coast would break upon or recede from the other coast. The world could not long continue to exist half free and half oppressed. Successful revolution in France would bring about emulation everywhere. Failure of the revolution in France would cause a revulsion against republicanism everywhere, including the United States. Jefferson's espousal of republicanism and democracy at home drove him relentlessly to the position of becoming a champion of republicanism and democracy abroad, especially in France. From that stand he could not, he dared not, recede.

He saw the situation clearly from the beginning of the revolution in France, as he explained in a series of letters to trusted friends. Early in 1791 he wrote to George Mason:

I look with great anxiety for the firm establishment of the new government in France, being perfectly convinced that if it takes place there, it will spread sooner or later all over Europe. On the contrary a check there would retard the revival of liberty in other countries. I consider the establishment and success of their government as necessary to stay up our own.

In the summer of that year he repeated the idea that the success of the American Revolution depended upon the outcome of the French Revolution. In a letter to Edward Rutledge he wrote:

I still hope the French revolution will issue happily. I feel that the permanence of our own leans in some degree on that, and that a failure there would be a powerful argument to prove there must be a failure here.

His faith in the French Revolution was put to a shocking test when the Jacobins seized power and began to butcher their opponents. Much as the killings outraged him, he did not let his repugnance to bloodshed blind him to the larger issue, namely, the success of the revolution. The terrible September massacres were a blind and violent method of defending the gains of the revolution against its armed enemies, foreign and domestic. When William Short, Jefferson's friend and protégé in Paris, wrote him bitter letters about the massacres in which he had lost dear friends, the Secretary of State replied with a vehement defense of the revolution. He said, in effect, What are the lives of a few people compared to the liberty of the world? In many ways it is perhaps the most remarkable letter Jefferson had ever penned:

In the struggle which was necessary, many guilty persons fell without the forms of trial, and with them some innocent. These I deplore as much as any body, & shall deplore some of them to the day of my death. But I deplore them as I should have done had they fallen in battle. It was necessary to use the arm of the people, a machine not quite so blind as balls and bombs, but blind to a certain degree. A few of their cordial friends met at their hands the fate of enemies. But time and truth will rescue & embalm their memories, while their posterity will be enjoying that very liberty for which they would never have hesitated to offer up their lives. The liberty of the whole earth was depending on the issue of the contest, and was ever such a prize won with so little innocent blood? My own affections have been deeply wounded by some of the martyrs to this cause, but rather than it should have failed I would have seen half the earth desolated. Were there but an Adam & an Eve left in every country, & left free, it would be better than as it now is.

16

In the meantime Hamilton was doing everything to make Jefferson's stay in the Cabinet disagreeable. He stigmatized him anonymously in the press and infuriated him at Cabinet meetings. Jefferson, sure of the justice of his views and the rightness of his ideas, wrapped himself in a mantle of imperturbability. But it was only a cloak, for underneath he quivered with suppressed emotions. His seeming impenetrability, however, may have acted as a spur on Hamilton, who never ceased his assaults, thrusting and slashing at his opponent like a dueling Cyrano. The aggressive Secretary of the Treasury probably enjoyed those assaults, but to Jefferson they were painful and humiliating. He and Hamilton, he said, were "pitted, like cocks."

The greatest blessing Jefferson could imagine was to retire from office and go home to live among his children, whom he missed poignantly. He wrote to his daughter Martha, who had recently made him a grandfather, that he wished he had a balloon so that he could fly—"instead of ten days, I should be within five hours of home." But the tyranny of circumstances kept him chained to his post.

When the rumor got around Philadelphia that the Secretary of State was planning to retire at the beginning of the new Administration in March, 1793, all manner of pressure was brought to bear upon him not to do so. Jefferson now felt painfully the burdens of a responsible leader of men. His followers, particularly the Republicans in Congress, urged him to stick it out. To retire under fire, they argued, would be playing into the hands of Hamilton and would give rise to the charge that he was a coward. He must not think solely of his personal comfort. There was his party—still loosely organized, to be sure, but nevertheless a reality—to think of, and there was the future to consider. Arguments like these dented Jefferson's resolution. "These representations have," he wrote to Martha in January, 1793, "for some weeks past shaken a determination which I had thought the whole world could not have shaken."

The President likewise repeated his appeal that he stay. Washington, fearing national disunity, did not wish to lose his Secretary of State, who symbolized the Southern viewpoint just as Hamilton represented the Northern interests. If the two men worked together, the President said, then the country could "coalesce." If Jefferson left now it would cause a new rent in the already strained ligaments that held the Union together. "He expressed his . . . apprehensions," Jefferson relates, "that my retirement would be a new source of uneasiness to the public."

The President asked him to consider some plan whereby he and Hamilton could work together on common measures. Hamilton, the President added, had already agreed to such an idea. Jefferson replied that he saw no possibility of collaborating with the Secretary of the Treasury. Their points of view were diametrically opposed, and neither was willing to give up his ideas in favor of the other. An aristocratic monarchist could not walk the same path with a democratic republican. He told the President:

That as to a coalition with Mr. Hamilton, if by that was meant that either was to sacrifice his general system to the other, it was impossible. We had both no doubt formed our conclusions after the most mature consideration and principles conscientiously adopted could not be given up on either side.

17

A wild gale blew across the Atlantic in the winter of 1793 and no ships sailed the ocean. For three months there was no news from Europe. Then, in April, 1793, when Washington's second Administration was only a month old, ships landed and brought news that set the country agog.

From travelers and old gazettes Americans learned that, in January last, the French had cut off the head of Louis XVI. That was the most sensational event of the generation. Other news was more important. Americans now learned for the first time that France, their ally for fifteen years, had declared war on Britain and Spain. That brought the conflict to the very doors of the United States. Finally there was the news that a French Minister Plenipotentiary had landed in Charleston, South Carolina, and was coming to Philadelphia to replace the royalist envoy, De Ternant.

The new Minister of the French republic was an excitable young civet named Edmond Charles Genet. Certain historians have long since pretended that Genet was a species of jackass and clown. That he was not. A man of aristocratic birth and a scholar, "Citizen" Genet had broken with royalism and aristocracy, although one of his sisters was the memoir-writing Madame de Campan, lady in waiting to Queen Marie Antoinette. He was a widely traveled intellectual, a man of scientific interests, a friend of thinkers like Condorcet, and above all, an enthusiastic republican. In June, 1792, he achieved the republican badge of honor by being expelled from the domain of serfdom by Catherine II of Russia. The fact that the Czarina did not approve of Genet's republicanism made him acceptable to democrats everywhere.

Citizen Genet was a man of faults. His chief defects were a lack of modesty and an absence of reserve. To him the French

Republic was not merely a *patrie*; it was a cause. He was not merely a representative of his country; he was a missionary for an idea. And being a zealot, he had no discretion.

Americans helped to fan the flames of his enthusiasm. From Charleston to Philadelphia, Genet traveled through the back country, where people showed their warm approval of the sister republic overseas. He was gaped at like a great personage and received like a hero. That did nothing to whittle down his vanity. "I live in the midst of continual parties," he wrote excitedly. "Old Washington is jealous of my successes, and the enthusiasm with which the whole town flocks to my house."

To give Genet his due, he was not sent to carry out the conventional diplomatic duties of an ambassador. His instructions were to use the United States as a center of operations against Britain. He was ordered to fit out privateers to prey upon British shipping, to recruit troops for the seizure of Spanish-held Florida and Louisiana, and to obtain the active participation of the United States in the war. His Government had instructed him to influence American opinion secretly—"to direct opinion by means of anonymous publications."

While Genet was coming to present his credentials to President Washington in Philadelphia, there was a clash of opinion in the Administration on the subject of his reception. Hamilton, who loathed the French Revolution, particularly since the execution of the King, argued against recognizing the regicide republic and against receiving its Minister. The Secretary of the Treasury advocated a break with France and a renunciation of the treaty of 1778, on the ground that since the monarch who had signed that treaty was dead, the alliance was no longer binding.

Hamilton was now on ground that was thoroughly familiar to the Secretary of State, and the latter had no difficulty in polishing off his opponent. Jefferson demolished Hamilton's position by stressing a few principles that were self-evident among liberal thinkers. The monarch, Jefferson pointed out, is not the state, but the agent of the state. Source of authority in any country, the Secretary of State emphasized, is not the king, who is transient, but the people, who are permanent. The monarch is merely the symbol of authority. "Consequently the Treaties between the U. S. and France, were not treaties between the U. S. & Louis Capet,[17] but between the two nations of America & France." So long as the two nations remain in existence, regardless of the change in the form of their government, their treaties are binding.

Having laid down these general propositions, Jefferson then raised questions that were lined with sarcasm. The American republic, he said, had been eager to ally with *despotic* France, but now that France was herself a republic some American gentlemen did not like her. Would these gentlemen, Jefferson asked sarcastically, never have allied with France if the latter had been a republic?

The Republic of the U.S. allied itself with France when under a despotic government. She changes her government, and declares it shall be a Republic, prepares a form of Republic extremely free, and in the mean time is governing herself as such, and it is proposed that America shall declare the treaties void, because "it may say with truth that it would not have allied itself with that nation, if it had been under the present form of government"! Who is the American who can say with truth that he would not have allied himself to France if she had been a republic? or that a Republic of any form would be as *disagreeable* as her antient despotism? . . . I conclude That the treaties are still binding, notwithstanding the change of government in France.

President Washington and Attorney-General Randolph agreed with the Secretary of State that the treaty with France was still valid, and it was decided to receive Genet. Hamilton ostentatiously joined the former French Minister, De Ternant, in putting on mourning for the guillotined Louis XVI. "A perfect Counter-revolutioner," was Jefferson's grim comment.

Early in May there arrived in Philadelphia the French frigate *L'Embuscade,* which had brought Genet to America. On the way from Charleston the frigate had captured a British ship and

[17] "Louis Capet" was the sobriquet which the French revolutionists contemptuously applied to Louis XVI. The latter resented it strongly (see the writer's *Life and Death of Louis XVI*, Appleton-Century, 1939, p. 293). Jefferson, ordinarily a scrupulous observer of conventions, probably used the nickname in order to annoy Hamilton.

brought her as a prize to port. The republican citizenry of Philadelphia, hating Britain and everything British, went mad with enthusiasm. *L'Embuscade* was received by a wildly cheering crowd. "Upon her coming into sight," Jefferson wrote to Monroe, "thousands & thousands of the *yeomanry* of the city crowded & covered the wharfs. Never before was such a crowd seen there, and when the British colours were seen *reversed*, & the French flying above them they burst into peals of exultation."

At about the same time Genet in person arrived in Philadelphia. He was received like a conquering hero. A "vast concourse of people," in the words of Jefferson, received him at Gray's Ferry and shouts of welcome thundered in the volatile Frenchman's ears. The rousing cheers went to his head and stayed there. His ardor was not quenched by President Washington's correct but not ardent reception. The Minister went to the Secretary of State and presented his credentials with the words: "We see in you the only person on earth who can love us sincerely & merit to be so loved." Jefferson was pleased. He felt that Genet would serve as a center around which pro-French opinion would crystallize.

But Genet brought only embarrassment and trouble to the Secretary of State. His presence and activities raised some pressing problems. To what extent was the United States bound by treaty to aid her ally France against Britain? Was the United States justified in permitting the fitting out of French privateers? What would be England's reactions if the Washington Administration permitted such privateering?

If Genet did not raise these questions, Hamilton emphatically did. During furious Cabinet squabbles, the Secretary of the Treasury warned the President against the dangers of being involved in war with a mighty Naval Power such as Britain. He urged not merely neutrality in the Anglo-French war, but an alliance with Britain, a country that the overwhelming majority of Americans distrusted and feared. Jefferson wrote Monroe:

H[amilton] is panic-struck if we refuse our breech to every kick which Gr. Brit. may chuse to give it. He is for proclaiming at once the most abject principles, such as would invite & merit habitual insults. And indeed every inch of ground must be fought in our councils to desperation in order to hold up the face of even a sneaking neutrality, for our votes are generally 2½ against 1½.

The "2½" were Hamilton and Secretary of War Knox, together with Attorney-General Randolph, who was the "½" of the trio. Randolph was a fine lawyer who hewed to a hairline of two-sidedness. His yes-but indecisiveness finally exasperated Jefferson. In a secret letter to Madison, the Secretary of State burst out against his fellow Virginian: "He is the poorest cameleon I ever saw, having no color of his own, and reflecting that nearest him. When he is with me he is a whig, when with H[amilton] he is a tory, with the P[resident] he is what he thinks will please him."

Jefferson argued that the least the Administration could do was to remain an honest neutral in the war, helping neither country. That was not fair to France, but it was safe for America. The President gave one ear to the Cabinet's "2½" and another ear to the Secretary of State. "If we preserve even a sneaking neutrality," Jefferson confessed early in May, "we shall be indebted for it to the President, & not to his counsellors." In the end an uneasy neutrality was agreed upon, for the young republic, even if it wished to aid France, was in no position to expose itself to attacks by the powerful British fleet.

Genet, convinced that public opinion was behind him, was not satisfied with passive neutrality. He felt that under the treaty of 1778 he had a right to demand positive assistance, such as the free use of American ports. Moreover, he asked for funds in the form of advance installments on the debt the United States owed to France.[18] In this the Secretary of the Treasury was thoroughly unco-operative. But the Secretary of State, the friend of France, proved in the end to be no more helpful.

"Sneaking neutrality" was not to Jefferson's taste or convictions, but since the situation demanded it and the President favored it, the Secretary of State could only obey. When Genet came to him and demanded that the treaty of 1778 be strictly executed, the uneasy Secretary of State sought refuge in juridical

[18] Between 1775 and 1782 France had advanced 18,000,000 livres in cash to the American colonies to help fight Britain.

subterfuge, a kind of chicanery that Jefferson despised in others. "This Secretary of State," Genet reported to Paris, "hunts excuses in the dusty tomes of Vattel and Grotius." [19]

Citizen Genet impatiently refused to accept Jefferson's juridical subtleties. France was fighting for life and liberty, as had the American colonies a decade back, and she needed aid. The United States was the ally of France; the American Secretary of State was the vaunted friend of France. Then why all these tortuous subterfuges when help was required? Genet wrote to Jefferson an angry letter:

Let us explain ourselves as republicans. Let us not lower ourselves to the level of ancient politics by diplomatic subtleties. Let us be as frank in our overtures, in our declarations, as our two nations are in their affections; and by this plain and sincere conduct arrive at the object by the shortest way. All the reasonings, sir, [in your letter] . . . are extremely ingenious; but I do not hesitate to tell you that they rest on a basis which I cannot admit. You oppose to my complaints, to my just reclamations . . . the private or public opinions of the President of the United States; and this aegis not appearing to you sufficient, you bring forward aphorisms of Vattel, to justify or excuse infractions committed on positive treaties. Sir, this conduct is not like ours.

Genet implied that such conduct was worthy neither of General Washington—"that celebrated hero of liberty"—nor of the American people. The Americans, he said, are a free people, "not attached to the glebe like the slaves of Russia." If free Americans wanted to aid France, and thereby the cause of liberty, they should be permitted to do so. Genet openly hinted that he would appeal to the American people over the head of the Government.

The words stung the Secretary of State. They also made him uneasy. No one, least of all a man as sensitive as Jefferson, likes to be scolded, particularly when the scolder is not altogether

[19] A few years later, Adet, another French Plenipotentiary to the United States, concluded that Jefferson, being an American, could be no real friend of France. "Jefferson, I say," Adet reported to Paris on Dec. 31, 1796, "is an American and hence he cannot be sincerely our friend. An American is the born enemy of all Europeans."—Turner, F. J., ed., *Correspondence of the French Ministers in the United States, 1792-97*, p. 982.

unjustified. Moreover, being intuitively attuned to trends in public opinion, Jefferson felt that the Frenchman's appeal to the people against the Administration might turn out to be a boomerang. Such a boomerang would not only crack the skull of the French Minister, but would also knock out France's American friends, chief of whom was the Secretary of State. Jefferson feared that the hotheaded Frenchman would upset the Republican apple cart and throw the apples right into the lap of Hamilton. "I am doing everything in my power," Jefferson confided to Monroe, "to moderate the impetuosity of his movements."

But the French Plenipotentiary would not be soothed into punctilious inactivity. He did not consider himself bound by the neutrality proclaimed by President Washington. Genet, moreover, felt that the American people loved France and wanted to help her, and he was sure that the Washington Administration was betraying the people. The impeccable Jefferson reasoned with the impetuous Minister patiently and somewhat pedagogically. He was trying to make him understand that certain things were not done in America. Under the Constitution, Jefferson explained, only the Executive could execute a treaty, and there was no legal appeal to Congress or to the people. A fine Constitution, Genet replied in effect, bowing with ironic humor to the Secretary of State.

Republican papers and Republican societies passionately supported Genet's cause, and Jefferson was thereby impaled on the proverbial horns of a dilemma. He did not wish to alienate his pro-French friends by putting the brakes on Genet, with whose country he sympathized, and he could not, as a public official, avoid enforcing the policy of neutrality. And Genet, by his unrestrained behavior, did nothing to improve Jefferson's painful position. The Secretary of State confessed unhappily to Madison:

Never in my opinion, was so calamitous an appointment made, as that of the present Minister of F[rance] here. Hot headed, all imagination, no judgment, passionate, disrespectful & even indecent towards the P[resident] in his written as well as verbal communications. . . . He renders my position immensely difficult.

After a time Jefferson realized that it was hopeless to argue with Genet, who was, the Secretary of State said, "incapable of correcting himself." If permitted to continue his activities unchecked, the stormy envoy would ruin them all, by disgusting Americans with France and Frenchmen in general. Already Hamilton and the Federalists were taking advantage of Genet's bull-in-the-china-shop tactics to strengthen their own position against the pro-French Republicans. Hamilton, in fact, subtly wanted Genet to appeal to the people so as to discredit him and thereby bring about a rupture with France. Genet, behaving like a "most furious Jacobin," was not averse to obliging his enemy, the Secretary of the Treasury. "I only wish our countrymen may distinguish between him [Genet] & his nation," Jefferson exclaimed.

Early in August, to the vast relief of the Secretary of State, the Cabinet decided to request the French Government to recall its Minister Plenipotentiary. "He will sink the republican interest if they do not abandon him," Jefferson told Madison.[20]

But Genet, like the shrew in Shakespeare, had the last word. Before being replaced, this man of trouble did exactly what Jefferson had been trying to persuade him not to do—he published some of his correspondence with the Administration, thereby appealing to the people against the Government. He also attacked President Washington, for whom Americans, even those who disagreed with him, entertained universal admiration. Criticizing the President was a privilege reserved for Americans, not foreigners. The effect of this "intermeddling by a foreigner" was, as Jefferson had foreseen, to alienate French sympathizers and to throw public opinion in the direction of the pro-British Federalists. To Jefferson's friends this was a calamity. Anti-French reaction was so widespread that even cool heads, such as James Madison, were distressed. Early in September, 1793, Madison reported to Jefferson:

[20] The French dictator, Robespierre, obliged the American Government by removing Genet. In return he asked that the United States recall its envoy, Gouverneur Morris. The latter was as active against the revolution in Paris as Genet was for it in Philadelphia. It was not an unfair exchange. But while Morris came back to America, Genet was too intelligent to return to France. He had no desire to make the acquaintance of the guillotine.

The effect is beginning to be strongly felt here in the surprise and disgust of those who are attached to the French cause, and viewed this minister as the instrument for cementing instead of alienating, the two Republics. These sensations are powerfully reinforced by the general and habitual veneration for the President. The Anglican [pro-British] party is busy as you may suppose in making the worst of everything, and in turning the public feelings against France, and thence in favor of England. The only antidote for their poison is to distinguish between the nation & its agent; between principles and events; and to impress the well meaning with the fact that the enemies of France & of Liberty are at work.

18

The Genet episode left unpleasant consequences in its wake and a bad taste in everybody's mouth. It fanned the sparks of opposition and frayed the nerves of leading men in the Government. Even the cool and patient Washington was affected by the strain of events, especially by criticism of his foreign policy in the Republican press. The President was only sixty-one, but the current of violent hates that was beating around him drained his health. Jefferson reported to Madison during the height of the Genet affair:

The President is not well. Little lingering fevers have been hanging about him for a week or ten days, and have affected his looks most remarkably. He is also extremely affected by the attacks made & kept up on him in the public papers. I think he feels those things more than any person I ever yet met with. I am sincerely sorry to see them.

Newspaper criticism shattered President Washington's poise. He was particularly incensed by the attacks upon him that appeared in the *National Gazette,* for Freneau did not follow his patron Jefferson in either accepting or condoning a policy of neutrality toward France. In his championship of the French Republic, the poet-editor did not spare the President. "The publications in Freneau's and Bache's papers are outrages in common decency," Washington exclaimed. He suggested that

Jefferson dismiss Freneau from his post in the Department of State. Jefferson refused. "But I will not do it," he wrote in his *Anas.* "His paper has saved our constitution which was galloping fast into monarchy. . . . It is well & universally known that it has been that paper which has checked the career of the Monocrats." [21]

A little later, at a Cabinet meeting, the exasperated President again raised the question of Freneau and his assaults. Washington, his nerves on edge, lost his temper and flew into one of his rare and terrifying rages. He "got," Jefferson records in his confidential diary, "into one of those passions when he cannot command himself . . . defied any man on earth to produce one single act of his . . . which had not been done on the purest motives . . . that *By god* he had rather be in his grave than in his present situation. He had rather be on his farm than to be made *emperor of the world*."

The Genet episode, the public reaction to the French Minister's antics, and the President's irritation—all these made Jefferson feel as if he were sitting on burrs. Hamilton, moreover, never ceased in his printed assaults on the Secretary of State and galled him as much as Freneau infuriated the President. The air resounded with fugues of bad feeling. "For God's sake, my dear Sir," Jefferson burst out with a plea to Madison, "take up your pen, select the most striking heresies and cut him [Hamilton] to pieces in the face of the public. There is nobody who can & will enter the lists with him." [22]

Like Washington, Jefferson reached the point where he felt that he would rather be on his quiet farm than "emperor of the world" and, again like the President, he was bitter at the wormy fruit he had to swallow while in office. He had been in the public service for almost a quarter-century, during which time he had neglected his estate and his personal affairs. What did he get out of office but hatred, misrepresentation, and a host of enemies? At the age of fifty, he decided, he was too old to cope

[21] The *National Gazette* had a circulation of about 1,500, but it was read in every State in the Union.

[22] On October 26, 1793, Freneau's *National Gazette* suspended publication for "want of money." This further limited the Republicans' channels for the influencing of public opinion.

with the political world. He was definitely through, he informed his friend Madison, and in June had painted a touching picture of the blessings of retirement and the curse of office.

The motion of my blood no longer keeps time with the tumult of the world. It leads me to seek for happiness in the lap and love of my family, in the society of my neighbors & my books, in the wholesome occupations of my farm & my affairs, in an interest or affection in every bud that opens, in every breath that blows around me, in an entire freedom of rest or motion, of thought or incogitancy, owing account to myself alone of my hours & actions. . . . worn down with labours from morning to night, & day to day; knowing them as fruitless to others as they are vexatious to myself, committed singly in desperate & eternal contest against a host who are systematically undermining the public liberty & prosperity, even the rare hours of relaxation sacrificed to the society of persons . . . of whose hatred I am conscious . . . cut off from my family & friends, my affairs abandoned to chaos & derangement, in short giving everything I love, in exchange for everything I hate.

He handed in his resignation to the President. Again Washington urged him to stay, but this time even the personal appeals of the weary President could not alter his determination. He consented to remain in office only until the end of the year 1793. The prospect of being a free man on January 1, 1794, enchanted Jefferson. He would go home to Virginia and be a veritable patriarch. He wrote exultantly to a friend, Mrs. Church, at the end of November, 1793:

I am then to be liberated from the hated occupations of politics, and to remain in the bosom of my family, my farm, and my books. I have my house to build, my fields to farm, and to watch for the happiness of those who labor for mine. I have one daughter married to a man of science, sense, virtue, and competence. . . . If the other shall be as fortunate, in due process of time I shall imagine myself as blessed as the most blessed of patriarchs.

Three days before Christmas, 1793, Washington made another personal appeal to his Secretary of State to remain in office. Jefferson's decision could not be shaken. "In this," he said, "I am now immovable by any considerations whatever."

On December 31, 1793, nearly four years after he had become Secretary of State, he sent in his resignation to the President: "I now take the liberty of resigning the office into your hands. . . . I carry into my retirement a lively sense of your goodness."

There was nothing for President Washington to do but to let his Secretary of State go. Reluctantly he accepted the resignation, and he sent Jefferson on his way with his blessings: "Let a conviction of my most earnest prayers for your happiness accompany you in your retirement."

CHAPTER XI

Vice-President

O N THE fifth day of the year 1794 Jefferson said farewell to Philadelphia—forever, he hoped. He was leaving politics and was going home to become a family patriarch and a farmer. On the sixteenth of January he climbed the winding road to Monticello, the peaceful nest that would shelter him from further storms. "The ascent of this steep, savage hill," Jefferson's friend George Ticknor once remarked, "was as pensive and slow as Satan's ascent to Paradise." To Jefferson it was Paradise.

He had taken a rough beating at the hands of Hamilton in the last three years, and now he came home with deep scars and distasteful memories. On his plantation, in the midst of his devoted family, he hoped to erase the former and forget the latter. Never again, he repeated, would he be enticed into the political arena, where jackals and wolves were in the habit of tearing at the vitals of a man's character and reputation. He felt himself old and ill. But he was neither old nor ill. At fifty he was as vigorous as ever, showing few signs of age except a graying around the temples. But he was weary and hurt. The cure for his soul-sickness was work in the open air.

Jefferson plunged into farming with a zeal he had never felt before. On the soil, away from political snipings and under-cover intrigues, a man could labor fruitfully without being in constant danger of having his teeth kicked in by an opponent. And he did not mind letting his political acquaintances in Philadelphia know that he did not miss their kind of work. "I return to farming," he wrote to John Adams, "with an ardor which I scarcely knew in my youth. . . . Instead of writing 10. or 12. letters a day, which I have been in the habit of doing as a thing of course, I put off answering my letters now, farmer-like, till a rainy day."

Farming was not simply a means of healing his spiritual wounds. Since he had given up the law some two decades back, farming was his sole means of support. He had no other income but that which his land was made to produce. Financially, he was broke, "money-bound," as he called it when he asked a man to lend him $100. The plantation was run down, and it needed hard work and careful cultivation to make it productive again. Jefferson possessed 10,000 acres of land, but only 2,000 were in use. The rest was uncleared timber, or otherwise unproductive. Two thousand acres in use sounds like a lot of land, but in reality it was little. These acres had to support not only Jefferson's family, including many relatives, but also one hundred and fifty-four slaves and their progeny. For the plantation depended upon slave labor.

Jefferson hated and dreaded the whole institution of slavery. He felt that it degraded both the master and the man. One of the most eloquent condemnations of slavery ever written is to be found in his *Notes on Virginia:*

The whole commerce between master and slave is a perpetual exercise of the most boisterous passions, the most unremitting despotism on the one part, and degrading submissions on the other. Our children see this, and learn to imitate it; for man is an imitative animal. . . . The parent storms, the child looks on, catches the lineaments of wrath, puts on the same airs in the circle of smaller slaves, gives a loose to the worst of passions, and thus nursed, educated, and daily exercised in tyranny, cannot but be stamped by it with odious peculiarities. The man must be a prodigy who can retain his manners and morals undepraved by such circumstances.

What was equally tragic about slavery, Jefferson felt, was that it destroyed the fiber and stamina of the South, by making the whites lazy and shiftless.

With the morals of the people, their industry also is destroyed. For in a warm climate, no man will labour for himself who can make another labour for him. This is so true, that of the proprietors of slaves a very small proportion indeed are ever seen to labour. And can the liberties of a nation be thought secure when we have removed their only firm basis, a conviction in the minds of the people that these liberties are of the gift of God? That they are not to be violated but with his wrath? Indeed I tremble for my country when I reflect that God is just: that his justice cannot sleep forever.

But there was not much that an individual planter could do about it. In a slave economy the planter had little choice but to continue using slave labor or to bankrupt himself by liberating his Negroes. Freeing the slaves, however, was no solution either, for such freedmen, unable to find free work in a slave world, would be certain to be exposed to beggary or starvation. Moreover, the slaves were neither morally nor technically prepared to make an independent living in a competitive world. Jefferson wrote to Dr. Edward Bancroft in 1789:

. . . to give liberty to, or rather, to abandon persons whose habits have been formed in slavery is like abandoning children. Many quakers in Virginia seated their slaves on their lands as tenants . . . but . . . the landlord was obliged to plan their crops for them, to direct all their operations during every season & according to the weather. But what is more afflicting, he was obliged to watch them daily & almost constantly to make them work, & even to whip them. A man's moral sense must be unusually strong, if slavery does not make him a thief. He who is permitted by law to have no property of his own, can with difficulty conceive that property is founded in anything but force.

Dominant opinion had it that the Negroes were incapable of independence and unable to take care of themselves. Many, possibly most, white people insisted that Negroes were inferior beings in every way, and hence it was "natural" that they be enslaved. Jefferson had strong doubts about the "natural" inferiority of Negroes. Indeed, when he met a Negro of culture and education (there were such even in those days), he welcomed him warmly and entertained him in his home as a guest.

Occasionally the author of the Declaration of Independence would receive letters from educated Negroes, pleading for equality. One such letter, written to him in 1791 by Benjamin Banneker, a Negro mathematician and astronomer, upbraided Jefferson for keeping slaves against his principles:

. . . we are a race of beings who have long laboured under the abuse and censure of the world . . . we have long been considered rather as brutish than human, and scarcely capable of mental endowment.

Sir, I hope . . . that you are a man far less inflexible in sentiments of this nature than many others, that you are measurably friendly and well disposed toward us. . . .

Now, Sir, if this is founded in truth, I apprehend you will readily embrace every opportunity to eradicate that train of absurd and false ideas and opinions which so generally prevails with respect to us, and that your sentiments are concurrent with mine, which are that our universal Father hath given being to us all. . . . [Here Banneker quoted the Declaration of Independence that "all men are created equal," and so on.]

. . . but, Sir, how pitiable it is to reflect that, altho you were so fully convinced of the benevolence of the Father of mankind . . . that you should at the same time counteract his mercies in detaining by fraud and violence so numerous a part of my brethren under groaning captivity and cruel oppression.

Jefferson's reply was that he realized that the so-called inferiority of colored people was due to their environment, that they had not been given a chance to raise themselves above their degraded status. He hoped that everything would be done to ameliorate this condition.

No body wishes more than I do to see such proofs as you exhibit, that nature has given to our black brethren, talents equal to those of the other colors of men, and that the appearance of a want of them is owing merely to the degraded condition of their existence, both in Africa & America. I can add with truth, that no body wishes more ardently to see a good system commenced for raising the condition both of their body & mind to what it ought to be, as fast as the imbecility of their present existence, and other circumstances which cannot be neglected, will admit.

He did everything he could to raise the physical and moral level of his slaves, and his considerate treatment of the colored folk on the plantation surprised many a visitor. To stimulate the slaves' initiative, Jefferson praised them when they did something well and rewarded them when they achieved something out of the ordinary. The slaves responded to their kind and patient master with abiding love.

On the Jefferson plantation there were also 249 heads of cattle, 390 hogs, 5 mules, and 34 horses. Of the latter, 8 or 9 were devoted exclusively to riding. It took Jefferson several months after his return from Philadelphia before he was able to borrow $50 to buy two or three score of sheep.

During his absence, Jefferson discovered, his lands had been ravaged to a "degree of degradation far beyond what I had expected." It was necessary, therefore, to heal the wounds of the soil and give the land a breathing-spell. To do that, Jefferson divided his lands under cultivation into four large farms. These farms were in turn subdivided into six fields of 40 acres each. This permitted a six-year period of rotation. For example, the first field would be planted to wheat, the second to corn, the third to rye or wheat, the fourth and fifth to clover, and the sixth to buckwheat. Rotation, together with contour plowing on hills to stop runoffs (Jefferson and Washington were among the American pioneers in this form of plowing), saved the land from exhaustion and wastage.

It was slow work, Jefferson wrote to Washington. "Time, patience & perseverance must be the remedy." Washington's words, "slow & sure," must be the maxim.

Jefferson brought system into management and invention into work. Each farm was an independent unit, directed by a steward and worked by four male slaves, four female slaves, four oxen, and four horses. But slaves and oxen were not the only ones cultivating the Jefferson lands. The master, with his lively sense of inventiveness, was one of the first Americans to use farming machinery. On the Jefferson plantation there was a threshing machine which was carried on a wagon, and weighed about a ton. It was capable of threshing as many as one hundred and fifty bushels a day. There was also a drilling machine, invented by one of Jefferson's neighbors. This instrument had a sharp iron that opened the furrows, and a small trough containing the sowing grain behind it.

Intelligent management and careful planning finally brought results. Within two years after his return from Philadelphia, the agricultural yield of Jefferson's plantation compared with the best in the State. It compares favorably, indeed, with the average of the State of Virginia today, as the following figures show:

YIELD IN VIRGINIA
(per acre)

	1796 [1]	1938 [2]
Wheat	8 bushels	14 bushels
Corn	18 bushels	25 bushels
Clover	1 ton	1.2 ton

Jefferson's agricultural yield is the more remarkable in that it was achieved without the benefit that the modern farmer gets from soil scientists and the more complicated farm machinery.

2

In his early fifties Jefferson was a lean, grizzled, quizzical farmer, as happy as a busy mortal and a loving parent can be. No political ambition slumbered in his breast, he was convinced. He shunned all "intermeddling with public affairs" and refused participation in political activities. "I have returned," he told a French friend, "with infinite appetite, to the enjoyment of my farm, my family & my books, and had determined to meddle in nothing beyond their limits."

But Jefferson deceived himself. He made a mistake when he assumed that the outside world would leave him alone with his books and his family. He also fooled himself into believing that he was nothing more than a farmer in retirement. It was as if

[1] 1796 is an approximate year. Jefferson may have had a similar crop yield in 1797, and 1798 also.
[2] These figures are taken from United States Department of Agriculture, *Agricultural Statistics*, 1939.

an Arabian thoroughbred pretended to be a dray-horse. Jefferson found it hard to admit, even to himself, that he could not resist the call of a good cause or the temptation of acting in an arena larger than Monticello. For all his patience and philosophic poise, he could not shut his susceptible mind to the clamor from the outside world. Up to the hill of Monticello there came a steady stream of letters, and many friends. Each was a living link with the world of action and the world of thought. Each was a challenge.

Despite his busyness on the farm, Jefferson followed events, especially political ones, with the liveliest curiosity. The course of the French Revolution still set him on edge with suppressed excitement and filled him with ardent hope for a better world. The activities of his enemies, the Federalists and Hamiltonians in Philadelphia, continued to stir him to smoldering anger. In brief, he was retired from "public affairs" in everything but his mind and his emotions.

His friends, especially Madison, played delicately upon these emotions to bring him out from his retirement. Madison was always dropping skillfully baited hints to stir up Jefferson's dormant ambitions. Judiciously distributed rumors to the effect that Jefferson was a candidate for the Presidency found their way into the newspapers. Such gossip was in turn relayed to Jefferson in letters.

Jefferson protested that he did not seek the Presidency, but his protests were couched in ambiguities. He insisted that he did not want the high office, but he never said emphatically that he would not take it. In a letter to Madison written in the spring of 1795 Jefferson disclaimed all political ambitions: "The little spice of ambition which I had in my younger days has long since evaporated, and I set still less store by a posthumous than present name." But at the same time he told his friend that he was interested in seeing that his own party, the Republican, did not lose votes in the next election. He also confessed to another one of his correspondents that he was "a warm zealot for the attainment & enjoyment by all mankind of as much liberty, as each may exercise without injury to the equal liberty of his fellow citizens." It is hard to square a desire for retirement from politics with a wish to see one's party victorious and one's fellow men in possession of full liberty. Both aims had to be fought for, and no one knew that better than Jefferson.

His letters show the inner struggle that he must have gone through—a conflict between a happy but politically inactive retirement and a strong ambition to direct events. To dampen the flame of obstinate ambition, he even went so far as to refuse to read newspapers. News from the political stage disturbed his peace of mind. "I read but little," he wrote to Mrs. Trist in the autumn of 1795, "take no [newspaper] that I may not have the tranquility of my mind disturbed by falsehoods & follies."

But try as he would, he could not drown out the political voices that reached all the way to Monticello. For one thing, his neighbors—good fellow Republicans—asked for opinion and advice. For another, when fundamental principles were involved Jefferson could not close his eyes and pretend that he did not care. He cared, deeply and passionately. For all his apparent poise, a basic issue made Jefferson quiver with desire to pitch in and fight it out, in his own way, of course.

This was particularly true where his old enemy Hamilton was concerned. At the end of 1794, after intolerable depredations upon American commerce by the British Navy and the impressment of American seamen, John Jay was sent to London to patch up some sort of peace. Jay brought back a treaty so disadvantageous to America that it dismayed the peace-loving President Washington. The treaty did not guarantee American vessels against seizure and impressment, but it assured American neutrality in the Anglo-French conflict. It was an obvious victory for the Anglophile Hamilton and his Francophobe friends.

But the country was neither Anglophile nor Francophobe, and Jefferson from a distance, as well as Hamilton on the spot (in more ways than one), realized that the Jay Treaty was dynamite. Jefferson, despite his retirement, jumped at the chance of burying Hamilton under an avalanche of popular disapproval. For the treaty, though reluctantly signed by Washington, was violently unpopular throughout the country. Hamilton, sensing danger, leaped to the defense of Jay's diplomatic bungling. A fellow Federalist named Noah Webster,[3] who sired the first American grammar and published a New York City newspaper, the *American Minerva*, printed twelve letters defending the Jay Treaty and signed himself, in the classical fashion of the day, "Curtius." Hamilton himself, in collaboration with Rufus King, published thirty-eight letters in defense of Jay's handiwork, under the classical name of "Camillus." One-third of these letters by "Camillus" were published in Webster's *American Minerva*.

News of this torrent of pro-Jay letters reached the newspaper-shunning Jefferson, who looked into them. The more he read, the hotter he got. Here, he realized with reluctant admiration, was powerful and effective stuff. He actually tested some of these printed letters upon his less sophisticated neighbors, and they fell for the "sophistry." If that was the case, then it was time to do something to stop such effective Federalist propaganda. The letters were so forceful that they led Jefferson to the conclusion that only one man could be their author. Only one man in the country was capable of writing like "Curtius" and "Camillus"—Alexander Hamilton.

If Hamilton was on the warpath, Jefferson thought it necessary, for the welfare of his own party, to stop him. Forgetting his retirement and his desire to avoid politics, Jefferson wrote to Madison urging him, "for god's sake," to take up the cudgels against Hamilton. The latter, Jefferson admitted frankly, was the ablest man of his party and a most formidable adversary. Only Madison could match swords with him.

Hamilton is really a colossus to the anti-republican party. Without numbers, he is an host within himself. They have got themselves into a defile, where they might be finished; but too much security on the republican part will give time to his talents & indefatigableness to extricate them. We have had only middling performances to oppose him. In truth, when he comes forward, there is nobody but yourself who can meet him. His adversaries having begun the attack, he has the advantage of answering them, & remains unanswered

[3] Jefferson had no high opinion of Noah Webster. In 1801 he wrote to Madison: "I view Webster as a mere pedagogue, of very limited understanding and very strong prejudices and party passions."

himself. . . . For god's sake take up your pen, and give a fundamental reply to Curtius and Camillus.

That was written in the autumn of 1795. Already Jefferson sniffed the political air and, despite his better judgment, began to quiver for action.

3

When the election year 1796 came around it was generally known that President Washington would be no candidate for a third term. He had accepted a second term with the utmost reluctance, and now he was weary, unwell, and utterly sick of politics. Newspaper criticism made him quiver with outraged indignation, and he never wanted to be exposed to such buffeting again.[4]

The question of a successor loomed dark on the national horizon. Public opinion was so acrimonious and national unity so precarious that it was vital that the President, to keep the loose national threads together, be neither an Anglophile nor a Francophobe, neither pro-North nor pro-South. With Washington retiring and Franklin dead, it seemed impossible to find a national leader who would be above party and beyond partisanship.

It was certain that the Vice-President, John Adams, would be a candidate for the Presidency. He would have the support of the Federalists and the conservative interests in general. But who would be the candidate of the Republicans and radical-democratic elements? The answer was obvious to Jefferson's friends and followers. To the planters of the South, the farmers of the West, the mechanics of the North, there was only one man to lead the Republican forces, and that was Thomas Jef-

[4] On June 26, 1796, Washington wrote to Hamilton that he was going to retire because of a "disinclination to be longer buffeted in the public prints by a set of infamous scribblers." On July 6 he complained to Jefferson of the "grossest and most insidious misrepresentations" made in the press against his Administration. He said bitterly that the newspapers were writing about him in "such exaggerated and indecent terms as could scarcely be applied to a Nero, a notorious defaulter, or even to a common pickpocket."

ferson. The chief problem was one of persuading him to accept the candidacy.

There were no formal nominating conventions in those days. Candidates were selected and programs adopted by a few leading figures in their political parties. Some such figures, like Aaron Burr of New York, were political bosses; others, like Alexander Hamilton, were leaders by dint of sheer intellectual weight.

As early as February, 1796, James Madison, who was to the Republican party what Hamilton was to the Federalist, urged Jefferson to come out and declare himself a candidate. Madison's appeal was based upon the hitherto unuttered ground of historical destiny. Although Madison must have felt that such talk smacked more of medieval theology than of eighteenth-century rationalism, he was so eager to nail Jefferson's candidacy that he actually told him that it was his "historical task" to run for the Presidency: "I intreat you not to procrastinate, much less abandon, your historical task"—Madison underlined the word. "You owe it to yourself, to truth, to the world."

Madison's plan was to have the Republican bigwigs draft Jefferson, thereby facing him with a fait accompli. His only fear, as he confessed to his fellow lieutenant in the Republican party, James Monroe, was that their candidate might balk publicly and thereby ruin the party in the election. Still Jefferson did not budge from the ground he had taken, that he wanted neither power nor position. "Politics, a subject I never loved, & now hate," he wrote to John Adams on the last day of February, 1796.

That spring Jefferson, in a confidential and indiscreet letter to an Italian friend, Philip Mazzei, expressed his opinion that though the mass of the American people was democratic, the Government was reactionary. He added significantly that a strong fight would have to be put up to preserve the liberties of the country. This could mean only that, in his heart of hearts, he was already prepared to take up the fight. The letter is revealing:

The main body of our citizens, however, remain true to their republican principles; the whole landed interest is republican, and so is a great mass of talents. Against us are the Executive,[5] the Judiciary, two out of three branches of the legislature, all the officers of the government, all who want to be officers, all timid men who prefer the calm of despotism to the boisterous sea of liberty, British merchants & Americans trading on British capitals, speculators & holders in the banks & public funds, a contrivance invented for the purposes of corruption, & for assimilating us in all things to the rotten as well as the sound parts of the British model. It would give you a fever were I to name to you the apostates who have gone over to these heresies, men who were Samsons in the field & Solomons in the council, but who have had their heads shorn by the harlot of England. In short, we are likely to preserve the liberty we have obtained only by unremitting labors & perils. But we shall preserve them; and our mass of weight & wealth on the good side is so great, as to leave no danger that force will ever be attempted against us.

This somewhat rash communication to Mazzei boomeranged and hit Jefferson smack on the nose. Somehow it was printed in the *Paris Moniteur* (January 25, 1798) and thence, with the swiftness of a poisoned arrow, it found its way to the United States. Jefferson's enemies made a loud ado about this letter in which he dared to criticize President Washington. Jefferson perforce kept an embarrassed silence.

4

Jefferson's political seclusion and his known disinclination to be a candidate for the Presidency did not fool his opponents. They suspected him of playing a crafty game. A Federalist pamphleteer, William Loughton Smith, ridiculed Jefferson for pretending to retire. According to Mr. Smith, Jefferson's retirement was merely a trick in order to "mature his schemes of concealed ambition, and at the appointed time, come forth the undisguised candidate for the highest honors."[6]

[5] President Washington.
[6] W. L. Smith, *The Pretensions of Thomas Jefferson to the Presidency Examined; and the Charges against John Adams Refuted*, Philadelphia, October, 1796. A copy may be found in the Rare Book Room of the Library of Congress.

As the period of election was approaching, Jefferson continued to play the sphinx. He wrote no political letters to his friends and never a word to the press. "From a very early period of my life," he confided to Monroe at this time, "I had laid it down as a rule of conduct, never to write a word for the public papers." He kept them guessing.

His ambiguous attitude was such that his enemies found it easy to accuse him of hypocrisy, a charge that dogged him during his life and clung to his reputation thereafter. But there was no hypocrisy in his behavior. The rawness of politics was a torture to him, but nevertheless he could not abstain. In his wish to have nothing to do with public affairs he was utterly sincere, but he was equally sincere in his desire to see his ideas triumph. If he loved his privacy greatly, he loved justice and liberty more. He believed deeply that what he did was not only right, but in the best interest of the public. If, therefore, there was deception in his course, it was nothing more than self-deception.

Autumn came and Jefferson was still noncommittal. Silence being taken for consent, the Republicans nominated him for the Presidency. Aaron Burr of New York was selected as his running mate. The Federalists chose John Adams and Thomas Pinckney. Jefferson accepted the nomination by the simple process of not protesting against it. To the world, and even to his own family, he gave the impression of indifference. "Ambition," he told his son-in-law Randolph, "is long since dead in my mind." He was then absorbed in a new threshing machine.

A presidential election in those days was neither simple nor direct. In each State the Electoral College voted for both offices, without designating which of the candidates was to get first place (the Presidency) and which second (the Vice-Presidency). The votes were then sent to the national capital to be counted. The candidate who had the highest number of votes was declared President and the next highest, Vice-President. If the two leading candidates had an equal number of votes, the election was to be decided by the House of Representatives, wherein each State cast one vote. Communication being slow and uncertain, it took several weeks for all the votes to come in from States so far apart as Georgia and Massachusetts. The intervening period was one of doubt and anxiety.

In the middle of December Jefferson had a feeling that the election would go against him. As a political strategist, he knew that elections cannot be won without careful groundwork, and he had done practically nothing to organize the campaign. He instructed Madison that in case of a tie the Republicans should give their vote to Adams. "I pray you and authorize you fully, to solicit on my behalf that mr. Adams may be preferred."

By that time Madison, who was pulling political strings at Philadelphia, sensed that Adams would get the Presidency and Jefferson would have to content himself with second place. Knowing Jefferson's sensitiveness, Madison was worried lest he would refuse the Vice-Presidency. That would hurt his political reputation. Madison, who was looking to the future, wrote him urgently: "You are bound to abide by the event whatever it may be. On the whole, it seems *essential* that you should not refuse the station which is likely to be your lot."

Jefferson, in the meantime, half hoped that he would be defeated. To a friend he confessed that if he lost: "I protest before my god, that I shall, from the bottom of my heart, rejoice." While the Presidency was tempting in one sense, it was frightening in another. He remembered the torments suffered by George Washington under attack. He knew that the presidential office was one in which the occupant was the whipping-boy for every irresponsible critic and the target of every venal scribbler. Such a prospect was not encouraging to a man who liked to plant corn in peace and who had no lust for power. "I have no ambition to govern men; no passion which lead me to delight to ride in a storm."

As soon as Jefferson received Madison's letter about the Vice-Presidency, he hastened to assure him that he would not be hurt at getting second place. No question of pride was involved in being second to a man as esteemed as John Adams. As for the position itself, he had no strong feelings about it either way:

. . . it is the only office in the world about which I am unable to decide in my own mind whether I had rather have it or not have it. Pride does not enter into the estimate; for I think with the Romans that the general of today should be a soldier tomorrow if necessary. I can particularly have no feelings which would revolt at a secondary position to mr. Adams. I am his junior in life, was his junior in Congress, his junior in the diplomatic line, his junior lately in our civil government.

To his rival John Adams, Jefferson wrote in similar terms. Without knowing the outcome of the election, he assured Adams of his friendship and of his conviction that he, Adams, would be elected. He, Jefferson, did not want the Presidency. The letter he wrote to Adams on December 28 is remarkable in the annals of American politics:

. . . our latest intelligence from Philadelphia at present is of the 16th inst. but tho' at that date your election to the first magistracy seems not to have been known as a fact, yet with me it has never been doubted. I knew it impossible you should lose a vote north of the Delaware, and even if that of Pennsylvania should be against you in the mass, yet that you would get enough South of that to place your succession out of danger. I have never one single moment expected a different issue; and tho' I know I shall not be believed, yet it is not the less true that I have never wished it. . . .

I leave to others the sublime delights of riding in the storm, better pleased with sound sleep and a warm birth [sic] below, with the society of neighbors, friends & fellow-laborers of the earth, than of spies & sycophants. No one then will congratulate you with purer disinterestedness than myself. . . . I have no ambition to govern men. It is a painful and thankless office. . . . that your administration may be filled with glory, and happiness to yourself and advantage to us is the sincere wish of one who . . . retains still for you the solid esteem of the moments when we were working for our independence.

The result of the election was as Jefferson had anticipated. When the electoral votes were finally counted in February, 1797, it was found that John Adams had 71 votes and Jefferson 68. That made Adams President and Jefferson Vice-President.

But the surprise of the election lay in the distribution of the votes. As Jefferson analyzed the ballot he realized that he had come within a hairbreadth of being elected. A shift of two votes would have given him the Presidency. For three votes of the

narrow margin which elected Adams were actually cast in solid
Jefferson States. Adams got a single vote in each of the States of
Pennsylvania, Virginia, and North Carolina; all the rest of the
votes in those States went to Jefferson.

That gave Jefferson an illuminating idea. In a flash he realized that the election of 1796 contained the key to future success. If the South could be kept solid for the Republicans—and
there was no reason to assume that it would not be—then all
that was needed to win in 1800, and subsequently, was Pennsylvania. He had just carried thirteen out of Pennsylvania's fourteen votes. Next time his party would make sure to win them
all. "Let us," he wrote in exultation to Madison, "cultivate
Pennsylvania, & we need not fear the universe."

5

On February 20, 1797, Vice-President-elect Thomas Jefferson left Monticello for Philadelphia. He drove a phaeton to
Alexandria and then, after sending his servant Jupiter home
with the horses, took a stagecoach to the capital. He arrived at
Philadelphia two days before the inauguration.

Having lost the Presidency by three votes, Jefferson viewed
the Vice-Presidency with a considerable degree of coolness. The
Vice-Presidency was a position of honor and of obscurity. In
1789 its first occupant, Vice-President John Adams, had written
to his wife: "My country has in its wisdom contrived for me the
most insignificant office that ever the invention of man contrived
or his imagination conceived." Perhaps the office was not as bad
as all that, but Jefferson felt no glow of enthusiasm in thinking
about his job.

The inauguration was not quite Jefferson's show, and so he
planned to slip into Philadelphia unobserved and without any
fuss. But his friends were on the lookout, and as soon as they
spotted him they fired artillery in his honor. A troop of militia
accompanied him to the city, carrying a banner: JEFFERSON, THE
FRIEND OF THE PEOPLE.

On the morning of Saturday, March 4, Jefferson entered the

Senate room to be sworn in as Vice-President, and President of the Senate. The fifty-four-year-old Vice-President, dressed in black, was an uncommon figure. Still as lean and bony as in his youth, there were now streaks of gray in his reddish hair. Long-limbed, long-chinned, long-browed, speaking in a low voice and without any gestures, he gave the impression of a strongly poised man who keeps his thoughts to himself. "He spoke," a contemporary who listened to him relates, "like one who considered himself entitled to deference."

His inaugural address to the Senate was brief and tactful. Listeners noticed that his face, while thoughtful, was a mask. He did not look at his audience; occasionally he stared at the ceiling as he spoke extempore in a low-pitched voice:

Gentlemen of the Senate: Entering on the duties of the office to which I am called, I feel it incumbent on me, to apologize to this honorable House, for the insufficient manner in which I fear they may be discharged. At an earlier period of my life . . . I have been a member of legislative bodies. . . . But much time has elapsed; since that, other duties have occupied my mind; in a great degree it has lost its familiarity with this subject. . . . If a diligent attention, however, will enable me to fulfil the functions now assigned me, I may promise that diligence and attention shall be sedulously employed. . . .

He promised the "most rigorous and inflexible impartiality" in applying the rules of procedure, and concluded with a tribute to John Adams, his predecessor as Vice-President, "whose talents and integrity have been known and revered by me through a long course of years."

After the address Jefferson went to the House of Representatives to witness the inauguration of the President. The new Vice-President was seated to the right of the Speaker of the House; below and in front sat the Chief Justice and the three members of the Supreme Court. As the tall, grave figure of the outgoing President, George Washington, entered the hall tumultuous applause broke out. His successor, the stocky John Adams, was also given a vigorous ovation.

After the oath of office had been administered, President

Adams delivered an oration of great eloquence. It must have been a puzzle to Jefferson, for Adams paid warm tribute to the "hearts and judgments of an honest and enlightened people." When Adams exclaimed, "What other form of government, indeed, can so well deserve our esteem and love?" the listening Jefferson must have recalled the occasions when Adams had ridiculed democracy and sneered at popular government.[7] Was this a change of heart, or was it just political applesauce?

President Adams's inaugural address surprised many of those who knew him. Hamilton condemned it as a "lure for the favor of his opponents at the expense of his sincerity." Jefferson kept his thoughts, but was not taken in. John Adams himself considered his performance the greatest masterpiece in American history. He wrote to his wife that his oration left "scarcely a dry eye but Washington's" and that "all agreed that, taken together, it was the sublimest thing ever exhibited in America."

A dramatic little incident occurred after Adams had delivered his tear-jerking "sublimest thing." As Adams left the hall, Vice-President Jefferson had started to follow when he noticed the tall figure of George Washington rising and making ready to leave. With quick courtesy the Vice-President fell back to let Washington pass. But the outgoing President was just as courteous; he insisted that the new Vice-President precede him. The embarrassed Jefferson did so, to the accompaniment of hearty cheers.

Later in the day Jefferson had a surprise waiting for him. He was in his room at Madison's, with whom he was staying, when a visitor was announced. It was President Adams. The two men had once been close friends, but the "rumbling noise of party calumny," to borrow Adams's phrase, had spoiled their relationship. They were still on polite terms, but fear and distrust lay between them. Politically they no longer saw eye to eye. Adams came to consult the Vice-President about foreign

[7] In his "Defence of the Constitution" John Adams wrote: "The proposition that the people are the best keepers of their own liberties is not true. They are the worse conceivable, they are no keepers at all; they can neither judge, act, think, or will, as a political body."

affairs, particularly America's relations with troublesome France, and to make him a strange proposition.

"I asked Mr. Jefferson," Adams relates, "what he thought of another trip to Paris, and whether he thought the Constitution and the people would be willing to spare him for a short time."

"Are you determined to send [an ambassador] to France?" Jefferson asked.

"Yes."

"That is right," Jefferson said, "but without considering whether the Constitution will allow it or not, I am so sick of residing in Europe, that I believe I shall never go there again."

"I own," Adams replied, "I have strong doubts whether it would be legal to appoint you; but I believe no man could do the business so well. What do you think of sending Mr. Madison? Do you think he would accept of an appointment?"

"I do not know," Jefferson answered. "Washington wanted to appoint him some time ago, and kept the place open for him a long time; but he never could get him to say that he would go."

President Adams may or may not have been entirely disinterested in his effort to send one or the other of the most important Republican leaders on a mission abroad. But the plan did not work. Jefferson had no desire to leave the United States and he did not wish to encourage Madison, his ablest lieutenant, to do so. After staying a while longer, Adams left. Extraordinary as it may sound, this was the last serious conversation the two men ever had. For the next four years the President and the Vice-President lived in worlds apart. "We parted . . . good friends," Adams tells, ". . . but we consulted very little together afterwards." Jefferson gives the same testimony—"he never after that said one word to me on the subject, or ever consulted me as to any measures of the government." [8]

[8] P. A. Adet, the French Minister Plenipotentiary, in his report to the Ministry of Foreign Affairs on Dec. 31, 1796, made the following keen observation: "Adams . . . is too jealous of his power to wish to share it, he is too much attached to his own opinions to wish to discuss them with anyone; he has too high an idea of his own knowledge to ask advice.

As Alexander Hamilton observed with malice, "the lion and the lamb" were not lying down together.

6

It was a stroke of good luck for Jefferson when Adams defeated him for the Presidency. In December, 1796, when Jefferson was protesting that he did not want the office, he had made a remarkable statement. He hoped, he told a friend, that Adams would win the election, because there were black clouds on the horizon. A heavy storm was brewing, Jefferson remarked, and it might be violent enough to destroy the new President— "our Eastern friend will be struggling with the storm which is gathering over us; perhaps be shipwrecked in it." It was an uncanny prediction.

The chief source of trouble, then as today, was foreign affairs. It is not out of place here to comment that the whole notion of "isolation," riveted upon the American mind by the massive authority of George Washington, has always been based upon nothing more solid than wishful thinking. The truth is that from her remotest beginnings America has been tied to Europe. The course of American history has often been twisted or altered by European events, and only rarely has Europe been stirred up by America. Every European crisis in the last two or three centuries has shaken America. Whether this has been good or bad for the United States is a problem that belongs in the realm of philosophical speculation. An interpreter of historical happenings can only remark that the wishful concept of "isolation" has a dream-world reality like the Golden Age. It is one of the indestructible national myths.

The French Revolution had not yet run its course. Napoleon had not yet started on his career of world conquest. The Franco-British world war was only in its initial stages. And the United States, anxious to remain neutral, was already deep in trouble. In

. . . Jefferson, under Adams, will play the same role as Adams under Washington." Turner, *Correspondence of the French Ministers to the United States, 1791-1797,* p. 982.

France the revolution was slicing off heads with a lack of squeamishness that was noteworthy. The revolutionists, following a time-hallowed practice, fell to killing each other. Dictator Robespierre chopped off the pock-marked head of ex-Dictator Danton. Others severed the prissy-faced head of Dictator Robespierre. The death of these men was France's gain, but America's loss, for both had been friendly to the United States. They were succeeded by power-lusting politicians who were more interested in personal profit than in liberty and more concerned with national expansion than with equality. At the time of the Adams-Jefferson Administration a Directory of five such politicians ruled France.

The Directory objected to the Jay Treaty with England under which American ports refused to harbor French privateers but allowed the British to seize ships destined for France. To the French Government such conduct was not merely unneutral but pro-British. In retaliation, French corsairs began to play havoc with American merchant shipping. By the middle of 1797 President Adams heard an appalling report from his Secretary of State that more than three hundred American ships had been seized by the French.

That did France's popularity in the United States no good. And when in 1798 an American diplomatic mission returned from Paris with alleged proof of corruption among high French government leaders, who asked for heavy bribes before they would negotiate, there was a storm of indignation throughout the country. Hatred for France spilled over upon the heads of the Jeffersonians, who were the champions of the French Revolution in America. National anger against France was reflected in the congressional elections of 1798, when Jefferson's party lost heavily and the Federalists won control of both the House and the Senate.

The country was split into bitter pro-French and pro-British factions. A rash of hostilities, dormant since the Genet affair, broke out again on the face of America. And Jefferson, regarded as the symbol of republicanism and revolution in America, was selected as a convenient target at which the pious and the righteous could aim their shafts.

Timothy Dwight, president of Yale and a fire-eating Calvin-
ist, in a Fourth of July sermon told his hearers that a victory
of Jeffersonianism meant lustful moral depravity—"our wives
and daughters the victims of legal prostitution; soberly dishon-
ored; speciously polluted." Anti-Jeffersonian verse was nearly
as bad as the sermons that were hurled at the head of the Vice-
President. In Connecticut a millionaire poet unburdened himself of the following:

> Long had the Jeffersonian band,
> Determin'd here to take their stand,
> To us, their vile intrigues impart,
> And old Connecticut subvert. . . .
>
> See Jefferson with deep dismay,
> Shrink from the piercing eye of day,
> Lest from the tottering chair of state,
> The storm should hurl him to his fate! [9]

In all this furore Jefferson kept wisely silent. Personal antipathy for squabbling apart, he was too adroit to fall into the
temptation of defending himself against attack. He knew that
unless hostile feelings were fed by provocations they tended to
die down. Silence was in itself a weapon of defense, for among
other advantages it kept the opposition in the dark. Jefferson's
seeming invulnerability was in itself a subtle form of victory.
He told a friend at this time:

> Were I to undertake to answer the calumnies of the newspapers,
> it would be more than all my own time, & that of 20. aids could
> effect. For while I should be answering one, twenty new ones would
> be invented. I have thought it better to trust to the justice of my
> country-men, that they would judge me by what they *see* of my
> conduct on the stage where they have placed me.[10]

[9]Richard Alsop, *The Political Green-house for the Year 1798: Addressed
to the Readers of The Connecticut Courant, Jan. 1st, 1799*, pp. 4, 8.
[10] It is interesting to observe that Abraham Lincoln took an almost identical position on the subject of criticism. Lincoln said: "If I were to try to
read, much less answer, all the attacks made on me, this shop might as well
be closed for any other business. I do the very best I know how—the very
best I can; and I mean to keep doing so until the end. If the end brings me
out all right, what is said against me won't amount to anything. If the

Jefferson took the long view. Few people knew better than he that sudden squalls of popular passion die out as fast as they burst forth. He had, moreover, a steadfast faith in the good sense of the people and enough patience to wait until that sense reasserted itself. If today his party was under attack and many adherents were falling away, tomorrow the horizon would clear and the doubters would return to the fold. The conviction that time and the course of history were with the democratic forces—symbolized by Jefferson's leadership—never deserted him.

In Jefferson's opinion history was decidedly not on the side of President Adams. "John Adams is a droll figure," his great-grandson Henry once remarked, and in a sense Jefferson might have approved of the comment. The President and the Vice-President had little except the most formal social contact, and from the neutral side lines of the Senate Jefferson coolly watched Adams commit the blunders he expected him to commit. Adams was an admirable man, learned, ruggedly honest, a devoted patriot, but he was too tactless to be an effective political leader. What was worse in Jefferson's eyes, he held views that were hopelessly reactionary and counter to the stream of events that was shaping in the world.

Adams made no secret of his hatred for the French Revolution (though he liked prerevolutionary France) and of his aversion for popular government. At a dinner at which the Vice-President was present, President Adams said bluntly that democracy was nothing better than anarchy: "That as to trusting to a popular assembly for the preserv[atio]n of our liberties it was the merest chimera imaginable . . . that anarchy did more mischief in one night than tyranny in an age." President Adams also coined later an antidemocratic aphorism: "A boy of 15. who is not a democrat is good for nothing, & he is no better who is a democrat at 20."

To Jefferson this was reminiscent of King Canute sitting on the shore and bidding the waves to recede. Jefferson was convinced that the waves that were beating in the world were dem-

end brings me out wrong, ten angels swearing I was right would make no difference."—Emanuel Hertz, *Lincoln Talks*, Halcyon House, N. Y. 1941, p. 277.

ocratic, and no combination of kings or Presidents could stop them. Jefferson had no doubt that a man who could not adjust himself to the new forces was bound to be "shipwrecked." And he was not unwilling to help a little in the wrecking. He once said to Letombe, the French Consul General in Philadelphia:

Mr. Adams is vain, suspicious, obstinate, excessively egoistic, not taking advice from anyone, and is even still nettled by the preference that had been shown to Franklin at Paris . . . But his Presidency will last only five [sic] years; . . . the whole American [political] system will change with him.

7

No longer protesting that he was through with politics, Jefferson, with measured steps, went about his plans for the demolition of the Federalists and their ideology. Two methods were available. One was to tighten the Republican party into a powerful fighting instrument. The other was to pounce like a hawk upon every Federalist blunder and make the most of it.

Jefferson had a fresh, and essentially democratic, view of the function of political parties. Others, including Washington, looked upon political parties with distaste, considering them as breeding-grounds of factionalism and cradles of strife. Jefferson, however, was one of the first great political leaders to realize that political parties were essential to self-government. Opposition parties were necessary not only as vehicles for the expression of political aims and passions, but also as checks upon the party in power. Without political parties there could be no self-government:

. . . in every free and deliberating society, there must, from the nature of man, be opposite parties, and violent dissensions and discords; and one of these, for the most part, must prevail over the other for a longer or a shorter time. Perhaps this party division is necessary to induce each to watch and to delate to the people the proceedings of the other.

He was, of course, no common partisan. He told Francis Hopkinson:

. . . I never submitted the whole system of my opinions to the creed of any party of men whatever, in religion, in philosophy, in politics or in anything else where I was capable of thinking for myself. Such an addiction is the last degradation of a free and moral agent. If I could not go to heaven but with a party, I would not go there at all.

To Jefferson a political party was a democratic instrumentality to be used, not an ecclesiastical institution to be revered. There were many good men in both parties, he said. His description of the two parties that were struggling for power has an air of pleasant and almost amused objectivity:

. . . the former of these [political parties] are called Federalists, sometimes Aristocrats or monocrats & sometimes Tories . . . the latter are still republicans, whigs, Jacobins, Anarchists, disorganisers, &tc. these terms are in familiar use with most persons. . . . The most upright and conscientious characters are on both Sides [of] the question, and as to myself I can say with truth that political tenets have never taken away my esteem for a moral and good man.

Jefferson conceived a political party as a tough and yet flexible instrument. In itself a party was not sufficient to win power. It needed a cause. And the Federalists were not slow in supplying it. Led by Hamilton, the Federalists urged President Adams to declare war on France. The President refused to do so, his aim being to extort respect for the American flag rather than to shed American blood. But a considerable defense program was inaugurated. Men-of-war were built, armed merchant vessels were put to sea, the regular army was greatly increased, a marine corps was raised, $7,000,000 was borrowed, and the treaty with France was abrogated. Vice-President Jefferson signed a contract with Eli Whitney, the Yankee inventor, for 10,000 muskets. The country was in a state of undeclared war with France.

But the defense program was accompanied by a fever of belligerency, and that in turn gave rise to the well-known diseases of intolerance and political witch-hunting. Excuses for intolerance and persecution were not lacking. The country was in a state of unrest, and fear gripped the members of the ruling elements. They blamed Jefferson, the Jacobins, and, above all, the foreigners. The country harbored many refugees, exiles, and agitators born abroad. Most of them were good men and a few among them, particularly the French and the Irish, were radicals. Among the more eminent foreign-born were Thomas Cooper, the English scientist; James Thomson Callender, the Scotch political writer; Du Pont de Nemours, the French economist and founder of the present-day Du Pont dynasty; Joseph Priestley, the English chemist; Albert Gallatin, the Swiss economist and statesman. Upon the heads of many of these people there descended a torrent of Federalist calumny.

Particularly hated by the pro-British Federalists were the Irish. A contemporary anti-Irish verse, written by a Federalist writer, well illustrates the spirit of intolerance that floated like scum on that particular "wave of the future":

> Like Hessian flies, imported o'er,
> Clubs self-create infest our shore.
> And see yonder western rebel band,
> A medley mix'd from every land;
> Scotch, Irish renegadoes rude,
> From Faction's dregs fermenting brew'd;
> Misguided tools of antifeds,
> With clubs anarchical for your heads.

Mad stories were being circulated about Irishmen and Jacobins arming to invade and overthrow the United States. One Federalist Senator said that the Commonwealth of Pennsylvania was full of "United Irishmen, freemasons, and the most God-provoking democrats this side of hell!" Professional patriots grew hysterical and club ladies (or their contemporary equivalents) were trembling with expectation. The upper classes, particularly in New England, "scared easy." Good ladies expected to be murdered in their beds, or meet a fate worse than death, at the hands of the godless Frenchmen and wild Irishmen. And who was to blame? That man Jefferson!

8

The epidemic of galloping xenophobia led to repressive legislation. In the summer of 1798 Congress, against the advice of
the cooler heads in the Federalist party, passed the Alien and
Sedition acts, designed to choke off agitation and to stifle criticism of the Adams Administration. The Alien Acts authorized
the President to expel all those whom he should "judge dangerous to the peace and safety of the United States" or should have
"reasonable grounds to suspect are concerned in any treasonable
or secret machinations against the government."

The Sedition Act provided for a fine of no more than $2,000,
and imprisonment of no more than two years, for the writing,
printing, uttering, or publishing of "any false, scandalous and
malicious writing or writings against the government of the
United States . . . with intent to defame . . . or to bring
them . . . into contempt or disrepute; or to excite against
them . . . the hatred of the good people of the United States,
or to stir up sedition within the United States, or to excite any
unlawful combinations therein."

The Federalists thus went hog-wild. The Sedition Act was
so broad and inclusive that it virtually abolished the Bill of
Rights. The Federalists were out to destroy republicanism, Jeffersonianism, Jacobinism, and radicalism in one fell swoop. If
in the process they also blasted away the democratic foundations
of the republic, so much the better, they thought.

These acts showed that the ruling class was blind to the consequences of the American and French revolutions, as well as
ignorant of the democratic aspirations stirring the common folk
of America. But Jefferson was neither blind to the one nor ignorant of the other. The acts were passed right under his gavel,
so to speak. As presiding officer of the Senate, however, he scrupulously refrained from interfering. He felt that the Federalists were doing their best to commit suicide, and he did not
think it his bounden duty to stop them. When the chariot of
one's enemy is galloping headlong toward the abyss it would be

the height of quixotism to arrest its plunge by throwing oneself in front of the wheels.

Not that he could have checked the outburst of reaction even if he had tried. To Jefferson's Republicans, the Alien and Sedition acts were, naturally, poison. Some of the more responsible Federalists agreed. John Marshall, for example, considered these acts useless and unwise. Alexander Hamilton, despite his hatred for Jeffersonianism and democracy, likewise feared the effects of the repressive legislation. "Let us not establish a tyranny," Hamilton urged. "Energy is a very different thing from violence." But these men were powerless to check the hysteria.

While Hamilton feared the consequences of the acts, Jefferson coolly waited for their effects. "For my own part," he said, "I consider those laws as merely an experiment on the American mind, to see how far it will bear an avowed violation of the constitution." He was certain there would be a terrific kickback. If the judges should try to execute the laws, which he regarded as infamous, he was convinced that the people would rise in their wrath and sweep the Federalists into the ash can of history.

9

Jefferson did not have long to wait for the reaction and counter-reaction to come. With the passing of the Sedition Act a "Federalist reign of terror," to quote Jefferson's words, descended upon the land. Within a few months after the act was passed, the Federalist judges created a sufficient number of martyrs to the cause of liberty to do Jefferson a world of good. That is what he had expected.

The first man to be convicted under the act, in October, 1798, was Matthew Lyon, a Jeffersonian Congressman from Vermont. He had been born in Ireland and had a fine record as a patriot and a soldier in Washington's army during the Revolution. Lyon's conviction was typical and scandalous. The indictment charged him with the intent "to stir up sedition, and to bring the President and government . . . into contempt." Actually he had not stirred up sedition; he had merely committed lèse majesté by criticizing President Adams. He had printed a statement that he could not support Adams when he saw "every consideration of the public welfare swallowed up in a continual grasp for power, in an unbounded thirst for ridiculous pomp, foolish adulation and selfish avarice," and "men of real merit daily turned out of office for no other cause but independency of sentiment," and the "sacred name of religion employed as a state engine to make mankind hate and persecute each other." This language may have been somewhat intemperate, but it was not treasonable—at least not under the Bill of Rights.

But Justice Patterson of the United States Supreme Court and the jury thought otherwise. In his defense, Lyon said that the Sedition Act was unconstitutional, his publication innocent, and its contents true. Point-blank he asked the Judge whether he had not often dined with President Adams and observed "his ridiculous pomp and parade." The Judge denied it, and instructed the jury to ignore the constitutional validity of the act (since juries could not pass upon that) and to decide merely whether the defendant had published "seditiously." The jury convicted Lyon and sentenced him to four months in prison and $1,000 fine. This conviction of a Revolutionary soldier, a patriot, and a member of Congress came as a tremendous shock to the nation. It was to be the first nail in the Federalist coffin.

The second conviction also took place in Vermont and was directly connected with Matthew Lyon. Anthony Haswell, the editor of the *Vermont Gazette,* printed an advertisement which Lyon had inserted. It was for a lottery to raise money to pay Lyon's fine. It stated that Lyon was "holden by the oppressive hand of usurped power in a loathsome prison, deprived almost of the right of reason, and suffering all the indignities which can be heaped upon him by a hard-hearted savage [the U. S. Marshal] who has, to the disgrace of Federalism, been elevated to a station where he can satiate his barbarity on the misery of his victims."

For this Haswell was indicted by the same judge and jury that convicted Lyon. Haswell offered evidence to prove that Lyon was being brutally treated by the Marshal. But the jury of New Englanders had no admiration for republicans and no love for foreigners. The English-born Haswell, father of seventeen children, was sentenced to two months in jail and $200 fine.

Still another victim of the "Federalist reign of terror" was Thomas Cooper, the English-born educator and scientist. In his capacity as an editor of a pro-Jeffersonian Pennsylvania newspaper, Cooper had criticized President Adams, saying that he was "hardly in the infancy of political mistake" and other such generalities. For this act of lèse majesté Cooper was indicted.

A student of the law, Cooper spoke in his own defense. He addressed the jury in dignified terms, pointing out that he had published only the truth, that his criticism was legitimate, and that he had expressed his opinions as a member of a lawful political party. It did him no good. In charging the jury, Justice Samuel Chase of the United States Supreme Court went out of his way to praise the Sedition Act—which it was not within his province or jurisdiction to do—and to attack the falsity of Cooper's statements. The jury found Cooper guilty—six months in prison and $400 fine.

Perhaps the most scandalous case under the Sedition Act took place in Jefferson's own Virginia. In Richmond, James Thomson Callender, a Scottish-born political writer, was indicted for the grave crime of criticizing President Adams. What made the case sensational, however, was the behavior of the judge. Three of the greatest lawyers in Virginia—William Wirt, Thomas Nicholas, and George Hay—volunteered to defend Callender. But Supreme Court Justice Chase, the same one who had convicted Cooper, was not impressed. In the court he did everything to show his contempt for the lawyers. He cut them short, cracked jokes, and made them shut up. When William Wirt started to tell the jury that the Sedition Act was unconstitutional, Justice Chase snapped, "Take your seat, sir." George Hay, the other lawyer, was so angered at the Justice's bullying tactics and insulting interruptions that he refused to go on with the case. Callender was convicted, sentenced to nine months in jail, and assessed a $200 fine. Virginia rocked with indignation, and Jefferson chalked off another mark against the Federal judiciary.

10

Jefferson was fighting mad. The Sedition Act, being a frontal assault upon the Bill of Rights and civil liberties, threatened to castrate the democratic features in the Constitution. For no one knew better than Jefferson that the right of free speech was basic to all other democratic rights. At the point where free opinion ceases, tyranny begins.

All over the country men were being jailed, fined, and persecuted because they dared to express their opinions freely. If that were permitted to continue, then republicanism was dead and freedom was dead and the United States nothing but a despotic oligarchy.

If this goes down we shall immediately see attempted another act of Congress, declaring that the President shall continue in office during life, reserving to another occasion the transfer of the succession to his heirs, and the establishment of the Senate for life.

As Vice-President, Jefferson could not openly do very much about the persecutions under the Sedition Act, but as leader of his party he could not abstain from acting. Throughout the country men and women—all those who were not zealous Federalists—looked up to Jefferson to raise his voice in protest and to supply the leadership against the raging reaction.

Jefferson acted in his own indirect way. Secretly, in collaboration with such friends and aides as George Nicholas and James Madison, he drew up a manifesto, the so-called Kentucky Resolution, which elaborated the theory of States' rights as a club with which to beat the Federalists. The theory was based upon three basic propositions—that the Federal Government was created by the individual States; that it was the agent of the States; and that its actions were subject to criticism, or even nullification, by the States. Underlying the long resolution there was a tone, faint but discernible, of rebellion, a threat of ultimate secession in the face of Federal tyranny—"these and successive acts of the same character, unless arrested at the threshold, [will] necessarily drive these states into revolution and blood."

The Kentucky Resolution was adopted, with virtual unanimity, by the Kentucky legislature. In Virginia, a similar resolution, drawn up by James Madison, was also overwhelmingly carried in the legislature. These resolutions were the first heavy shots fired in the war on the Federalists. That Jefferson was the instigator and coauthor of the resolutions few people knew, but many suspected.

Jefferson continued to preside over the Senate with scrupulous impartiality and impressive serenity. Only his most intimate friends knew of his plans. To many lieutenants of his party throughout the country he wrote letters of advice and encouragement, urging them to keep calm and steady. That he was a candidate for the Presidency, the center and hope of resistance to the Federalists, was a wide-open secret. But his was a low-visibility strategy that disconcerted the opposition. He left no crack open into which they could shoot an arrow.

In the darkest days of Federalist reaction Jefferson's function was that of inspirer, stimulator, and clarifier. He wanted his friends and followers to understand the basic issues involved and to act upon them in the light of reason. His object was to educate the people, so that they could not fall victim to phony arguments and false appeals. For this purpose he wrote long letters which he knew would be read in circles, around stoves, in stores, in taverns, in shops.

One of his letters, written to his vacillating republican friend Elbridge Gerry of Massachusetts in January, 1799, is a fine example of epistolary precampaign literature. It sets the keynote to his aims, explains his objectives, and states his basic beliefs. One might entitle it "Credo of a Democrat."

I am for preserving to the States the powers not yielded by them to the Union . . . and I am not for transferring all the powers of the States to the general government. . . .

I am for a government rigorously frugal & simple, applying all the possible savings of the public revenue to the discharge of the national debt; and not for a multiplication of officers & salaries merely to make partisans, & for increasing, by every device, the public debt, on the principle of it's being a public blessing.

I am for relying, for internal defence, on our militia solely, till actual invasion, and for such a naval force only as may protect our coasts and harbors from such depredations as we have experienced; and not for a standing army in time of peace, which may overawe the public sentiment; nor for a navy, which, by it's own expenses and the eternal wars in which it will implicate us, will grind us with public burthens, & sink us under them.

I am for free commerce with all nations; political connection with none; & little or no diplomatic establishment. And I am not for linking ourselves by new treaties with the quarrels of Europe; entering that field of slaughter to preserve their balance, or joining in the confederacy of kings to war against the principles of liberty.

I am for freedom of religion, & against all maneuvres to bring about a legal ascendancy of one sect over another: for freedom of the press, & against all violations of the constitution to silence by force & not by reason the complaints or criticisms, just or unjust, of our citizens against the conduct of their agents.

And I am for encouraging the progress of science in all it's branches; and not for raising a hue and cry against the sacred name of philosophy; for awing the human mind by stories of raw-head & bloody bones to a distrust of its own vision, & to repose implicitly on that of others; to go backwards instead of forwards to look for improvement; to believe that government, religion, morality, & every other science were in the highest perfection in ages of the darkest ignorance, and that nothing can ever be devised more perfect than what was established by our forefathers.

To these I will add, that I was a sincere well-wisher to the success of the French revolution, and still wish it may end in the establishment of a free & well-ordered republic; but I have not been insensible under the atrocious depredations they have committed on our commerce.

He concluded this statement with a moving declaration of pure and disinterested patriotism:

The first object of my heart is my own country. In that is embarked my family, my fortune, & my own existence. I have not one farthing of interest, nor one fibre of attachment out of it, nor a single motive of preference of any one nation to another, but in proportion as they are more or less friendly to us.

CHAPTER XII

Candidate

1800

THE CAMPAIGN of 1800 was unlike anything ever known in America before. For sheer virulence and bitterness it has hardly been surpassed since. It was an all-out campaign, with both sides wielding every club that was handy. It was not a gentlemanly campaign, though gentlemen were the candidates. The gloves were off. On the Federalists' side it was a struggle to preserve power for the rich and the privileged. On the Jeffersonian side it was a battle to keep America a democracy, with liberty and opportunity for all the people.

Each side knew what was at stake. The upper classes, frozen in their status and narrow in their outlook, meant to hang on to what they had, not yield an inch. The poorer people hoped for a better life, and wanted to keep the doors of freedom and opportunity open. Feeling ran deep on both sides. The hate-filled bitterness of the reactionaries, always easily stirred in a crisis, was matched by the ardent militancy of the humble.

Jefferson was in dead earnest. It was a resolute battle for the dream of his life, for the ideas and hopes that he had written into the Declaration of Independence twenty-four years back. Jefferson was afraid that a Federalist triumph would mean a victory for the enemies of freedom, a destruction of the Bill of Rights, and possibly a disruption of the Union. As Claude Bowers has said in a fine phrase: "Jefferson was not playing ping-pong—he was out with a meat cleaver."

There was a surprising political awareness on the part of

simple artisans, farmers, workers, and little people in general. To them, as to millions of later Americans, America "was promises." Adams, Hamilton, and other conservatives despised the common people, and made no secret of their contempt. But Tom Jefferson championed their cause and spoke in their name. He not only formulated their inarticulate hopes, but also believed in their intelligence, trusted their judgment, respected their character. Tom Jefferson wanted every man to have a chance for life, liberty, and the pursuit of happiness. And every humble man from Maine to Georgia knew that Jefferson voiced his sentiments.

The common people's trust in Jefferson is something to marvel at. He was famous, to be sure, but he was personally known to only a few. Except for his immediate neighbors, he had literally no contact with the masses, and he sought none. Unlike Patrick Henry, he had never made any public speeches. The people who were behind him had never seen him. They had never heard him speak. They had never shaken his hand. And yet to hundreds of thousands of them Tom Jefferson was a symbol and a hope.

Here was a great paradox. The aristocrat of impeccable taste and of exquisite manners, the hypersensitive gentleman who was shy of meeting with the common people in the mass, was the man who had devoted his life to the popular cause. He was the strangest leader of democracy ever known.

2

He was also, in the strictest and noninvidious sense of the word, the master politician of the age. For sheer political adroitness Jefferson has probably never been excelled in America, except possibly by Abraham Lincoln, whose physical and mental resemblance to Jefferson, frequently overlooked, is startling. Like the far better known Lincoln, Jefferson had the knack of crystallizing popular ideas and aspirations in unforgettable words. Again like Lincoln, Jefferson had the priceless gift of knowing how to get along smoothly with those who were ambitious for power and prestige. And like Lincoln, Jefferson knew when and where to strike the telling blow.

The way Jefferson organized the campaign of 1800 was a masterpiece of political strategy. Every move was calculated in advance, with an eye to the maximum political effectiveness. Each step was carefully weighed by Jefferson's chief aides, particularly Madison and Monroe. No possible advantage was overlooked; no flank was left exposed. In every section of the Union key figures were set in motion by the Vice-President. They kept in touch with Jefferson by correspondence, and occasionally through personal contact. Among these men were Albert Gallatin and Thomas McKean of Pennsylvania; Charles Pinckney of South Carolina; John Taylor of North Carolina; Robert R. Livingston and George Clinton of New York. They made up a sort of Jeffersonian general staff.

The actual work of winning over the voters and of keeping them in line was entrusted to local agitators and political bosses. Jefferson carefully cultivated and inspired these men, writing them letters which contained judicious mixtures of advice and encouragement. They were a tough lot, used to shouting their arguments in taverns and country stores. But they were as American as homespun, stanch and aggressive individualists who despised the silk-breeched gentry. Jefferson was brought up among such men, and he had a deep-rooted appreciation of their worth. His father had been such a homespun frontier type of American. And if the Randolph in Jefferson winced a bit at the manners of some of his lieutenants, he may have reflected that he was not taking them to a ball. He was taking them to victory.

They were hard-bitten, hard-driving men, these Jeffersonian leaders. In North Carolina, Timothy Bloodworth, a "red Republican," did yeoman work for the Jeffersonian cause. Bloodworth rose from the masses. He had no education or social position. Starting as a cobbler, he ended as a United States Senator. In Georgia there was James Jackson, another man without birth or position. By sheer will and ability Jackson became a lieutenant-colonel in the Revolutionary War, Governor of Georgia, and United States Senator. He had been born in England and was a stout democrat. Perhaps the toughest political boss in the Jeffersonian party was Benjamin Austin of Boston. Austin of Boston was a member of the Massachusetts Senate and a first-rate democratic speaker. A lean, lank, lantern-jawed figure, he was the terror of the blue-blooded Federalists. He would flood town meetings with his followers, men "who looked as if they had been collected from all the Jails on the continent," according to John Quincy Adams.

3

Jefferson also made systematic use of the press and the printed word. As far back as 1799, one year before the campaign actually got under way, Jefferson wrote to Madison:

We are sensible that this summer is the season for systematic energies and sacrifices. The engine is the press. Every man must lay his purse and his pen under contribution. . . . Let me pray and beseech you to set apart a certain portion of every post-day to write what may be proper for the public.

Note the expression "what may be proper for the public." It is a good definition of propaganda, for which Jefferson had a twentieth-century appreciation.

The newspapers in those days were not altogether clean instruments. Both the Republican and the Federalist newspapers were unrestrained and vindictive. Their contents, after being read by a few, spread by word of mouth, gathering poison from tongue to tongue. An example of the journalism of those days, taken from William Cobbett's *Political Censor*, is the following: "that lump of walking tallow, streaked with lamp-black, that calls itself Samuel F. Bradford, has the impudence to say that my wardrobe consisted of my old regimentals."

The press was bad, but self-righteous Federalists made it out to be worse than it was. They attacked the newspapers, particularly the Jeffersonian ones, as crude and vulgar. Noah Webster, the lexicographer who edited the stuffy *Minerva*, solemnly "averred" that no government "can be durable and quiet under the licentiousness of the press that now disgraces our country."

John Ward Fenno, who succeeded his father as editor of the dull and pedantic *Gazette of the United States,* waxed hot when he contemplated the state of the press. Wrote he wrathfully:

The American newspapers are the most base, false, servile and venal publications, that ever polluted the fountains of society—their editors the most ignorant, mercenary, and vulgar automatons that ever were moved by the continually rusting wires of sordid mercantile avarice.

A New England editor, Joseph Dennie of the Walpole (New Hampshire) *Farmer's Weekly Museum,* agreed with his Federalist colleague of Philadelphia. Quoth Dennie:

. . . the majority of American newspapers fully deserve the severity of Mr. Fenno's reproof. He has described a large class of our Journals with truth, accuracy and acumen. From a most painful experience of four years, the writer of this article can abundantly testify to the plagiarisms, mawkishness, dreariness, and gross folly of many of those weekly things, which profess to convey novelty and amusement to gaping readers. The fact is, there are three or four good papers published, upon which all the rest live.

But Jefferson was not running a school of journalism. He was running for political office. To him the press, with all its shortcomings, was a weapon in the battle for democracy. He planned his campaign from behind the scenes, striking swift, invisible blows. When he suggested to one of his lieutenants that he distribute several dozen copies of a certain pamphlet in "every county comm[itt]ee in the state," he added a warning that his sponsorship of the pamphlet should be kept secret. "You will readily see what a handle would be made of my advocating their contents." Secrecy was his strategy and his predilection. In describing the political situation in North Carolina, he explained that Republican propaganda there should be carried out under cover. "The medicine for that State must be very mild & secretly administered. But nothing should be spared to give them true information."

He used pamphlets like ammunition. One of the Jefferson-inspired pamphlets was Thomas Paine's *Rights of Man.* Jefferson also dropped hints and suggestions into the ears of political organizers and editors. One of his ideas which speakers and writers were asked to take up and hammer at was government expenditure. Jefferson suggested to his followers that they keep on assailing the Adams Administration on the ground of costliness and extravagance. This, he said coolly, would "open the eyes of the nation." It did.

The Jefferson writers—Freneau, Duane, Callender, Cooper—and the Jefferson organizers played together like a superlative orchestra under the master's baton. And when the campaign was over, the outmaneuvered and outgeneraled John Adams was to pay bitter tribute to the political skill of the Jeffersonians: "A group of foreign liars, encouraged by a few ambitious native gentlemen, have discomfited the education, the talents, the virtues, and the property of the country."

4

In the spring of 1800, after Congress adjourned, Jefferson and Burr were unanimously nominated by a congressional caucus. "The campaign," Jefferson wrote to John W. Eppes, "will be as hot as that of Europe, but happily we deal in ink only; they in blood."

In taverns and courthouses, at meetings and barbecues, men began to exchange arguments, handbills, and blows. But the central figure around whom all the heat was generated never made any public appearance. He remained at Monticello busy with his nail factory and his brick kiln. He made no speeches, shook no hands, but calmly continued with his routine. A young man named Thomas Lee Shippen visited Jefferson during the campaign and was struck by his charm and serenity. Jefferson invited Shippen to join him and Madison in a little outing. There was no campaign talk or worry. "I never knew men more agreeable than they were," Shippen tells. "We talked and dined and strooled [sic] and rowed ourselves in boats, and feasted on delicious crabs."

Jefferson needed all the philosophy and self-confidence he

could muster to ride through the campaign storm. He was made the target of such abuse and defamation as was never before heaped upon any public figure in America. The Federalists portrayed him as a thief, a coward, a libertine, an infidel, and an atheist. The religious issue was dragged out, and stirred up flames of hatred and intolerance. Clergymen, mobilizing their heaviest artillery of thunder and brimstone, threatened Christians with all manner of dire consequences if they should vote for the "infidel" from Virginia. This was particularly true in New England, where the clergy stood like Gibraltar against Jefferson. In Virginia itself the clergy had no overpowering influence. In Jefferson's home State gentlemen were inclined to be agnostic, and ordinary folk were imbued neither with theological prescience nor with intolerance. There is the anecdote about the Reverend Mr. Garrettson, a Methodist clergyman, who while traveling through the Virginia backwoods met a man and asked him whether he was acquainted with Jesus Christ. "Sir," came the unexpected reply, "I know not where the gentleman lives."

The most violent attack on Jefferson's religion was made by William Linn in a pamphlet entitled *Serious Considerations on the Election of a President.* Linn, who was a Dutch Reformed minister in New York City, accused Jefferson of the heinous crimes of not believing in divine revelation and of a design to destroy religion and "introduce immorality." Linn set out to show that Jefferson was a "true infidel," quoting from Jefferson's writings, real and imaginary, to prove his case. He quoted Jefferson as saying that "It does me no injury for my neighbor to say there are twenty gods, or no god. It neither picks my pocket nor breaks my leg." [1] Linn wrote that Jefferson once pointed to a dilapidated church and remarked, "*It is good enough for him that was born in a manger.*" Such a remark, the Reverend Mr. Linn concluded, could "issue from the lips of no other than a deadly foe to His name and His cause." Does Jefferson ever go to church? the Reverend asked. "How does he spend the Lord's day? Is he known to worship with any

---

[1] Linn quoted correctly. The quotation is to be found in Jefferson's *Notes on Virginia,* Query XVII.

denomination of christians?" The answer was a resounding
NO!

Let the first magistrate to be a professed infidel, and infidels will
surround him. Let him spend the sabbath in feasting, in visiting or
receiving visits, in riding abroad, but never in going to church; and
to frequent public worship will become unfashionable. Infidelity will
become the prattle from the highest to the lowest condition in life,
and universal desoluteness [sic] will follow.

An infidel like Jefferson could not, should not, be elected.
The Reverend Mr. Linn concluded his pamphlet with a fiery
appeal to Christians to defeat the "infidel" from Virginia:

Will you then, my fellow-citizens, with all this evidence . . .
vote for Mr. Jefferson? . . . As to myself, were Mr. Jefferson
connected with me by the nearest ties of blood, and did I owe him a
thousand obligations, I would not, and could not vote for him. No;
sooner than stretch forth my hand to place him at the head of the
nation, "Let mine arms fall from my shoulder blade, and mine arm
be broken from the bone." [2]

The Jeffersonian side did not make the mistake of underestimating the effectiveness of Linn's pamphlet. Cogently stated,
it undoubtedly sounded convincing to thousands of sincere
Christians. In an age when ministers were the most potent members of the community, an accusation of infidelity was dynamite.
The pamphlet put Jefferson on the defensive and made it necessary for his followers to clear his religious character. A number
of vigorous pamphlets were issued in reply to Linn's *Serious
Considerations*. Perhaps the best of them was Tunis Wortman's
*A Solemn Address to the Christians and Patriots upon the Ap-
proaching Election of a President of the United States*. Wortman started out by establishing the propositions that Jefferson
was a fine republican citizen and a good Christian:

That the charge of deism . . . is false, scandalous and malicious
—That there is not a single passage in the Notes on Virginia, or any

[2] Job XXXI, 22. Another pamphlet that repeated Linn's charges was
John Mitchell Mason's *The Voice of Warning to Christians in the Ensuing
Election*. It was a trumpet blow in Zion, asking for the defeat of the Vir-
ginia "infidel."

of Mr. Jefferson's writings, repugnant to christianity; but on the contrary, in every respect, favourable to it.

Wortman praised Jefferson, whom he described as the "sage of Monticelli" [sic], as a great scholar, a great patriot, a great scientist, and a great statesman. He pointed out that the religious issue was nothing more than what a later generation has called a "red herring," in order to confuse and mislead the people. His conclusion was eloquent:

People of America, patriots and electors, be assured that it is not religion, but the state which is in jeopardy—Jefferson, who has been the object of so much unmanly but unavailing calumny, is one of the strongest bulwarks of its safety; remember that at this moment, your liberty, your constitution, your families; your children, the fate of the empire, depend upon the rectitude of your decision.

De Witt Clinton, Jefferson's New York ally, likewise came to his defense in *A Vindication of Thomas Jefferson, against the Charges Contained in a Pamphlet Entitled "Serious Considerations."* Clinton's aim was to make out the difficult case that "we have the strongest reasons to believe that he is a *real Christian.*" He argued that Jefferson was a highly moral man of lofty character. "I feel persuaded that he is a believer." "I feel happy to hail him a Christian." And he clinched his argument with

And let me add . . . that he has for a long time supported out of his own private revenues, a worthy minister of the Christian church—an instance of liberality not to be met with in any of his rancorous enemies, whose love of religion seems principally to consist in their unremitted endeavors to degrade it into a handmaid of faction.

Another defender of Jefferson's religious character was John James Beckley, whose *Address to the People of the United States* lauded Jefferson for having established the Statute of Religious Freedom in Virginia:

Read, ye fanatics, bigots, and religious hypocrites, of whatsoever clime or country ye be—and you, base calumniators, whose efforts to traduce are the involuntary tribute of envy to a character more pure and perfect than your own, read, learn, and practice the RELI-

GION OF JEFFERSON, as displayed in the sublime truths and inspired language of HIS ever memorable "Act for establishing religious freedom."

In days when religion was firmly tied to morals, a man accused of irreligion was automatically branded a moral outcast. If you did not believe in God, so the clergy argued, you were ipso facto a thief and a seducer. If you did not attend church regularly, you naturally hated your mother and beat your wife.

They accused Jefferson of everything. If the sermons of the clergy were to be believed, there was no crime in the calendar of which Jefferson was not guilty and no unspeakable evil which he had not committed. One clergyman, the Reverend Cotton Mather Smith, accused Jefferson of having obtained his property by fraud and of having robbed widows and orphans. Others warned their congregations that their Bibles would be confiscated if the Republican ogre were elected. They compared him to Rehoboam, the evil son and successor of King Solomon, from whom the ten tribes revolted:

And Rehoboam the son of Solomon reigned in Judah. Rehoboam was forty and one years old when he began to reign, and he reigned seventeen years in Jerusalem, the city which the Lord did choose out of all the tribes of Israel, to put his name there. And his mother's name was Naamah an Ammonitess.

And Judah did evil in the sight of the Lord, and they provoked him to jealousy with their sins which they had committed, above all that their fathers had done.

For they also built them high places, and images, and groves, on every high hill, and under every green tree.

And there were also sodomites in the land: and they did according to all the abominations of the nations which the Lord cast out before the children of Israel.

The clerical fulminations did not budge Jefferson from his determination to ignore them. He had too great a contempt for his detractors to dignify them with a reply. To Uriah McGregory of Connecticut he wrote:

From the moment that a portion of my fellow citizens looked towards me with a view to one of their highest offices, the floodgates of calumny have been opened upon me.' . . . I know that I might have filled the courts of the United States with actions for these slanders, and have ruined perhaps many persons who are not innocent. But this would be no equivalent to the loss of character. I leave them therefore, to the reproof of their own consciences.

But from friends he could not conceal his anger at the clerical character-assassins. At the height of the campaign of vilification, Jefferson gave voice to one of his angriest yet immortal statements. In a letter to Dr. Rush he wrote: "they [the clergy] believe that any portion of power confided to me, will be exerted in opposition to their schemes. And they believe rightly; for *I have sworn upon the altar of god, eternal hostility against every form of tyranny over the mind of man.*" [3]

The religious issue—freedom versus intolerance—undoubtedly had its educational effect upon many people. Whether it influenced any votes is another question, and one that it is not possible to answer either way. It is certain, however, that so much mud was hurled at Jefferson that some of it stuck. For generations many communities, particularly in the North, continued to regard Thomas Jefferson as Antichrist. As late as 1830 the Philadelphia Public Library refused to keep any works dealing with the life or writings of Jefferson. In New England he was pursued by relentless clerical hatred. A Puritan clergyman during a baptism asked the father for the child's name. "Thomas Jefferson," the father replied. "No such unchristian name!" thundered the clergyman. "John Adams, I baptize thee."

5

The religious question that was raked up was only a side issue. The real struggle was over popular government. It was a battle for democracy.

The frankness with which the opposing sides faced the issue of democracy versus oligarchy is astonishing to modern ears that are accustomed to sounds which do not mean what they

---

[3] Italics mine. S.K.P. Incidentally, these words are engraved on the Jefferson monument now in the process of completion in Washington, D. C.

seem to mean. In 1800 the men who fought the war of democracy against privilege, and of privilege against democracy, minced no words; they said exactly what they thought. Both sides hated and feared each other too much to pretend to have any other feelings. In the Jeffersonian ranks there were men who did not conceal their conviction that the moneybags and the aristocrats were ripe for the ax. Among the Federalists there was a blunt contempt for and fierce hatred of the "rabble."

It took courage to be a democrat, a follower of Jefferson. A democrat had no caste and no character. He was not respectable, did not belong to the best clubs, wore no silk on Sunday. A democrat, a follower of Jefferson, was a common man, an ordinary American who worked with his hands and hoped for a better life. The Federalists regarded such men as the lowest dregs of humanity. Henry Adams, the great-grandson of John Adams, has given the following mental picture of Jeffersonian democrats as conceived by the Federalists:

Every dissolute intriguer, loose-liver, forger, false-coiner, and prison-bird; every hare-brained, loud-talking demagogue; every speculator, scoffer, and atheist,—was a follower of Jefferson; and Jefferson was himself the incarnation of their theories.

The Federalists, terrified at the prospect of propertyless people winning the campaign, made the mistake of overlooking an elementary fact in arithmetic—a fact that Lincoln well knew when he said that God must love the common people because he made so many of them. The Federalist campaign was based upon an appeal to men of property and a searing contempt for men without much property. It happened that men without much property were in the majority.

The Federalists made another mistake: every time they attacked Jefferson as a leader of democracy, they identified him with democracy. And the common people were quick to draw the conclusion, if any were needed, that Jefferson must be their friend, since he too believed in self-government for ordinary folk.

The Federalists indulged in a spree of hatred for democracy that intoxicated them. They marshaled antidemocratic arguments that appealed to an upper-class minority which needed no convincing. They did not reach, or even try to reach, the common people. Dennie's *Portfolio* wrote:

A democracy is scarcely tolerable at any period of national history. Its omens are always sinister. . . . It is on its trial here, and the issue will be civil war, desolation, and anarchy. No wise man but discerns its imperfections, no good man but shudders at its miseries, no honest man but proclaims its fraud, and no brave man but draws his sword against its force.

This was reprinted in all the Federalist newspapers.

Everywhere Federalists struck out savagely. Fisher Ames, the New England lawyer, openly raged against the poor and the underprivileged. To him viciousness and poverty were interchangeable terms. The duty of government, he exclaimed, was to protect property against the enemies of society, the poor. His hatred for Jefferson and Madison, the leaders of the democratic forces, was apoplectic. He called them "those apostles of the race-track and the cock-pit."

At a dinner in New York City, Alexander Hamilton struck his hand on the table and shouted to a man who had expressed a democratic sentiment: "Your people, sir,—your people is a great *beast!*"

The *Columbian Centinel* of Boston wrote that the State of Virginia was full of "mad Democrats" and that the "common people are . . . cruelly misled." This Federalist newspaper issued frantic warnings against the insidious wiles of the Jeffersonian "Jacobins":

By their art they can make *black* appear *white* even to sound Federal eyes; this shows in a striking light their *actual* influence and our *real* danger. . . . Let not Federalists then any longer confide in their boasted superiority of numbers. What are thousands of honest, unsuspicious, inactive, sleeping souls, opposed to a few secret, insidious and even active spirits combined against them! . . . Be aroused from your lethargy, before death, *unexpected* death, overtake you . . . Your farms, your houses, your wives, and your children, will be miserable comforters, when the day of your political salvation is no more!

As the election of Jefferson seemed to be more and more of a certainty, the hysteria of the Federalist press redoubled in violence. The *Columbian Centinel* exclaimed that the election of Jefferson was "equivalent to a Revolution" and warned the country: "Citizens beware, you are on the margin of a precipice." An appeal was made to the citizens to "crush the monster" before it was too late.

The *Centinel* refused to consider that Jefferson had any right to run for the Presidency. It even denied that he had had much to do with the Declaration of Independence:

Let us attend to a few of the arguments of these wise-acres. . . . the sum total of Mr. Jefferson's merit, his paramount and indefensible claim to the President's chair, is his concern in the Declaration of Independence. What concern? Did he move it in Congress? No— Mr. Adams was the first who made the motion. . . . He signed it then? To be sure and so did all the members present. . . . On the whole, it is fair to presume that the credit attached to it as a *composition*, principally belongs to Mr. Jefferson. So the facts stand. JOHN ADAMS and others made the independence of America. THOMAS JEFFERSON put their doings on paper. "By gar," said ——, "it was the Frenchman who invented the ruffle for the shirt." "True," said John Bull, "but it was the Englishman who put the shirt to it."

"The Jeffersoniad," an anonymously written essay in thirteen installments, raked Jefferson's character with fanatical savagery. It smeared the Republican candidate as an anarchist and a coward, and even went so far as to start a hopeful rumor of his death.

During the height of the campaign the *Columbian Centinel* printed a bitter "Creed of a Full Blooded Jacobin." The word "Jacobin," it should be recalled, carried the connotation of "Communist" today. The "Creed" summarized all the evil things that Jefferson and the Jeffersonian were supposed to believe in, including universal suffrage. It read:

I believe in Thomas Jefferson, the father, and founder of our sect; the author of the first attack on Christianity in this country, the promoter of French principles, the advocate of gallic depredations, and sworn foe of Great Britain:—I believe that the Federal Constitution was begotten in fraud and conceived in corruption—

that it is inimical to the rights of man. . . . I believe in the indiscriminate right of suffrage,[4] the perpetual rotation in office, and the frequency of revolution.

There was a concerted drive to deprive Jefferson of every shred of credit as a patriot. This was true even of the Southern Federalists. On July 4 the Federalists of Charleston, South Carolina, celebrating Independence Day, praised "our worthy President" John Adams for his work on the Declaration of Independence. Jefferson's work was minimized,´ so the *State Gazette* of July 7 reports:

Thomas Jefferson was accredited for the elegance of language with which it was clothed; and much more than that he never merited, for that excepted, the American people are unacquainted with any acts which can exalt him or benefit him.

Even in Jefferson's home State there were some publications that accused him of fostering disorder. The *Virginia Herald* of Fredericksburg on July 1 attacked the Jeffersonians as anarchists and worse:

What security have we for the protection and preservation of our properties, our liberties, our lives? None. Are the people . . . determined forever to shut their eyes and ears against truth, and to countenance men who wantonly and contumeliously trample justice under foot, and whose object palpably is to subvert all regular government, and to throw our country into anarchy and distraction?

6

During all this excitement, throughout the spring and the summer of 1800, Jefferson stayed home at Monticello and attended to his private affairs. He neither orated nor campaigned. The only evidences of his participation in the campaign were a gift of $50 to the political writer James T. Callender (victim of

[4] This was really true. Jefferson did believe in universal suffrage. On Aug. 14, 1800, he wrote to Jeremiah Moor: . . . "my opinion has always been in favor of it [a general suffrage]. . . . I believe we may lessen the danger of buying and selling votes, by making the number of voters too great for any means of purchase: I may further say that I have not observed men's honesty to increase with their riches."

the Sedition Act) and a subscription to an extra newspaper or two. Otherwise he followed his routine with unshatterable serenity. He never doubted the outcome of the struggle.

In the latter part of November Jefferson left Monticello for Washington, which (since June) was the capital of the nation. As Vice-President, he had to be in Washington for the opening of the Congress. In the swampy village on the Potomac Jefferson awaited the result of the election with cool confidence. In this he differed from the rest of the country, which was on tenterhooks. News of the election was trickling in slowly, in inconclusive fragments. Early in December Jefferson learned that he had carried Virginia by a smashing plurality. Out of 27,335 votes cast, he received 21,111. This was a great personal triumph, particularly since the Federalists had been using the potent name of George Washington (who had died in 1799) against Jefferson.

A few days later Jefferson learned that he had carried South Carolina. "I believe we may consider the election as now decided," he wrote. Soon it was known that the Republican party had swept the country and had won majorities in both houses of Congress. Du Pont de Nemours, Jefferson's French friend, was quick to congratulate him with a Gallic compliment (in French, as he always wrote Jefferson): "Behold you at the head of your wise nation. She has freely placed her greatest man in her greatest position."

The Jeffersonians began a round of celebrations with speeches, songs, and toasts.

> Calumny and falsehood in vain raise their voice
>   To blast our Republican's fair reputation;
> But Jefferson still is America's choice,
>   And he will her liberties guard from invasion.
>   'Tis the wretches who wait
>   To unite Church and State,
>   That the name of McKean,[5] Burr, and
>   Jefferson hate.
> But ne'er will the sons of Columbia be slaves
> While the earth bears a plant or the sea rolls its waves.

[5] Thomas McKean was the Jeffersonians' candidate for Governor of Pennsylvania. He routed the Federalists in one of the most bitterly fought elections in that State.

This song, "Jefferson and Liberty," was sung at the Green Tree Tavern in Philadelphia, where toasts were drunk with enthusiasm.

But the celebrations were premature. When the electoral vote was counted, it was found that though Adams was defeated, Jefferson was not elected. This paradoxical situation was the result of the confused electoral law, which did not stipulate that the electors should specify which of the candidates was to be President and which Vice-President. Each elector voted for two candidates, and the one with the highest number of votes was declared President. It was true that Adams and Pinckney were defeated—with 65 and 64 electoral votes respectively—but it was likewise true that Jefferson did not get a majority over his running mate, Aaron Burr. The Republican vote stood 73 electoral votes for Jefferson and 73 electoral votes for Burr— a new experience for America.

The Jeffersonians thus had a majority of the total vote cast, but they had no President. The election now had to be thrown into the House of Representatives, which, under the Constitution, had the power to break the tie. This was a heaven-sent opportunity for the Federalists. They considered the election of Jefferson to be a national calamity and were determined to do everything to prevent it. Although it was universally known and assumed that Jefferson, and not the figurehead Burr, was the presidential candidate, and although the people had voted for Jefferson, and not for Burr, for President, the embittered Federalists in Congress were resolved to throw their votes to Burr.

Not all the Federalists, however, were willing to be a party to this unscrupulous scheme. The two greatest, John Adams and Alexander Hamilton, would have nothing to do with the intrigue. In view of the hatred that both men bore Jefferson, their behavior in this instance was a tribute to their patriotism. Perhaps they did not object so much to the dishonesty of the plot to defeat Jefferson as to the character of Burr. For Aaron Burr was not famous for virtue or steadfastness of character, and the idea of such a man's occupying the presidential chair was disturbing to responsible men.

To Alexander Hamilton, Burr was "bankrupt beyond redemption." When that arch-Tory, Gouverneur Morris, told Hamilton that "Burr must be preferred to Jefferson" because the latter was "infected with all the cold-blooded vices," Hamilton gave a determined No. The career of the machine politician Burr, he replied, proved that he had "formed himself upon the model of Cataline, and that he is too cold-blooded and too determined a conspirator ever to change his plan."

Before the election was thrown into the House of Representatives, Hamilton announced that he would support Jefferson against Burr. He did that because he considered Jefferson to be the lesser of two great evils. Hamilton's letter in which he explains his support is full of vindictive hatred of Jefferson. He wrote to Bayard:

I admit that his politics are tinctured with fanaticism; that he is too much in earnest in his democracy[!!!]; that he had been a mischievous enemy to the principal measures of our past administration; that he is crafty and persevering in his object; that he is not scrupulous about the means of success, nor very mindful of truth, and that he is a contemptible hypocrite.

Hamilton thus favored a "contemptible hypocrite" against a man whom he considered to be totally devoid of scruples. He felt that Burr was capable of anything, while Jefferson was too shrewd a politician to sell out his country, since it would not be to his advantage to do so:

Nor is it true, that Jefferson is zealot enough to do anything in pursuance of his principles, which will contravene his popularity or his interest. He is as likely as any man I know, to temporize; to calculate what will be likely to promote his own reputation and advantage.

This maliciously distorted picture, needless to say, is more of a reflection upon the character of Hamilton than upon that of Jefferson.

As for John Adams, in this crucial struggle he felt less strongly about Jefferson, whose principles he disliked, than he did about Burr, whom he feared and despised. Jefferson, despite his ardent democratic views which were anathema to Adams, was at least honest and a gentleman, Adams knew. But Burr, in Adams's eyes, was a "humiliation" to America.

Jefferson may have known of the underground intrigues that were designed to rob him of victory, but he went about his vice-presidential duties as if the election concerned two other fellows. Before the House of Representatives took up the balloting, Jefferson visited President Adams on official business. In the breast of Adams, the defeated candidate, there dwelt no love for Jefferson. But the President was a gentleman, and he spoke to his visitor words of magnanimity which he did not feel.

"Well," the President said to the Vice-President, "I understand that you are to beat me in this contest, and I will only say that I will be as faithful a subject as any you will have."

Jefferson did not think that this was the right interpretation of events. To him the election was not a matter of persons but of principles.

"Mr. Adams," he said, "this is no personal contest between you and me. Two systems of principles on the subject of government divide our fellow citizens into two parties. . . . Were we both to die to-day, to-morrow two other names would be in the place of ours." . . .

"I believe you are right," Adams admitted, "that we are but passive instruments, and should not suffer this matter to affect our personal dispositions."

But he did not really feel magnanimous. The defeated President was bitter and unforgiving.

7

On February 11 the House of Representatives in Washington began to ballot in order to break the Jefferson-Burr tie. Each of the sixteen States was allowed one vote. Nineteen times the ballot was taken on that day, and nineteen times the result was the same—eight States cast their votes for Jefferson, six for Burr, and two were divided. Neither candidate had a clear majority. On February 12 the ballot was taken nine times, and the result was the same. On February 13, 14, and 16, the House of Representatives voted six times. And the results were identical. The Federalists were determined to subvert the will of the people and to defeat Jefferson at all costs.

At the height of the bitter deadlock President Adams said to Jefferson with an undertone of anger: "Sir, the event of the election is within your own power. You have only to say you will do justice to the public creditors, maintain the navy, and not disturb those holding office, and the government will instantly be put into your hands."

Jefferson replied quietly: "I will not come into the government by capitulation."

"Then," Adams said, "things must take their course."

Jefferson was like steel against any kind of capitulation. He knew himself to be the lawful choice of the majority of the people, and he would not under any circumstances be a party to any kind of compromise with the enemies of democracy. "Many attempts," he informed Monroe, "have been made to obtain terms & promises from me. I have declared to them unequivocally, that I would not receive the government on capitulation, that I would not go into it with my hands tied."

The Federalists' intrigues to deprive him of the Presidency were so blatant that there was fear of secession in case the House of Representatives voted for Burr. As a matter of fact, the Jeffersonians, whose leader in Congress was the intelligent Albert Gallatin, declared openly and firmly that if the House did so, there would be an armed uprising in the Middle States.

Intransigent animosity on one side was matched by resolute loyalty on the other. Joseph H. Nicholson, a Congressman from Maryland, is a case in point. While the House was voting, Nicholson was gravely ill. But, nursed by his wife, he had himself daily carried in a litter to the Capitol and scribbled *Jefferson* on every ballot. Other Republican Congressmen were equally stanch. That winter Jefferson lived with thirty Republican members of Congress at Canaird's boardinghouse, in an atmosphere of comradeship and democratic simplicity. When someone suggested that the Congressmen give their fellow

boarder Jefferson, who after all was Vice-President of the
United States and the leader of their party, a seat of honor at
the long table, they replied with affectionate laughter that "he
must not be allowed to forget that he is one of the people and
that all were equal." Jefferson was proud of his pupils in democracy.

But outside of the Republican ranks, the atmosphere in Washington reeked with hostility. Jefferson felt as if he were living
in an enemy land. To his daughter Martha he wrote:

I long to be in the midst of the children, and have more pleasure
in their little follies than in the wisdom of the wise. Here, too, there
is such a mixture of bad passions of the heart that one feels themselves in an enemy's country.

To his younger daughter Maria he expressed himself in a
similar vein. Two days before the final balloting, he wrote
Maria that he was yearning to be with his children, who were
the only reason for his political ambition, but that he owed a
duty to his "republican principles" and to his country.

The scene passing here makes me pant to be away from it; to fly
from the circle of cabal, intrigue, and hatred, to one where all is
love and peace. . . . I feel no impulse from personal ambition to
the office now proposed to me, but on account of yourself and your
sister and those dear to you. I feel a sincere wish indeed to see our
Government brought back to its republican principles, to see that
kind of government firmly fixed to which my whole life has been
devoted. I hope we shall now see it so established, as that when I
retire it may be under full security, that we are to continue free and
happy.

The Federalists "who figure," as Jefferson described them,
were of the "violent kind" and they were "personally bitter."
In this category belonged President Adams, who did everything to embarrass Jefferson. A few days before the final vote
in the House, President Adams appointed John Marshall, who
hated Jefferson with an ardent hate, to the Supreme Court. The
President also put a number of other Tories, Federalists all, into
lesser judicial posts. These appointments were a contemptuous

challenge flung into the face of Jefferson, for the new judges disliked both his person and his ideas. Adams's action could undoubtedly be defended on legal grounds, but to saddle a new President with hostile judges, appointed for life, was not altogether cricket. Jefferson did not consider it fair.

By this time there was a secessionist air in Washington, and many people, especially the more responsible Federalists, began to fear that the anti-Jeffersonian intrigue might lead possibly to a dissolution of the Union and certainly to widespread unrest. Under pressure of opinion and upon the urgent advice of Hamilton, some Congressmen shifted their votes, and broke the week-long deadlock. On the thirty-sixth ballot ten States finally cast their votes for Jefferson and four for Burr. Two voted blank.[6]

This took place on February 17, 1801. On that day, after thirty-one hours of balloting, Jefferson was elected third President of the United States. It was nearly a quarter-century since he had written the Declaration of Independence.

8

Jefferson's election was a great victory for the democratic forces, but it was black Tuesday to the thousands of Federalists who honestly believed that the Republican leader was an atheistic anarchist and who feared that his Administration would be that of a bloody-handed revolutionist. Throughout America, while many rejoiced, some mourned.

The day on which it announced Jefferson's victory, the Georgetown triweekly, the *Washington Federalist*, came out with a picture of the American eagle turned upside down. And the *Columbian Centinel* of Boston, in its inaugural issue of March 4, published an obituary on the Federal Government:

[6] New York, New Jersey, Pennsylvania, Virginia, North Carolina, Georgia, Kentucky, Tennessee, Vermont, and Maryland voted for Jefferson. Massachusetts, Connecticut, Rhode Island, and New Hampshire voted for Burr. Delaware and South Carolina voted blank.

YESTERDAY EXPIRED
Deeply regretted by MILLIONS of grateful Americans,
And by *all* Good Men
THE FEDERAL ADMINISTRATION
Of the
GOVERNMENT OF THE UNITED STATES
Its death was occasioned by the
Secret Arts, and Open Violence;
Of Foreign and Domestic Demagogues.

EVEN before the bitterness of the campaign had died down, Americans realized that with the election of Jefferson something unusual had happened to the United States. Free men, casting their votes uncoerced and despite virulent opposition, had chosen a leader who believed in equality for all men, in opportunity for all men, in toleration for all men, and above all in government by all men. It was a victory for democracy, perhaps the greatest in the history of America up to that day.

The victorious candidate was quietly and deeply exultant. He said that his election was a great revolution—"a pacific revolution, as real as that of 1776, a revolution not of form but of principles." But, he insisted, his victory was not personal. It was the victory of a great ideal. The election meant that the forces of freedom had routed the forces of bigotry. Freedom-loving Americans had swept into the junk heap of history the powers of darkness in order to make way for a true and enlightened democracy.

Jefferson's postelection letters breathed a spirit of enthusiasm and of triumph. He was conscious that something "new under the sun" had taken place. To the English scientist Joseph Priestley, whom he invited to settle in the United States and become the apostle of science, he wrote:

As the storm is now subsiding, and the horizon becoming serene, it is pleasant to consider the phenomenon with attention. We can no longer say there is nothing new under the sun. For this whole chapter in the history of man is new. The great extent of our Republic is new. Its sparse habitation is new. The mighty wave of public opinion which has rolled over it is new.

He wrote in a similar strain to Nathaniel Niles:

The times have been awful, but they have proved an useful truth, that the good citizen must never despair of the commonwealth. How many good men abandoned the deck, and gave up the vessel as lost. It furnishes a new proof of the falsehood of Montesquieu's doctrine, that a republic can be preserved only in a small territory. The reverse is the truth. Had our territory been even a third only of what it is, we were gone. But while frenzy and delusion like an epidemic, gained certain parts, the residue remained sound and untouched, and held on till their brethren could recover from the temporary delusion.

To John Dickinson, his old friend of the Continental Congress, he wrote that the election meant that the democratic ship, after a fierce battering by a gale, had come through victorious and had proven its viability:

The storm through which we have passed, has been tremendous indeed. The tough sides of our Argosie have been thoroughly tried. Her strength has stood the waves into which she was steered. . . . We shall put her on her republican tack, & she will now show by the beauty of her motion the skill of her builders.

And he added a thought that was frequently in his mind: that the successful functioning of American democracy would serve as a beacon and as a model for the rest of mankind.

A just and solid republican government maintained here, will be a standing monument & example for the aim & imitation of the people of other countries.

He was thus conscious of a double responsibility: to the American people and to the rest of the world.

Congratulations and some warnings poured in. Most succinct and pointed message came from Sam Adams, the old revolutionary democrat from Boston: . . . "you must depend upon being hated yourself," the seventy-nine-year-old patriot warned Jefferson, "because they hate your principles."

2

"They" hated him worse than ever, but the common people of America hailed him as their champion and their hope. They sang a new "Jefferson and Liberty" song which stirred the hearts of democrats all over the land.

> The gloomy night before us flies,
>   The reign of terror now is o'er;
> It's gags, Inquisitors, and spies,
>   It's hordes of Harpies are no more.
>   Rejoice! Columbia's Sons, rejoice!
>   To Tyrants never bend your knee,
>   But join with heart and soul and voice
>   For Jefferson and Liberty. . . .
>
> Hail, long expected, glorious day!
>   Illustrious, memorable morn,
> That Freedom's fabric from decay
>   Rebuilds, for millions yet unborn.
>   Rejoice! Columbia's Sons, &c.
>
> His country's surest hope and stay,
>   In virtue and in talents try'd,
> Now rises, to assume the sway,
>   O'er Freedom's Temple to preside.
>   Rejoice! Columbia's Sons, &c. . . .
>
> Here Strangers from a thousand shores,
>   Compelled by Tyranny to roam,
> Shall find, amidst abundant stores,
>   A nobler and a happier home.
>   Rejoice! Columbia's Sons, &c. . . .
>
> Here, free as air's expanded space,
>   To ev'ry soul and sect shall be
> The sacred priv'lege of our race,
>   The Worship of the Deity.
>   Rejoice, Columbia's Sons, &c. . . .
>
> Let Foes to Freedom dread the name,
>   But should they touch the sacred Tree,

Twice fifty thousand swords shall flame
For Jefferson and Liberty.
Rejoice, Columbia's Sons, &c.

From Georgia to Lake Champlain,
From seas to Mississippi's shore,
The Sons of Freedom loud proclaim,
The reign of Terror now is o'er.
Rejoice! Columbia's Sons, rejoice!
To Tyrants never bend your knee,
But join with Heart, and Soul and Voice
For Jefferson and Liberty.

3

The inauguration took place in a bleak and deserted city. John Adams, frustrated and embittered, left Washington the night of March 3. His wife Abigail had preceded him by a few weeks. The defeated old President would not do his hated successor the honor of being present at his installation, and Adams's example was followed by other high officials and gentlemen. The gentry ostentatiously turned its collective back on the victorious apostle of democracy.

Washington, the capital since the preceding summer, was a swampy village that accentuated the bleakness of the occasion. The settlement was without any proper streets or urban facilities. It possessed a few wretched houses, "most of them small, miserable huts," according to Oliver Wolcott, Adams's Secretary of the Treasury. Gouverneur Morris described it ironically as "the best city in the world for a *future* residence. We want nothing here but houses, cellars, kitchens, well informed men, amiable women, and other trifles of this kind, to make our city perfect."

The inauguration was as extraordinary as the capital itself. On the morning of March 4 the sun was shining over the mud of the capital. Jefferson rose and donned green breeches, gray woolen stockings, and a gray waistcoat. The tall, bony President-elect left the boardinghouse and walked the two blocks to the unfinished Capitol as if he were performing an ordinary errand.

He was accompanied by a number of friends and colleagues, also on foot. This was in striking contrast to John Adams, who in 1797 had ridden ceremoniously to the inauguration in a coach and six.

Jefferson entered the Senate Chamber as unostentatiously as he came. The Republican members of Congress rose and greeted him warmly. There were few visitors present. He walked up to the table, shook hands with Vice-President Burr. A Bible lay on the table. Near by stood a tall, thin, black-haired man. He was a Virginian named John Marshall, whom Adams had appointed Chief Justice of the Supreme Court. Marshall and Jefferson, although distant kinsmen, felt a deep aversion for each other. But the august occasion left no room for the play of antipathy. The Chief Justice delivered the oath of office to his enemy, and his enemy repeated the sacred oath to uphold and defend the Constitution of the United States.

After a brief pause, Jefferson—President Jefferson—began to read his inaugural address in a clear, well-modulated voice. It was a beautiful speech, an eloquent appeal for national unity and conciliation. He stretched out a friendly hand to all his opponents and all those who hated him. "We are all republicans; we are all federalists," he exclaimed. He reminded the country that the rights of the minority were as sacred as those of the majority. He reassured the people that there would be no injustice and no persecution, and he appealed to the whole country to unite with "one heart and one mind."

It is a mystery why Jefferson's first inaugural address is not at least as well known as some of Lincoln's speeches. It deserves to be. Today, one hundred and forty years later, it is still a great speech. It is a declaration of the principles of democracy.

4

Friends & Fellow Citizens [1]
Called upon to undertake the duties of the first Executive office of our country, I . . . declare a sincere consciousness that the task

[1] In this quotation the abbreviations of the original (y^e, y^t, w^{ch}, and the like) have been written out to make the reading easier.

is above my talents, & that I approach it with those anxious & awful presentiments which the greatness of the charge, & the weakness of my powers so justly inspire. . . .

All too will bear in mind this sacred principle, that though the will of the Majority is in all cases to prevail, that will to be rightful, must be reasonable: that the Minority possess their equal rights, which equal laws must protect, & to violate would be oppression.

Let us, then, fellow citizens, unite with one heart & one mind; let us restore to social intercourse that harmony & affection, without which Liberty & even Life itself, are but dreary things. And let us reflect that having banished from our land that religious intolerance under which mankind so long bled & suffered we have yet gained little if we countenance a political intolerance as despotic, as wicked & capable of as bitter & bloody persecution. . . .

But every difference of opinion, is not a difference of principle. We have called, by different names, brethren of the same principle. We are all republicans; we are all federalists. . . .

I know indeed that some honest men have feared that a republican government cannot be strong; that this government is not strong enough. But would the honest patriot, in the full tide of successful experiment abandon a government which has so far kept us free & firm on the theoretic & visionary fear that this government, the world's best hope may, by possibility, want energy to preserve itself? I trust not.

I believe this, on the contrary, the strongest government on earth. I believe it the only one where every man, at the call of the law, would fly to the standard of the law; would meet invasions of public order, as his own personal concern. Some times it is said that man cannot be trusted with the government of himself.—Can he then be trusted with the government of others? Or have we found angels in the form of kings to govern him? . . .

Let us pursue with courage & confidence our own federal and republican principles, our attachment to our Union and Representative government. Kindly separated by nature, & a wide ocean, from the exterminating havoc of one quarter of the globe . . . Possessing a chosen country, with room enough for all descendants to the 100th & 1,000th generation; Entertaining a due sense of our equal right, to the use of our own faculties, to the acquisitions of our own industry, to honor & confidence from our fellow citizens resulting not from birth, but from our actions . . . With all these blessings, what more is necessary to make us a happy and a prosperous people?

Still one thing more, fellow citizens—a wise & frugal government, which shall restrain men from injuring one another, shall leave them otherwise free to regulate their own pursuits of industry & improvement, and shall not take from the mouth of labor the bread it has earned. This is the sum of good government, & this is necessary to close the circle of our felicities.

About to enter, fellow citizens, on the exercise of duties, which comprehend everything dear & valuable to you, it is proper that you should understand what I deem the essential principle of this government, and consequently those which ought to shape it's administration. I will compress them in the narrowest compass they will bear, stating the general principle. . . .

Equal & exact justice to all men, of whatever state of persuasion, religious or political:

Peace, commerce, & honest friendship with all nations, entangling alliances with none:

The support of the State governments in all their rights, as the most competent administrations for our domestic concerns, and the surest bulwarks against anti republican tendencies;

The preservation of the General government, in it's whole constitutional vigor, as the sheet anchor of our peace at home, & safety abroad.

A jealous care of the right of election by the people, a mild and safe corrective of abuses, which are lopped by the sword of revolution, where peaceable remedies are unprovided.

Absolute acquiescence in the decisions of the Majority, the vital principle of republics, from which is no appeal but to force, the vital principle & immediate parent of despotism.

A well disciplined militia, our best reliance in peace, & for the first moments of war, till regulars may relieve them:

The Supremacy of the Civil over the Military authority:

Economy in public expense, that labor may be lightly burdened:

The honest paiment of our debts and sacred preservation of the public faith:

Encouragement of Agriculture, & of Commerce as it's handmaid:

The diffusion of information, & arraignment of all abuses at the bar of the public reason:

Freedom of Religion, freedom of the press, & freedom of Person under the protection of the Habeas corpus;

And trial by juries, impartially selected.

These Principles form the bright constellation which has gone

before us, & guided our steps thro' an age of Revolution and Reformation: The wisdom of our Sages, & blood of our Heroes, have
been devoted to their attainment: they should be the Creed of our
political faith, the Text of civil instruction, the Touchstone by which
to try the services of those we trust. . . .

And may that infinite power which rules the destinies of the universe lead our councils to what is best, and give them a favorable
issue for your peace & prosperity.

5

When the tall man in gray finished speaking he bowed to
the applauding audience and left the Senate Chamber. Two or
three gentlemen who lived with him in the same boardinghouse
accompanied him to his room.

There was no celebration of any kind. Jefferson's fellow
boarders made no fuss over him, and he occupied the same
place at the bottom of the table. But he was in fine humor. At
dinner a guest from Baltimore, not knowing about the com-
radely egalitarianism that prevailed in the boardinghouse, asked
permission to congratulate the new President. Jefferson smiled.
"I would advise you," he jested, "to follow my example on
nuptial occasions, when I always tell the bridegroom, I will
wait till the end of the year before offering my congratulations."

6

Thus began Jefferson's Administration, in a boardinghouse.
There the President remained for another two weeks, and then
moved into the still unfinished President's House, which later
came to be called the White House. It was an imposing structure, a clean jewel of light-colored sandstone set in a sea of
mud. Jefferson thought it too big for a simple republican and
too ambitious for a modest republic. He described the mansion
jestingly as a "great stone house, big enough for two emperors,
one pope, and the grand lama into the bargain."

If the President's House seemed ludicrously big to Jefferson, the capital city was funny to a lot of other people. Satirists everywhere poked fun at the pathetic little village on the Potomac. Pennsylvania Avenue was called the "great Serbonian bog." Someone quipped that near-by Georgetown was a "city of houses without streets" and Washington a "city of streets without houses." Thomas Moore, the Irish poet who visited Washington, had a fine time ridiculing Jefferson's capital.

The little Irish snob wrote some mocking verse:

> In fancy now beneath the twilight gloom,
> Come, let me lead thee o'er this "second Rome!"
> Where tribunes rule, where dusky Davi bow,
> And what was Goose-Creek once is Tiber now:—
>
> This embryo capital, where Fancy sees
> Squares in morasses, obelisks in trees;
> Which second-sighted seers, ev'n now, adorn
> With shrines unbuilt and heroes yet unborn.

7

To old Sam Adams of Boston, Jefferson explained his plans and his program. The letter was a subtle tribute to the New England patriot:

In meditating the matter of that [inaugural] address, I often asked myself, is this exactly in the spirit of the patriarch of liberty, Samuel Adams? . . . Will he approve of it? . . . However, the storm is over, and we are in port. The ship was not rigged for the service she was put on. We will show the smoothness of her motions on her republican tack. I hope we shall once more see harmony restored among her citizens, & an entire oblivion of past feuds. . . . I hope the great body of our fellow citizens will do it. I will sacrifice everything but principle to procure it. A few examples of justice on officers who have perverted their functions to the oppression of their fellow citizens, must . . . be made. But opinion, & the just maintenance of it, shall never be a crime in my view: nor bring injury on the individual.

At the same time the victorious President revealed another facet of his character and another side of his conduct in a letter to Catherine Church. In reply to her letter of congratulations, he wrote:

There is something within us which makes us wish to have things conducted in our own way and which we generally fancy to be patriotism. This ambition is gratified by such a position. But the heart would be happier enjoying the affections of a family fireside.

8

The tall, angular, sinewy man who moved into the President's House in March, 1801, was fifty-eight years old and at the height of his mental and physical powers. He was conscious of his democratic mission and mellowed by a quarter-century of political experience.

His was, beyond a doubt, the most capacious and impressive intellect in the country, and possibly in the Western Hemisphere. His was also one of the subtlest minds in America. The range of his interests was astonishing. Apart from his vast knowledge of law and great knowledge of literature, he was also a botanist, an agronomist, a paleontologist, a zoologist, an anthropologist, a geologist, a mathematician, a metereologist, an astronomer, a surveyor, a gardener, an architect, and a musician. In some of these sciences, such as botany and paleontology, he excelled; in others, such as architecture and mathematics, he was highly skilled; in still others, such as astronomy and zoology, he was adept. He was also an expert mechanic and inventor. There were few things in which he was not interested. For eighteen years he was President of the American Philosophical Society (founded by Benjamin Franklin), the most distinguished body of learned men and scientists in the country.

He was a genuinely modest and genuinely warmhearted man. He liked people for their own sake, and his ruddy face, reserved in repose, would light up with inner fire at any expression of friendship or the floating spark of an idea. Political conflicts apart, he was completely devoid of prejudice, racial, religious, or social. He judged people only on the basis of their worth and their character. Snobs he despised; reactionaries he hated. Honest folk he loved and intelligent minds he admired.

Despite his modesty, Jefferson was aware that the election had made him the most powerful man in America. His victory had been complete and, from the point of view of popular support, overwhelming. The masses of the people, particularly in the West and in the South, were stanchly behind him.[2] His party had majorities in both houses of Congress and he was the leader of his party, as well as its greatest figure. Not only were the Federalists routed throughout the country, but in Jefferson's own party there was no one willing or able to challenge his authority.

Although Jefferson said that his election was a revolution, he was not actually a revolutionist in practice. He had no intention of changing any property relations. He had no desire to alter the fundamental laws or institutions of the United States. His aims were both more modest and more ambitious. He wished to strengthen the republic and set it along a truly democratic course. He meant to perpetuate the Constitution and the free institutions guaranteed by it. His ideal was a republic composed of small property-owning citizens with a sense of civic responsibility and a decent regard for the rights of their neighbors. Jefferson's dream was the creation of a republic of virtuous men acting according to justice and reason, and not according to hate and passion. He wrote to Amos Marsh:

. . . the Constitution of the United States [is] the result of the collected wisdom of our country. That wisdom has committed to us the important task of proving by example that a government, if organized in all its parts on the Representative principle unadulterated by the infusion of spurious elements, if founded, not in the fears & follies of man, but on his reason, on his sense of right, on the predominance of the social, over his dissocial passions, may be so free as to restrain him in no moral right, & so firm as to protect him from every moral wrong.

[2] In Virginia it was dangerous to criticize Jefferson. According to the *Virginia Gazette and General Advertiser*, any person "who should dare to open his lips against Jefferson or Paine, would run the risk of being grossly maltreated or put to death and no magistrate would be found who would make the least attempt to prevent it."

Perhaps the dream was unrealizable, but Jefferson was great enough to try to carry it out. Moreover, unlike Plato and other well-intentioned spinners of verbal utopias, Jefferson was in a position of power and authority. He could do something with his vision.

He not only could, but did. And he knew how. Despite the calumnies of his enemies, there was no hotheaded radicalism about President Jefferson. He had a philosopher's respect for time, and he did not hurry unduly. He meant to teach by precept and example, not to antagonize by haste and violence. Teaching people democracy was Jefferson's primary aim, and one did not teach democracy by cracking people's skulls or calling them names. One proceeded firmly, step by step. During his first month as President he wrote Dr. Walter Jones:

I am sensible how far I should fall short of effecting all the reformation which reason would suggest, and experience approve, were I free to do whatever I thought best; but when we reflect how difficult it is to move or inflect the great machine of society, how impossible to advance the notions of a whole people suddenly to ideal right, we see the wisdom of Solon's remark, that no more good must be attempted than the nation can bear.

Always he was conscious of having to set examples of republican virtue, of democratic simplicity, of reasonable behavior. For that was the essence of democratic living—virtue based upon reason. Jefferson was convinced that the people would learn from good examples, and he conceived one of his functions as President to be that of the nation's teacher and moral guide. Political activities, springing from the narrow exigencies of the occasion, quickly pass into oblivion, but good examples live forever.

Jefferson rejected all suggestions of presidential pomp and public subservience to officials. He informed Monroe:

I am decidedly against it, as it makes the citizen in his own eyes exalting his functionary and creating a distance between the two, which does not tend to aid the morals of either. I think it a practice which we ought to destroy and must destroy and, therefore, must not adopt as a general thing even for a short time.

9

Still, the President had to play politics. His immediate and most pressing problem was what to do with the Federalist office-holders. His own party insisted that John Adams's appointees be dismissed. Jefferson knew that many, possibly most, Federalist appointees, particularly those holding judicial posts, were his personal enemies and, in general, no friends of democracy. Yet he felt ashamed to have to throw men out of their jobs simply because he disagreed with their ideas.

James Monroe, writing from Richmond, warned the President to proceed cautiously in the matter of removals. "The principle," Monroe advised, "is sound that no man ought to be turned out for mere difference of political sentiment. . . . By retaining them in office you will give a proof of tolerance, moderation & forbearance, which must command the respect of the benevolent." That was good advice and in principle Jefferson agreed. He wrote to John Dickinson that he had no intention of punishing men for their opinions:

My principles, and those always received by the republicans, do not admit removing any person from office merely for a difference of political opinion. Malversations in office, & the exerting of official influence to control the freedom of election are good causes for removal.[3]

The theory was excellent, but it clashed with the needs of the occasion, as well as with the larger aims. Jefferson felt that the welfare of the republic required that its avowed enemies be ferreted out of office. The country, he said, was in the "enemies' hands."

About the Federalist judges who were appointed for life, the President could do nothing; but he could sweep out Adams's

[3] Jefferson consistently maintained this attitude. On November 3, 1806, he wrote to C. Parker: "I have never had a wish to control the right of private opinion or of suffrage in the officers of the government. I have only believed it wrong where they disapproved those principles of administration which the will of the nation has sanctioned, that they should employ the influence of their office in aid of an active opposition to them."

district attorneys and marshals. Removing people from office was an ordeal. "In this horrid drudgery," Jefferson once confessed to William Short, "I always felt myself as a public executioner."

One of Jefferson's earliest acts was to nullify the appointments made by Adams in December, 1800, when the President knew already that he had been defeated at the polls. Among those "midnight appointments," as Jefferson dubbed them contemptuously, were forty-two justices of the peace. Jefferson ousted seventeen of them. At that time there were 316 Federal offices at the disposal of the President. When Jefferson took over power, all of these officials were Federalists. Within two years he removed 105 of them—collectors of customs, marshals, district attorneys, and consuls. But of the 105, only 9, according to Jefferson, were removed for purely "political principle." He explained to his friend Du Pont de Nemours:

It was my destiny to come to the government when it had for several years been committed to a particular political sect. . . . I found the country entirely in the enemies hands. It was necessary to dislodge some of them. Out of many thousands of officers in the U.S. 9. only have been removed for political principles, and 12. for delinquencies chiefly pecuniary. The whole herd have squealed out, as if all their throats were cut.

By the end of Jefferson's first Administration, a total of about one-third of the officials appointed by Adams were removed. In their place Jefferson appointed men who were friendly to his ideals and on whose loyalty he could rely.[4] An example is a letter he wrote to his Secretary of the Treasury, Albert Gallatin:

[4] In a letter to Mrs. John Adams, written on June 13, 1804, Jefferson explained that he resented her husband's "midnight appointments" because he did not consider it fair to be burdened with officials who were hostile to him and his ideas: "I can say with truth, that one act of Mr. Adams's life, and one only, ever gave me a moment's personal displeasure. I did consider his last appointments to office as personally unkind. They were from among my most ardent political enemies, from whom no faithful co-operation could ever be expected; and laid me under the embarrassment of acting thro' men whose views were to defeat mine, or to encounter the odium of putting others in their places. It seemed but common justice to leave a successor free to act by instruments of his own choice."

Is Jonas Clark, proposed as collector of Kennebunk, a Republican? . . . if he is not, we must be inflexible against appointing Federalists till there be a due portion of Republicans introduced into office. It gives just offence to those who have been constantly excluded heretofore to be still excluded by those who have been brought in to correct the system.

He also did what he could to reward faithful party workers and place them in Federal positions. In another letter to Gallatin he wrote:

With respect to Gardner and Campbell . . . I think we are bound to take care of them. Could we not procure them as good berths as their former at least, in some of the custom-houses?

These removals infuriated the Federalists, particularly in New England. Even a partial application of the "spoils system" seemed like a full-blown revolution to the defeated party. As Jefferson said, they squealed as if their throats were being cut.

One of the removals that caused an uproar was that of Elizur Goodrich, whom Adams had appointed Collector of Customs at New Haven, Connecticut, two weeks before his retirement from the Presidency. Jefferson nullified the appointment and replaced Goodrich with Judge Samuel Bishop, Mayor of New Haven. The merchants of New Haven, an ardent Federalist town dominated by the ecclesiastical-minded Yale College, protested to the President. Bishop, they said, was incompetent. Jefferson's reply was masterful. It had the double object of making the protestants ridiculous by demolishing their arguments and of explaining to the people the principles on which his appointments and removals were based. He wrote ironically:

He [Bishop] is said to be the town clerk, a justice of the peace, mayor of the city of New Haven, an office held at the will of the legislature, chief judge of the court of common pleas for New Haven county, a court of high criminal and civil jurisdiction wherein most causes are decided without the right of appeal or review, and sole judge of the court of probates, wherein he singly decides all questions of wills, settlement of estates, testate and intestate, appoints guardians, settles their accounts, and in fact has under his jurisdiction and care all the property real and personal of persons dying.

The two last offices, in the annual gift of the legislature, were given to him in May last. Is it possible that the man to whom the legislature of Connecticut has so recently committed trusts of such difficulty & magnitude, is "unfit to be the Collector of the district of New Haven," tho' acknoleged in the same writing, to have obtained all this confidence "by a long life of usefulness"?

And he concluded with the principle that the "only questions concerning a candidate shall be, is he honest? Is he capable? Is he faithful to the Constitution?"

Such letters did nothing to endear the President to die-hard New Englanders. Their hatred for Jefferson was relentless and unforgiving. While the Goodrich-Bishop matter was still fresh, Theodore Dwight, a prominent Federalist politician and brother of Timothy the hyperorthodox president of Yale, delivered himself of an oration in which he castigated the Jefferson Administration as the horrible work of Satan:

We have now reached the consummation of Democratic blessedness. We have a country governed by blockheads, and knaves; the ties of marriage, with all its felicities, are severed, and destroyed; our wives and our daughters are thrown into the stews; our children are cast into the world from the breast, and forgotten; filial piety is extinguished. . . . Can the imagination paint any thing more dreadful on this side hell?

Another Jefferson-hater was twenty-year-old Daniel Webster, who in an address at Dartmouth College attacked the President as a dangerous democrat. Said the youthful orator in the lush phrases that remind one of his future verbal prowess: "let neither tergiversation or seduction attach us to the systems of those opinionated visionaries who mistake the fantastic dreams of their own minds for the oracles of philosophy." Daniel Webster's father, Ebenezer, felt about Jefferson the way his son did. When he was taken ill in a New England village that had committed the crime of having voted for Jefferson, Ebenezer Webster exclaimed: "Carry me back home! I don't want to die in a Republican town."

In the North they had fantastic notions of the new President. Shortly after his election, Jefferson was out riding in the vicinity of Washington. There was nothing conspicuous about the brown-clad horseman except his horse, which was exceptional.[5] A traveling man from Connecticut stopped him and politely inquired what about a horse trade. The two men fell into conversation and the stranger from Connecticut said to the stranger from Washington that in the last election he had voted for Adams and that he had no use for that man Jefferson. The latter raised some mild objections.

"Come, come, mister," said the man from Connecticut, "I guess you don't see the moral sin of niggery; but it ain't only that. This Thomas Jefferson—did you ever see him?"

Jefferson nodded.

"Well, that's more luck than I've had; but that doesn't matter. Now I hear that this Jefferson is a very wasteful chap with our hard-earned money. . . . They tell me he never goes out but he's got clothes on his back that would sell for a plantation . . . he's a couple of watches or more . . . rings on all his fingers; and a frill to his shirt." . . .

Here was the genuine vox populi, and Jefferson, who himself relates the story, burst out laughing. He said to the Connecticut Yankee that the President was no better dressed than himself. The Yankee was dubious. By this time they had approached the President's House and Jefferson invited the stranger in. As they entered, one of the servants addressed Jefferson as "Mr. President." The truth suddenly dawned upon the man from Connecticut. He stood stock-still from the shock, then he turned and fled.

10

To his Postmaster-General, Gideon Granger, Jefferson wrote that he wanted only men of "talents and virtue" in office.

My wish is to collect in a mass round the administration all the abilities & respectability. . . . To give none of them [the offices]

[5] Horses were one of Jefferson's major passions. As President, he started out with five. The price of the horses varied from $300 to $500. His favorite, "the magnificent Wildair," cost $300. The presidential lover of horseflesh could hardly ever resist a horse trade.

to secondary characters. Good principles, wisely and honestly administered cannot fail to attach our fellow citizens to the order of things
which we espoused.

On one point the President was adamant. He absolutely refused to appoint kinsmen. Nepotism was a hateful idea. It was
also bad politics. No one, Jefferson said, would believe that a
relative was given a job because he happened to have merit.
Rightly or wrongly, people were cynical in their interpretation
of the appointments of relatives to political offices, and Jefferson
considered political cynicism an enemy of democracy. He said:
"I . . . laid it down as a law of conduct for myself, never to
give an appointment to a relation."

Jefferson, who was not hard-boiled, disliked the task of making appointments to office. He found it disagreeable to have to
disappoint people, and yet there were not enough jobs to go
around. The worst of it was that every position that he filled
caused enmity on the part of those who did not get the job.

But the task of appointment is a heavy one indeed. He on whom
it falls may envy the lot of a Sisyphus or Ixion. Their agonies were
of the body: this of the mind. Yet, like the office of the hangman it
must be executed by some one.[6]

The Cabinet, when it was finally constituted, reflected Jefferson's dual aim: to achieve national unity and to surround
himself with men of ability. As a gesture of friendship and
appeasement, he chose half of his Cabinet from New England.
And to avoid the kind of conflict that disrupted Washington's
Cabinet, Jefferson chose men whose ideas did not clash with his.

For Secretary of State, he appointed James Madison. For
Secretary of the Treasury, he chose Albert Gallatin. The Sec-
retaryship of War went to Henry Dearborn. The position of
Attorney-General was given to Levi Lincoln. The Postmaster-
Generalship was obtained by Gideon Granger. The recently
created Secretaryship of the Navy was filled by Robert Smith.

[6] Abraham Lincoln used to make similar complaints. He once said: "To
remove a man is very easy, but when I go to fill his place, there are *twenty*
applicants, and of these I must make *nineteen* enemies."—Carl Sandburg,
Abraham Lincoln: The War Years, 4 vols., Harcourt, Brace, 1939, Vol. 4,
p. 102.

Secretaries Dearborn, Lincoln, and Granger were New Englanders. Smith was from Maryland. Gallatin was a Swiss, via
Pennsylvania. The only Southerner in the Cabinet was Madison.
In so choosing his Cabinet, Jefferson wanted to show the country that his was not a factional or sectional Administration, but
a truly national one.

Secretary of War Dearborn was born in New Hampshire,
where he had once practiced medicine, but was a resident of
Maine, which State he had represented in Congress. He had
had a fine war record, and had achieved the rank of colonel.
A big and imposing man, he was cool-tempered and able. Levi
Lincoln, the Attorney-General, was in his early fifties, Massa-
chusetts-born and Harvard-bred. By profession he was a lawyer
and by conviction an ardent Jeffersonian Republican. Like Dearborn, he also had been a member of Congress. Gideon Granger,
the Postmaster-General, being only thirty-four, was the youngest member of the Cabinet. He was born in Connecticut and
was a Yale graduate. By profession a lawyer and by inclination
a politician, he was a member of the State legislature, where,
despite his youth, he had achieved distinction for his energy and
efficiency. Robert Smith, the Secretary of the Navy, succeeded
his brother Samuel after the latter had served a few months
under Jefferson in the same post. The forty-four-year-old
Smith was a lawyer from Maryland, and his family, particularly his brother Samuel, was intimate with Jefferson. The
Smiths came from an eminent family of Baltimore and they
knew something about shipping and finance. Robert Smith,
being a man of elegant manners and distinguished appearance,
was popular with the navy people.

But the ablest and most interesting members of the Cabinet
were not the men from New England or from Maryland, but
a Virginian and a Swiss. In ability, as well as rank, Secretary
of State James Madison excelled all others except the President.
The two were lifelong and devoted friends. "You have been a
pillar of support through life," Jefferson told Madison a few
months before his death. Madison combined a massive intellect
with a jolly disposition. The homely little Secretary of State
was both a fine scholar and an amusing storyteller. Sir Augus-

tus Foster, the British Minister, said of Madison that he was better informed even than Jefferson himself—a superb compliment, even if not altogether true—and, moreover, "a social, jovial and good-humoured companion, full of anecdotes, sometimes rather of a loose description, but often of a political and historical interest." Unlike the President, Madison was also a cogent speaker. He had a top-notch legal brain. Only his appearance was against him. Washington Irving's description of him is famous. "But as to Jemmy Madison—ah, poor Jemmy—he is but a withered little Apple-john."

If "Jemmy" Madison was physically unimposing, his wife, Dolly, made up for it in sparkle and looks. Washington Irving said of her admiringly: "Mrs. Madison is a fine, portly, buxom dame who has a smile and a pleasant word for everybody." Jefferson being a widower, the "buxom dame" was his official hostess. The famous Dolly was perhaps the liveliest lady in Washington.

In Secretary of the Treasury Albert Gallatin, Jefferson had a real jewel. Neither Jefferson nor his party, made up as it was of agrarians and mechanics, was famous for knowledge of finance or intimacy with commerce. But when it came to figures and finance, Gallatin was a wizard. In the realm of money he was as smart as a Yankee trader and as tough as Alexander Hamilton.

Like Hamilton, Gallatin was foreign-born. It is a peculiar coincidence that the two ablest financiers of their day should have been born abroad; both of them left a deep imprint upon their adopted country, particularly in the realm of financial administration. Gallatin was born in Geneva, Switzerland, of an aristocratic family, and came to America in his teens. Unlike Hamilton, the noble-born Gallatin was an ardent democrat. He was also a first-rate administrator. In appearance he was tall, long-nosed, long-faced, blue-eyed, and bald-headed. There was great power and drive in that long figure. His eyes were those of a man who knew the value of money.

For his chief, President Jefferson, Gallatin had an admiration that amounted to reverence. He always kept a portrait of Jefferson on his desk. The latter, in turn, held Gallatin in warm

esteem and was deeply grateful for his efficient handling of the
national finances. Gallatin, Jefferson said, was a man "of a pure
integrity, and as zealously devoted to the liberties and interests
of our country as its most affectionate native citizen." Jefferson's
admiration and affection for the Secretary of the Treasury lasted
a lifetime. As late as 1823 Jefferson, a very old man, wrote to
Gallatin that a visit from him to Monticello would be a "day
of jubilance" and added: "I shall love you forever, and rejoice
when you rejoice, and sympathize in your evils."

It was, on the whole, a remarkable Cabinet, and it functioned
in exceptional harmony. Largely this was due to Jefferson's tact
and his graciousness; he knew how to handle difficult individuals with silk gloves. The President's cheerful disposition, his
genuine affection for those who worked with him, and his will-
ingness to discuss ideas on their merit, kept the Cabinet clicking
like a well-oiled machine. Every member, moreover, recognized
and bowed to the President's intellectual superiority.

Jefferson held a loose rein over the Cabinet. "I have no pleasure in the exercise of power," he told one of his political lieutenants. He never interfered or dictated except in cases of exceptional gravity. At Cabinet meetings, even when matters of
unusual importance were discussed, the President acted only as
primus inter pares. In true democratic fashion, he retained for
himself an equal vote with the others, and decisions were made
on the basis of majority opinion. "So that," Jefferson explained
to one of his intimates, "in all important cases the Executive is
in fact a directory, which certainly the President might control;
but of this there was never an example."

Jefferson was at the beck and call of the members of his Cabinet. They were encouraged to ring the doorbell of the Executive Mansion any time something important came up. There
was no need, he told them, to wait for ceremony, appointments,
or protocol. They were told to "call on me at any moment of
the day which suits their separate convenience." His Cabinet,
Jefferson later said,

presented an example of harmony in a cabinet of six persons, to
which perhaps history has furnished no parallel. There never arose,
during the whole time, an instance of an unpleasant thought or word

between the members. We sometimes met under differences of opinion, but scarcely ever failed, by conversing and reasoning, so to modify each other's ideas, as to produce a unanimous result.

II

Jefferson's first Administration began under a lucky star. For the first time in years, no vital problems plagued the country. Business was good, the people were comparatively well off, and there was no threat of war. The French Revolution had run its convulsive course. Its frustrated hopes and distorted idealism were seized upon by a swarthy little Italian adventurer who dreamt a typical "Fascist" dream of a new order in the world. The new order was to be shaped by the ambitious Corsican, who had a genius for political brigandage, for the exclusive benefit of himself, his family, and his professional condottieri. Napoleon's lust for domination was to plunge the world into fourteen years of violence and bloodshed. Its reverberations were to be felt in the United States and to affect President Jefferson as deeply as the French Revolution had shaken President Washington. But now, during Jefferson's first years in office, Bonaparte had signed a truce with the British and was not at war with the world.

Broadly speaking, Jefferson pursued two general lines of policy: economy at home, peace abroad. Although he was personally in debt, the notion of a public debt was repugnant to him. Not being an economist, he viewed economic problems from a political angle. He considered it an axiom that "Debt & revolution are inseparable as cause and effect." A rising national debt was like a flood. If permitted to go on unchecked, it would destroy the whole fabric of society—"if the public debt should once more be swelled to a formidable size," he once wrote to Gallatin ". . . we shall be committed to the English career of debt, corruption and rottenness, closing with revolution."

Jefferson was convinced that a government that owed a lot of money to private individuals was no longer free but a pawn of its creditors. Under no circumstances must the United States

Government borrow so much money as to become obligated to the bankers and thereby lose its freedom. Economy, he said, meant liberty; borrowing spelled servitude.

There was another reason why Jefferson, the agrarian democrat, abhorred the idea of a big national debt. It was clear that debt meant interest, interest called for higher taxes, and higher taxes involved a reduction in the standard of living of the common people. Coddling the bankers and robbing the toilers was not Jefferson's idea of the good society. He once explained in a letter to Samuel Kercheval:

> If we run into such debts, as that we must be taxed in our meat and in our drink, in our necessaries and our comforts, in our labors and our amusements, for our callings and our creeds, as the people of England are, our people, like them, must come to labor sixteen hours in the twenty-four, give the earnings of fifteen of these to the government for their debts and daily expenses; and the sixteenth being insufficient to afford us bread, we must live, as they now do, on oatmeal and potatoes; have no time to think, no means of calling the mismanagers to account; but be glad to obtain subsistence by hiring ourselves to rivet their chains on the necks of our fellow-sufferers.

The President and his Secretary of the Treasury attacked the problem of economy along three lines. There was to be no more borrowing. The national debt was to be extinguished by systematic payments of principal and interest. Expenditures were to be drastically reduced. Wherever possible, Jefferson tried to shift the burden of taxation from the poor to the rich. A large portion of the Government's income came from imposts on imported goods and shipping. This, in Jefferson's eyes, was as it should be, since he believed that it affected mainly those who could best afford to pay. "I wish," he told Gallatin in 1802, "it were possible to increase the impost on any articles affecting the rich chiefly, to the amount of the sugar tax, so that we might relinquish that at the next session."

One of the direct taxes that Jefferson abolished was the excise on distilled liquors. This did not make him unpopular with the whisky-drinkers. Wine-imbibers, who belonged to the upper crust, continued to pay a tax and to curse the President.

Jefferson inherited a national debt of over $80,000,000. To cut into this sum, the President and Gallatin elaborated a system whereby $7,500,000 was set aside annually for the payment of principal and interest. This worked so well that by the end of Jefferson's Administration—despite the purchase of Louisiana, wars, and losses due to the Embargo—the national debt was decreased by $27,500,000. This economizing was achieved, to some extent, at the expense of the army and the navy. The army was reduced from 4,000 to 2,500 men. Jefferson was not a lover of the arts of violence.

In the realm of finance, the Jefferson Administration instituted two major reforms. Under Hamilton and his successors, government finances had been handled in the English way—an account was given to the legislature after the money had been spent. In Jefferson's eyes, such a system was both undemocratic and potentially corrupt. He believed that Congress should know beforehand what the Government intended to spend in the coming year. The representatives of the people should have the power to approve or disapprove of each detailed item. This, in Jefferson's opinion, was the only way the people could control the Government and check upon its actions. He therefore proposed to Gallatin that he institute a system of strict accounting and submit to Congress detailed appropriations bills. The President made his proposals with his customary indirection—as a suggestion, rather than an order. But men like Gallatin were familiar with their chief's mind and acted upon his hints. Jefferson wrote Gallatin in 1804:

Would it not be useful also to oblige our successors, by setting the example ourselves, of laying annually before Congress a . . . calendar of the expenditures 1. for the civil, 2. the military, 3. the naval departments, in a single sum each?

The greatest security against the introduction of corrupt practices and principles into our government, which can be relied on in practice, is to make the continuance of an administration depend on their keeping the public expenses down to their minimum. The people at large are not judges of theoretic principles, but they can judge on comparative statements of expense of different epochs.

12

In foreign affairs Jefferson's course was as simple as his economics. To him the United States was a splendid experiment in democracy and a great island of freedom in the midst of a world of tyranny. He blessed the Almighty Being for the fact that America was "separated by a wide ocean from the nations of Europe" and he hoped to keep it that way. "We have a perfect horror at everything like connecting ourselves with the politics of Europe," he wrote to William Short.

If Jefferson had been able, he would have put up a Chinese wall around America, not as a bulwark against invaders, but as a means of keeping out the Old World's patterns of hate and injustice. This was not chauvinism or narrow patriotism. Jefferson's love of country was, indeed, tinged with the universal. He loved America as a wise father proud of his offspring, not as an anxious lover jealous of his mistress. He was so proud of America that he wanted his land to be a beacon of freedom to mankind. Always he was conscious of world opinion. He knew that if the democratic experiment succeeded in America it would be followed elsewhere. In 1802 he wrote to Governor Hall:

We have the same object, the success of representative government. Nor are we acting for ourselves alone, but for the whole human race. The event of our experiment is to shew whether man can be trusted with self-government. The eyes of suffering humanity are fixed on us with anxiety as their only hope, and on such a theatre for such a cause we must suppress all smaller passions and local considerations.

Jefferson also wanted America to be a haven for the world's oppressed. In his first Annual Message to Congress, he made an eloquent appeal for an open door for refugees:

And shall we refuse the unhappy fugitives from distress that hospitality which the savages of the wilderness extended to our fathers arriving in this land? Shall oppressed humanity find no asylum on this globe?

He drew a sharp dividing line between the European peoples and their governments. The latter were tyrannical at home and belligerent abroad. The peoples, on the other hand, were essentially decent, unhappy victims of oppression. Jefferson wanted them to have a chance of life and liberty, and he hoped that they would revolt against their masters.

But he did not desire any large-scale immigration to America, fearing that men brought up in the school of despotism would not make ideal citizens of a free republic. "In proportion to their numbers," he had written in 1792, "they will share with us the legislation. They will infuse into it their spirit, warp and bias its directions, and render it a heterogeneous, incoherent, distracted mass." Jefferson preferred small groups of immigrants, particularly skilled artisans and craftsmen. Such men, no matter whence they came, would be easily absorbed and would enrich America by teaching it "something we do not know."

Of all emigrating peoples, Jefferson preferred Italians. They were among the world's finest artisans and artists, as well as energetic farmers and viticulturists. He felt that skilled and hard-working Italians could transform many areas of America from a wilderness into a garden. In connection with another emigrating people, the Germans, Jefferson played with the idea of carrying on an experiment to compare German labor with Negro labor. He wanted to import "as many Germans as I have grown slaves" and to settle them "and my slaves, on farms of 50 acres each, intermingled." He was sure that, given a chance, the German immigrants, particularly their children, would become "good citizens."

It was the European aggressors and oppressors that Jefferson wanted to keep out of America. One way of doing it was to cut contact with the outside world down to an irreducible minimum. Such an aim sounds quixotic in the radio- and airplane-encircled world of the 1940's, but it was not altogether visionary in the sailing-vessel days of the early 1800's. Jefferson wanted no truck with Europe, except a minimum of necessary trade. He meant to let all the existing treaties die and to make no new ones; and if an emergency should arise, he would send a representative abroad to settle it, and then have him return home. There would be no permanent American diplomatic agents abroad.

In this instance policy coincided with a certain bias. Knowing many diplomats, Jefferson distrusted them as deeply as he disliked bankers. He regarded diplomats with suspicion as the spoilers of peace and their craft as the smithy of war. They were professional troublemakers, and the more trouble they brewed, the greater was their prestige and importance. To his friend William Short, who was in the diplomatic service, the President wrote: "I have ever considered diplomacy as the pest of the peace of the world, as the workshop in which nearly all the wars of Europe are manufactured."

Gradually the President liquidated America's diplomatic missions in Europe. He called in the diplomats, not like a mother hen anxious for her chicks, but like a cautious businessman closing his foreign branches because they did not pay; . . . "as we wish not to mix in the politics of Europe," the President stated, "but in her commerce only, Consuls would do all the business we ought to have there." He withdrew William Smith from Portugal, William Murray from Holland, John Quincy Adams from Prussia. He intended to withdraw the rest—Rufus King was in London and Robert R. Livingston in Paris—but Napoleon's international adventures threw a monkey wrench into Jefferson's plans.

13

Events beyond the control of Presidents or philosophers nullified Jefferson's dream of political isolation from the rest of the world. But the destruction of the President's isolationist fences brought to America a gift of priceless value and incomparable importance. In the spring of 1803 the paths of two great ambitions met for a brief moment, and a bargain was struck. Napoleon, ambitious to build a personal dynasty, sold territory that was of no use to his family. Jefferson, ambitious to secure a free republic for posterity, bought the territory that was of use to his people.

The background of the story, involving the greatest real-estate deal in history, was essentially geographic and commercial. West of the Mississippi, and extending a thousand miles to the Rocky Mountains, lay a vast no man's land of forests and rivers and prairies and bison. It was a wilderness paradise, full of scenic wonders and overflowing with natural resources; and except for several thousand Indians and a few hardy whites, there was no one to admire the one or to exploit the other. Over this tremendous area, since 1763, had flown the flag of decaying and decrepit Spain.

Louisiana was the name of the whole region. Out of it were subsequently to be carved the States of Arkansas, Colorado, the Dakotas, Iowa, Kansas, Louisiana, Minnesota, Missouri, Montana, Nebraska, Oklahoma, and Wyoming. The Louisiana Territory comprised an area of more than a million square miles— about the size of the Argentine. The region was so big that all of Western Europe, including Scandinavia, could be tucked away in it.

The gate to the territory was New Orleans at the mouth of the Mississippi River. The latter, in turn, was the life line of the commerce of the American West. He who controlled New Orleans was in a position to affect the destinies of the American people who did not live on the Atlantic seaboard. So long as a feeble Spain held the key to New Orleans, the American West could grow and trade without fear of effective interference. But should New Orleans fall into the hands of a powerful and ambitious state, then the United States would face the choice of either submitting to dictation and a permanent status of inferiority, or fighting for the control of the Mississippi and the West. As Jefferson said categorically, any foreign Power that controlled New Orleans was the "natural and habitual enemy" of the United States. This was elementary politics, dictated by the stubborn facts of geography.

Napoleon, bent on building an empire in the Old World as well as in the New, pounced upon the Louisiana Territory at his first opportunity. In October, 1800, by the secret treaty of San Ildefonso, he obtained Louisiana and the adjoining Floridas from Spain. Since he did not take immediate possession, the treaty was kept secret for about a year. But late in 1801 the news leaked out. It came as a cruel shock to Jefferson. In one blow it knocked out all his hopes for isolation from European affairs.

With painful clarity the peace-loving President saw that the French occupation of New Orleans meant inevitable war with Napoleon. But the United States had neither enough troops nor sufficient warships, and so Jefferson faced the bleak prospect of having to ally with England, the nation he most distrusted, against France, the nation he most liked. It was a bitter choice. The day, Jefferson said grimly, that Napoleon's troops set foot on the soil of New Orleans, that day "we must marry ourselves to the British fleet and nation." Shades of isolationism!

To Robert R. Livingston, the American Minister in France, Jefferson wrote a long letter remarkable for its revelation of his Realpolitik. Although the President was greatly disturbed by the Louisiana situation, his analyses of political courses to be pursued and alternatives to be chosen were as cool as a scientific report:

The session [sic] of Louisiana and the Floridas by Spain to France works most sorely on the U.S. On this subject the Secretary of State has written to you fully. Yet I cannot forbear recurring to it personally, so deep is the impression it makes in my mind. It completely reverses all the political relations of the U.S. and will form a new epoch in our political course.

Of all nations of any consideration France is the one which hitherto has offered the fewest points on which we could have any conflict of right. . . . From these causes we have ever looked to her as our *natural friend.* . . . Her growth, therefore, we viewed as our own, her misfortunes ours.

There is on the globe one single spot, the possessor of which is our natural and habitual enemy. It is New Orleans, through which the produce of three-eighths of our territory must pass to market, and from its fertility it will ere long yield more than half of our whole produce and contain more than half of our inhabitants. France placing herself in that door assumes to us the attitude of defiance.

Spain might have retained it quietly for years. Her pacific dispositions, her feeble state, would induce her to increase our facilities there, so that her possession of the place would be hardly felt by us. . . . Not so can it ever be in the hands of France. The impetuousity of her temper, the energy and restlessness of her character, placed in a point of eternal friction with us . . . these circumstances render it impossible that France and the U.S. can continue long friends when they meet in so irritable a position. They as well as we must be blind if they do not see this; and we must be very improvident if we do not begin to make arrangements. . . .

The day that France takes possession of N. Orleans . . . From that moment we must marry ourselves to the British fleet and nation. We must turn all our attentions to a maritime force . . . and . . . make the first cannon, which shall be fired in Europe the signal for tearing up any settlement she may have made, and for holding the two continents of America in sequestration for the common purposes of the united British and American nations. This is not a state of things we seek or desire. It is one which this measure, if adopted by France, forces on us.

It was an astonishing letter in more ways than one. In it the pacific Jefferson actually threatened Napoleon with war if he should carry out his bargain with Spain. The Anglophobe President, furthermore, bluntly warned that he was ready to ally with Britain to keep the French out of New Orleans. Finally, and this is perhaps the most novel aspect of the letter, Jefferson here first mentioned the doctrine—later to be made famous by Monroe—that the United States, with the aid of Britain, should prevent European Powers from intervening in the Americas. Here his phrasing was deliberately blunt and unequivocal—he said that the United States and Britain should hold the "two continents of America in sequestration for the common purposes" of these countries. In other words, he put up a Keep Out sign.

To make sure that this letter of warning would reach Napoleon and his Foreign Minister Talleyrand, Jefferson sent it by his friend Du Pont de Nemours, who was then returning to France. The letter was given to Du Pont unsealed, because, the President told him, it was urgent that he read it and acquaint himself with the situation. He repeated that he was the last man in the world to want war with France, but—!

I wish you to be possessed of the subject, because you may be able to impress on the government of France the inevitable consequences of their taking possession of Louisiana . . . this measure will cost France, & perhaps not very long hence, a war which will annihilate her on the ocean. . . . I wish the present order of things to continue. . . . I value highly a state of friendship between France & us. . . . You know . . . how much I value peace, and how unwillingly I should see any event take place which would render war a necessary recourse. . . . I am thus open with you, because I trust that you will have it in your power to impress on that government considerations, in the scale against which the possession of Louisiana is nothing. . . . if you can be the means of informing the wisdom of Bonaparte of all it's consequences, you [will] have deserved well of both countries. Peace and abstinence from European interferences are our objects.

Jefferson instructed Minister Livingston that in case the French insisted that they needed to keep all of Louisiana, they should cede the island of New Orleans and the Floridas to the United States. This was absolutely the least concession the United States would accept before "taking immediate measures" against Napoleon.[7]

14

Public opinion was not prepared for the bad news about the transfer of Louisiana to France, and when it leaked out there was great agitation through the land. In the autumn of 1802 the country heard that the Spanish authorities in New Orleans had withdrawn the "right of deposit" from American merchants. This meant more than the mere loss of $1,000,000 worth of produce annually; it meant stunting the growth of the West by choking its outlet. Throughout the country there was an outburst of indignation, particularly among Jefferson's own stanch supporters, the men of the West.

[7] Jefferson was determined to achieve his object by peace if possible, by war if necessary. "Nothing but the failure of every peaceable mode of redress," he wrote to William Dunbar, on Mar. 3, 1803, "nothing but dire necessity, should force us from the path of peace which would be our wisest pursuit, to embark in the broils and contentions of Europe and become a satellite to any power there. Yet this must be the consequence if we fail in all possible means of re-establishing our rights."

Jefferson, having foreseen the emergency, gave the country an impressive example of calm and imperturbability. He knew exactly what he was about, and he was taking steps to carry into effect his determination either to buy New Orleans or to fight for it.

In the meantime, Jefferson's advisers raised the question of constitutionality. Did the President have the legal right to acquire territory and then incorporate it into the Union? Jefferson, taking the long view, replied in effect, We will settle that question when we come to it. "There is no constitutional difficulty as to the acquisition of territory," he told Gallatin, "and whether, when acquired, it may be taken into the Union by the Constitution as it now stands, will become a question of expediency."

Quietly he had Congress pass a mysterious appropriation of $2,000,000 to be used in the "intercourse between the United States and foreign nations." Then, in March, 1803, he sent James Monroe as envoy extraordinary to France to help Livingston make a deal with Bonaparte. Monroe was instructed to offer Napoleon as much as 50,000,000 francs for New Orleans and the Floridas, or two-thirds of that sum for the island of New Orleans alone. The least the American negotiators were to insist upon was a permanent guarantee of the rights of navigation on the Mississippi. If the French refused, Jefferson instructed his envoys to play for time and get secretly in touch with the British. The instruction that was sent to Monroe and Livingston read:

. . . as soon as they find that no arrangement can be made with France, to use all possible procrastination with them, and in the mean time enter into conference with the British government, through their ambassador at Paris, to fix principles of alliance, and leave us in peace till Congress meets; and prevent war till next spring.

As it turned out, this was not necessary, for Napoleon moved quicker than Jefferson could have hoped. While Monroe was sailing for France, Livingston had begun to negotiate with Napoleon and his Foreign Minister, the venal Talleyrand. The American Minister, who spoke French poorly and was hard of hearing to boot, got nowhere at first. Neither the imperious

First Consul nor his corrupt Foreign Minister paid much attention to the patrician Livingston with his upright manners. The
sincere republican from America was probably unaware that
Talleyrand was making a fortune out of his office. Three months
after he entered the Ministry of Foreign Affairs, Talleyrand
had piled up a nest egg of 12,000,000 francs which he received
in the form of "gifts" from foreign Powers that were currying
favor with Napoleon.

The first thing that the cynical Talleyrand said to the gentlemanly Livingston was, "Have you any money?"

"I do not understand," stammered Jefferson's shocked plenipotentiary.

"In this country," Talleyrand said blandly, "matters are difficult to manage without it. With the aid of an abundance of
money all difficulties are surmounted. Reflect well on this." [8]

In the meantime the uneasy Franco-British truce was rapidly
deteriorating and a renewal of war between Napoleon and Great
Britain was imminent. Since in case of war the British fleet could
easily capture New Orleans, Napoleon thought it a clever idea
to sell the territory to the United States and get money for
something that would be a dead loss anyhow. The First Consul
acted quickly. On April 11, 1803, he deliberately insulted Lord
Whitworth, the British Ambassador in Paris, and raised his
hand as if to strike him. Whitworth gripped his sword. Later
in the day Talleyrand called in Livingston and asked him
whether the United States wanted to have the "whole of
Louisiana."

"No," the surprised Livingston replied, "our wishes extend
only to New Orleans and the Floridas."

Without New Orleans, Talleyrand explained, the rest of the
territory was of little value. He wanted to know what America
would be willing to pay for the whole. Livingston was completely unprepared to make an offer, since Monroe had not yet
arrived with instructions from Jefferson. But he tentatively
offered Talleyrand 20,000,000 francs. "Too low," said the For-

[8] J. W. Thompson and S. K. Padover, *Secret Diplomacy*, London, 1937,
p. 207.

eign Minister, and asked Livingston to think it over and see him tomorrow. The following day brought Monroe to Paris, and Livingston went to see Talleyrand with a new offer, but the Foreign Minister was evasive, perhaps because there was nothing in it for him. On April 13, which was Jefferson's birthday, Livingston had an interview with Marbois, the Minister of Finance, into whose hands Napoleon had put the negotiations. Marbois told Livingston that Napoleon had said to him: . . . "let them [the Americans] give you one hundred millions of francs, and pay their own claims and take the whole country."

Livingston would not commit himself without Monroe. On the following day the two Americans went to see Marbois and made an offer of 50,000,000 francs. Marbois thought it was not enough, but Livingston and Monroe, knowing that France was on the verge of war and in need of the sinews of war, decided to bide their time before giving away any more money than they had to. On the last day of April the two American representatives and the French Ministers came to terms. Two days later, on May 2, the historic treaty was signed. For the price of 60,000,000 francs—about $15,000,000—Napoleon ceded the whole Louisiana Territory to the United States.[9]

It was a phenomenal bargain. After Livingston had signed his name to the treaty he exclaimed prophetically: "From this day the United States take their place among the powers of the first rank."

The haggling and the signing over, Napoleon invited the Americans to dinner. He felt fine and wanted to know all about *Monsieur* Jefferson.

"Well," Napoleon asked, "Mr. Jefferson, how old is he?"

Monroe: "About sixty."

Napoleon: "Is he married or single?"

Monroe: "He is not married."

Napoleon: "Then he is a *garçon*?"

Monroe: "No he is a widower."

---

[9] Fifteen million dollars was of course a lot of money in those days. Since wages in a city like New York amounted to about $10 a month, one may roughly estimate the value of the dollar then to be about ten or twelve times what it is today.

Napoleon: "Has he children?"

Monroe: "Yes, two daughters who are married."

Napoleon: "Does he reside always at the federal city?"

Monroe: "Generally."

Napoleon: "Are the publick buildings there commodious, those for the Congress and the President especially?"

Monroe: "They are."

Napoleon: "You the Americans did brilliant things in your war with England, you will do the same again."

Monroe: "We shall I am persuaded always behave well when it shall be our lot to be in war."

Napoleon: "You may probably be in war with them again."

Monroe replied cautiously that he did not know, that that was an important question to decide when there would be an occasion for it.

Livingston urged Jefferson that the treaty be immediately ratified, lest Napoleon change his mind. Though questions of constitutionality were raised again, Jefferson's party was strong enough in the Senate to overcome opposition. On October 17, 1803, the Senate ratified the treaty by a vote of 24 to 7.

Before the year was out, the country was given a memorable Christmas present. On December 20, the French authorities handed over the Louisiana Territory to the United States, and Jefferson's "island of freedom" thereby became an empire of liberty, stretching from the Atlantic to the Rockies. It was President Jefferson's crowning glory.

He could not suppress his feeling of triumph. In one stroke, and with superlative luck, he had doubled the territory of his country, not by war but through purchase—an achievement rarely, if ever, excelled in recorded history. The Louisiana Territory, Jefferson was convinced, would be opened to immigration, and the new settlers would bring prosperity to the United States and happiness to themselves.[10] "I confess," Jefferson

[10] Jefferson was a strong believer in immigration and settlement. In criticizing Thomas Robert Malthus for overlooking immigration as a check upon population, he wrote: "Were half the money employed under the poor laws in England, laid out in colonizing their able-bodied poor both the emigrants and those who remained would be the happier."

wrote to Joseph Priestley, "I look to this duplication of area for the extending a government so free and economical as ours, as a great achievement to the mass of happiness which is to ensue."

15

Doubling the area of freedom was easier than ensuring it. In the third year of his Administration, Jefferson at long last came to grips with the Federal judiciary. It was the first conflict of its kind in the United States; the last, so far, took place in 1937. The struggle is not yet over, for neither Thomas Jefferson in 1803-04 nor Franklin D. Roosevelt in 1937-38 can be said to have achieved brilliant success in his conflict with the judiciary.

Jefferson's struggle with the Federal judiciary was not something arbitrary, willful, or easily avoidable. He was driven to the conflict by the dynamics of his ideas, as well as by the logic of his position. The Federalists, especially John Adams, had packed the judicial posts with their own appointees. These judges liked neither Jefferson nor his type of democracy. The antipathy, needless to say, was reciprocal. Jefferson's lack of affection for the lawyers' trade applied also to the lawyers' goal: judgeships.

How Jefferson felt about the judiciary can be gathered from an anecdote. A few years after he retired from the Presidency, Jefferson entertained at dinner a number of guests, including his enemy Chief Justice John Marshall. The conversation turned to the training of lawyers. Jefferson criticized the narrow, legalistic education of lawyers and said that they should have "More general science, and more common sense." Then he told of an experiment that he had made when he was President.

To fill the Supreme Court of the Michigan territory, Jefferson had chosen three utterly different men from different parts of the country. Only one of them was a lawyer—"a dry technical lawyer," Jefferson remarked smiling, "and would not believe two and two made four, unless you could prove it by an adjudged case." The second, Woodward of Virginia, was a philosopher and a scientist, a "visionary." The third was a "large strong-handed and strong-minded Vermont farmer" who never saw a textbook and despised legal learning.

Chief Justice Marshall, who had been listening quietly, looked up and asked ironically: "And how did your plan operate, Mr. President; did your machine go well?"

"Upon my word," Jefferson replied candidly, "it would not go at all."

From the beginning of his Administration Jefferson had intended to put a bridle on the judiciary. The draft of his first message to Congress, in December, 1801, carried a concealed bomb that was designed to blow up the powers and pretensions of the judges. In that original draft the President declared the Sedition Act of the Adams Administration unconstitutional and denied the Supreme Court the exclusive right to construe the Constitution.

But the bomb was not placed. At the last moment the President changed his mind. The nation, he knew, had not yet recovered from the election; bitterness still lingered in many parts of the country. Jefferson's primary aim was to heal the wounds and to unite the country by conciliating all honest men, regardless of their political principles. The time was not ripe to start a judicial war. Hence Jefferson struck out the passage in the speech that might give offense to the moderates among the Federalists.

I am perfectly satisfied the effect of the proceedings of this session of Congress will be to consolidate the great body of well meaning citizens together, whether federal or republican. . . . I do not mean to include royalists or priests, their opposition is unmovable.

His speech to the Congress was conciliatory and soft-spoken. It was, to borrow a phrase used by the *Republican Advocate*, "like the oil of the good Samaritan to the wounded stranger, gratefully healing to the public mind." The "oil" worked. When the next congressional election came around, Jefferson's party carried the country overwhelmingly. "We are all federalists"—the President had said in his inaugural—"we are all republicans." And the country was with him on that.

Jefferson, who had an exquisite sense of timing, was still waiting for the proper moment to solve the problem of the judiciary. But while he was biding his time, his judicial opponents jumped the gun. This came about in an incident which did not lack drama. The story, fateful in its influence on American history, is famed as the case of *Marbury* v. *Madison*.

William Marbury was a petty Federalist politician. In the last hours of his Administration, President Adams had appointed him justice of the peace for the District of Columbia. The Senate ratified the appointment. The Secretary of State (who was John Marshall) signed and sealed the commission. Everything went according to schedule, but there was one slip-up. The outgoing Administration was so busy making arrangements to move out that it failed to deliver the commission to Marbury.

When the new Administration came in, Marbury asked for his commission, which was still lying on the Secretary of State's desk. Jefferson, who resented Adam's "midnight appointments," ordered Madison, his Secretary of State, not to deliver it. Marbury took the case to court. He applied to the Supreme Court for a writ of mandamus, under Section 13 of the Judiciary Act of 1789, to order Secretary Madison to give him his commission. In February, 1803, Chief Justice Marshall delivered his decision in the case of *Marbury* v. *Madison*. It turned out to be epoch-making.

The case gave the Chief Justice a glorious opportunity to spank Jefferson and at the same time assert the judicial power of the Supreme Court. Marshall seized his chance. He did it with a subtlety worthy of Jefferson himself. The problem Marshall faced was this: He could not reject Marbury's claim without admitting the powerlessness of the judiciary. On the other hand, he dared not uphold Marbury's claim because Jefferson would ignore it (as he certainly would have done) and make a fool out of the Supreme Court. Marshall solved the dilemma with extraordinary astuteness. By a bold maneuver the Chief Justice succeeded in eating the cake and having it.

First of all, Marshall pointed out, Marbury's commission was valid, regardless of whether it was delivered or not. Madison acted illegally in withholding the commission. Therefore Marbury had the right to seek a remedy—the writ of mandamus. Round one for Marbury.

The real problem, the Chief Justice argued, was whether the Supreme Court was competent to grant Marbury the mandamus he was seeking under Section 13 of the Judiciary Act of 1789. Here came the crux of Marshall's decision. The subtle Chief Justice pointed out that under the Constitution the Supreme Court had no power to issue writs against executive officers. Should, therefore, the court follow Section 13 of the Act of 1789, or should it follow the Constitution? Marshall's answer was obvious. "It is a proposition too plain to be contested," he wrote, "that the Constitution controls any legislative act repugnant to it." In other words, the Constitution was superior to Section 13. In other words, Section 13 was unconstitutional. In other words, the Supreme Court decides what legislative act is unconstitutional. Round two was thus against Marbury (who was only a pawn, anyhow) but for the Supreme Court.

Thus Marshall asserted the supremacy of the Supreme Court and at the same time rebuked Jefferson, without leaving the latter a legal opening at which to strike. The "crafty chief judge," as Jefferson called him, had delivered a hard blow. Incidentally, Justice Marshall passed judgment upon a case in which he had been previously involved, since he himself had signed Marbury's commission. Not everybody considered this ethical.

The dangerous implications of the Marshall decisions were not lost on Jefferson, who was quick to see that this was a permanent threat to free government in the future. A court that usurped the power—never granted by the Constitution—to pass upon legislative acts endangered the whole structure of democracy and challenged, in effect, the right of the people to legislate unhindered for themselves.

Jefferson struck back at the judges. One Federal judge, notorious for his intemperance, was impeached. Others were threatened with impeachment wherever their conduct warranted it. The President was out to show the judiciary that they were not above the law and the will of the people.

In battling the judiciary, Jefferson followed a definite constitutional theory. His theory was—and James Madison, the "Father of the Constitution," agreed with him—that the framers of the Constitution had intended the three branches of the Government to check, not to dominate, each other. Jefferson had no desire to interfere with the judges when they were doing their duty. On the other hand, he had no intention of permitting them to interfere with the acts of the legislative or the executive branches. Any presumption of power on the part of one against the other, he considered as despotism. He expressed this idea clearly when he granted pardons to the victims of the Sedition Act. In a letter to Abigail Adams (he was no longer on speaking terms with her husband) he explained:

The judges, believing the law constitutional, had a right to pass a sentence of fine and imprisonment; because that power was placed in their hands by the Constitution. But the Executive, believing the law to be unconstitutional, was bound to remit the execution of it; because that power has been confided to him by the Constitution. The instrument meant that its co-ordinate branches should be checks on each other. But the opinion which gives to the judges the right to decide what laws are constitutional . . . would make the judiciary a despotic branch.

Jefferson's greatest attempt to break the power of the judiciary was the impeachment of Justice Samuel Chase of the Supreme Court. This was the same highhanded Chase who had presided at the trial of Thomas Cooper and James Thomson Callender. It was the same bullying judge who had told some of Virginia's most eminent attorneys in court to shut up. It was the same Justice who once ordered the Federal Marshal to strike off the panel "any of those creatures or persons called democrats." It was the same Chase who, in addressing a grand jury in Baltimore, went out of his way to attack the new Maryland constitution because it provided for manhood suffrage, which, he said, would "certainly and rapidly destroy all protection to property and all security to personal liberty, and our republican Constitution will sink into a mobocracy."

Chase was, in short, an intemperate reactionary of exceptional virulence who reveled in outraging public opinion. As far back as 1778 he had been, in the words of Alexander Hamilton, "universally despised" (because he had tried to corner the market on flour). Now Jefferson decided that the time had come when this embittered enemy of democracy should meet his proper deserts at the hands of the representatives of the people whom he reviled.

The President, in a letter to Congressman Nicholson, urged that the House impeach Chase, and early in 1804 a committee was appointed to "enquire into the judicial conduct of Samuel Chase." A year later the House, by a vote of 73 to 32, voted to impeach the Justice on eight counts of misfeasance and malfeasance. The brilliant John Randolph of Roanoke acted as prosecutor for Congress. Five of the greatest lawyers of the day appeared on behalf of Chase.

The trial took place in the Senate, which was set up like the English House of Lords. A majority of two-thirds was necessary for conviction on any one of the eight counts. Of the thirty-four Senators who acted as the court in the impeachment, twenty-five belonged to Jefferson's party, and nine were Federalists. Since only twenty-three were necessary for conviction, it looked as if Justice Chase's goose was cooked. But it happened that the President was either unable or unwilling to crack the whip. Six of the Republican Senators refused to follow the majority of their party.

The trial, which lasted for nearly a month, was the most sensational of its day. The drama was heightened by the fact that the man who presided at the trial was the Vice-President of the United States, Aaron Burr. He had just slain Alexander Hamilton in a scandalous duel and was a fugitive from public indignation and from justice.

On a number of counts a majority of the Senate found Chase guilty—but no two-thirds majority could be found. Article 4, for example, charging that Chase's conduct in the Callender case was marked by "manifest injustice, partiality and intemperance," got 18 Senators for conviction, and 16 against. On Article 8, accusing Chase of delivering "an intemperate and inflammatory political harangue" before the grand jury at Baltimore, the vote was 19 guilty, 15 not guilty. The upshot was that the impeachment fell through. It is possible that what saved Justice Chase was a "trade-union" feeling on the part of the lawyers in the Senate. They did not like to set a dangerous precedent against one of their kind, and in not finding Chase guilty they also nullified the value of impeachment as a check on officeholding lawyers. After the Chase case Jefferson said that impeachment was a "farce."

The failure of the Senate to impeach Chase was a defeat for Jefferson. If the Justice had been convicted, the President would probably have followed it with an impeachment of the whole Supreme Court. But as it was, he saw no reason for repeating the "farce." What was left of Federalist power now sought entrenched shelter behind the battlements of the Supreme Court, where the judiciary bided its time to tear Jeffersonian idealism to rags and tatters.

16

If Jefferson failed in his attempt to put a permanent curb on the judiciary, he succeeded in scaring it stiff. For the time being, the Federal judges were on the run. None of them liked to face even the threat of impeachment and the consequent notoriety; many ran to cover. Chase himself, properly squelched, delivered but one opinion afterward. Richard Peters, a District of Columbia judge who had sat with Chase in the trial of Callender, was so frightened by the threat of impeachment that for five years he refused to sign an order to carry out a decision that he himself had made in the District Court.

But while the judiciary was momentarily silenced, the Federalist press was not. Their numbers dwindling and their influence waning, the desperate Federalists fought a bitter last-ditch press campaign against "that man" who had driven them from power. Die-hard Federalists carried on a guerrilla war against the President, sniping at his Administration and besmirching his character. One of their toasts was "Damnation to Jefferson forever!" [11]

Jefferson's patience was severely tried and his democratic philosophy was put to a hard test. The temptation to strike back, to punish the libelers and to silence the calumniators, was exceedingly strong. But Jefferson, conscious of his mission and convinced that the eyes of the world were upon his democratic "experiment," resisted the temptation to curb the offenders. The test of freedom of speech, he well knew, was in its practice, not in its theory. No matter how greatly the newspapers abused their freedom, Jefferson felt, it was vital for democracy that that freedom be not checked.

In thus acting, Jefferson taught a whole generation of Americans to respect the principle of freedom of expression. Even highly partisan newspapers gave at least lip service to the idea. Wrote the *Republican Advocate:* "Kind and salutary as the dew of heaven to the productions of nature, is the freedom of the press to the plant of liberty."

Jefferson, furthermore, never failed to hammer home the lesson in the practice of freedom. Carefully he formulated the reasons underlying his behavior, so that his fellow citizens would have something to go by. He wrote to a friend:

. . . they [the Federalists] fill their newspapers with falsehoods, calumnies, and audacities. . . . We are going fairly through the experiment whether freedom of discussion, unaided by coercion, is not sufficient for the propagation and protection of truth, and for the maintenance of an administration pure and upright in its actions and views. No one ought to feel, under this experiment, more than myself. Nero wished all the necks of Rome united in one, that he might sever them at a blow. So our ex-federalists, wishing to have a single representative of all the objects of their hatred, honor me with that post, and exhibit against me such atrocities as no nation had ever

[11] *Republican Advocate,* Mar. 11, 1803. "The remains of federalism, like the remains of royalty in France during the revolution, now smell offensively to every honest man. The true patriot, and upright statesman, hold their noses as they pass by them. It is full time that the carcase should be buried."— *Ibid.,* Jan. 14, 1803.

before heard or endured. *I shall protect them in the right of lying and calumniating.*[12]

Jefferson had confidence in the good sense of the people and was convinced that they would not be permanently blinded by a biased press. In 1803 he wrote:

Indeed the abuses of the freedom of the press here have been carried to a length never before known or borne by any civilized nation. But it is so difficult to draw a clear line of separation between the abuse and the wholesome use of the press, that as yet we have found it better to trust the public judgment, rather than the magistrate, with the discrimination between truth and falsehood. And hitherto the public judgment has performed that office with wonderful correctness.

The President suffered deeply from the poisoned barbs of the printers, whose favorite target he was. "You know," he wrote wryly to Thomas Cooper, "that if I write as a text that two and two are four, it serves to make volumes of sermons of slander and abuse." Nevertheless, he was determined that nothing should block the "experiment" in freedom. He used the word "experiment" in this connection with such frequency that it is clear that he acted with purposive deliberation. He wrote to John Tyler:

No experiment can be more interesting than that we are now trying, which we trust will end in establishing the fact that man may be governed by reason & truth. Our first object should therefore be to leave open to him all the avenues to truth. The most effectual hitherto found is the freedom of the press. It is therefore the first shut up by those who fear the investigation of their actions. The firmness with which the people have withstood the late abuses of the press, the discernment they have manifested between truth & falsehood shew that they may safely be trusted to hear everything true and false & to form a correct judgment between them.

And again he wrote:

I have lent myself willingly as the subject of a great experiment, which was to prove that an administration, conducting itself with integrity and common understanding, cannot be battered down, even

[12] Italics mine. S. K. P.

by the falsehoods of a licentious press, and consequently still less by the press, as restrained within the legal & wholesome limits of truth. This experiment was wanting for the world to demonstrate the falsehood of the pretext that freedom of the press is incompatible with orderly government.

Madison was right when he told Lafayette, after Jefferson's death, that "no man more than Mr. Jefferson, regarded the freedom of the press as an essential safeguard to free Govt."

Alexander von Humboldt, the great German world traveler, when on his tour of exploration of the Western Hemisphere went hundreds of miles out of his way to visit the city of Washington. He wanted to meet the great man who was President of the young Republic. In Jefferson's study Humboldt was surprised to see a newspaper that was filled with abuse of the President. "Why are these libels allowed?" the Prussian visitor asked. "Why is not this libelous journal suppressed, or its editor at least fined and imprisoned?"

Jefferson smiled. "Put that paper in your pocket, Baron," he said, "and should you hear the reality of our liberty, the freedom of our press, questioned, show this paper and tell where you found it."

17

Jefferson also taught the country democratic manners. After all the talk about a monarchy under Washington and the hullabaloo about pomp under Adams, Jefferson decided to set the country a deliberate example of republican simplicity. One of his earliest acts as occupant of the President's House was to abolish the weekly levee, a pompous institution borrowed from monarchy. As practiced under Washington and Adams, the levee meant that once a week starch-bosomed ladies would appear before the President to do homage to the throne. Here was the incubation of snobbery, and Jefferson considered it unseemly in a democracy.

The President did away with the levee in a manner worthy of a play by Molière. When the word spread that Jefferson would no longer hold any levees, the ladies of Washington put on their best dresses and "mustered in force" at the President's House. But they found no President. He was out riding. Grimly they waited; they would have their levee whether the President liked it or not.

He came from his ride booted, spurred, dusty, hat in hand. Seeing the ladies, he beamed at them with all the suavity of a courtier and the graciousness of a Virginia gentleman. What a splendid surprise! What a delightful visit! He was overjoyed to see them! And would they not stay a bit longer? Speechless and bewildered, the ladies left in a hurry. Some had the humor to laugh at their discomfiture. The country laughed too. And the levee was buried forever after.

Jefferson also put the rules of precedence and etiquette, which had been rigidly observed under Washington and Adams, under the ax. He abolished formal state dinners and entertained only privately. At the table, which was round so that no one should claim precedence over the other, everyone was seated alike. The idea was, Jefferson said, that "nobody shall be above you, nor you above anybody."

Not without malice, for he despised snobs, the President instituted what he called the rule of "pêle mêle" which meant that no individual, regardless of his rank or importance, was to have precedence in going from one room to another. Women in the mass simply preceded men in the mass, on the principle that "When brought together in society, all are perfectly equal." This principle knocked the bottom from under the social climbers and caused at least one minor international incident.

The droll affair involved Anthony Merry, the British Minister in Washington, who did not understand how a diplomat could function without precedence and without gold lace. It was not dignified. It was not cricket. And it just was not done. But the dreadful thing did happen to Mr. Merry. When he arrived in Washington, Secretary of State Madison took him to see the President. Merry, resplendent in full regalia, gold lace, dress sword, and all, expected a formal state reception. Instead, he found the audience hall empty. This was his first surprise. But the real shock came when Madison led him, through a narrow passageway, to the President's study and introduced him. Jefferson was cordial, but his appearance—! The amazed Merry, clinging to his dress sword, saw before him a man, he tells indignantly, "not merely in an undress, but actually standing in slippers down at the heels, and both pantaloons, coat and underclothes indicative of an indifference to appearance." The British minister considered Jefferson's appearance a studied insult to His Majesty. Perhaps it was. When Jefferson was introduced at the court in London in 1786, George III had been deliberately rude.

This did not end the Merry affair. Jefferson invited Merry and his wife—a shrew and a snob, whom the President privately called a "virago"—to dinner. Among the other guests were the Spanish Minister, the Marquis de Yrujo, and his hoity-toity wife (née Sally McKean of Philadelphia); the French Minister, Louis Pichon, and his wife; and James Madison and his wife Dolly. Minister Merry had not been warned about "pêle mêle" and he, the diplomat representing the ranking Power, expected to be given precedence and be seated ahead of the other guests. Instead, Jefferson calmly offered his arm to Dolly Madison and seated her on his right; the others were left to follow and seat themselves "pêle mêle."

This was too much for the infuriated Merrys. They considered themselves outraged, demeaned, affronted, humiliated, and never so insulted in their lives. Merry protested the "incivility" to his Government in London and asked for further instructions. Jefferson, who was quietly amused at all this ado, tried to soothe the British Minister. He told him that this was a democracy and that everybody was equal. No insult was intended. He wrote James Monroe, who was American Minister at London:

We have told him that the principle of society as well as of government, with us, is the equality of the individuals composing it. That no man here would come to a dinner, where he was to be marked with inferiority to any other. That we might as well attempt to force our principles of equality at St. James's as he his principle of precedent here.

But it was no use; the Merrys would not be appeased. Never again did they appear socially at the President's House. Mrs.

Merry wept outraged tears when uncouth American democrats visited her house and sometimes stepped on her gown. They also commented occasionally on her diamonds. The city of Washington under President Jefferson was, indeed, a veritable Calvary for the Merrys, the Yrujos, and the Sally McKeans.

The Merrys were not the only visitors to be offended by Jefferson. There was also Tom Moore, the Irish poet. When Merry introduced Moore to the President, the latter, from his towering height, looked down upon the perfumed little dandy (he had never heard of him before), courteously acknowledged the introduction, and passed on to other matters. Moore, hypersensitive as short men are apt to be, was cruelly stung. Later he traduced the President and castigated America in savage verse.[13]

Moore's description of the President was, nevertheless, fair and graphic:

He is a large man; in fact, I never met a man of loftier stature. He has a noble face, with a Scotch-Irish cast of feature, and with curly hair of a reddish tint, although greatly mixed with gray. His mouth is large and firm set, while his nose is of the true Scottish type and unusually wide at the nostrils. As to his eyes, I would say that they are of a grayish and light blue tint mixed, and steely in expression. His brow is broad and white and very free from wrinkles. His whole appearance denotes a man of vigorous actions, and did I not know that he was President of the United States, I would judge him to be a gentleman of landed property, with all the inclinations of a fox-hunting squire.

Another Briton, Sir Augustus Foster, secretary of the British Legation, did not like Jefferson's slippers. Indeed, Jefferson *en pantoufles* seems to have had an upsetting effect upon certain people. Foster, impressed by the President's stature, thought that he looked like a ruddy farmer:

[13] In his *Epistles* (2d ed., 1806) Moore thus slandered Jefferson:

> "The weary statesman for repose hath fled
> From halls of council to his Negro's shed,
> Where blest he woos some black Aspasia's grace,
> And dreams of freedom in his slave's embrace!"

To make sure that he would not be misunderstood, the poet explained in a footnote that this allusion was to the President of the United States.

. . . he was a tall man, with a very red freckled face, and grey neglected hair; his manners goodnatured, frank, and rather friendly, though he had somewhat of a cynical expression of countenance. He wore a blue coat, a thick grey-coloured hairy waistcoat, with a red under-waistcoat lapped over it, green velveteen breeches with pearl buttons, yarn stockings, and slippers down at the heels; his appearance being very much like that of a tall, large-boned farmer.

Slippers were not the only thing for which Jefferson was criticized. One of the presidential guests in 1802 was Thomas Paine, the freethinker who shocked the pious, the radical who scandalized the Tories. Jefferson welcomed him warmly and appeared with him on the street arm in arm. The stuffed shirts in and around Washington were outraged. One citizen suggested that the President and his "blasphemous crony" should be hanged on the same gallows. While Paine was staying at the President's House, a new Senator, William Plumer of New Hampshire, came to pay his respects to the President. Plumer had never met Jefferson. He relates:

. . . a tall, high-boned man came into the room. He was dressed, or rather undressed, in an old brown coat, red waistcoat, old corduroy small clothes much soiled, woollen hose, and slippers without heels. I thought him a servant, when General Varnum surprised me by announcing that it was the President. I tarried with him about twenty minutes. He was easy of access, and conversed with great ease and freedom.

The shock of being received by a President in slippers was as nothing compared to seeing Thomas Paine in the Executive's house. While Jefferson was talking to Senator Plumer, Paine entered the room and behaved, the scandalized New Englander remarked, with the familiarity of "an equal." Plumer was upset. "Can virtue," he asked himself indignantly, "receive sufficient protection from an administration which admits such men as Paine to terms of intimacy with its chief?" The Senator thought not, and had no use for Jefferson afterward.

18

The President's House was fitted out in the utmost comfort, designed for living and not for show. Every room reflected Jefferson's tastes, habits, and interests. His working hours, and they were long, were spent in the study. Here the walls were lined with books, maps, and charts. In the window recesses were plants and flowers. Among the geraniums and the roses hung a cage containing a mockingbird, which Jefferson loved for its melodious voice and its devotion to him. The bird was his faithful companion during work. When there were no callers, the President let the bird fly freely about the room. Frequently it would perch on his shoulder while he was working and sing in his ear. It ate from his lips. And when Jefferson went to his room for a rest the affectionate bird would hop after him and chirp.

The Presidency, although not yet as burdensome as it was to become a century later, nevertheless absorbed virtually all of Jefferson's time. He complained to his friends that he did not have a free moment. The job compelled him to give up his favorite studies and books, as well as to interrupt his correspondence on scientific and speculative subjects. "It is rare I can indulge myself in the luxury of philosophy," he confessed to Du Pont de Nemours in 1802. As for mechanics and mathematics, two of his favorite subjects, he told Thomas Paine: "I am obliged to abandon them entirely."

His purchases in the field of books and instruments were confined largely, if not exclusively, to the practical. The President found little time to read, and when he did read, it was poetry. He read and reread Homer and Tasso, Shakespeare and Milton, Dryden and Pope; also the British ballads, particularly Ossian, the favorite of his youth. Occasionally he would clip verses from newspapers and, with his usual methodicalness, paste them in a scrapbook. Among the papers from which he clipped were the *American Citizen*, the *Political Observatory*, the *Boston Gazette*, the (Philadelphia) *Aurora*, the *Trenton True Ameri-*

can, and the *New York Daily Advertiser.* In Jefferson's scrapbook there is a stanza from Thomas Sackville's *Mirror for Magistrates,* a poem first published nearly two centuries before the President was born:

> What doth avail to have a princely place,
> A name of honour, and a high degree;
> To come by kindred of a noble race,
> Except we princely, worthy, noble be!
> The fruit declares the goodness of the tree.
> Do brag no more of birth, or lineage then;
> For virtue, grace and manners make the man.

Characteristically, Jefferson thought this a great poem. In the margin of the scrapbook he remarked: "As good now as when it was written."

The President's greatest pleasure was giving little dinners to friends, acquaintances, and interesting companions. "I have only the evening in which I can indulge in the society of my friends," he wrote to Paine. These dinners combined the best features of relaxation and business.

Under Jefferson the President's House became renowned for its hospitality and its manner of living. There was more good talk and good cheer at the President's round table than, probably, at any other place in North America. Often there were as many as twelve guests at the table, but never more. The guests were selected for their suitability, not for their rank or position. The food was excellent and so was the wine, particularly the Madeira and the Champagne. During his first four years as President, Jefferson spent an average of $2,130 annually on wine. The annual consumption of Jamaica "syrop of punch" (a mixture of lemon juice, sugar, and alcohol) was 40 gallons. In 1804 he ordered 400 bottles of Champagne at $1 a bottle.[14] Warmed by the drinks and encouraged by the ever cheerful host, everybody had a great good time at the presidential dinners.

At the table Jefferson was dressed in snowy linen and in black garments whose severe simplicity only underlined their ex-

[14] In ordering the Champagne, Jefferson asked his agent not to disclose his name, since the merchants asked a higher price from him.

pensive quality.[15] His genuine liking for people was reflected in his face, which, according to a contemporary, "beamed with benevolence and intelligence." It was a face marked with generosity and humankindness. In personal matters he could not say No; "it is so much pleasanter to *give* than to *refuse*," he used to say, smiling.

The President was a vivacious host. At the table the conversation was kept on a level of generality so that everyone could participate, and everyone did. Jefferson subtly took the lead and tactfully encouraged his guests to display what talents and information they possessed. If any guest was neglected, the President went out of his way to pay him special attention and to draw him out. Once a guest who had just returned from a long residence abroad found himself a silent and unnoticed stranger. Jefferson suddenly turned to him and said so that everybody could hear: "To you, Sir, we are indebted to this benefit; no one more deserves the gratitude of his country." The guests turned in surprise to the silent stranger and the subtle President said: "Yes, Sir, the upland rice which you sent from Algiers and which thus far succeeds, will, when generally adopted by the planters, prove an inestimable blessing to our Southern States." The stranger, himself surprised, immediately became a center of attention.

The dinners were not exclusively for pleasure. They were also one of Jefferson's methods of governing the country. Washington was a "little village in the midst of the woods," as Senator Plumer remarked. There were no amusements, and the members of Congress were furiously bored. In the midst of the social desolation that was Washington, the President's House was one of the places where Congressmen and Senators could go for relaxation, good wine, and genial talk. And Jefferson took advantage of this situation.

[15] The old clothes and heelless slippers which so struck Merry and other visitors were worn by the President on democratic principle. Actually Jefferson possessed and wore fine and expensive clothes. He spent a considerable amount of money on his wardrobe. His accounts show that he paid as much as £13 sterling ($65 today) for a suit and 50s. ($12.50 today) for a hat. A pair of lace ruffles, bought in France, cost him 120 francs.

Sir Augustus Foster, the British diplomat whose disgust with Washington made him see matters through the clear eyes of hatred, remarks with great acumen:

> . . . he [Jefferson] could not have appeared in a great town, as he did at Washington, without attendants, when he took a ride, and, fastening his horse's bridle himself to a shop-door, as I have once witnessed, when his nail was torn off in the operation, or in yarn stockings and slippers when he received company; neither could he anywhere else have had the members of the legislature so dependent upon him and the rest of the administration for the little amusement and relief which they could obtain after public business; his house and those of the Ministers being in fact almost necessary to them, unless they chose to live like bears, brutalised and stupefied . . . from hearing nothing but politics from morning to night.

Congressmen and Senators, in effect, had little choice but to visit the President's House, and Jefferson, with his exquisite tact and insinuating manners, rarely failed to put over his point of view. The dinners, delightful as they were in themselves, thus also served as political instruments.

The President was fond of using the person-to-person method in overcoming opposition. He would invite an opponent or a potential opponent for a confidential chat, and the two would iron out their difficulties in the mellow atmosphere of the President's study. Once, for example, when Nathaniel Macon, the Speaker of the House of Representatives, was said to be planning to support a bill that Jefferson opposed, the latter wrote him the following note:

> My dear Sir
> Some enemy, whom we know not, is sowing tares among us. Between you & myself nothing but opportunities of explanation can be necessary to defeat these endeavours. . . . I must therefore ask a conversation with you. This evening my company may stay late: but tomorrow evening, or the next I can be alone. I mention the evening because it is the time at which alone we can be free from interruption: however take the day & hour most convenient to yourself. Accept my affectionate salutations.

When the President wanted to discuss something confidential, he would have only a few members of Congress at the table, and no listening waiters or prying servants. Near each guest was placed a dumb-waiter which contained the whole dinner, from soup to wine, and each guest served himself, the while talking freely and uninterruptedly.

Usually there would be about ten legislators at the table, Federalists one time and Republicans another. Jefferson rarely mixed them, for he disliked discord and had a prejudice against argumentative talk. He would state his opinions in a quiet, persuasive fashion, without undue emphasis; and he would listen patiently and sympathetically to opposing ideas. He refused to argue a point if anyone differed with him; discussion, he said, did not change opinions but riveted them. Moreover, he was tolerant of every point of view. He once told his grandson:

When I hear another express an opinion which is not mine, I say to myself, he has a right to his opinion, as I to mine; why should I question it? His error does me no injury, and shall I become Don Quixote, to bring all men by force of argument to one opinion? . . . If he wants information, he will ask it, & then I will give it in measured terms; but if he still believes his own story, & shows a desire to dispute the fact with me, I hear him & say nothing.

This method of listening sympathetically and not arguing was one reason for Jefferson's success and popularity.

The only man in the Jefferson circle who liked a good verbal fight was gay little James Madison, who peppered his brilliant talk with amusing anecdotes. Senator Plumer wrote to his wife in December, 1802:

Yesterday I dined with the President. His rule is to have about ten members of Congress at a time. We sat down to the table at four, rose at six, and walked immediately into another room, and drank coffee. . . . The wine was the best I ever drank, particularly the champagne, which was indeed delicious. I wish his French politics were as good as his French wines; but to me, at least, they have by no means so exquisite a flavor.

From a financial point of view, Jefferson could hardly afford the Presidency. His manner of living went beyond his income.

In the first year in office he spent $32,634, while his salary was only $25,000. In that year he derived around $3,000 from the sale of tobacco, so that he had to borrow more than $4,000 to make up the deficit. It might be argued that he could have economized on Madeira and Champagne, but then he also spent a considerable sum on charity—nearly $1,000 in 1801 and $1,585 in 1802. He could rarely make both ends meet and was therefore financially strained. When a friend asked him for a loan of $1,000, the President replied wistfully:

. . . no man is less in condition to aid his friends pecuniarily than myself. I have always endeavored so to live as just to make both ends meet; but imperfect calculations disappoint that endeavor, and occasion deficiencies which accumulating, keep me always under difficulties. My resources of every kind have for some time been on the stretch so that I can with truth assure you that at this time they could not be made to place one thousand dollars at my command.

19

The election year 1804 found Jefferson at the top of his political career. He was riding the wave of immense popularity. The people were prosperous. The country was at peace. "Never," said John Randolph in after years, "was there an administration more brilliant than that of Mr. Jefferson up to this period. We were indeed in the 'full tide of successful experiment!' Taxes repealed; the public debt amply provided for, both principal and interest; sinecures abolished; Louisiana acquired; public confidence unbounded."

Public confidence in Jefferson, despite the screechings of Federalist newspapers, was indeed "unbounded." On February 25, 1804, a congressional caucus in Washington unanimously nominated the President for re-election. Vice-President Burr was ignored. In his stead, the Republicans selected George Clinton, also of New York. The Jeffersonians had not forgotten that in the bitter election of 1800 Burr had permitted himself to be used by the Federalists in their attempted knifing of Jefferson, and now they would have nothing to do with him. And since Vice-President Burr had slain Alexander Hamilton, and was under indictment for murder both in New York and in New Jersey, the opposition party would not touch him either.

There was a pathetic scene in the President's House. Burr had decided to return to New York politics, but he knew that he could get nowhere without the approbation of the powerful President. He went to see Jefferson and pleaded with him for a token of public approval. If only the President would say a good word for him, he, Burr, could recoup his fortunes in New York. Jefferson was not encouraging. He had a feeling that he was dealing with a dangerous and desperate man. He had never quite trusted him, anyhow. "His conduct"—the President was speaking of early days—"very soon inspired me with distrust. I habitually cautioned Mr. Madison against trusting him too much." [16]

Jefferson's enjoyment of the triumph of his unanimous renomination was dampened by a personal tragedy. His beautiful young daughter Maria, a brilliant and gifted girl whose aim in life had been to be worthy of her father, was gravely ill. In the spring the anxious father hurried to Monticello to be at her bedside. He came just in time. Maria's death was a merciless blow to her father. Jefferson, now sixty-one and with only one surviving child, was shaken as he had not been since his wife had gone. For hours after the young woman died, the stricken President stayed in her room with a Bible in his hand. Once again he was alone with his soul in the presence of inexorable death.

To his boyhood friend John Page, now Governor of Virginia, Jefferson poured out his overburdened heart. The letter to Page is a mixture of grief and philosophic reflections, with undertones of bitterness:

[16] Jefferson frankly admitted that, despite his distrust, he had accepted Burr as a running mate purely as a political reward: "When I destined him for a high appointment, it was out of respect for the favor he had obtained with the republican party by his extraordinary exertions and successes in the N. Y. election in 1800."

Others may lose of their abundance, but I, of my want, have lost even the half of all I had. My evening prospects now hang on the slender thread of a single life.

He wondered bitterly whether he was destined to lose even that last "cord of parental affection." Death was cutting down his generation. The men he had known earlier in life—Samuel Adams, Edmund Pendleton, Alexander Hamilton—were dead.

Where are all the friends who entered it with us, under all the inspiring energies of health and hope? As if pursued by the havoc of war, they are strewed by the way, some earlier, some later, and scarce a few stragglers remain to count the numbers fallen.

For an awful moment the President doubted whether, under the circumstances, it was worth while carrying on.

Is it a desirable thing to bear up through the heat of the action, to witness the death of all our companions, and merely be the last victim? I doubt it. We have, however, the traveller's consolation. Every step shortens the distance we have to go; the end of our journey is in sight, the bed wherein we are to rest, and to rise in the midst of the friends we have lost.

There was not much campaigning that summer. The fury of the anti-Jeffersonian press, so fierce in 1800, had subsided to a low growl in 1804. The leadership of the Federalists was demoralized and their ranks were depleted by desertions to the Jeffersonian cause. Everywhere the Republicans were on the march, conscious of their democratic strength and believing in their democratic mission. Their leader, who had successfully planned the defeat of the Federalists, was the most commanding figure in America. Nobody in the land had even a fighting chance of beating Jefferson. He was loved by common men as few leaders had been loved before. And the Federalist candidates who opposed him, General Charles Cotesworth Pinckney of South Carolina and former Senator Rufus King of Massachusetts, were cultured and able gentlemen, but not national heavyweights.

The election turned into a pitiful rout of the Federalists. Of the seventeen States that voted (including Ohio, recently admitted to the Union), Jefferson got fifteen. In most States there was not even a contest; they simply went to Jefferson. The President even carried Massachusetts, where John Adams, who was one of the electors, voted for Jefferson, perhaps because he got tired of playing King Canute to the democratic tide. Except for Connecticut and Delaware, Jefferson got nearly all the votes that were cast—162 out of 176.

It was an overwhelming triumph for Jefferson and a vindication of his democratic ideas. His popularity was so phenomenal that some observers, such as John Adams, thought that the President would be elected again in 1808. But Jefferson had no such intentions. He was convinced that there was a danger to democracy in more than two terms. Before the votes were counted he told a friend that he would not run for a third term:

I determined to withdraw at the end of my second term. The danger is that the indulgence & attachments of the people will keep a man in the chair after he becomes a dotard, that reelection through life shall become habitual, & election for life follow that. General Washington set the example of voluntary retirement after 8 years. I shall follow it.

20

Accompanied by enthusiastic citizens and militia, Jefferson went down muddy Pennsylvania Avenue, which he had planted with poplars, to Capitol Hill to deliver his second inaugural address. It was a simply written speech delivered in so low a voice that only a few people in the crowded auditorium were able to hear it. The sixty-two-year-old President gave an account of his national stewardship, and his barely audible words reflected a sense of quiet pride in his genuine achievements.

He told how he had cultivated friendship with all nations. He explained how the abolition of unnecessary offices had enabled the Government to eliminate internal taxes—"what farmer, what mechanic, what laborer, ever sees a tax-gatherer of the United States?" the President asked. The acquisition of Louisiana, Jefferson continued, enlarged the area of republicanism and secured the opposite bank of the Mississippi through the future settlement of "our own brethren and children." Freedom of the press, despite its abuse of the President, had been upheld, in order to prove to the world that self-government could function without suppression. That policy had been vindicated by the electorate.

Jefferson dwelt at some length on his successful policy of conciliating the Federalists. The election showed what great unity now prevailed throughout the country, and the President hoped that the rest of the Federalists would lose the "veil" from their eyes. He ended with an appeal for even greater national unity and for the aid of "that Being in whose hands we are."

Our wish . . . is that the public efforts may be directed honestly to the public good, that peace be cultivated, civil and religious liberty unassailed, law and order preserved; equality of rights maintained. . . . let us cherish them [the Federalists] with patient affection; let us do them justice, and more than justice . . . and we need not doubt that truth, reason, and their own interests, will at length prevail, will gather them into the fold of their country, and will complete their entire union of opinion, which gives to a nation the blessing of harmony, and the benefit of all its strength.

21

Jefferson's second Administration, which began in an aura of goodwill and peace, was pock-marked with trouble and ended in adversity.

One of the troubles that caused greater annoyance than harm was the Aaron Burr conspiracy against the unity and welfare of the United States. The Burr plot is still cloaked in considerable mystery; its details are blurred and its motivations are vague. Perhaps only the student of adventure yarns will want to dig deeper into Burr's efforts to build himself a Western realm. The historian, especially at this late date, finds the story relatively unimportant.

It seems that after Burr left the Vice-Presidency, discredited as a man, ruined as a politician, he approached Jefferson's

enemies with offers to do harm to the President and the coun-
try. One of those approached was Merry, the British Minister,
who still smarted from having been kicked in his dignity by
Jefferson's slippers. Merry actually advised his Government in
London to give Burr $500,000 for a promise to detach the
Western States from the Union. Burr also got in touch with the
Spanish Minister Yrujo, as well as a number of high United
States Army officers, among them General William Eaton (who
gave away the scheme to Congress), General James Wilkinson,
and General Andrew Jackson. The former Vice-President was
also active among certain people in the West, on the Ohio, on
the Mississippi, and in New Orleans. The schemes that were
hatched and the promises that were made sound more like a
Grade B Hollywood thriller than veracious history.

Wind of the intrigues and machinations reached Jefferson
sometime in 1806. Among those who warned the President of
Burr's devious doings was the same General Wilkinson who had
originally lent an ear to the conspiracy. In the autumn of 1806,
after the incredulous President was convinced that the Burr
intrigue was not altogether a comic-opera affair, he issued an
order for the arrest of the former Vice-President. Burr was
seized and brought to Richmond for trial on a charge of treason.

Fortunately for Burr, the man who presided at the trial was
Chief Justice John Marshall, and it was almost a foregone conclusion what the verdict would be. It was sufficient for the Chief
Justice to know that Jefferson desired a conviction to do everything—within technical legal limits—in favor of Burr. The
Chief Justice showed marked friendliness to Burr, and he actually sat at the same table with one who was arraigned as a
traitor. The whole trial was turned into a joke at Jefferson's
expense, and Burr was acquitted because Chief Justice Marshall's calculated definition of treason was such that it could not
apply to the defendant.

Although the Chief Justice acquitted Burr, and although
the upper-class ladies of Richmond treated the former Vice-
President like a conquering hero, the people still considered
Burr a traitor. So deep was the popular aversion for him that

in some places he was almost lynched, and finally he had to flee the country—"there is not a man in the U.S.," Jefferson wrote, "who is not satisfied of the depth of his guilt." Regardless of what a Justice of the Supreme Court said, Burr was still regarded as a traitor, and the people were still with Jefferson.

22

The President's real difficulties originated not with traitors at home but with enemies abroad. Two empires, the British and the French (under Napoleon), were locked in a mortal struggle for world supremacy. They were trying to strangle each other by blockade and counterblockade, both being naval Powers. The Atlantic Ocean was one of the major areas of battle.

Facing the belligerent empires across the ocean was the United States. It too was a marine Power, although not a significant naval one. It too was an Atlantic country depending upon the salt water for most of its exports and imports. Of the approximately 6,000,000 people in the United States, about 80 per cent lived in States that fronted the Atlantic. When the two leviathans, as Jefferson called them, churned the ocean with their powerful tails, they threw up waves high enough to inundate the American Atlantic shore and affect the lives of the great majority of the American people.

The situation that confronted Jefferson, who loved peace, was how to defend American shipping and American rights from the Anglo-French predators, who did not love peace. The problem was further complicated by the fact that the United States had no navy to speak of. Without a strong navy, Jefferson was in no position to play off one belligerent against the other. That the President was a lover of peace did not necessarily endear him to Napoleon or make the British Tories respect him. In a world of violence only violence was respected. The British in particular, having crippled Napoleon's navy at Trafalgar, ruled the waves and, on the seas, waived the rules.

One of the rules the British suspended, and the one that most infuriated and humiliated Americans, was that against impressment of American sailors on the high seas. Being engaged in a life-and-death fight with the conqueror of Europe, a war in which naval power played a preponderant role, the British were frequently shorthanded as to sailors. To recruit their navy, the British therefore resorted to impressment, which is a polite word for abduction.

The theory behind the abductions was that the sailors thus seized—"impressed" into service—were British citizens. There was enough truth in the claim to make the situation cruelly complicated. Many British subjects actually served in the American merchant marine, for the simple reason that they earned higher wages under the Stars and Stripes than under the Union Jack. A number of them were naturalized American citizens—only a little over half of the *Constitution's* crew of 419, however, were United States citizens in 1807—but on the high seas this was difficult to prove. Any sailor with a British accent was liable to be taken off an American ship, and many were, even just outside New York Harbor. And all that American captains could do about it was to protest to Washington; Washington protested to London, and London sometimes ordered the release of the unfortunates who had been abducted. This was one of the country's earliest lessons in the folly of being unarmed in a world at war. It also caused Jefferson to suffer a succession of severe headaches—sure sign of strain and tension.[17]

The most scandalous case of impressment occurred in the summer of 1807 when the American frigate *Chesapeake* (38 guns) was hailed by the British man-of-war *Leopard* (50 guns) outside Chesapeake Bay. The *Leopard* demanded permission to "search for deserters" on the American frigate. Commodore Barron refused, and the British frigate opened fire, killing three men and wounding eighteen. The *Chesapeake*, her decks cluttered and her guns unprepared for action, struck her flag.

The news of the attack on the *Chesapeake* caused a burst of anger throughout the land. Commodore Barron and a number of his officers were court-martialed for negligence, but this did

[17] Madison to Monroe, Mar. 10, 1806: "The President is just taken with one of his afflicting periodical headaches. We hope . . . that it will be less severe than his former ones."

not lessen the tension, or diminish the gravity of the outrage. If Jefferson had wanted to declare war on Britain he would have had a solidly united country behind him. But the President kept his head, knowing that the United States was in no position to wage war against a powerful enemy. He protested to London and demanded both apology and reparation. He promptly ordered British warships out of American waters.[18] At the same time he asked Congress for money to build 188 gunboats to add to the existing miniature fleet of 69 gunboats.

Jefferson's gunboats, which he built upon the advice of naval experts, were a contemporary joke, and the Federalists never tired of making jests about them. These gunboats, like Ford's Tin Lizzies of a later date, easily lent themselves to rich humor. They were so small and light that a high wind could lift them and deposit them on land—a high wind once did with one. Each vessel carried two guns, and their weight was such that the whole works capsized in foul weather. The best that can be said for this pathetic ersatz fleet is that it did no one any harm.

"We have borne patiently a great deal of wrong," the President wrote to Madame de Staël a few days after the *Chesapeake* outrage, "on the consideration that if nations go to war for every degree of injury, there would never be peace on earth." But, he added, his patience had limits.

Jefferson's attitude of hostility toward Great Britain was forced upon him by the blind and vindictive behavior of the British Tories and their contemptuous treatment of the young republic. Actually, Jefferson loved and admired the British people. What he hated was their government. As far back as 1775 he told John Randolph: "Believe me, dear Sir, there is not in the British Empire a man who more cordially loves a union with Great Britain, than I do." And again: "I . . . would rather be in dependence on Great Britain, properly limited, than on any other nation on earth." But Britain was not "properly limited" in Jefferson's time; it was a country corrupted by a "pampered aristocracy" and a greedy merchant class.

[18] Even Jefferson's bitterest critics approved of his prompt action. He was so surprised at their praise that he exclaimed with the Psalmist: "Lord, what have I done that the wicked should praise me."

"The English have been a wise, a virtuous and truly estimable people. But commerce and a corrupt government have rotted them to the core."

Jefferson always hoped that the British Tories would relent in their hostility and stretch out a hand of friendship. He was eager to grasp such an offer and ally with England—"the land of our own language, morals, manners, & habits," as he called it. In 1804, he wrote to Richard Rush:

No two nations on earth have so many interests pleading for a cordial frdshp, and we have never had an executive which was not anxious to have cultivated it, if it could have been done with any regard to self-respect.

He repeated similar sentiments two years later, in a letter to James Monroe, who was then Minister in London:

No two countries upon earth have so many points of common interest & friendship; & their rulers must be great bunglers indeed, if, with such dispositions, they break them asunder. . . . If . . . she [England] is just to us, conciliatory, and encourages the sentiment of family feelings & conduct, it cannot fail to befriend the security of both. . . . We ask for peace & justice from all nations; & we will remain uprightly neutral in fact, tho' leaning in belief to the opinion that an English ascendancy on the ocean is safer for us than that of France.

But the British Tories were too blind to see the outstretched hand of a friend across the Atlantic.

23

The British ignored Jefferson's protests and actually intensified their hostile acts (royal proclamation of October 17, 1807). And the French, although not in a position to do the same amount of damage as the British, were no more friendly. Napoleon sneeringly referred to the American flag as "only a piece of striped bunting."

Between the British blockade of France and the French counterblockade of Britain, American commerce was caught in the jaws of an iron pincers. Napoleon sealed the European ports against England. In retaliation, the British issued Orders in Council (November 11, 1807) declaring that all European ports that excluded the British should henceforth be "subject to the same restrictions."

Napoleon countered with a declaration that his navy would capture any ship that had permitted itself to be searched by British warships or that sailed from a British port. This was a blow to neutral shipping in general and American shipping in particular. American vessels were now caught in a crushing dilemma. They could obey the British Orders in Council and thereby run the risk of capture by Napoleon's privateers; or they could adhere to Napoleon's decrees and expose themselves to seizure by the British.

Faced with a heads-you-win-tails-I-lose situation, what could Jefferson do? To protect American rights and interests against repeated outrages and contemptuous violations was beyond the physical resources of the Government. A nation of 6,000,000 people, most of them making their living from agriculture, could not wage war against the two greatest empires in the world, or even against one of them. Yet to ignore the violations was to invite more of the same.

Lacking a strong fleet and an effective fighting force, the country could not go to war, even assuming that Jefferson believed in war as an instrument for settling international disputes, which he did not. Once, to be sure, Jefferson had used force to settle a difficulty. The action took place in the Mediterranean where Moroccan, Algerian, and Tripolitan pirates levied tribute and ransom on Occidental merchants. The Moslem marauders had collected about $2,000,000 from Americans in ten years, and the economizing Jefferson thought that the money could be used to better advantage at home. He sent a naval squadron to the Mediterranean, and after a series of gallant actions on the part of the American sailors, the Barbary corsairs agreed to respect the American flag. It was one thing, however, to teach a lesson to a handful of barbarians, and another to make two world empires at war obey the rules of civilized behavior.

But was there no substitute for war? Jefferson was convinced that there was. The substitute was known as the Embargo.

Behind the policy of the Embargo lay a sound theoretical idea. Since the object of war was to defeat an opponent, or to make him respect your rights, it followed that any method that achieved this aim was good. Guns were the conventional mode of waging war. But suppose another weapon were used—an economic weapon? A weapon that would withold vital supplies from, and cut off the trade with, the enemy. Would it not beat the opponent as effectively as a gun? Jefferson, the philosopher and apostle of peace, thought it was worth trying. He was perhaps the first important statesman in the world to carry out the experiment of waging a nonmilitary war.

The President was influenced in his by some of his European observers. J. Barnes, an American consul stationed at Leghorn, Italy, wrote to Jefferson that an embargo would cause so much deprivation and want in England that the Government would be compelled to knuckle under:

In fine, we have only to *Shut* our ports & *remain firm*—the *People* of *England* would *do* the *rest*—for British manufacturers being precluded from the Continent of Europe almost entirely, their chief resource is the U. S. consequently about 150,000 Manufacturers being thrown out of Bread would *rise* in Mass and *compel* the Minister to open our Ports at *any price,* or they would Massacre him.

The idea of an economic Embargo was excellent, but its success depended upon two factors, and Jefferson miscalculated both. One of them was the assumption that Britain's trade with the United States was of such importance that its lack would gravely damage her economy and impair her military position. This turned out to be far from the case. The other miscalculation was that the Embargo could be enforced. Jefferson assumed that the merchants of New York and New England would forgo profits and co-operate with the Government.

On December 22, 1807, the Congress, after receiving a brief message from the President, passed the Embargo Act by an overwhelming vote. Immediately thereafter Secretary of the Treasury Gallatin dispatched messengers to New York and

Boston and Norfolk and New Orleans and all other ports that had been doing a thriving business despite British provocations —to tie up all American ships until further notice.

The shipping interests promptly struck back. They began a systematic, almost joyful, sabotage of the Government's efforts. This, at last, was their chance to get even with "that man" in the President's House. Within a week after the Embargo Act was passed Jefferson received the following characteristic letter from New York: "We are the shipping interest and we will take care that [it] shall not be destroyed by your attachment to France, your implacable enmity to G[reat] B[ritain], and in short, by your madness & folly."

The shipowners and merchants met the Embargo Act (and the supplementary Non-Importation Act of April 16, 1808) with contempt and derision. Profits in illegal trading soared, and systematic smuggling became a big business. Goods from Britain were smuggled in by way of Canada, Florida, and the West Indies. And soon the anti-British blockade—for that is what the Embargo amounted to—was shot so full of holes that it became worse than futile.

Smuggling, however, was no compensation for lawful trade, and the Embargo boomeranged on the American people, preventing them from exporting their cotton, tobacco, and wheat. The pity of it was that the chief sufferers were the people Jefferson most wanted to help and protect—the little folk, the farmers, traders, and mechanics. The big companies weathered the crisis very well.   •

Except for smuggling, business, which in America of Jefferson's day meant small business, was hit severely. Ports were idle, ships dismantled. Exports dropped from $110,000,000 to $20,000,000 in the first year of the Embargo. In five months there were one hundred and twenty-five bankruptcies in New York City.

The distress in the country was not only visible but vocal. Even the British heard of it. George Canning, the British Foreign Secretary, remarked with devastating wit that England was willing to help Jefferson do away with the Embargo Act because it was a "measure of inconvenient restriction upon the American people."

The President stuck unswervingly to his policy. He hoped that the "present paroxysm of the insanity of Europe," as he called it, would not last forever, and in the meantime he would strive to keep out of war, regardless of provocations. To D. B. Warden he wrote:

Our eyes are turned with anxiety towards Europe to know whether after bearing so much from them they will let us live in peace. In truth I consider Europe but as a great mad house, & in the present deranged state of their moral faculties to be pitied and avoided. There is no bravery in fighting a maniac.

This, indeed, might have been his motto—"There is no bravery in fighting a maniac."

To another correspondent he wrote: "I think one war enough for the life of one man: and you and I have gone through one." Fighting the insolent British Tories or the "maniac" Napoleon, whom Jefferson loathed above all other men in the world, made no sense to the pacifist philosopher in the President's House.

The hardships caused by the Embargo, as well as the President's long-range patience under provocation, brought down a stream of vituperation upon his head. For the third time in less than two decades Jefferson found himself the central receiving-station of verbal sewage and the main target of sizzling animosities.

Most of the verbal violence came from New England, a region that, owing to its commercial economy, suffered most under the Embargo. A typical letter from New England, addressed to the President of the United States, read: "You Infernal Villain, How much longer are you going to keep this damned Embargo on to starve us poor people." New England's bitterness against Jefferson and his Embargo was perhaps best expressed in a poem written by a boy of fourteen named William Cullen Bryant. The poem was entitled "The Embargo."

Ill-fated clime! condemn'd to feel th' extremes,
Of a weak ruler's philosophic dreams;

Driven headlong on, to ruin's fateful brink,
When will thy country feel, when will she think! . . .

Curse of our nation, source of countless woes,
From whose dark womb unreckon'd misery flows;
Th' Embargo rages like a sweeping wind,
Fear lowers before and famine stalks behind. . . .

Go, wretch, resign the Presidential chair;
Disclose thy secret measures, foul or fair.
Go, search with curious eye, for horned frogs,
Mid the wild wastes of Louisianian bogs.

24

Little William Cullen Bryant's exhortation to Jefferson, "Go, wretch, resign the Presidential chair," was not only gratuitous but unnecessary. Long before the Embargo policies brought a hailstorm of hatred upon the President, he was determined to retire from public life at the end of his second term. In William Plumer's *Memorandum of Proceedings in the United States Senate* there is the following entry under date of February 6, 1807:

James Turner one of the senators from North Carolina informed me this day, that in a conversation he had with the President, he took the liberty to ask him Whether he would gratify the general wishes of the people, by standing candidate for another presidential term.

He said Mr. Jefferson assured him that he had made up his mind not to permit his name to be used as a candidate—That Genl Washington had established a precedent, of standing only for *two elections* —That it was a precedent which he thot was obligatory upon himself—& from which he could not depart. That he has himself uniformly advocated the principle of rotation in high offices. . . . That the most effectual method he can take to . . . prove the sincerity of his profession of rotation in office, will be, now he has the power, to imitate the great Washington, & not suffer himself to be a third time a candidate.

To the legislatures of Vermont and North Carolina, which asked him to run for a third term, Jefferson replied (December 10, 1807, and January 10, 1808) in a similar vein—that he did not wish to violate the two-term precedent set by President Washington, his "illustrious predecessor."

Jefferson's views on the limits of presidential terms were not immutably fixed. He changed his mind many times. At first he favored a single period of seven years with perpetual ineligibility thereafter. Then he abandoned the seven-year idea in favor of two four-year terms, as he explained to John Taylor in 1805:

> I have since become sensible that seven years is too long to be irremovable, and that there should be a peaceable way of withdrawing a man in midway who is doing wrong. The service of 8. years, with a power to remove at the end of the first four, comes nearly to my principle as corrected by experience.

A few years later he again reverted to a single term of service, both for Presidents and for Senators. He thought that Presidents, like Senators and Justices, served too long. To James Martin he wrote in 1813:

> Your quotation . . . alludes, as I presume, to the term of office to our Senate; a term, like that of the judges, too long for my approbation. I am for responsibilities at short periods, seeing neither reason nor safety in making public functionaries independent of the nation for life, or even for long terms of years. On this principle I prefer the Presidential term of four years, to that of seven years, which I myself had at first suggested, annexing to it, however, ineligibility forever after.

His final opinion, as expressed in the *Autobiography*, was that a two-term period of four years each was wise, particularly if precedent barred a third term:

> My wish . . . was that the President should be elected for 7 years & be ineligible afterwards. . . . But the practice adopted I think is better allowing his continuance for 8 years, with a liability to be dropped at half way of the term, making that a period of probation. . . . The example of 4 Presidents voluntarily retiring at the end of their 8th year, & the progress of public opinion that the

principle is salutary, have given it in practice the form of precedent & usage.

The "no-third-term" precedent was only one of a variety of causes that led Jefferson to reject the idea of remaining in Washington for an additional four years. "My determination to retire," he told his friend William Short, "is the result of mature reflections, and on various considerations." One of the motives for his eagerness to leave office was, he said, declining physical vigor. Although he enjoyed good health, Jefferson was nevertheless in his middle sixties, and the burdens of the Presidency were beginning to be felt. To John Dickinson he wrote early in 1807: ". . . yet two years to endure. I am tired of an office where I can do no more good than many others. . . . To myself, personally, it brings nothing but unceasing drudgery & daily loss of friends. Every office becoming vacant, every appointment made, me donne un ingrat, et cent ennemis." A year later he wrote to Monroe: "My longings for retirement are so strong, that I with difficulty encounter the daily drudgeries of my duty."

The world, too, had changed for the worse. Bitter criticism, personal abuse, and an international situation riven by violence made Jefferson more eager than ever to hand over the reins to a younger man. At sixty-five it was particularly painful to be exposed to the "flagitiousness" of the press that was full of "atrocious lies," or to feel comfortable in a world trampled by Napoleon. The newspapers continued to flay the President with merciless abandon, the oceans were the prey of Powers that behaved like pirates, and Europe was convulsed with strife. So dark was the world outlook that Jefferson, usually so buoyant and sanguine, sometimes despaired of the outcome. "Those moral principles and conventional usages which have heretofore been the bond of civilized nations," he wrote sadly to the Ketocton Baptist Association, ". . . have given way to force, the law of Barbarians, and the nineteenth century dawns with the Vandalism of the fifth."

It was time, he felt, to retire and let a younger man take over. The country was on the verge of revolt against the Embargo;

New England definitely threatened secession. Jefferson's own party was badly split, and his popularity took a nose dive. But the President was still powerful enough to select James Madison as his successor. In the election of 1808 Madison won by a comfortable majority, but only after a promise that the Embargo would be repealed.

Three days before his term expired, on March 1, 1809, Jefferson approved the bill repealing the Embargo. He had carried on a bold experiment and had lost. He had tried to save the country from losses, but the Embargo had ruined at least $50,000,000 worth of business. He had tried to spare the people humiliation, but he had only brought national wrath upon himself. But he was not convinced that the embargo policy was wrong. He left the presidential office under a cloud murky with disapprobation—but there was a surplus in the national treasury and the finances were sounder than ever before. On March 2 he wrote Du Pont de Nemours:

Within a few days I retire to my family, my books and farms, and having gained the harbor myself, shall look on my friends still buffeting the storm, with anxiety indeed, but not with envy. Never did a prisoner, released from his chains, feel such relief as I shall on shaking off the shackles of power.

The thought that in a few days he would be in the midst of his family in Monticello, away from strife, bitterness, and abuse, filled him with joy. But he was sorry for his friend James Madison, who was taking over all the burdens and perplexities of the presidential office. For that matter, Madison was sorry for himself.

A crowd of ten thousand flocked to Washington to attend Madison's inauguration. Jefferson accompanied his protégé and successor to the inaugural, this time in a carriage, and escorted by cavalry. Times had changed. Another sign of the times was an inaugural ball. It was held that evening at Long's Hotel in Georgetown and was attended by a brilliant assembly of four hundred guests. The center of attraction was not the black-garbed new President, nor his "portly, buxom" wife Dolly, bright in yellow velvet and a turban, but the lanky Jefferson. The outgoing President sparkled with joy and enchanted the guests with his jests and laughter. At the same time President Madison flitted about like a wraith, weary and worried. He knew that he had nothing to be gay about.

Jefferson mounted his sorrel and rode out of Washington under a bleak sky. Slowly he made his muddy way through the hills to Monticello, encountering a severe snowstorm on the way. Along the road the solitary traveler expected to be received with hostility. To his surprise, Virginia farmers thronged to meet and cheer "Old Tom." They drank his health and vigorously toasted "Thomas Jefferson—the Statesman, the Patriot and the Sage." To Virginians Jefferson was already a legend.[19]

He got to Monticello in the middle of March and his neighbors in Albemarle County flocked to give him a rousing wel-

[19] How Virginia felt about her famous son can be judged from the Farewell Address which both houses of the legislature passed on February 7, 1809. After acknowledging Jefferson's services and bidding him a "respectful and affectionate farewell," the address continued:

"We have to thank you for the model of an administration conducted on the purest principles of republicanism; for pomp and state laid aside; patronage discarded; internal taxes abolished; a host of superfluous officers disbanded; the monarchist maxim 'that a national debt is a national blessing,' renounced, and more than thirty-three millions of our debt discharged; the native right to nearly one hundred millions of acres of our national domain extinguished; and, without the guilt or calamities of conquest, a vast and fertile region added to our country. . . .

"In the principles on which you have administered the government, we see only the continuation and maturity of the same virtues and abilities, which drew upon you in your youth the resentment of Dunmore. From the first brilliant and happy moment of your resistance to foreign tyranny, until the present day, we mark with pleasure and with gratitude the same uniform, consistent character, the same warm and devoted attachment to liberty and the republic, the same Roman love of your country, her rights, her peace, her honor, her prosperity.

"How blessed will be the retirement into which you are about to go! How deservedly blessed will it be! For you carry with you the richest of all rewards, the recollection of a life well spent in the service of your country, and proofs the most decisive, of the love, the gratitude, the veneration of your countrymen.

"That your retirement may be as happy as your life has been virtuous and useful; that our youth may see in the blissful close of your days, an additional inducement to form themselves on your model, is the devout and earnest prayer of your fellow citizens who compose the General Assembly of Virginia."

come. The tall, gray former President had tears in his eyes as he addressed them:

Of you, then, my neighbors, I may ask, in the face of the world, "whose ox have I taken, or whom have I defrauded? Whom have I oppressed, or of whose hand have I received a bribe to blind mine eyes therewith?" On your verdict I rest.

```
┌─────────────────────────────────────────────────┐
│                                                   │
│                CHAPTER XIV                        │
│                                                   │
│                   Sage                            │
│                                                   │
│   1809                              July 4, 1826  │
│                                                   │
└─────────────────────────────────────────────────┘
```

CHAPTER XIV

Sage

1809   July 4, 1826

AT LAST Jefferson had reached a permanent port and, despite storms raging abroad, he could look forward to years of unbroken serenity on his farm in the midst of his family. "I am supremely happy in being withdrawn from these turmoils," he said. Forty years ago he had begun to build his brick eyrie on top of the hill, but only now, at the age of sixty-six, did he have any prospect of inhabiting it without interruption. This time, come what may, he was wedded to his beautiful home until his earthly days were over.

He was happy now and carefree and full of zest, humming as he walked and smiling at the world around him. For forty years, on and off, he had been in the service of his State and his country. Virtually every high office within the gift of his fellow citizens had been his. He had been State legislator and Congressman and Governor and Minister and Secretary of State and Vice-President, and President twice. It was a record never equaled in America before.

His life had been full and fruitful. He had experienced some defeats and many triumphs, and his name, he knew, was imperishably linked with the story of his country. He had doubled the territory of the United States, and had welded, from loose and scattered materials, a powerful political party. His ideals of liberty were graven into the law of the land, and his measures—the coinage, for example—were among the permanent institutions of the country. He had achieved all this by means of peace and persuasion. No one in all the land could say that Thomas Jefferson had shed blood or had inflicted injury upon his fellow men. "I have the consolation to reflect," Jefferson told Count Dugnani, the Papal Nuncio, in 1818, "that during the period of my administration not a drop of the blood of a single fellow citizen was shed by the sword of war or of the law."

The years of struggle and turmoil had given him an immense reservoir of moral strength. Time, like fire, having purified whatever weaknesses lurked in his character, he could face the opinion of his contemporaries and the judgment of history with equal serenity. Well past middle age, he was now that most rare of human species, a balanced and harmonious man capable of viewing the world with detached compassion and serene wisdom. Few men in history ever achieved such philosophical balance and spiritual harmony as did Jefferson in his later—his postpolitical—years. One of the few individuals who can compare with him in this respect was his contemporary, the German poet Goethe. "My temperament," Jefferson said at the age of sixty-seven, "is sanguine. I steer my bark with Hope in the head, leaving Fear astern."

And so, upon his retirement, he became what men called a sage—the Sage of Monticello. At that period, the period of Napoleonic wars and international reaction, the country needed just such a figure to act, or rather to live, as an example of spiritual elevation and mellow wisdom. If there was still some lingering bitterness against him as the founder and leader of a victorious political party, the country remembered him for the great role he had played. To a younger generation of Americans the still hale and vigorous Virginian was a piece from the tapestry of history—the author of the Declaration of Independence and the friend and associate of the now revered George Washington. And who can say that during this, the last period of Jefferson's life, he was not as useful to his country, as a symbol of national unity and wise counsel, as he had been during his years of activity?

2

Even if Jefferson's reputation had not inspired veneration, his appearance would have done so. He was nearly seventy-five inches of lean muscle, his body straight as a gun barrel. The face, fresh and unwrinkled under its white hair, was as serene as that of a Buddha. What struck visitors most, in fact, was the tranquillity of him.

Margaret Bayard Smith, wife of the editor of the *National Intelligencer and Washington Advertiser,* an ardent Jeffersonian triweekly, visited Monticello about four months after Jefferson's retirement and left a thoughtful record of her visit. She remarked of Jefferson:

There is a tranquillity about him, which an inward peace alone could bestow. . . . His tall and slender figure is not impaired by age. . . . His white locks announce an age his activity, strength, health, enthusiasm, ardor and gayety contradict. His face owes all its charm to its expression and intelligence; his features are not good and his complexion bad, but his countenance is so full of soul and beams with much benignity. . . . His low and mild voice harmonizes with his countenance rather than his figure. But his manners— how gentle, how humble, how kind. . . . To a disposition ardent, affectionate and communicative, he joins manners timid even to bashfulness, and reserved even to coldness.

One evening Mrs. Smith had an interesting conversation with the former President. Stimulated by an intelligent and sympathetic feminine listener, Jefferson spoke about himself. He admitted frankly what is, in perspective, clear to his biographer —that his whole life was a conflict between private inclination and public duty:

The whole of my life has been a war with my natural taste, feelings and wishes; domestic life and literary pursuits were my first and my latest inclinations—circumstances and not my desires led me to the path I have trod, and like a bow though long bent, which when unstrung flies back to its natural state, I resume with delight the character and pursuits for which nature designed me. The circumstances of our country, at my entrance into life, were such that every honest man felt himself compelled to take part, and to act up to the best of his abilities.

Now that he no longer had to worry about politics, Jefferson could devote himself to the art of living. He kept himself in perfect physical shape, and his daily regimen was worthy of a young athlete. Every day the old gentleman rose at dawn and made his own fire from dry wood which he kept in a box near the fireplace. He bathed his feet in ice-cold water and then dressed with neatness and simplicity. Ordinarily he wore short breeches, but in later years he substituted pantaloons. When preparing to ride he donned overalls.

After dressing he would write and read until breakfast. Then he would mount his favorite horse and ride for several hours, six or eight miles daily, but sometimes as many as forty miles. Before mounting the horse he would wipe its mouth and flanks with a white handkerchief to see whether the animal was clean. "From breakfast, or noon at latest, to dinner," he told his good friend Dr. Benjamin Rush, "I am mostly on horseback, attending to my farm . . . which I find healthful to my body, mind and affairs."

After a hard ride he would dine, at about three, on some meat and many vegetables. He drank water at least once a day and ate sparingly, though heartily, because he believed that one should always rise from the table a little bit hungry. He never smoked or played games of chance. After dinner he worked in his study, reading sometimes and writing often. He was, he said, "devoured by correspondences." At nine he retired to his room and read for about an hour, using spectacles at night but rarely during the day. Usually he went to bed at about ten and slept from five to eight hours.

3

He never wasted time and did not understand the meaning of idleness. Always he was doing something, and happy in what he was doing. His activities, he said, kept him "busy as a bee ın a molasses barrel." He was often either drawing or designing or sketching or outlining. Now it was a plow, now a carriage, now a building, now a fence, now a garden. A lover of flowers, he laid out a garden and planted rare specimens. An architect, he drew blueprints for many buildings, some of which still stand as monuments to the many-sided genius of their creator.[1] An inveterate inventor, he monkeyed with innumerable gadgets and improvements. He invented polygraphs, pontographs, and new-fangled plows. He designed a cunning dumb-waiter. He built himself a handy weathervane. He experimented with a hundred and one gimcracks.

Since his farms and those of his neighbors were located far from cities, Jefferson built a number of industrial establishments to make himself and his friends reasonably self-sufficient. His most ambitious undertakings in this respect were a flour mill and a nail factory. The flour mill, which he designed and built, was four stories high and made of stone. A canal three-fourths of a mile long led to the dam above the mill and cost several thousand dollars. The mill lost money.

The nail factory, begun before Jefferson's retirement from politics, was more profitable. It employed ten workers who earned $2 a day, a high wage for those days. Jefferson's nailery supplied the near-by stores as well as his neighbors, including James Monroe, with nails. It closed in 1812, when it was unable to obtain rods. There was also a small cotton mill which manufactured homespun from cotton obtained in Richmond. Three spinning machines wove cloth for all of Jefferson's slaves. Wagonloads of homespun were also sold to merchants. The plantation had a smithy and a furniture shop.

But Jefferson's primary activity was farming, for agriculture was his sole means of support. It was also the only way he could hope to pay his debts, especially those he had accumulated as President. "In a couple of years more," he wrote early in 1810, "I shall be able to clear out all the difficulties I brought on myself in Washington."

[1] Apart from Monticello, the best examples of Jeffersonian architecture are the Capitol in Richmond and the University of Virginia in Charlottesville. These are worth a special trip to the Old Dominion to see.

As a farmer, Jefferson was fortunate in possessing a scientific son-in-law. Thomas Mann Randolph, the brilliant and high-tempered husband of Martha Jefferson, was of immense help to his father-in-law. It was Randolph, according to Jefferson, who pioneered in plowing horizontally around hills to save soil and water from runoffs. "For this improvement," Jefferson said, "we are indebted to my son-in-law, Mr. Randolph, the best farmer, I believe, in the United States, and who has taught us to make more than two blades of corn to grow where only one grew before."

But growing two blades where one grew before did not spell prosperity. It was actually ruinous, as farmers have discovered from time to time in periods of crises. The world war then in progress, with its devastating blockades and counterblockades, knocked the bottom from agricultural prices, a development that had been further aggravated by Jefferson's Embargo policy; by a common irony Jefferson thus was the victim of his own work. Neither wheat nor tobacco, the crops of which he increased by 50 per cent, brought enough cash to pay for articles that he had to buy. The market for such products was shot to pieces and, Jefferson said in discouragement, you might as well burn the stuff or feed it to the animals. He complained:

I shall be like Tantalus up to the shoulders in water, yet dying with thirst. We can make indeed enough to eat, drink and clothe ourselves; but nothing for our salt, iron, groceries and taxes which must be paid in money. For what can we raise for the market? Wheat? we can only give it to our horses, as we have been doing ever since harvest. Tobacco? it is not worth the pipe it is smoked in. Some say whiskey; but all mankind must become drunkards to consume it.

4

Early in 1812, when Jefferson was in his sixty-eighth year, he received from a man of seventy-six a letter that gladdened his heart. There was not, to be sure, much to the letter. The writer simply informed Jefferson that he was sending him specimens of homespun and that his family was fine. But the signature was what mattered. The letter was signed—"with sincere Esteem your Friend and Servant"—John Adams. Thus began a classic correspondence in American history.

For eleven years, ever since the campaign of 1800, the two men had not been on speaking terms. Their estrangement, however, had not altered the fundamental admiration that each entertained for the other. Time had blunted the sharp edges of their political differences, and now that both were in retirement they could resume a friendship that was started way back when they were both comparatively young "rebels" against the British crown.

The conciliation of the two friends was the work of Dr. Benjamin Rush, the Philadelphia physician who was also one of the signers of the Declaration of Independence. Dr. Rush, who loved and admired both Jefferson and Adams, wanted the only living former Presidents, and the two greatest living American patriots, to pick up the threads of their friendship that had been broken under the stress of party politics. Jefferson said that he had forgotten all bitterness he had once felt and that his esteem for Adams was as high as ever. Adams, when approached by Rush, was also eager for the renewal of the friendship. He told Rush, surely there had been differences between Jefferson and him on political matters, but they were "miserable frivolities." Jefferson, Adams said with characteristic humor, believed in "liberty and straight hair. I thought curled hair was as republican as straight." Anyhow, why worry about all that? "His administration and mine are passed away into the dark backwards." And he added, "I have always loved him [Jefferson] as a friend."

After this admission, Adams wrote to Jefferson the letter about the homespun. Jefferson was deeply moved. The voice of Adams, coming from faraway Quincy, Massachusetts, was a voice from Jefferson's youth, bringing back the great and crucial days of the Revolution. He remembered how stanchly and loyally Adams had battled for the Declaration of Independence. He recalled how Adams, eight years his senior, had been active in a hundred patriotic causes. His reply to the older man was therefore full of eagerness and warmth. It was a rambling letter, covering many points which, Jefferson knew, Adams would be eager to take up.

A letter from you calls up recollections very dear to my mind. It carries me back to the time when . . . we were fellow-laborers in the same cause, struggling for what is most valuable to man, his right of self-government. . . . Still we did not expect to be without rubs and difficulties; and we have had them. . . . As for France and England, with all their preëminence in science, the one is a den of robbers, and the other of pirates. And if science produces no better fruits than tyranny, murder, rapine and destitution of national morality, I would rather wish our country to be ignorant, honest and estimable, as our neighboring savages are.

Then he wrote about himself, how he spent the day, what he was doing and reading.

I have given up newspapers in exchange for Tacitus and Thucydides, for Newton and Euclid, and I find myself much happier. Sometimes, indeed, I look back to former occurrences. . . . Of the signers of the Declaration of Independence, I see now living not more than half a dozen on your side of the Potomac, and on this side, myself alone.[2] You and I have been wonderfully spared, and myself with remarkable health. . . . I am on horseback three or four hours of every day. . . . I walk little, however, a single mile being too much for me, and I live in the midst of my grandchildren. . . . I salute you with unchanged affection and respect.

This letter inaugurated a series of communications that are remarkable for brilliance and bold adventuring in the realm of ideas. The two old gentlemen, both men of massive learning and vast intellectual curiosity, poured out their ideas with the zeal and zest of youngsters. To the intimacy of their letters they entrusted their innermost hopes and fears and prejudices and convictions and indignations. No one who is interested in the history of America should miss this record of two noble minds.

[2] In January, 1812, when Jefferson wrote this letter, only ten of the fifty-six signers of the Declaration of Independence were still alive. These were besides Jefferson and Adams: Charles Carroll (Maryland), George Clymer (Pennsylvania), William Ellery (Rhode Island), William Floyd (New York), Elbridge Gerry (Massachusetts), Thomas McKean (Delaware), Robert Treat Paine (Massachusetts), and Benjamin Rush (Pennsylvania). Of the seventeen Southern signers, only Jefferson and Carroll were alive.

They continued writing to each other until the end of their days. At least one hundred and fifty bulging envelopes marked "President Adams" and "President Jefferson" passed to and fro Monticello and Quincy. Jefferson wrote fewer letters than Adams, but the latter did not care. He was so eager to share his thoughts with Jefferson and to hear from him that even an occasional letter was an event. "Never mind," Adams told Jefferson, "if I write four letters to your one, your one is worth more than four of mine."

5

What did they write about? Practically everything. And everything they wrote has the freshness of youth and the permanency of what is nobly felt. Jefferson's letters reveal a consistent championship of democratic ideas and a systematic view of life. They are lively and forthright. Those of Adams are characteristically eccentric, full of tangy expressions, sharp with a Johnsonian bias. The letters of both are fruit-caked with learning, and they make lively reading. For instance, Adams quotes what Theognis said about aristocracy, then adds his own comment:

"My friend Curnis, when we want to purchase horses, asses, or rams, we inquire for the well-born, and every one wishes to procure from the good breeds." . . . Has science, or morals, or philosophy . . . shown . . . that the idea of the "well-born" is a prejudice, a phantom, a point-no-point, a Cape Flyaway, a dream? I say it is the ordinance of God Almighty, in the constitution of human nature, and wrought into the fabric of the universe.

And Jefferson took up the challenge. Of course, he said, there are differences among men. But a distinction must be made between a natural aristocracy and an artificial one. Natural aristocrats are people of good quality and decent virtues; such citizens are always valuable, but particularly so in a democracy. Artificial aristocrats are those who inherit birth or position; they are often useless and generally harmful. He wrote Adams:

I agree with you, that there is a natural aristocracy among men. The ground of this are virtues and talents. . . . But since the invention of gunpowder has armed the weak as well as the strong with missile death, bodily strength, like beauty, good humor, politeness and other accomplishments has become but an auxiliary ground for distinction. There is also an artificial aristocracy, founded on wealth and birth, without either virtue or talents. . . .

The natural aristocracy I consider as the most precious gift of nature, for the instruction, the trusts, and government of society. . . . The artificial aristocracy is a mischievous ingredient in government, and provision should be made to prevent its ascendency. . . .

I think the best remedy is exactly that provided by all our constitutions, to leave to the citizens the free election and separation of the aristoi from the pseudo-aristoi, of the wheat from the chaff. . . . In some instances, wealth may corrupt, and birth blind them; but not in sufficient degree to endanger the society.

They also discussed religion. Jefferson had written to Dr. Joseph Priestley that he considered the Christian philosophy "the most sublime & benevolent, but most perverted system, that ever shone on man." Adams was somewhat skeptical of this generalization. He wrote Jefferson:

That it is the most sublime and benevolent, I agree; but whether it has been more perverted than that of Moses, of Confucius, of Zoroaster, of Sanchoniathon, of Numa, of Mahomet, of the Druids, of the Hindoos, &c., &c., &c., I cannot as yet determine, because I am not sufficiently acquainted with these systems.

Jefferson picked up the argument. His quarrel was not with Christianity, the religion which he professed with devotion, but with its ministers—the "intolerant brethern, the Cannibal priests"—who had perverted the beautiful and simple ethics of Jesus.[3] To Adams he wrote:

It is too late in the day for men of sincerity to pretend they believe in the Platonic mysticisms that three are one, and one is three; and yet that the one is not three, and the three are not one. . . . But this constitutes the craft, the power and the profit of the priests.

[3] "History, I believe," Jefferson wrote to Alexander von Humboldt in 1813, "furnishes no example of a priest-ridden people maintaining a free civil government."

Sweep away their gossamer fabrics of factitious religion, and they would catch no more flies. We should all then, like the Quakers, live without an order of priests, moralize for ourselves, follow the oracle of conscience, and say nothing about what no man can understand, nor therefore believe.

Nor was Jefferson less severe in his condemnation of Calvinism. He confided to Adams:

I can never join Calvin in addressing *his God*. He was indeed an atheist, which I can never be; or rather his religion was daemonism. If ever man worshipped a false God, he did. The being described in his five points, is not the God whom you and I acknowledge and adore, the creator and benevolent governor of the world; but a daemon of malignant spirit. It would be more pardonable to believe in no God at all, than to blaspheme him by the atrocious attributes of Calvin. Indeed, I think that every Christian sect gives a great handle to atheism by their general dogma, that, without a revelation, there would not be sufficient proof of the being of a God.

The two old gentlemen also debated the question of life and death. In one letter Adams, aged eighty-one, asked Jefferson: "Would you go back to your cradle, and live over again your seventy years?" Jefferson replied that he was not sure that he would want to live all his life over again. The earlier years, yes. But the later years meant gradual physical decline, like the running-down of an unwound clock. Why perpetuate a worn-out mechanism?

Would I agree to live my seventy-three years over again forever, I hesitate to say. . . . from twenty-five to sixty, I would say yes; and I might go further back, but not come lower down. For at the latter period, with most of us, the powers of life are sensibly on the wane; sight becomes dim, hearing dull, memory constantly enlarging its frightful blank . . . spirits evaporate, bodily debility creeps on, palsying every limb, and so faculty after faculty quits us, and where, then, is life? . . .

There is a ripeness of time for death, regarding others as well as ourselves, when it is reasonable we should drop off, and make room for another growth. When we have lived our generation out, we should not wish to encroach on another.

I enjoy good health. I am happy in what is around me; yet I assure you, I am ripe for leaving all, this year, this day, this hour.

This question ceased to be academic when, in 1818, Abigail Adams died and her husband, at eighty-three, was left alone with his memories of a great and noble woman. Jefferson wrote his afflicted friend a letter of condolence that was hushed with sadness:

Tried myself in the school of affliction, by the loss of every form of connection which can rive the human heart, I know well, and feel what you have lost, what you have suffered, are suffering, and have yet to endure. The same trials have taught me that for ills so immeasurable, time and silence are the only medicines. . . . it is of some comfort to us both, that the term is not very distant, at which we are to deposit in the same cerement, our sorrows and suffering bodies, and to ascend in essence to an ecstatic meeting with the friends we have loved and lost, and whom we shall still love and never lose again.

"While you live," Adams replied, "I seem to have a bank at Monticello, on which I can draw for a letter of friendship and entertainment."

6

Although Jefferson, in search of tranquillity, preferred reading Horace and Tacitus to contemporary newspapers, he could not escape hearing the echoes of a very much disturbed world. Friends came to him when in trouble, and the occupant of the President's House in Washington sought his advice when in perplexity, which was not infrequently.

President Madison was a reasonable and sensible man, but he lacked fire and Jefferson's genius for politics and leadership. The times, moreover, were even worse than they had been under Jefferson, for the Franco-British world war was reaching its climax of fury. The whole world was agitated by this struggle between Napoleon, the most insolent dictator of his day, and the British Tories, who were not famous for their regard for the rights of others.

As Jefferson looked over the world scene he saw only gloom —a "conqueror roaming over the earth with havoc and destruction, a pirate spreading misery and ruin over the face of the ocean." He hoped that America would remain the "bed of roses" it was in contrast to Europe, but the whole conduct of Europe toward the United States continued to be, he said, "an atrocious and insulting tyranny." Jefferson counseled peace and patience to the harassed Madison, but the situation got out of hand and in June, 1812, Congress declared war against Britain.

The war was something bitter and distasteful for Jefferson to swallow, but he supported it and gave Madison strong encouragement. He had come to the reluctant conclusion that under certain circumstances war was preferable to a tortured and humiliating peace. The seventy-year-old Jefferson wrote sadly:

But our lot happens to have been cast in an age when two of the most powerful nations in the world, abusing their force . . . have dared to . . . substitute set up force instead of reason as the umpire of nations, degrading themselves . . . into lawless bands of robbers & pirates . . . Against such banditti, war had become preferable [and] less ruinous than peace, for their peace was a war on one side only.

For one of these international "banditti" Jefferson reserved a special and, for him, unique hatred. To Jefferson, Napoleon was the "Attila of the age" and he wrote about him with scathing contempt:

The Attila of the age . . . the ruthless destroyer of ten millions of the human race, whose thirst for blood appeared unquenchable, the great oppressor of the rights and liberties of the world. . . . In civil life a cold-blooded, calculating, unprincipled usurper, without a virtue.

And when Napoleon was at last safely caged on the rocky island of St. Helena Jefferson rejoiced that the Corsican's "inflated career" had ended miserably and meanly. "I considered him," Jefferson wrote to S. Cathalan, the American consul at Marseille, "as the very worst of all human beings, and as having inflicted more misery on mankind than any other who had ever lived."

Even the news that in his windswept island prison Napoleon was dying of an incurable disease did not soften Jefferson's hostility for the would-be ruler of the world. The author of the Declaration of Independence felt no pity for the destroyer of the liberties of France. He wrote George Ticknor:

The penance he is now doing for all his atrocities must be soothing to every virtuous heart. It proved that we have a god in heaven. That he is just, and not careless of what passes in this world. And we cannot but wish to this inhuman wretch, a long, long life, that time as well as intensity may fill up his sufferings to the measure of his enormities. But indeed what sufferings can atone for his crimes against the liberties & happiness of the human race; for the miseries he has already inflicted on his own generation, & on those yet to come, on whom he has rivetted the chains of despotism!

In a letter to the Papal Nuncio, Count Dugnani, Jefferson expressed similar sentiments:

. . . thanks be to God the tiger who revelled so long in the blood and spoils of Europe is at length, like another Prometheus, chained to his rock, where the vulture of remorse for his crimes will be preying on his vitals and in like manner without consuming them.

With the defeat of Napoleon in 1815 peace broke out, and the futile Anglo-American war came to an end too. During that war the President's House in Washington was burned, the small United States Navy trounced the veteran British fleet, and Andrew Jackson made his reputation at New Orleans. All the while Jefferson maintained an impressive outward tranquillity.

When young Randolph, Jefferson's grandson, rushed in from Charlottesville with the wonderful news of Andrew Jackson's astounding victory over the British at New Orleans, he found that his grandfather had gone to bed. Randolph dashed up to the old gentleman's bedroom with the newspaper, but Jefferson would not open the door. He told the excited young man that the news could wait until morning.[4]

4 In this connection it should be noted that Jefferson always had a prejudice against Andrew Jackson, mainly because he disliked military types. In 1824,

The Napoleonic wars and their consequent effect upon the United States wrought a revolution in one of Jefferson's fundamental ideas. From his youth on he had been an ardent agrarian, hostile to industry and somewhat contemptuous of urban dwellers. He hoped that the people of America would tend the soil and leave trade and commerce to the "corrupt" English and other European merchants. He prayed that America would never develop a class of merchants and manufacturers. In his *Notes on Virginia* (Query XIX) he had penned an eloquent tribute to agriculturists and a scathing denunciation of those who did not "labor in the earth":

Those who labour in the earth are the chosen people of God, if ever he had a chosen people, whose breasts he has made his peculiar deposit for substantial and genuine virtue. It is the focus in which he keeps alive that sacred fire, which otherwise might escape from the face of the earth. Corruption of morals in the mass of cultivators is a phaenomenon of which no age nor nation has furnished an example. It is the mark set on those, who not looking up to heaven, to their own soil and industry, as does the husbandman, for their own subsistence, depend for it on casualties and caprice of customers. Dependence begets subservience and venality, suffocates the germ of virtue, and prepares fit tools for the designs of ambition. . . .

. . . generally speaking the proportion which the aggregate of the other classes of citizens bears in any state to that of its husbandmen, is the proportion of its unsound to its healthy parts, and is a good enough barometer whereby to measure its degree of corruption. While we have land to labour then, let us never wish to see our citizens occupied at a work-bench, or twirling a distaff. Carpenters, masons, smiths, are wanting in husbandry: but, for the general oper-

when Jackson was the Republican candidate for the Presidency, Jefferson refused to endorse him. He said: "I feel much alarmed at the prospect of seeing General Jackson President. He is one of the most unfit men I know of for such a place. He has had very little respect for laws or constitutions, and is, in fact, an able military chief. His passions are terrible. When I was President of the Senate he was a Senator; and he could never speak on account of the rashness of his feelings. I have seen him attempt it repeatedly, and as often choke with rage. His passions are no doubt cooler now . . . , but he is a dangerous man."

Jefferson also said that "One might as well make a sailor of a cock, or a soldier of a goose, as a President of Andrew Jackson." But Jefferson did not come out publicly against General Jackson, and the General was elected.

ations of manufacture, let our work-shops remain in Europe. It is better to carry provisions and materials to workmen there, than bring them to the provisions and materials, and with them their manners and principles. The loss by the transportation of commodities across the Atlantic will be made up in happiness and permanence of government. The mobs of great cities add just so much to the support of pure government, as sores do to the strength of the human body.

Industry, he had reasoned, would corrupt and undermine American democracy. It would also, he feared, lead to war because it would attempt to sell its manufactured goods in a competitive international market. This, Jefferson told John Jay, is what would happen once American merchants began to ship goods abroad:

Their property will be violated on the sea, & in foreign ports, their persons will be insulted, imprisoned, &c. for pretended debts, contracts, crimes, contraband, &c., &c. These insults must be resented, even if we had no feelings, yet to prevent their eternal repetition; or, in other words, our commerce on the ocean & in other countries, must be paid for by frequent war.

But bitter experience shattered Jefferson's hopeful assumption that it was possible for the United States to remain a purely agricultural nation. A quarter-century of wars, blockades, counterblockades, impressments, seizures, piracies, and embargoes had taught Jefferson the folly of economic isolation. It had taught him that in a world where war was a frequent—nay, an institutional—occurrence, it was madness to depend upon foreign Powers for industrial necessities and manufactured goods. Early in 1815 Jefferson admitted his mistake in a letter to the French economist Jean Baptiste Say, whom he encouraged to come to America and open a cotton mill:

I had . . . persuaded myself that a nation, distant as we are from the contentions of Europe, avoiding all offences to other powers . . . might expect to live in peace, and consider itself merely as a member of the great family of mankind; that in such case it might devote itself to whatever it could best produce, secure of a peaceable exchange of surplus for what could be more advantageously furnished by others. . . . But experience has shown that continued peace depends not merely on our own justice and prudence, but on that of others also; that when forced into war, the interception of exchanges which must be made across a wide ocean, becomes a powerful weapon in the hands of an enemy domineering over that element, and to the other distresses of war adds the want of all those necessaries for which we have permitted ourselves to be dependent on others, even arms and clothing. This fact, therefore, solves the question by reducing it to its ultimate form, whether profit or preservation is the first interest of a State?

For Jefferson this viewpoint was a veritable mental revolution. In fact, he was so startled by his own conclusion that "we must now place the manufacturer by the side of the agriculturist" that he felt apologetic. "There is perhaps a degree of duty to avow a change of opinion called for by a change of circumstances," he explained to Benjamin Austin, the man who had been his political lieutenant in the campaign of 1800. It was in a letter to Austin that Jefferson fully explained his position and his drastic change of mind. Austin, Jefferson knew, would pass on his views to his followers.

You tell me I am quoted by those who wish to continue our dependence on England for manufactures. There was a time when I might have been so quoted with more candor, but within the thirty years which have since elapsed, how are circumstances changed! We were then in peace. . . . A commerce which offered the raw material in exchange for the same material after receiving the last touch of industry, was worthy of welcome to all nations. It was expected that those especially to whom manufacturing industry was important, would cherish the friendship of such customers by every favor, by every inducement, and particularly cultivate their peace by every act of justice and friendship. Under this prospect the question seemed legitimate, whether, with such an immensity of unimproved land, courting the hand of husbandry, the industry of agriculture, or that of manufactures, would add most to the national wealth? . . .

This was the state of things in 1785, when the "Notes on Virginia" were first printed. . . . But who in 1785 could foresee the rapid depravity which was to render the close of that century the disgrace of the history of man? Who could have imagined that the two most distinguished in the rank of nations, for science and civilization, would have suddenly descended from that honorable eminence, and setting at defiance all those moral laws established by the Author of nature between nation and nation, as between man and man, would cover earth and sea with robberies and piracies, merely because strong enough to do it with temporal impunity; and that . . . we should have been despoiled of a thousand ships, and have thousands of our citizens reduced to Algerine slavery.

Yet all this has taken place. One of these nations interdicted to our vessels all harbors of the globe without having first proceeded to some one of hers, there paid a tribute proportioned to the cargo, and obtained her license to proceed to the port of destination. The other declared them to be lawful prize if they had touched at the port, or been visited by a ship of the enemy nation. Thus were we completely excluded from the ocean.

Compare this state of things with that of '85, and say whether an opinion founded in the circumstances of that day can be fairly applied to those of the present. We have experienced what we did not then believe, that there exists both profligacy and power enough to exclude us from the field of interchange with other nations: that to be independent for the comforts of life we must fabricate them ourselves. We must now place the manufacturer by the side of the agriculturist . . .

Shall we make our own comforts, or go without them, at the will of a foreign nation? He, therefore, who is now against domestic manufacture, must be for reducing us either to dependence on that foreign nation, or to be clothed in skins, and to live like wild beasts in dens and caverns. I am not one of these; experience has taught me that manufactures are now as necessary to our independence as to our comfort.

Thus Jefferson accepted the inevitable. Ultimately the growth of American industrialization led to the ruin of the agricultural South. Even in Jefferson's lifetime Congress passed a tariff which hit him and his fellow agrarians hard. Jefferson had to pay three times the prewar prices for shirtings, for example.

Jefferson's change of position on the subject of industrialization illustrates a basic quality of his mind, that of flexibility. He viewed the world as mutable. In his eyes nothing was permanent and nothing was rigidly fixed. Men changed, institutions changed, ideas changed. There was constant growth, and constant decay. The life cycle applied to nature as well as to institutions. Even the Constitution of the United States, which was the bulwark of American freedom, was not immutable. At the age of seventy-three Jefferson said that the Constitution was not "too sacred to be touched" but was a human institution that should be revised periodically when needed:

Some men look at constitutions with sanctimonious reverence and deem them like the arc of the covenant, too sacred to be touched. They ascribe to the men of the preceding age a wisdom more than human, and suppose what they did to be beyond amendment. . . . I know . . . that laws and institutions must go hand in hand with the progress of the human mind. . . . As . . . new discoveries are made, new truths disclosed, and manners and opinions change with the change of circumstances, institutions must advance also, and keep pace with the times. We might as well require a man to wear still the coat which fitted him when a boy, as civilized society to remain ever under the regimen of their barbarous ancestors. . . . Each generation . . . has . . . a right to choose for itself the form of government it believes most promotive of its own happiness. . . . a solemn opportunity of doing this every nineteen or twenty years, should be provided by the constitution.

His final conclusion in the matter of laws and institutions was that they were perpetually subject to change for the benefit of humanity. "Nothing then," he told Major John Cartwright in 1824, "is unchangeable but the inherent and unalienable rights of man."

7

News of war was not all that disturbed the tranquil retreat of the white-haired sage. He was also troubled by letters, which consumed precious time, and invaded by visitors, who drained his budget. Letters came unceasingly. In an average year Jefferson received about a thousand, and in some years the number reached nearly thirteen hundred. At Jefferson's death, his grandson Thomas Jefferson Randolph found twenty-six thousand letters and sixteen thousand answers on file.

To answer these letters was a stupendous task. Jefferson conscientiously replied to as many as he could, but it was crushing drudgery. "Is this life?" he groaned as he looked at the stacks of communications awaiting a reply. "At best it is but the life of a mill-horse, who sees no end to his circle but in death. To such a life, that of a cabbage is paradise."

Laborsaving devices and timesaving methods helped some. Jefferson invented a polygraph, an ingenious multiwriting machine that was useful in producing stereotyped letters. For job-seekers, particularly those who wanted him to intercede with the Administration in Washington, he had circulars printed stating that he was sorry but must decline "to exercise his influence with the President concerning appointments to office." When an appeal for a Federal job came in, Jefferson replied with one of those printed blanks, simply filling in date, address, and signature.

Visitors were a more difficult problem to solve and a considerably greater burden. Poor and rich alike flocked to Monticello. Some came to ask favors, others to request advice, still others to enjoy comfortable board and room. To all Jefferson gave unstintedly of his time, his money, and his resources.

Many people came to Monticello simply to look at the great man. Often strangers would plant themselves in the passageway near the study to see the Sage of Monticello as he came out to eat dinner. Once a woman broke a windowpane with her parasol in order to get a better view of him. Curious men and women would pass near the house to catch a view of Jefferson as he sat in the shade of the portico.

Those who came out of curiosity were a compliment at best and a nuisance at worst. But the visitors who stayed were a problem. Guests were so numerous and so frequent that Monticello sometimes looked like a big resort hotel at the height of the summer season. There were fifty beds for guests on the premises. At one time as many as seventy people were put up overnight. When the invasion became too great, Jefferson would travel a hundred miles to escape it—to Poplar Forest, a farm he owned near Lynchburg.

Usually he entertained his guests with that hospitality for which he was renowned, particularly when they were people he liked. Many guests have left records of their visits. In 1815 the New England historian George Ticknor, on his way to study in Germany, stopped off in Monticello to spend several

SAGE 381

days with Jefferson. Ticknor has described the life at Monticello as a beehive of regularity:

. . . everything is done with such regularity, that when you
know how one day is filled, I suppose you know how it is with the
others. At eight o'clock the first bell is rung in the great hall, and
at nine the second summons you to the breakfast room. . . . After
breakfast every one goes, as inclination leads him, to his chamber,
the drawing-room, or the library. The children retire to their school-
room with their mother, Mr. Jefferson rides to his mills on the
Rivanna, and returns at about twelve. At half past three the great
bell rings, and those who are disposed resort to the drawing-room
and the rest go to the dining-room at the second call of the bell,
which is at four o'clock. The dinner was always choice, and served
in the French style; but no wine was set on the table till the cloth
was removed. The ladies sat until about six, then retired, but returned with the tea-tray a little before seven, and spent the evening
with the gentlemen; which was always pleasant, for they are obviously accustomed to join in the conversation, however high the topic
may be. At about half past ten . . . I went to my chamber, found
there a fire, candle, and a servant waiting to receive my orders for
the morning, and in the morning was waked by his return to build
the fire.

Young Ticknor (he was then twenty-four) was impressed by
two things in the "extraordinary character" of his host. First,
Jefferson's clothes were unique; he wore sharp-toed shoes,
corduroy smallclothes, and a red waistcoat made of stiff wool.
This gave the rangy host a queer appearance. Second, Ticknor
was struck with Jefferson's conversation, deep, discursive, many-
sided, full of paradox, yet dominated by "sobriety and cool
reason."

Jefferson was a charming host, regardless of the race or position of his guests. What counted with him was character, not
pedigree. He entertained a cultured Negro with the same
warmth and courtesy as he did a French marquis—more so, in
fact. One of Jefferson's guests, in 1815, was Julius Melbourn,
a mulatto who had been born a slave. When Melbourn entered
the room, Jefferson rose with pleasure and evident curiosity.
He had heard of Melbourn as a learned man and he was eager

to see in the flesh the proof of what he always suspected—that colored folk were not inherently inferior to whites.[5]

According to Melbourn, the two men had a long and sympathetic talk on many learned topics. Jefferson told his mulatto guest that he was thinking of establishing a university in Virginia where there would be no bar to any sect or color. He spoke warmly of "our colored brethren." He discussed the political philosophy of Montesquieu, whose principles he did not admire, and the British constitution, which he liked even less. He also talked of David Hume, the influential English philosopher, who was Jefferson's bête noire in the realm of ideas.[6]

Another guest who left a record of his visit to Monticello was the French Baron de Montlezun. The Baron was struck by the youthful appearance of his host who, at seventy-three, "looks like sixty-three," and by his scientific interests. The products of Jefferson's paleontological and anthropological curiosity were stored in a small museum where the Baron admired such "excessively rare" objects as the head of a gigantic ram, an Indian

[5] In 1791 Jefferson wrote to Benjamin Banneker: "No body wishes more than I do to see . . . proofs that nature has given to our black brethren, talents equal to those of the other colors of men, and that the appearance of a want of them is owing merely to the degraded condition of their existence, both in Africa & America. I can add with truth, that no body wishes more ardently to see a good system commenced for raising the condition both of their body & mind to what it ought to be."

In 1809 he wrote to the Abbé Grégoire: ". . . no person living wishes more sincerely than I do, to see a complete refutation of the doubts I have myself entertained and expressed on the grade of understanding allotted to them [Negroes] by nature, and to find that in this respect they are on a par with ourselves."

[6] Jefferson had a prejudice against Hume because he thought him a narrow-minded reactionary who had "sold out" to the upper classes. To Melbourn he said: "It is painful that so profound a thinker, and so able a philosopher as David Hume, should have finally settled down in the professed belief that the fitness of things required that an immense majority of men should be slaves to a pitiful minority of their brethren. His veneration and love for the aristocracy, increased, perhaps, by his pecuniary interest, induced in his mind conclusions which rendered him a traitor to human nature."

In 1824 Jefferson wrote to Cartwright: "Hume, the great apostle of toryism, says . . . 'it is belied by all history and experience that the *people are the origin of all just power.*' And where else will this degenerate son of science, this traitor to his fellow men, find the origin of *just* powers, if not in the majority of the society?"

painting on five square feet of buffalo hide, and an upper jaw-bone of a mammoth.

To the Baron we are also indebted for a description of Jefferson's art collection. Of prints that hung on the walls at Monticello, De Montlezun observed portraits of Washington, Lafayette, John Adams, Sir Walter Raleigh, Franklin, Vespucius, Columbus, Francis Bacon, Locke, and Newton. Of busts, there were those of Cleopatra, Voltaire, Turgot, Czar Alexander I, Napoleon, Washington, Franklin, Lafayette, and John Paul Jones. There were also a number of indifferent paintings and at least three valuable ones. The latter included Poussin's "Ascension," Raphael's "Holy Family," and Rubens's "Flagellation of Christ."

Everywhere there were books, thousands of them. But guests did not leave Jefferson much time for reading, "my greatest of all amusements." He said: "Dr. Franklin used to say that when he was young and had time to read he had not books; and now when he had become old and had books, he had no time."

8

The world did not leave Jefferson alone in his retirement; on the other hand, it cannot be said that he kept thoroughly aloof from matters that were going on outside Monticello. He did not, to be sure, interfere with the policies of the Government in Washington; nor did he offer gratuitous advice. During the sixteen years that his two friends and disciples, Madison and Monroe, were in the Presidency, Jefferson scrupulously abstained from any intervention by word or deed. When Madison and Monroe asked his advice, which they not infrequently did, he gave it, but he left the initiative to them.

Nevertheless, Jefferson was active in influencing public opinion in his own way. As a matter of fact, in view of his position, his range of friendships, and his temperament, he could not help affecting the minds of others. This he did not only through conversation but, essentially, by means of letters. These superb letters were written with zest and frankness, for Jefferson loved ideas and was often carried away by them, especially when communicating with friends.

When we are pouring our inmost thoughts into the bosom of a friend we lose sight of the world, we see ourselves only as in confabulation with another self; we are off our guard; write hastily hazard thoughts of the first impression; yield to elementary excitement, because if we err, no harm is done, it is to a friend we have committed ourselves, who knows us, who will not betray us; but will keep to himself what, but for this confidence, we should reconsider, weigh, correct, perhaps reject, on the more mature reflection . . . of our reason.

Jefferson expressed himself with particular fullness and almost with impetuousness on subjects that were close to his heart —the judiciary, America's international policies, and religion. The years did not soften his hostility to the judges; if anything, conditions sharpened the severity of his opinions. Gradually, as Jefferson had foreseen, the judiciary was arrogating to itself powers never granted by the Constitution. He watched the process with helpless indignation. All he could do was to write letters to his friends, sharply critical records of his undying opposition to all forms of unchecked power.

. . . to consider the judges as the ultimate arbiters of all constitutional questions [is] a very dangerous doctrine indeed, and one which would place us under the despotism of an oligarchy. Our judges are as honest as other men, and not more so. They have, with others, the same passions for party, for power, and the privilege of their corps. Their maxim is *"boni judicis est ampliare jurisdictionem,"* and their power the more dangerous as they are in office for life. . . . The constitution has erected no such single tribunal, knowing that to whatever hands confided, with the corruptions of time and party, its members would become despots.

Three months later he wrote his famous letter to Thomas Ritchie:

The judiciary of the United States is the subtle corps of sappers and miners constantly working under ground to determine the foundations of our confederated fabric. . . . I will say, that "against this every man should raise his voice," and more, should uplift his arm. . . .

Having found, from experience, that impeachment is an impracticable thing, a mere scare-crow, they consider themselves secure for life; they sculk from responsibility to public opinion. . . . An opinion is huddled up in conclave, perhaps by a majority of one, delivered as if unanimous, and with the silent acquiescence of lazy or timid associates, by a crafty chief judge, who sophisticates the law to his mind, by the turn of his own reasonings. . . .

A judiciary independent of a king or executive alone, is a good thing; but independence of the will of the nation is a solecism, at least in a republican government.

The fear of a tyrannical Supreme Court, unchecked by anybody or anything, continued to haunt Jefferson's last years. He wrote to Judge Roane in the spring of 1821:

The great object of my fear is the federal judiciary. That body, like gravity, ever acting, with noiseless foot, and unalarming advance, gaining ground step by step, and holding what it gains, is ingulphing insidiously the special governments into the jaws of that which feeds them.

He wrote in the same vein to his son-in-law, John Wayles Eppes:

It is the Judiciary I fear, independent as they feel themselves of the Nation and all its authorities. They already openly avow the daring and impudent principle of consolidation and arrogate to themselves the authority of ultimately construing the constitution for all the other departments and for the nation itself.

As a correction to the danger to democracy inherent in a Supreme Court whose members were appointed for life, Jefferson proposed a six-year term:

Let them be appointed for the Senatorial term of six years, reappointed by the President with the approbation of *both* houses. Their official doctrines will be reviewed every six years, their conduct undergo the ordeal of debate and if they pass examination they will have heard strictures and criticism warning them to keep straight.

But such a proposal had no chance of acceptance in a Congress composed of many lawyers, some of whom hoped to be judges.

In part, Jefferson's hostility to the Federal judiciary is explainable on the ground of States' rights. Justices like John Marshall favored a strong central government at the expense of the individual States. Jefferson, on the other hand, was convinced that strong governments always tended to become tyrannical. He looked upon the individual States as barriers to centralized power and as checks upon Federal usurpation. The United States, moreover, was far too big to be efficiently governed from one central authority. Jefferson was sure that complete centralization would perforce lead to inefficiency, bribery, and corruption—as was the case with such large administrative areas as Russia and China. To Gideon Granger, the man who was to become his Postmaster-General (and job dispenser), Jefferson had written in 1800:

Our country is too large to have all its affairs directed by a single government. Public servants at such a distance, & from under the eye of their constituents, must, from the circumstance of distance, be unable to administer & overlook all the details necessary for the good government of the citizens, and the same circumstance, by rendering detection impossible to their constituents, will invite the public agents to corruption, plunder & waste. And I do verily believe, that if the principle were to prevail, of a common law being in force in the United States . . . it would become the most corrupt government on earth. . . .

What an augmentation of the field for jobbing, speculating, plundering, office-building & office-hunting would be produced by an assumption of all the state powers into the hands of the general government. The true theory of our constitution is surely the wisest & best, that the states are independent as to everything within themselves, & united as to everything respecting foreign nations. Let the general government be reduced to foreign concerns only . . . and our general government may be reduced to a very simple organization, & a very unexpensive one; a few plain duties to be performed by a few servants.

Jefferson thought that a balance of powers between the central government and the States would be the best safeguard of the liberties of the citizens, but only on condition that each respect the other and that no encroachment be permitted:

It is a fatal heresy to suppose that either our State governments are superior to the federal, or the federal to the States. The people, to whom all authority belongs, have divided the powers of government into two distinct departments, the leading characters of which are *foreign* and domestic; and they have appointed for each a distinct set of functionaries. These they have made co-ordinate, checking and balancing each other, like the three cardinal departments in the individual States: each equally supreme as to the powers delegated to itself, and neither authorized ultimately to decide what belongs to itself, or to its coparcenor in government. As independent, in fact, as different nations, a spirit of forbearance and compromise, therefore, and not of encroachment and usurpation, is the healing balm of such a constitution.

But "our blessed system," as Jefferson called it, gradually gave way to the inexorable march of commerce and industry on a national scale—which necessitated greater and greater centralization of power in Washington. This development, with its consequent encroachment upon the jealously guarded rights of the States, caused Jefferson considerable distress in his old age. At the age of eighty-two he wrote:

I see . . . with the deepest affliction, the rapid strides with which the federal branch of our government is advancing towards the usurpation of all the rights reserved to the States, and the consolidation in itself of all powers, foreign and domestic; and that too, by constructions [on the part of the judiciary] which, if legitimate, leave no limits to their power. . . . it is but too evident, that the three ruling branches . . . [of the Federal Government] are in combination to strip their colleagues, the State authorities, of the powers reserved by them.

He was deeply worried by the drift towards centralization, which the Federal judiciary helped along, and, frankly, he did not know how to solve the difficulty. He dreaded the possibility that further Federal encroachment upon the rights of the States might some day lead to armed uprising.

And what is our resource for the preservation of the constitution? Reason and argument? You might as well reason and argue with the marble columns encircling them. The representatives chosen by ourselves? They are joined in the combination, some from incorrect

views of government, some from corrupt ones, sufficient voting together to out-number the sound parts . . .

Are we then *to stand to our arms* . . . ? No. That must be the
last resource, not to be thought of until much longer and greater
sufferings. If every infraction of a compact of so many parties is to
be resisted at once, as a dissolution of it, none can ever be formed
which would last one year. We must have patience and longer endurance then with our brethren while under delusion; give them
time for reflection and experience of consequences; keep ourselves
in a situation to profit by the chapter of accidents; and separate from
our companions only when the sole alternatives left, are the dissolution of our Union with them, or submission to a government without
limitation of powers. Between these two evils, when we must make
a choice, there can be no hesitation.

But in the meanwhile, the States should be watchful to note every
material usurpation on their rights; to denounce them as they occur
in the most peremptory terms; to protest against them as wrongs
to which our present submission shall be considered, not as acknowl-
edgments of precedents of right, but as a temporary yielding to the
lesser evil, until their accumulation shall overweigh that of separation.

Here, prophetically, was the foreshadowing of a problem that
was to tear the United States to pieces within one generation.

9

In another realm, that of the policy of the United States
toward Latin America, Jefferson's advice met with more success. Moved by the belief that the Western Hemisphere was a
new world, offering chances for happiness to oppressed mankind, Jefferson always felt that there should be greater co-
operation among all the Americas. His vision of American unity
ranks him as one of the major prophets of Pan-America.

Before any such co-operation could be effective, it was im-
perative that the Latin American peoples attain independence
from Spain and freedom for themselves. But emancipation from
Spain was child's play compared to the attainment of an enlightened liberty internally. About that Jefferson had no illusions. He knew that centuries of Spanish misrule, accompanied

as it was by bigotry and obscurantism, had left their fatal mark upon the southern neighbors of the United States. In 1813 he wrote to Lafayette:

I join you sincerely . . . in wishes for the emancipation of South America. That they will be liberated from foreign subjection I have little doubt. But the result of my enquiries does not authorize me to hope they are capable of maintaining a free government. Their people are immersed in the darkest ignorance, and brutalized by bigotry & superstition. Their priests make of them what they please, and tho' they may have some capable leaders, yet nothing but intelligence in the people themselves can keep these faithful to their charge.

Their efforts I fear therefore [Jefferson concluded prophetically] will end in establishing military despotisms in the several provinces. Among these there can be no confederacy. A republic of kings is impossible. But their future wars and quarrels among themselves will oblige them to bring the people into action, & into the exertion of their understandings. Light will at length beam in on their minds and the standing example we shall hold up, serving as an excitement as well as a model for their direction may in the long run qualify them for self-government. This is the most I am able to hope for them.

"For I lay it down as *one of the impossibilities of nature that ignorance should maintain itself free against cunning*.[7]

Jefferson repeated this warning to Lafayette, who was an active friend of South American freedom, four years later:

I wish I could give better hopes to our southern brethren. The achievement of their independence of Spain is no longer a question. But it is a very serious one, what will then become of them? Ignorance and bigotry, like other insanities, are incapable of self-government. They will fall under military despotism, and become the murderous tools of the ambition of their respective Bonapartes.

But despite these doubts, Jefferson never gave up the idea of co-operating with South America and of putting up a barrier along the Americas against European powers. He had been tirelessly advocating such an American Wall for decades. In 1820 he wrote to an anonymous friend:

[7] Italics mine. S. K. P.

I hope . . . [for] a cordial fraternization among all the American nations and . . . their coalescing in an American system of policy, totally independent of and unconnected with that of Europe. The day is not distant when we may formally require a meridian of partition thro' the ocean which separates the two hemispheres, on the hither side of which no European gust shall ever be heard, nor an American on the other; and when during the rage of the eternal wars of Europe, the lion and the lamb within our regions shall lie down together in peace. . . .

And I hope no American patriot will ever lose sight of the essential policy of interdicting in the seas and territories of both Americas, the ferocious and sanguinary contests of Europe. . . . *I should rejoice to see the fleets of Brazil and the United States riding together as brethren of the same family and having the same interests.*[8]

Jefferson's warnings and suggestions struck responsive chords in the minds of many an influential American, particularly in James Monroe. A year before Monroe, who was Madison's Secretary of State, was inaugurated President, Jefferson advised him that the South Americans, then struggling to free themselves from Spain, should be given every possible aid.

Every kindness which can be shown the South Americans, every friendly office and aid within the limits of the law of nations, I would extend to them. . . . Interest . . . would wish their independence, and justice makes the wish a duty. They have a right to be free, and we a right to aid them, as a strong man has a right to assist a weak one assailed by a robber or murderer.

In October, 1823, when Jefferson was well past his eightieth birthday, he received a startling letter from President Monroe. The President asked his advice on a matter of grave international importance, that of co-operating with Great Britain to keep European Powers out of the Americas. The United States and Britain, it must be remembered, had been on terms of virtually uninterrupted hostility for half a century. Now Britain's Foreign Minister, George Canning, actually proposed friendly co-operation. Canning was motivated by the news that the reactionary Holy Alliance (Russia, Prussia, Austria, Spain, and Bourbon France) was planning to reconquer South America for

[8] Italics mine. S. K. P.

the greater glory of monarchy and the benefit of bigotry. He quickly got in touch with Monroe. Monroe communicated with Jefferson, and the latter, amazed at and pleased with the offer from Britain, urged immediate acceptance of Canning's proposition:

The question . . . is the most momentous which has ever been offered to my contemplation since that of Independence. . . . Our first and fundamental maxim should be, never to entangle ourselves in the broils of Europe. Our second, never to suffer Europe to intermeddle with cis-Atlantic affairs.

America, North and South, has a set of interests distinct from those of Europe, and peculiarly her own. She should therefore have a system of her own, separate and apart from that of Europe. While the last is laboring to become the domicil[e] of despotism, our endeavor should surely be, to make our hemisphere that of freedom. One nation, most of all, could disturb us in this pursuit; she now offers to lead, aid, and accompany us in it. By acceding to her proposition, we detach her from the bands [of despots], bring her mighty weight into the scale of free government, and emancipate a continent at one stroke. . . . Great Britain is the nation which can do us the most harm of any one, or all on earth; and with her on our side, we need not fear the whole world. With her then, we should most sedulously cherish a cordial friendship; and nothing would tend more to knit our affections than to be fighting once more, side by side, in the same cause. . . .

I could honestly, therefore, join in the declaration proposed, that we aim not at the acquisition of any of those possessions, that we will not stand in the way of any amicable arrangement between them and the mother country; but that we will oppose, with all our means, the forcible interposition of any other power, as auxiliary, stipendiary, or under any other form or pretext, and most especially, their transfer to any power by conquest, cession, or acquisition in any other way. I should think it, therefore, advisable, that the Executive should encourage the British government to a continuance in the dispositions expressed in these letters, by an assurance of his concurrence with them.

Jefferson even hinted that he favored going to war, in alliance with Britain, to keep Europe out of the Western Hemisphere. Thus once again his isolationism crumpled under the impact of Realpolitik.

Monroe accepted Jefferson's advice, and even his line of reasoning. Jefferson's letter was written on October 24. On December 2, President Monroe sent a message to Congress in which he announced that the United States should declare any attempt of European Powers "to extend their system to any portion of this hemisphere as dangerous to our peace and safety."

Thus, fathered by Jefferson, was born the Monroe Doctrine.

10

In his retirement, the white-haired Sage of Monticello missed no opportunity to preach tolerance and to hammer at bigotry, one of the seemingly unavoidable barnacles on the structure of organized religion. Although churches today no longer play the preponderant role they did in an earlier century, Jefferson's forthright letters on the subject are far from being outdated. No student of American democracy, least of all one interested in Jefferson, will want to miss them. Many churchmen were intolerant and bigoted, and Jefferson thought it necessary to fight them for the sake of enlightenment and freedom.

Be it stressed that Jefferson, although no churchgoer, was a sincere Christian, "a *real Christian*," as he called himself. He did not oppose the church but certain churchmen. He fully accepted the moral principles of Jesus, whom he regarded as one of the greatest figures in all history. What Jefferson rejected was sectarianism:

An eloquent preacher . . . is said to have exclaimed aloud to his congregation, that he did not believe there was a Quaker, Presbyterian, Methodist, or Baptist in heaven. . . . He added, that in heaven, God knew no distinctions, but considered all good men as his children, and as brethren of the same family. I believe, with the Quaker preacher, that he who steadily observes those moral precepts in which all religions concur, will never be questioned at the gates of heaven, as to the dogmas in which they all differ. . . . Of all the systems of morality, ancient or modern . . . none appear to me so pure as that of Jesus.

He once cut out the words of Jesus and pasted them, on blank pages, in chronological and subject order. The result was extremely impressive. "A more beautiful or precious morsel of ethics I have never seen," he told Charles Thomson; "it is a document in proof that *I* am a *real Christian*,[9] that is to say, a disciple of the doctrines of Jesus." And to another correspondent he wrote in the same vein:

> The sum of all religion as expressed by its best preacher, "fear God and love thy neighbor" contains no mystery, needs no explanation. But this wont do. It gives no scope to make dupes; priests could not live by it.

In his eightieth year, writing to Dr. Benjamin Waterhouse, the famous medical scientist of Boston, Jefferson thus summarized the doctrines of Jesus:

> The doctrines of Jesus are simple, and tend all to the happiness of man.
> 1. That there is only one God, and he all perfect.
> 2. That there is a future state of rewards and punishments.
> 3. That to love God with all thy heart and thy neighbor as thyself, is the sum of religion.

These pure principles, Jefferson added, had been corrupted and perverted by such men as Athanasius and Calvin, with their "*deliria* of crazy imaginations" which are "as foreign from Christianity as is that of Mahomet." Jefferson hoped that Americans, who had surrendered their conscience "to neither kings nor priests," would return to the unspoiled doctrines of Jesus. This would make the United States a Unitarian country.

Upon receipt of this blunt letter, Dr. Waterhouse asked Jefferson for permission to publish it, but the Sage, having more than once experienced the full fury of clerical rage, smilingly declined. At eighty he did not feel like having his repose disturbed by thunderous fulminations from a thousand pulpits.

> No, my dear Sir, not for the world. Into what a nest of hornets would it thrust my head! . . . Don Quixote undertook to redress the bodily wrongs of the world, but the redressment of mental

---

[9] Italics Jefferson's.

vagaries would be an enterprise more than Quixotic. I should as soon undertake to bring the crazy skulls of Bedlam to sound understanding, as inculcate realism into that of an Athanasian. I am old, and tranquility is now my *summum bonum*. Keep me, therefore, from the fire and faggots of Calvin and his victim Servetus.

Jefferson's letters on religion, though they delighted those who received them, were never made public during his lifetime. Many of his correspondents begged to be allowed to publish some of his letters, but he was adamant in his refusal. In 1816 he told Mathew Carey:

I write nothing for publication, and last of all things . . . on the subject of religion. On the dogmas of religion as distinguished from moral principles, all mankind, from the beginning of the world to this day, have been quarrelling, fighting, burning and torturing one another, for abstractions unintelligible to themselves and to all others, and absolutely beyond the comprehension of the human mind. Were I to enter on that arena, I should only add an unit to the number of Bedlamites.

To another correspondent, Judge Thacher of Massachusetts, Jefferson wrote at the age of eighty-one:

You press me to consent to the publication of my sentiments and suppose they might have effect even on Sectarian bigotry. But have they not the Gospel? If they hear not that, and the charities it teacheth, neither will they be persuaded though one rose from the dead. Such is the malignity of religious antipathies that, altho' the laws will no longer permit them, with Calvin, to burn those who are not exactly of their Creed, they raise the Hue & cry of Heresy against them, place them under the ban of public opinion, and shut them out from all the kind affections of society. I must pray permission therefore to continue in quiet during the short time remaining to me.

It was not, he said, that he was afraid of the clergy, but that he thought it crazy, at his age, to get himself mixed up in a public fight with people he despised:

You judge truly that I am not afraid of the priests. They have tried upon me all their various batteries, of pious whining, hypocritical canting, lying & slandering, without being able to give me one moment of pain. I have contemplated their order from the Magi of the East to the Saints of the West, and I have found no difference of character.

He had a special contempt for certain kinds of clergymen, especially those who disfigured the "genuine and simple religion of Jesus." He referred to the clergy as the "*genus irritabile vatum*" and as "mountebanks calling themselves the priests of Jesus." Their business in life, Jefferson said, was to confuse mankind with their "Abracadabra." He compared them to scuttlefish, which have the "faculty of shedding darkness . . . thro' the element in which they move, and making it impenetrable to the eye of a pursuing enemy, and there they will skulk."

To dissipate clerical obscurantism and its accompanying disease of intolerance, Jefferson believed that it was vital to practice religious freedom and to enlighten the people through universal education. "Religious freedom," he told Dr. De La Motta, rabbi of the Jewish synagogue at Savannah, Georgia, "is the most effectual Anodyne against religious dissension." To another man of the Jewish faith, Joseph Marx, Jefferson expressed his regrets that the Jewish sect, "parent and basis of all those of Christendom," should have been, in the past, singled out by Christians "for a persecution and oppression which proved they have profited nothing from the benevolent doctrines of him whom they profess to make the model of their principles and practice." The twin evils of bigotry and persecution could be avoided in the United States by a vigorous policy of enlightenment. "To penetrate and dissipate these clouds of darkness, the general mind must be strengthened by education," Jefferson concluded.

II

And so, in his old age, Jefferson developed a plan for public education in a democracy and gave the last years of his life to its realization. "I am now," he wrote at the age of seventy-four to George Ticknor, "entirely absorbed in endeavours to effect the establishment of a general system of education in my native state." He had long pondered on the subject of education. For years he had been reading up on educational methods and techniques in other lands; he also consulted specialists. He told his nephew Peter Carr in 1814:

I have long entertained the hope that this, our native State, would take up the subject of education, and make an establishment . . . where every branch of science, deemed useful at this day, should be taught in its highest degree. With this view, I have lost no occasion of making myself acquainted with the organization of the best seminaries in other countries, and with the opinions of the most enlightened individuals.

By 1817 Jefferson had the last detail of his plan worked out. It was one of the most ambitious projects ever designed for education in a free republic. He divided his educational system into three parts—elementary school, high school, and university. The elementary schools were to provide instruction in reading, writing, arithmetic, and geography. They were to be free to all children, for Jefferson insisted that it was the duty of government "to provide that every citizen . . . should receive an education proportioned to the condition and pursuits of his life."

In this connection it is noteworthy that Jefferson, ever the lover of liberty, hesitated to make attendance in elementary schools compulsory. Coercion of any kind was so distasteful to him that he would not see it applied even in so vital a matter as public education:

Is it a right or a duty in society to take care of their infant members in opposition to the will of the parent? How far does this right and duty extend?—to guard the life of the infant, his property, his instructions, his morals? The Roman father was supreme in all these: we draw a line, but where? —public sentiment does not seem to have traced it precisely. Nor is it necessary in the present case. It is better to tolerate the rare instance of a parent refusing to let his child be educated, than to shock the common feelings and ideas by the forcible asportation and education of the infant against the will of the father.

The high schools were to teach sciences and languages, and to provide, at public expense, preparation for the professions.

These high schools were to be established throughout the State, within one day's ride of every inhabitant.

The crown of the whole system was to be the university. It was to be composed of a number of professional schools, giving instruction in what Jefferson called "useful" branches of science. These professional schools were to train architects, musicians, sculptors, gardeners, economists, military and naval scientists, horticulturists, agronomists, physicians, historians, clergymen, and lawyers.

People thought Jefferson's educational plan visionary, and when it was introduced in the State legislature, it was, as Jefferson expected, rejected. Legislators, commented the Sage of Monticello dryly, "do not generally possess information enough to perceive the important truths, that knoledge is power, that knoledge is safety, and that knoledge is happiness."

But Jefferson was too seasoned a political maneuverer and too patient a philosopher to be discouraged by a first failure. He knew that it was a tough task to persuade many simple people, farmers and artisans, that a good system of education in a democracy was not a luxury, as some thought, but a need. Realization of the difficulties involved in "selling" his idea to the legislature only spurred the seventy-five-year-old Sage to greater efforts. He remarked to Joseph C. Cabell, who was his stanch supporter in the educational experiment:

A good system of education in the abstract is among the most difficult of problems. . . . So many biases are to be humored, local, party, personal, religious, political, economical, and what not. Still I have great faith in the observation of Lord Coke, that he had never known a good proposition made to parliament, but that, however often rejected, it prevailed at last. So the general education, altho' it was rejected at the last session, may be at this, & perhaps at the next, it will obtain in the long run. In the mean time we must observe the scriptural precept "never to be wearied with well-doing."

Early in 1818, the Virginia legislature appropriated the munificent sum of $45,000 for elementary education for the poor and the generous sum of $15,000 for the endowment and support of a university. This was the first crack in the wall of indifference. And Jefferson was an expert at widening such fissures.

The legislature provided that twenty-four Commissioners be appointed to discuss the organization and location of the university. Among these Commissioners were former President Jefferson, former President Madison, and President Monroe. The three men met at Monticello and quietly made plans for the founding of the university at near-by Charlottesville.

In August, 1818, when Jefferson was in his seventy-fifth year, he rode to the lush-green Blue Ridge Mountains to meet the other Commissioners and decide upon the plans for a State university. The meeting took place at Rockfish Gap, in a modest inn but in a scenic setting of incomparable beauty. Among the twenty-one eminent Virginians who were present in the low-ceilinged, whitewashed, rustic room, Jefferson was easily the most impressive figure. Not only was his appearance distinguished, but his prestige was overpowering. "It was remarked by the lookers on," comments a contemporary, "that Mr. Jefferson was the principal object of regard, both to the members and spectators; that he seemed to be the chief mover of the body—the soul that animated it."

The Commissioners' primary problem was where to place the university. Each section of the State had its advocates. Jefferson favored Charlottesville, and had come prepared to make an astute defense of his choice. His arguments were unexpected and unorthodox. He told the gentlemen present that the university should be at Charlottesville because the climate in that region was very salubrious. To prove the salubrity, Jefferson calmly produced a list of octogenarians who lived in Albemarle County, where Charlottesville was located.

Then he surprised the Commissioners with a cardboard shaped in the form of the map of Virginia. This showed that Charlottesville was in the geographical center of the commonwealth. Then he brought forth another cardboard map listing the inhabitants in every county. This revealed that Albemarle County was also the population center of the State. Finally, he pointed out that Charlottesville already had, in its so-called Central College (to which Jefferson had contributed $1,000), the nucleus of a higher institution around which the State university

could be built. The Commissioners, overwhelmed by such a
wealth of shrewdly piled up evidence, agreed unanimously that
Central College at Charlottesville should become the University of Virginia. Half a year later the State legislature approved
the choice.

For the next six years Jefferson lived and breathed only for
the University of Virginia. The institution was to be the crowning glory of his life, and upon it he lavished all that was in him,
his energies, his talents, his hopes. He turned himself into a
one-man construction plant, a one-man architectural firm, a one-
man apprentice school, and a one-man planning board. He did
everything himself. He raised money. He drew up the architectural plans. He procured the workmen, including the importation of sculptors from Italy. He prepared all the details of
construction. Since there was a shortage of skilled labor, he also
taught bricklayers how to work and carpenters how to measure.

One visitor, D. P. Thompson, tells that in 1822 he was on
the university grounds and saw Jefferson take a chisel from an
Italian sculptor and show him how to turn a volute on a pillar.
Then the old gentleman approached the visitor with "an elastic
step and serene countenance" and greeted him with a "sweet,
winning smile." After inviting Thompson to Monticello, Jefferson mounted his blooded horse "with the agility of a boy."

Daily the white-haired gentleman rode down the mountain
to Charlottesville to supervise the construction of his pet project.
These rides, four or five miles each way, were becoming hazardous as Jefferson reached his eighties. But despite his age and
broken wrists, he insisted upon riding Eagle, a thoroughbred so
spirited that it frequently threw him.

The proud old horse was tied to a staple outside of Jefferson's
study and could hardly contain itself until its master appeared.
When Eagle heard Jefferson's footsteps it stopped pawing,
turned its arched neck in his direction, and neighed in greeting.
In his eighties, Jefferson could no longer rise from stirrup. He
mounted Eagle from a low terrace; all the while the intelligent
horse stood still, knowing that its master was old and a little
helpless. Despite his swollen wrists (the result of a fall from
Eagle), Jefferson rode to Charlottesville alone. When his fam-

ily pleaded with him to take a servant, he said that if they insisted he would give up riding altogether.

The sight of the thin old man and his old horse carefully picking their way through slippery mud and fording a treacherous river was unforgettable. Rider and horse were recognized by everybody and were constantly stopped. Friends and neighbors greeted them all along the way. They inquired after his health and asked how things were getting along. Some stopped the rider to ask his advice, and he always responded cheerfully.

Jefferson's greatest difficulty in building the university was not physical, but financial. He designed his institution on a scale so ambitious that to some of the legislators he appeared like a Kubla Khan with his Xanadu. The legislature had appropriated an original sum of $15,000. That amount of money was, of course, a joke. Jefferson proceeded as if he could extract ten or even twenty times as much from the reluctant legislators. At every session he asked for more money. Bit by bit the money was voted, under protest. It was like pulling teeth. On more than one occasion the legislature, shocked at the realization that they had already sunk a fortune in the Charlottesville institution, refused appropriations altogether. But the legislature was no match for Jefferson's cajolery. He argued patiently and outmaneuvered strategically. He appealed to patriotism and pride —how would it look to the world if Virginia permitted a dozen fine public buildings to stand without roofs and without doors? Unless the buildings were finished, the whole investment would be a dead loss. With the resigned air of those throwing good money after bad, the legislature grudgingly voted Jefferson his money, piecemeal.

Jefferson was too astute to ask for large grants outright. When friends asked him why he demanded only small appropriations, he replied, with a twinkle, that no one likes to have more than one hot potato at a time crammed down his throat. The "hot potato" crack caused some resentment in Richmond, but Jefferson's prestige in the State was so great that he could get away with any number of indiscreet remarks. By the time he finished constructing the principal buildings, he had spent $300,000—a tremendous sum for those days.

But the university was a sight worth seeing. Built entirely according to Jefferson's architectural plans and specifications, the red-brick University of Virginia rose from the red soil against the green mountain backdrop as one of the most beautiful institutions in the land. It made a powerful impression even upon those who, like George Ticknor, had studied at Harvard and at Göttingen.

The university was set on 250 acres of high ground, commanding a superb view. There were ten houses for professors (annual rent estimated at $600 a year), four refectories, four lecture halls, and one hundred and eight apartments for students. The dominant building of the campus was the library, topped by a magnificent rotunda, on the model of the Parthenon. Flowing down from both sides of the rotunda, so as to form a rectangle, were the apartments for students and professors, as well as the lecture rooms. All the buildings were connected by a continuous portico held up by massive and graceful white columns.

But Jefferson well knew that what makes a university is teachers, and not structures. The problem of assembling a faculty was difficult. There were not many universities in the United States, and few of those trained scholars in sufficient numbers, or of sufficiently high caliber, to supply the domestic need. Jefferson wanted only the best men in their fields, and the best were available mainly abroad, particularly in England, "the land of our own language, morals, manners, and habits." He sent an American scholar, Francis Walker Gilmer, to Britain to ransack the universities of Oxford, Cambridge, and Edinburgh in search of first-rate scholars who would be willing to undertake the arduous journey to America. He also set in motion his powerful connections in England to help him get the professors he wanted.

To Samuel Parr, the eminent Oxford classicist, he wrote: "We are anxious to place in it none but professors of the first grade of science in their respective lines." And he asked him to assist Gilmer to find the men. To Dugald Stewart, the famous Scottish metaphysician, Jefferson made the same request in almost identical words—"anxious to recieve [sic] none but of the highest grade of science in their respective lines."

After many troubles, Jefferson succeeded in assembling an excellent faculty of seven professors, only one of whom was a native American. This was John Tayloe Lomax of Virginia, who was given the chair of law. The others included George Tucker, a native of Bermuda, professor of moral philosophy; George Long of Cambridge, England, professor of ancient languages; George Blättermann, a German, professor of modern languages. Apart from these Georges, there were Thomas Hewitt Key, an Englishman, professor of mathematics; Charles Bonnycastle, also an Englishman, professor of natural philosophy; and Robley Dunglison, likewise an Englishman, professor of anatomy and medicine. The salary of the professors was $1,500 a year, plus a rent-free house, plus a fee of $20 from each student.

One appointment only caused trouble. It was that of Thomas Cooper, a liberal-minded scientist. The clergy promptly raised what Jefferson called a "Hue and cry" against Cooper, and forced the Board of Visitors to cancel the appointment. Jefferson, furious at the "Holy Inquisition," as he called it, of the Virginia Presbyterians, was nevertheless unable to save Cooper, since the university was a tax-supported institution.

The university was scheduled to open on the first day of February, 1825, six years after it was begun. It was an exciting moment for Jefferson, who at the age of eighty-two was to see the last great dream of his life realized. But to his dismay three of the European professors did not arrive. He was so much upset that he exclaimed that he was "dreadfully non-plused"— a vigorous colloquialism that shows the depth of his agitation. The opening had to be postponed until March, by which time the professors had arrived, after a hazardous crossing. Jefferson received them warmly. One of the European professors relates:

The venerable ex-President presented himself and welcomed us with that dignity and kindness for which he was celebrated. He was then eighty-two years old, with his intellectual faculties unshaken by age. . . . He sympathized with us on the discomforts of our long voyage, and on the disagreeable journey we must have passed over the Virginia roads.

The old gentleman continued his keen interest in the university until the end. Two or three times weekly he invited the professors to dine at Monticello, and not only fed them good meals but also stimulated them with his rich and subtle conversation. Students were also invited to Monticello, especially on Sundays. They were awe-struck by the lively, thin, white-haired gentleman, so tactful and so wise. When the students were at the table, Jefferson would eat by himself in a small recess in the dining-room, because, being a little deaf, he did not want to spoil the enjoyment of the young men while they were talking among themselves. There was nothing he would not do for these students, for they were the new generation that would carry on the things he believed in and the ideals he had labored for. He told his collaborator Cabell at the time of the opening of the university:

It is from posterity, we are to expect remuneration for the sacrifice we are making for their service. . . . The multitude of fine young men whom we shall redeem from ignorance, who will feel that they owe to us the elevation of mind, of character, and station, they shall be able to attain from the result of our efforts, will ensure us their remembering us with gratitude.

They did. Not only did the university students remember the founder with reverence, but they also went out into the world equipped to play their part. Jefferson sowed wisely, and the country reaped a rich harvest. From the red-brick classrooms of Jefferson's university there came, in the course of time, poets such as Edgar Allan Poe, scientists such as Walter Reed, and statesmen such as Woodrow Wilson. The founder would have been proud of this "multitude of fine young men."

12

Students and professors were not the only guests at Monticello. There were many others. The number of visitors was so constant and so great that in the end they practically ate Jefferson out of house and home. The specter of poverty began to haunt his remaining years. As early as 1814 he said to his grandson Thomas Jefferson Randolph, according to the latter, that "if he lived long enough he would beggar his family, that the number of persons he was compelled to entertain would devour his estate; many bringing letters from his ancient friends, and all coming with respectful feelings—he could not shut his door in their faces."

To maintain what amounted to a virtual hotel and to support his large family of grandchildren, cousins, in-laws, and all manner of kinsfolk, Jefferson had to resort to borrowing. There was little else that he could do. His farms brought in just about enough cash to pay taxes and interest. "Our means," he complained, "are ever absorbed as soon as received."

Debt and poverty began to weigh upon his old shoulders like an incubus. Despite the magnificent appearance of Monticello and the generous hospitality practiced there, evidences of poverty were visible all over the place. There were silver drinking cups on the table (marked "G.W.[10] to T.J."), but the chairs had holes in them. "The first thing which attracted our attention," writes Francis Calley Gray, who visited Monticello in the winter of 1814, "was the state of the chairs. They had leather bottoms stuffed with hair, but the bottoms were completely worn through and the hair sticking out in all directions."

To raise money, Jefferson was ultimately driven to deprive himself of the things he cherished most—his books. After the British had burned Washington, including the books that belonged to the Government, in 1814, Jefferson offered to sell to the Congress his own private library. He had a magnificent collection of about ten thousand volumes, the fruit of fifty years of collecting in the book marts of Europe. Most of the books were bound, and many were rare items dealing with America. Jefferson offered his collection to Congress at any price that the latter thought fair. Fortunately for the country, Congress accepted, and paid Jefferson $25,000.[11] The money was a godsend, al-

[10] George Wythe, who made Jefferson his heir.

[11] Jefferson's collection formed the nucleus of the Library of Congress in Washington, which is today probably the greatest library in the world. Among the books were volumes on history, zoology, anatomy, surgery, medicine, technics, agriculture, botany, mineralogy, chemistry, physics, geography, ge-

though the former President was able to keep only about one-third of it. More than $15,000 went to his creditors in Philadelphia and Georgetown.

Financial disaster and the threat of bankruptcy hovered over Jefferson's gray head like an evil phantom. Gradually he sank deeper into the morass of debt, and his chances of extricating himself from the financial swamp dimmed with the years. In 1819 a severe financial blow struck him. He had, with his customary generosity, endorsed a $21,200 debt of Wilson Cary Nicholas, one of his distant kinsmen. Nicholas failed, and ruin stared Jefferson in the face. He had no means whatever of paying that debt.

13

The future of the debt-ridden Jefferson's large family of grandchildren was a constant worry. A few days before his eightieth birthday he drew up an account of his debts and his income. It was a discouraging birthday present. The balance sheet showed that Jefferson owed a total debt of $40,262.44 (including $5,250 to the Bank of the United States). The interest alone amounted to $2,121.90 in 1823. Since his farms brought him only $10,400 in that year, the interest alone consumed well over one-fifth of his income.

And all the while there was a growing family to support. Jefferson's daughter Martha, wife of Thomas Mann Randolph, had eleven living children.[12] These children had children in turn. Anne Bankhead, one of Jefferson's grandchildren, had three sons and one daughter who lived near Monticello. Another grandchild, Thomas Jefferson Randolph, had seven offspring. The whole big family of grandchildren and great-grandchildren was centered around the adored figure of Jeffer-

ology, astronomy, mathematics, geometry, ethics, religion, law, politics, design, epics, romances, drama, rhetoric, oratory, criticism, philosophy, bibliography, and polygraphy. See the Jefferson Catalogue in the Library of Congress.

[12] Jefferson himself named four of his male grandchildren after his friends —James Madison, Benjamin Franklin, Meriwether Lewis, and George Wythe. The oldest grandson was named Thomas Jefferson. The girls' names were Anne, Ellen, Cornelia, Virginia, Mary, and Septimia.

son. "Among these," he said at the age of seventy-seven, "I live like a patriarch of old."

Martha Jefferson Randolph, Jefferson's sole surviving child and matriarch of the whole family, was a remarkable woman; she resembled her father in many ways. She was blue-eyed, stately, cheerful, and nearly as tall as Jefferson. Like her father, she was in the habit of humming a tune while working. From her father she acquired the habit of being constantly occupied. She had her father's happy disposition, his winning smile, and his imperturbability.

Jefferson was a loving patriarch among his grandchildren and great-grandchildren. His favorite was his namesake, Thomas Jefferson, Martha's oldest son. Upon that grandson, Jefferson, who never had a son, lavished all his affections. "Yourself particularly, dear Jefferson," the grandfather said to him, "I consider as the greatest of the Godsends which heaven has granted me." It was this same grandson who, after Jefferson's death, loyally assumed his grandfather's whole debt and in the course of time paid it off.

Grandson Thomas Jefferson was a colossus of a man, the delight not only of his grandfather but of all who beheld him. He was taller than his grandfather and physically as powerful as Jefferson's father, Colonel Peter. They certainly bred them big and strong in the mountains of Virginia. When the gigantic Thomas Jefferson Randolph visited Boston in the spring of 1826 and went to see his grandfather's old friend John Adams, little John Adams, a man of ninety-one, was greatly impressed with the size of the young Virginian. "How happens it," he wrote to Jefferson, "that you Virginians are all sons of Anak? We New Englanders are but pygmies by the side of Mr. Randolph."

Jefferson taught his grandchildren gentlemanly behavior and imbued them with his high moral standards. Once when he and grandson Thomas Jefferson were out riding, a colored man took off his hat and bowed. Jefferson returned the salute with the same grave courtesy, but his grandson ignored the colored man. Jefferson rebuked the boy: "Do you permit a Negro to be more of a gentleman than yourself?"

Jefferson's ideas for the education of his grandchildren are condensed in a letter he wrote to another grandson, Francis Eppes. He was the sole surviving child of Jefferson's deceased daughter Maria, and the grandfather supervised the orphan's education with loving scrupulousness. When Francis, at the age of fifteen, went away to the academy, his grandfather gave him some thoughtful advice. After telling the boy that for a gentle- man learning was not enough but must be combined with character, Jefferson continued:

Honesty, disinterestedness and good nature are indispensable to procure the esteem and confidence of those with whom we live, and on whose esteem our happiness depends. Never suffer a thought to be harbored in your mind which you would not avow openly. When tempted to do anything in secret ask yourself if you would do it in public. . . . In little disputes with your companions, give way rather than insist on trifles . . . Above all things, and at all times, practice yourself in good humor. Whenever you feel a warmth of temper rising check it at once, and suppress it, recollecting it will make you unhappy within yourself and disliked by others. Nothing gives one person so great advantage over another as to remain always cool and unruffled under all circumstances.

The grandchildren idolized him. They followed him around the grounds and garden, talking and playing. The old gentleman directed their games and picked fruit for them with a stick to which was attached a hook and bag. He supervised the children's games and races. His favorite was the "stealing goods" game. The children would lay down their personal belongings —coats, hats, pocket knives—and then divide into two parties. The idea was for one group to try to steal from the other, and those who got caught were made prisoners. The old patriarch loved to watch that game, laughing heartily. He also liked to see the children run races around the lawn. He arranged the tots according to size and age, the youngest and smallest being given a head start. Jefferson held up a white handkerchief for a signal, and upon the count of three, they ran. The winner got fruit as a reward.

The children thought Grandfather adorable. And no wonder.

He not only played with them, he also seemed to divine the secret longings of the little girls and the hidden ambitions of the boys, and lo, at the proper moment he fulfilled them. One little girl would suddenly receive from Grandfather a much-hoped-for silk dress, another an ardently desired guitar. According to the recollections of Virginia, one of the granddaughters:

On winter evenings when it grew too dark to read, in the half hour which passed before candles came in, as we all sat round the fire, he taught us several childish games, and would play them with us. . . . When the candles were brought, all was quiet immediately, for he took up his book to read; and we would not speak out of a whisper, lest we should disturb him, and generally we followed his example and took a book; and I have seen him raise his eye from his own book, and look round on the little circle of readers and smile, and make some remark to mama about it.

14

Gradually, very gradually, the energies of the old philosopher slowed down, but only one of his senses, hearing, lost its strength. He concerned himself much with the state of his health, observing the slow, barely perceptible decline with the curiosity of a scientist. Although he dwelt frequently upon small attacks of illness, he was constantly surprised that his physical machinery was as good as it was. To the end of his days he had every tooth in his mouth. At the age of seventy-three he wrote to his friend Charles Thomson:

I retain good health, am rather feeble to walk much, but ride with ease. . . . My eyes need the aid of glasses by night, and with small print in the day also; my hearing is not quite so sensible as it used to be; no tooth shaking yet, but shivering and shrinking in body from the cold we now experience.

In the same year he informed Charles Pinckney that his health was holding up surprisingly well:

I weaken very sensibly, yet with such a continuance of good health as makes me fear I shall wear out very tediously, which is not what one would wish. I see no comfort in outliving one's friends, and remaining a mere monument of the times which are past.

At the age of seventy-four, he expressed to Abigail Adams his philosophical ideas on death:

. . . the Being who presides over the world is essentially benevolent. Stealing from us, one by one, the faculties of enjoyment, searing our sensibilities, leading us like the horse in his mill, round and round the same beaten circle . . . until satiated and fatigued with this leaden iteration, we ask our own *congé*.

When he was seventy-five, he gave, in a letter to Dr. Vine Utley, a curiously detached and full account of his physical condition and habits:

I have lived temperately, eating little animal food, and that not as an aliment, so much as a condiment for the vegetables, which constitute my principal diet. I double, however, the Doctor's glass and a half of wine, and even treble it with a friend; but halve its effects by drinking the weak wines only. The ardent wines I cannot drink, nor do I use ardent spirits in any form.[18] Malt liquors and cider are my table drinks, and my breakfast . . . is of tea and coffee. I have been blest with organs of digestion which accept and concoct, without ever murmuring, whatever the palate chooses to consign to them, and I have not yet lost a tooth by age.

I was a hard student until I entered on the business of life . . . and now, retired, and at the age of seventy-six, I am again a hard student. Indeed, my fondness for reading and study revolts me from the drudgery of letter writing. And a stiff wrist, the consequence of an early dislocation, makes writing both slow and painful. I am not so regular in my sleep . . . devoting to it from five to eight hours, according as my company or the book I am reading interests me; and I never go to bed without an hour, or half hour's previous reading of something moral, whereon to ruminate in the intervals of sleep. But whether I retire to bed early or late, I rise with the sun. I use spectacles at night, but not necessarily in the day, unless in reading small print. My hearing is distinct in particular conversation,

[18] Jefferson was always an enemy of hard liquor, believing it to be an enemy of health and society. He wished that people would drink wine rather than whisky. "I have . . . seen the loathsome and fatal effects of whisky, destroying the fortunes, the bodies, the minds & morals of our citizens," he wrote to William H. Crawford in 1818.

but confused when several voices cross each other, which unfits me for the society of the table.

I have been more fortunate than my friend [Dr. Rush] in the article of health. So free from catarrhs that I have not had one (in the breast, I mean) on an average of eight or ten years through life. I ascribe this exemption partly to the habit of bathing my feet in cold water every morning, for sixty years past. A fever of more than twenty-four hours I have not had above two or three times in my life. A periodical headache has afflicted me occasionally, once, perhaps, in six or eight years, for two or three weeks at a time, which seems now to have left me. . . . I enjoy good health; too feeble, indeed, to walk much, but riding without fatigue six or eight miles a day, and sometimes thirty or forty.

He faced the inevitable future with the same philosophic objectivity as he observed the gradual slowing up of his body. He wrote William Short:

My business is to beguile the wearisomeness of declining life, as I endeavor to do, by the delights of classical reading and of mathematical truths, and by the consolations of a sound philosophy, equally indifferent to hope and fear.

The fire in him died down. At the age of seventy-two he received a letter from the dim, dead past—it was from Maria Cosway, the woman he had loved in Paris. Whether from love for Jefferson or for some other causes, the unhappy woman had long ago sought refuge in a convent. Jefferson did not reply to her letter for more than a year and a half, and when he did, it was in the form of a philosophic consolation: "the religion you so sincerely profess," he wrote to the woman he had loved thirty-four years back, "tells us we shall meet again; and we have all so lived as to be assured it will be in happiness."

Sentimental emotions were only cold embers now. Even poetry, once a great passion, no longer interested him. "I have no imagination," he said at the age of eighty. And when Samuel Judah, a New York poet, sent him his works, Jefferson acknowledged the receipt politely and added—"the chill of 80 winters has so completely extinguished his [Jefferson's] sensibility to the beauties of poetry, as to leave him no longer competent either to enjoy or judge them."

He made an attempt, at the age of seventy-seven, to recapture his memories by putting them down on paper. On January 6, 1821, he began an autobiography with the following sentence: "At the age of 77, I begin to make some memoranda, and state some recollections of dates and facts concerning myself, for my own more ready reference, and for the information of my family." After writing about forty thousand words of autobiography, he gave up. He had, he said, an "invincible repugnance" to talk about himself, especially about his public activities. To his son-in-law John Wayles Eppes, he gave a further explanation:

I am too old to begin any serious work. It had always been my intention to commit to writing some notes and explanations of particular and leading transactions, which history should know, but in parting with my library to Congress, I parted with my whole collection of newspapers, journals, state papers, documents, etc., without the aid of which I have been afraid to trust my memory.

The old gentleman's vigor and sprightliness surprised all those who saw him. James Madison, who was eight years younger than Jefferson, remarked in 1822: "Mr. Jefferson approaches his *octogenary climacteric* with a *mens sana in corpore sano*. The vigor of both is, indeed, very remarkable at his age."

In 1824 George Ticknor revisited Monticello and he was amazed to see how little change time had wrought in Jefferson's appearance. Browere's life mask, taken when Jefferson was eighty-two, corroborates Ticknor's description by showing Jefferson's face without a wrinkle. Ticknor wrote to his fellow historian William H. Prescott:

He is now eighty-two years old, very little altered from what he was ten years ago, very active, lively, and happy, riding . . . every day, and talking without the least restraint, very pleasantly, upon all subjects. In politics, his interest seems nearly gone . . . but on all matters of literature, philosophy, and general interest, he is prompt and even eager. He reads much Greek and Saxon. I saw his Greek Lexicon, printed in 1817; it was much worn with use. . . .

Mr. Jefferson seems to enjoy life highly, and very rationally; but he said well of himself the other evening, "When I can neither read nor ride, I shall desire very much to make my bow."

He continued to read Greek and to ride thoroughbreds. His legs would no longer carry him farther than the garden, but he rode regularly and steadily.

15

The year 1824, when Jefferson had passed his eighty-first birthday, was memorable because of a visit from an old and cherished friend. It was the year when Lafayette made his triumphant tour of the United States. Jefferson looked forward to the visit of his friend with keen excitement. They had not seen each other for about thirty-five years, during which time the world had been through many revolutions and many wars.

Lafayette arrived at Monticello accompanied by an escort of Virginia gentlemen with Revolutionary banners. There was a fanfare of martial trumpets. The cavalcade stopped on the lawn in front of the portico where the long, thin, white-haired man was standing. As Lafayette got out of the carriage, Jefferson descended the steps of the portico. It was a dramatic scene. Jefferson could barely walk. Lafayette was lame. "As they approached each other," Thomas Jefferson Randolph recalls, "their uncertain gait quickened itself into a shuffling run, and exclaiming, 'Ah Jefferson!' 'Ah Lafayette!' they burst into tears as they fell into each other's arms." Hundreds of people witnessed the scene; there was not a dry eye among them.

The friends spent two happy weeks together. They had been through much, had done much, and the things they had to say to each other—on slavery, on South America, on democracy in Europe, on life and on death—were well-nigh inexhaustible.

Before his departure, Lafayette was given a banquet at Charlottesville. It was a memorable occasion because, among other eminent guests, there were present Jefferson, Madison, and President Monroe. Toasts were drunk to Lafayette and to Jefferson, and the latter delivered a speech by proxy. "My friends, I am old, long in the disuse of making speeches, and without voice to utter them." The brief and rare address praised Lafayette for all that he had done for the cause of American liberty, especially for the splendid aid he had given Jefferson in Paris:

. . . this friend . . . was my most powerful auxiliary and advocate. He made our cause his own. . . . His influence and connections there were great. All doors of all departments were open to him at all times. . . . I only held the nail, he drove it. Honor him then.

Lafayette thought that there never was anybody like his friend Jefferson. He told a friend that the "history of the human race tells us of no one who has ever had a broader mind, a loftier soul, a stronger republicanism" than the Sage of Monticello.

Lafayette symbolized America's past. Another visitor who came to Monticello a few months after the Frenchman represented America's future. This was a chesty, massive, immaculately clad New England politician and orator whose name was Daniel Webster. Webster enjoyed Jefferson's generous hospitality and his frank talk for five days.[14] Afterward he put everything down on paper in minute detail.

Like other short men, Webster was particularly impressed by Jefferson's lean size. He described him as long, "thin and spare," with an expression full of "contentment and benevolence."

His limbs are uncommonly long; his hands and feet very large, and his wrists of an extraordinary size. His walk is not precise and military, but easy and swinging. He stoops a little. . . . When sitting, he appears short, partly from a rather lounging habit of sitting, and partly from the disproportionate length of his limbs . . . His general appearance indicates an extraordinary degree of health, vivacity, and spirit.

---

[14] It was to Webster that Jefferson expressed his unflattering opinion of Andrew Jackson as a man "most unfit" for the Presidency. General Jackson, Jefferson said to Webster, "is a dangerous man." This was four years before Jackson was elected President.

16

His health continued to be amazingly good, but financial worries were poisoning his last days. He was near bankruptcy and was in danger of losing his home and his fields.[15] At the age of eighty-three he faced the terrifying prospect, not only of being without a home, but also of leaving his daughter and grandchildren utterly without means.

In February, 1826, on the eve of his eighty-third birthday, Jefferson wrote to Madison a letter that was a cry of pain. To pay his pressing debts, he proposed the idea of selling some of his properties around Monticello at auction. This was a practice resorted to before the Revolution, but now needed the approval of the legislature. If he could not get such permission, he explained to Madison, "I must sell everything here, perhaps considerably in Bedford, move thither with my family, where I have not even a log hut to put my head into." He was not sure, he added bitterly, that he would have left any "ground for burial."

He begged his old friend's pardon for troubling him with these dreadful details. But to whom could he turn? His only consolation in these dark days was the knowledge that he and Madison had fought together for fifty years to build a democracy in America. He hoped that posterity would not forget them in the days to come.

But why afflict you with these details? Indeed, I cannot tell, unless pains are lessened by communication with a friend. The friendship which has subsisted between us, now half a century, and the harmony of our political principles and pursuits, have been sources of constant happiness to me through that long period. . . . It has also

[15] In November, 1826, Madison, in a letter to Lafayette, thus explained Jefferson's financial difficulties: "The expences of his numerous household, his extensive hospitalities, and a series of short crops and low markets, to which are to be added old debts contracted in public service abroad and new ones for which private friendship had made him responsible; all these causes together, had produced a situation of which he seems not to have been fully aware, till it was brought home to his reflections by the calls of creditors."

been a great solace to me, to believe that you are engaged in vindi-
cating to posterity the course we have pursued for preserving to them,
in all their purity, the blessings of self-government, which we had
assisted too in acquiring for them. If ever the earth has beheld a
system of administration conducted with a single and steadfast eye
to the general interest and happiness of those committed to it, one
which, protected by the truth, can never know reproach, it is that
to which our lives have been devoted. To myself you have been a
pillar of support through life. Take care of me when dead, and be
assured that I shall leave with you my last affections.

It was a farewell letter. This was the last time Jefferson communicated with his old friend.

To sell his lands through a lottery—a method that would
enable him to retain Monticello and one farm—was, he said "a
question of life and death." But there were doubts whether the
legislature would authorize such a method of sale, and Jefferson
was almost frantic with fear at the prospect of being thrown out
of his home and left without any means of support. He wrote
to his grandson Thomas Jefferson Randolph:

You kindly encourage me to keep up my spirits. But oppressed
with disease, debility, age, and embarrased affairs, this is difficult.
For myself I should not regard a prostration of fortune, but I am
overwhelmed at the prospect of the situation in which I may leave
my family. My dear & beloved daughter, the cherished companion
of my early life and nurse of my age, and her children, rendered as
dear to me as if my own from having lived with me from their
cradle, left in a comfortless situation, hold up to me nothing but
future gloom, and I should not care were life to end with the line
I am writing, were it not that in the unhappy state of mind which
your father's misfortunes have brought upon him I may yet be of
some avail to the family. . . .
Without you what could I do under the difficulties now environ-
ing me. This has been produced in some degree by my own unskil-
ful management and devoting my life to the service of my country,
but much also by the unfortunate fluctuations in the value of our
money and the long continued depression of the farming business.
But for these last I am confident my debts might be paid leaving me
Monticello and the Bedford estate. But where there are no bidders
property however great offers no resource for the payment of debts.

And the old philosopher concluded his letter with the characteristic consolation that his life had been so rich and happy that he had no right to complain of the misfortune that had befallen his last days:

I duly acknolege that I have gone thro' a long life, with fewer circumstances of affliction than are the lot of most men. Uninterrupted health, a competence for every reasonable want, usefulness to my fellow citizens, a good portion of their esteem, no complaint against the world which has sufficiently honored me, and above all a family which has blessed me by their affectn and never by their conduct given me a moment's pain; and should this my last request be granted I may yet close with a cloudless sun a long and serene day of life.

"This my last request" referred to the lottery bill before the legislature. A few days later the bill was passed, with few dissenting votes. But the bill was not necessary. When news reached the outside world that the Sage of Monticello was in dire straits, offers of help came from every part of the Union. The country was deeply moved at the plight of the author of the Declaration of Independence. Mass meetings were held everywhere, North and South.[16] All over the nation people cried that it was a national shame that the old patriot should be allowed to be thrown out of his home in his old age. New York City raised $8,500 in no time. Philadelphia promptly collected $5,000. Baltimore citizens donated $3,000. Other cities contributed their share.

These spontaneous gifts from all parts of the country overjoyed the ailing old patriot. He had refused a gift from the State, but this was different. It was, he said, "the pure and unsolicited offering of love." Which it was. It was also perhaps the greatest tribute he had ever received—a vindication of his lifelong belief in the goodness of the people and his devotion to their cause. "I have spent three times as much money and

[16] In New York City, Mayor Philip Hone held a large public meeting "to take measures of relief, from debt, of Mr. Jefferson's estate." Another big meeting was held at historic Faneuil Hall, at Boston, to raise funds for "the relief of Mr. Jefferson." A mass meeting was also held at Richmond. See *Niles Weekly Register*, May 6, 1826, p. 172, and June 17, p. 284.

given my whole life to my countrymen," he said, "and now they nobly come forward, in the only way they can, to repay me and save an old servant from being turned like a dog out of doors."

17

In February, 1826, Jefferson had a severe attack of diarrhea, but he minimized his pain in order not to alarm his family. He could not overcome his reluctance to being nursed, and would not have any member of the family watch in his room while he was sleeping. To reassure the anxious family, he tried to be up and about, and even to ride for a short time, pretending heroically that he was not gravely ill.

But he knew that he was dying. In the middle of March he drew up his will, writing the whole document in his own hand, clear, precise, and steady. The will bequeathed most of the real property to two of his grandsons, Francis Eppes and Thomas Jefferson Randolph. The latter was also given all of Jefferson's papers. A codicil to the will made the following provisions:

A gold-mounted walking staff of animal horn, to "my friend James Madison . . . as a token of the cordial and affectionate friendship which for nearly now an half century, has united us in the same principles and pursuits of what we have deemed for the greatest good of our country." His library (which he collected after the one he sold to the Congress) to the University of Virginia. A gold watch to each grandchild, to be given to the girls at the age of sixteen and the boys at twenty-one. To his personal colored servants Jefferson was particularly generous:

I give to my good, affectionate, and faithful servant Burwell, his freedom, and the sum of three hundred Dollars to buy necessaries to commence his trade of painter and glazier, or to use otherwise as he pleases. I give also to my good servants John Hemings and Joe Fosset their freedom at the end of one year after my death: and to each of them respectively all the tools of their respective shops or callings: and it is my will that a comfortable log-house be built for each of the three servants so emancipated on some part of my lands convenient to them with respect to the residence of their wives.

Although he could barely move about, his mind retained its vigor undimmed. He read a great deal, especially the Greek dramatists (in the original) and the Bible. His speech was as vivacious and animated as usual.

Toward the latter part of June the ailing Jefferson received a letter of invitation from General Roger Weightman, Mayor of Washington, to attend the celebration of the fiftieth anniversary of the Declaration of Independence. The invitation only served to remind Jefferson of his great age—a full half-century had passed since he had written that clarion call in Philadelphia. And now, of all the fifty-six signers, only he and John Adams and Charles Carroll were still alive; and they belonged to history, not really to the living. The invitation moved Jefferson deeply. His reply to General Weightman, dated June 24, is an outburst of democratic faith; it is also the last letter he ever wrote:

Respected Sir,—The kind invitation I receive from you . . . as one of the surviving signers of an instrument pregnant with our own, and the fate of the world, is most flattering to myself. . . . It adds sensibly to the sufferings of sickness, to be deprived by it of a personal participation in the rejoicings of that day. . . .

I should, indeed, with peculiar delight, have met and exchanged there congratulations personally with the small band, the remnant of that host of worthies, who joined with us on that day, in the bold and doubtful election we were to make for our country, between submission or the sword; and to have enjoyed with them the consolatory fact, that our fellow citizens, after a century of experience and prosperity, continue to approve the choice we made.

May it be to the world, what I believe it will be . . . the signal of arousing men to burst the chains under which monkish ignorance and superstition had persuaded them to bind themselves, and to assume the blessings and security of self-government. . . .

All eyes are opened, or opening, to the rights of man. The general spread of the light of science has already laid open to every view the palpable truth, that the mass of mankind has not been born with saddles on their backs, nor a favored few booted and spurred, ready to ride them legitimately, by the grace of God.

18

Toward the end of June Jefferson grew worse. Although life was visibly ebbing away, he continued to converse in his usual cheerful fashion. He reverted often to the scenes of the Revolution. Death was ever present, and he faced it calmly. "Do not imagine for a moment," he said to his grandson, "that I feel the smallest solicitude about the result; I am like an old watch, with a pinion worn out here, and a wheel there, until it can go no longer." To the physician he said, "A few hours more, Doctor, and it will be all over."

Awakened from sleep by a noise in the room, he thought that it was the Reverend Mr. Hatch, the clergyman of the parish, who entered. When informed that it was not Hatch, he said: "I have no objection to see him, as a kind and good neighbor." His meaning was quite clear; he had no objections to Mr. Hatch as a neighbor, but did not want his visit as a clergyman.

The dying man's last visitor was Henry Lee, the son of General Henry Lee. Martha Randolph told him that he could not see her father, but Jefferson overruled her. Lee was surprised at the sick man's energy and lively conversation. "He talked of the freshet which was then prevailing in the James river—of its extensive devastation. . . . He soon, however, passed to the university, expatiated on its future utility . . . commended the professors, and expressed satisfaction at the progress of the students."

The conversation shifted to the imminence of death. Jefferson referred to it calmly, "as a man would to the prospect of being caught in a shower—as an event not to be desired, but not to be feared." Always the host, he asked his visitor to stay for dinner. Lee was reluctant. "You *must* dine here," Jefferson said with a touch of impatience, "my sickness makes no difference."

On July 2 he called in his family for a final farewell. He spoke with calm composure, as if he were leaving on a short journey. Pursue virtue, be loyal, be true, were his parting admonitions. One of his little grandsons, a boy of eight, was seemingly bewildered at the solemn scene. The dying man turned to the boy's older brother with a smile: "George does not understand what all this means."

He took a private and deeply moving farewell of his beloved daughter Martha. This was in the form of a brief poem, which was in a little casket that he handed her:

A DEATH-BED ADIEU FROM TH.J. TO M.R.

Life's visions are vanished, its dreams are no more;
    Dear friends of my bosom, why bathed in tears?
I go to my fathers: I welcome the shore
    Which crowns all my hopes or which buries my cares.
Then farewell, my dear, my lov'd daughter, adieu!
The last pang of life is in parting from you!
Two seraphs await me long shrouded in death; [17]
I will bear them your love on my last parting breath.

He slept through the night, and when he awoke he remarked, "This is the Fourth of July." It was only the third. He was fighting with every ounce of his ebbing energy to live until the Fourth of July. When Dr. Robley Dunglison came in the morning to give him his medicine (laudanum), Jefferson said in a husky and indistinct voice, "Ah! Doctor, are you still there?" Then he asked, "Is this the Fourth?" Dr. Dunglison replied, "It soon will be."

The night of July 3-4 he was disturbed and partly delirious. He went through the motions of writing, and muttered about the Committee of Public Safety and that it should be warned. At eleven o'clock in the morning of July 4 his lips moved, and his grandson Thomas Jefferson Randolph, who did not leave his bedside, applied a wet sponge to his mouth. Then the sick man lost consciousness.

Death came to him two hours later, fifty minutes past noon of the Fourth of July, 1826. It was fifty years, to the day, after the Declaration of Independence.

At that moment, throughout the length and breadth of the United States, the people were celebrating the fiftieth anniversary of independence. At that moment, hundreds of thousands

[17] This refers to his wife and daughter Maria.

of people were listening to thousands of Fourth of July orations. In every town bells were ringing and cannon were booming.

At that moment, in Quincy, Massachusetts, John Adams was dying. He did not know that his friend at Monticello had already gone. "Thomas Jefferson still survives," Adams exclaimed, and with these words on his lips he died.

It was a rainy day when they buried Thomas Jefferson in the family plot near his wife. He had written his own epitaph. It was found in a drawer in his desk. Visitors to Monticello can read the words engraved on the gray granite obelisk over his grave:

Here was Buried

THOMAS JEFFERSON

Author of the
Declaration
of
American Independence
of the
Statute of Virginia
for
Religious Freedom
and Father of the
University of Virginia

This is all that he wanted to be remembered for.

Perhaps a few words may be added to his epitaph: He had lived triumphantly a full and rich life, the fruit of which will feed and inspire countless generations of Americans to come.

Of the thousands of tributes that were paid to the departed patriot, the following three are perhaps characteristic:

Secretary of the Navy Samuel L. Southard ordered that every navy yard and ship pay funeral honors to the "venerable Patriarch of the Revolution" by firing twenty-one guns and by lowering the flag at half-mast for a week.

The British publication *John Bull* (August 6, 1826) paid its respects to Jefferson and Adams in these words:

By a curious coincidence, Adams and Jefferson, two of the revolted colonists, who signed the Declaration of American Independence, died on the 4th of July, that being the fiftieth anniversary ot their *rebellious triumph* over their mother country. This coincidence is, however, rendered less curious by a statement which has reached us, that these patriarch *malcontents* brought on their sympathetic deaths by too liberal *potations* in honor of their unnatural gratitude.

And the true words as to Thomas Jefferson were pronounced by James Madison:

. . . he lives and will live in the memory and gratitude of the wise & good, as a luminary of Science, as a votary of liberty, as a model of patriotism, and as a benefactor of human kind.

References

The numbers in heavy type are those of the pages of this book. First words, and where necessary for clearness last words, of the quotation follow, then the source (in italics), and volume and page number. *Ford, Congress,* and *Monticello* when used alone designate the editions of Jefferson's *Writings.* Names of other statesmen designate their *Works* or *Writings. Randolph* indicates *The Domestic Life of Thomas Jefferson; Mass. Hist. Soc., The Jefferson Letters* in *Massachusetts Historical Society Collections,* Ser. 7, Vol. 1; *Randall,* his *The Life of Thomas Jefferson; Parton,* his *Life of Thomas Jefferson; N.Y.P.L.,* the typescript copy of letters made by Ford. Consult the Bibliography for details of all these. *Woodfin* indicates his chapter in *Essays in Honor of William E. Dodd* (University of Chicago Press, 1935); *Morison and Commager,* their *The Growth of the American Republic* (Oxford University Press, 1930).

CHAPTER I

1. The tradition, *Ford,* 1: 1-2. **2.** My father's, *loc. cit.;* Henry, *loc. cit.* **5.** to search . . . I would, *Ibid.,* 1: 388-89. **6.** So much, *Ibid.,* 9: 358. **7.** He [father], *Ibid.,* 1: 3; on Jefferson's family background see also *William and Mary Quar. Hist. Mag.,* Jan. 1924, pp. 14-15 and *Tyler's Quar. Mag.,* 1925, pp. 199ff.

CHAPTER II

8. whole care, *Ford,* 9: 231. **9.** Sir, *Ibid.,* 1: 340. **10.** During the festivity, *Ibid.,* 9: 339. **12.** a man profound, *Ibid.,* 1: 4. **12-13.** my faithful, *Ibid.,* 1: 5. **13.** amici . . . quarree, *Ibid.,* 1: 4; the ablest, *loc. cit.* **14.** At these dinners, *Monticello,* 14: 231-32; this rude bard, *Ford,* 1: 413. **15.** Man was destined, *Ibid.,* 4: 428-29; No, no, *Randolph,* 37. **16.** Last night, *Ford,* 1: 353. **17.** When I recollect, *Ibid.,* 9: 231. **18.** When I was, *Ibid.,* 1: 361; appeared to me, *Ibid.,* 1: 6. **19.** I would have cried, *Ibid.,* 1: 343; Jane Nelson, *Bookman,* 31: 648; How does R. B., *Ford,* 1: 346-47. **20.** you advise, *Ibid.,* 1: 348; a few broken . . . I asked, *Ibid.,* 1: 353-54; Perfect happiness, *Ibid.,* 1: 349; I have been, *Ibid.,* 1: 357; n. the world, *Ibid.,* 3: 338. **21.** Once more, *Bookman,* 31: 648-49. **21-22.** most affectionate . . . into the practice, *Ford,* 1: 4.

CHAPTER III

23. Well, it is hard, *Randolph,* 40. **24.** I should apologize, *Congress,* 9: 489-90; lawyer's trade, *Ford,* 1: 82; Our ancestors, *Ibid.,* 1: 444.

25. I was, *Bernard, Retrospections,* 238. **26.** I was, *Ford,* 1:372. **27.** the *cost, Ibid.,* 1:370; August 4, *Commonplace Book,* 2; **n.** folios, *Monticello,* 19:129. **28.** Mr. Wayles, *Ford,* 1:6; In every scheme, *Ibid.,* 1:399. **29.** 1771, Dec. 24, *Scribner's,* 12:510. **30.** They were, *Randolph,* 44. **31.** handsome . . . doubled, *Ford,* 1:6. **32.** I have, *Madison (Hunt),* 1:21. **33.** Being a young man, *Ford,* 1:369n. **34.** Not thinking, *Ibid.,* 1:78. **36.** The perfection, *Commonplace Book,* 18-19. **37.** we must, *Ford,* 1:9; we cooked up, *Ibid.,* 1:10; The people met, *Ibid.,* 1:12. **38.** an attack, *Ibid.,* 1:11; with some uncertainties, *Ibid.,* 1:421. **39-40.** his Majesty, *Ibid.,* 1:429-47. **41.** Whether Mr. Henry . . . things, *Ibid.,* 1:13.

CHAPTER IV

42. an indolent, *Adams,* 3:31; **n.** none was, *Ford,* 10:59. **43.** This accident, *Ibid.,* 1:454. **44.** he was, *Adams,* 2:514. **45.** I prepared, *Ford,* 1:17; We . . . find nothing, *Ibid.,* 1:18. **46.** Gentlemen may, *Morgan, Patrick Henry,* 191; There is, *Ford,* 1:18. **47.** America was conquered, *Ibid.,* 1:430; I would, *Ibid.,* 1:484; domestic ease, *Ibid.,* 1:482. **48.** there is not, *Ibid.,* 1:493. **50.** flaming . . . reasoning, *Washington (Bicentennial),* 4:297; No writer, *Ford,* 10:183; March 31, *Diary;* In that parlor, *Ford,* 10:346. **51.** who could calculate, *Parton,* 164; during the whole time, *loc. cit.;* that these, *Ford,* 1:18-19. **51-52.** That the people . . . time, *Ibid.,* 1:19-20. **52.** not yet matured, *Ibid.,* 1:24. **53.** which impelled us . . . error, *Ibid.,* 1:25-26. **54.** The committee, *Ibid.,* 1:24; Neither, *Ibid.,* 10:343. **54-60.** Declaration of Independence, *facsimile.* **61.** June 11, *Scribner's,* 12:515-16; Their alterations, *Ford,* 1:27. **62.** a passive auditor, *Ibid.,* 10:268; fighting fearlessly, *loc. cit.* **62-63.** I was sitting, *Ibid.,* 10:120n. **63.** The *Thing, Lee, Letters,* 1:210. **64.** July 4th, *Scribner's,* 12:516; God knows, *Ford,* 4:84; for God's sake, *Va. Mag. of Hist. and Biog.,* 8:114. **65.** I am sorry, *Ford,* 2:61; I hope, *Woodfin,* 34.

CHAPTER V

66. The laboring oar, *Ford,* 1:71. **67.** When I left, *Ibid.,* 1:57-58. **68.** The transmission, *Ibid.,* 1:49; To annul this, *loc. cit.* **69.** No violence, *loc. cit.;* His virtue, *Congress,* 1:114; a man of the first order, *Ford,* 1:55-56; he acquired, *Ibid.,* 1:57. **71.** he was cool, *Ibid.,* 1:50. **73.** that to compose, *Ibid.,* 1:59; perhaps the most severe, *Madison (Hunt),* 9:257. **73-74.** In the execution, *Ford,* 1:60-61. **74.** a Model, *Madison (Hunt),* 9:288; if the eldest, *Ford,* 1:60. **76.** I think, *Congress,* 2:7-8. **77.** How far, *Ford,* 2:99-100. **78-79.** The rights, *Ibid.,* 3:263-66. **79.** the endless quibbles, *Ibid.,* 1:62. **80.** unwearied, *loc. cit.* **80-81.** Well aware, *Ibid.,* 2:237-39. **81.** We, the General Assembly, *Ibid.,* 2:239. **82.** to comprehend, *Ibid.,* 1:62; I considered, *loc.*

cit.; **n.** accumulation . . . self-government, *Ibid.*, 1:69. **83.** In whose hands, *Ambler, Sectionalism*, 33.

CHAPTER VI

84. a fat man, *Adams*, 2:422. **85.** It had, *Ford*, 2:187. **85-86.** In a virtuous, *loc. cit.* **86.** sincere, *Washington (Bicentennial)*, 15:401; It may be said, *Madison (Hunt)*, 9:260-61; I wish, *Woodfin*, 37; he is, *Morgan, Life of Monroe*, 74-75. **88.** The public treasury, *Gay, James Madison*, 20; I have had, *Tyler, Patrick Henry*, 273-74. **89.** It is essentially, *Washington (Bicentennial)*, 18:263; we have reason, *Ford*, 2:384; **n.** But is an enemy, *Randolph*, 31. **91.** Short inlistments, *Washington (Bicentennial)*, 19:195; to this we may, *Ibid.*, 19:374; North Carolina, *Congress*, 1:242. **92.** What is, *Ibid.*, 1:253; I have, *Washington (Bicentennial)*, 19:470; we are, *Ford*, 2:333. **93.** to call on, *Ford*, 2:406. **94.** The papers, *Randall*, 1:300n. **94-95.** Were it possible, *Ford*, 3:43. **95.** necessity, *Washington (Bicentennial)*, 22:189. **97.** strict orders . . . inhabitants, *Ford*, 5:38. **98.** The very thought, *Ibid.*, 3:234. **98-99.** That at, *Eckenrode, The Revolution in Va.*, 226. **99-100.** 5th Objection, *Randall*, 1:354-55. **100-01.** no information . . . censure, *Woodfin*, 41. **101.** I find, *Ford*, 5:78. **102.** Great as, *Madison (Hunt)*, 1:207-08; **n.** Your kindness, *Monroe*, 1:8-9. **102-103.** Before I ventured, *Ford*, 3:56-57. **103.** It were contrary, *Ibid.*, 58-59.

CHAPTER VII

104. I had folded, *Ford*, 3:65; The play, *Morison and Commager*, 1:109. **105.** If there is . . . observe, *Ford*, 2:158-59; **n.** Emigrants, *Va. Mag. of Hist. and Biog.*, 8:115. **108.** Unwilling to expose, *Ford*, 3:70. **108-10.** Before we condemn . . . we can, *Ibid.*, 3:158, 195n, 225, 254, 266-69, 279. **111.** Mr. Jefferson, *Curtis, The True Thomas Jefferson*, 34; state of . . . If in, *Randolph*, 41. **112-13.** Your letter, *Ford*, 3:64-65. **113.** I cannot, *Ibid.*, 3:297-98. **114.** To merit, *Washington (Bicentennial)*, 26:118; we lost, *Ford*, 3:299; we got, *Ibid.*, 3:301. **115.** a most amazing, *Ibid.*, 3:301; Congress, *Ibid.*, 3:309; the Hon. . . . service, *Ibid.*, 3:315. **116.** Take things, *Ibid.*, 10:93. **117.** morbid rage . . . listen, *Ibid.*, 1:81. **117-18.** Our body, *Ibid.*, 1:81-82. **119-20.** the following . . . creatures, *Ibid.*, 3:345-46. **119.** I hope, *Randolph*, 70; I omitted, *Ibid.*, 71; I am anxious, *Ford*, 3:378. **120.** I had left, *Amer. Hist. Rev.*, 12:76-77.

CHAPTER VIII

121. Those who labour, *Ford*, 3:268; All the world, *Ibid.*, 3:422; I made, *Ibid.*, 1:84-85. **122.** We had . . . rough, *Brooks, Dames*, 183; than which, *Ford*, 4:5; We should, *Brooks, op. cit.*, 184. **124.** I live

. . . tribe, *Ford*, 4: 11-12; the best, *Brooks, op. cit.*, 185.   **125.** one of the most . . . women, *Ford*, 10: 332-33.   **125-26.** He dined, *Ibid.*, 10: 333.   **126.** Well, my dear, *Randolph*, 51.   **127.** I have had, *Ford*, 4: 41; **n.** During, *Monticello*, 11: 64.   **128.** phosphoric . . . value, *Ford*, 4: 14; While in Paris, *Ibid.*, 9: 486; **n.** Progress, *Henry Adams, History*, 1: 279.   **129.** dearth, *Monticello*, 19: 6; Of political, *Ibid.*, 19: 11-12; Titus Livius, *Randolph*, 85.   **129-30.** I do not like . . . contrivance, *Ford*, 4: 373.   **130-31.** My dear Polly, *Ibid.*, 4: 97-98.   **131.** Dear Papa (three), *Randolph*, 104.   **132.** It is . . . successor, *Ford*, 5: 292; Among many, *Ibid.*, 4: 413-14; **n.** He is, *Adams*, 9: 524; **n.** I am more, *Letters of Lafayette and Jefferson*, 69.   **132-33.** My duties, *Ford*, 1: 90.   **133.** It may be, *Commonplace Book*, 316.   **133-34.** You ask, *Ford*, 4: 104-105.   **134.** We have, *Ibid.*, 4: 88.   **135.** I sincerely, *Ibid.*, 4: 59; I do love, *Ibid.*, 4: 61; Indeed, *Congress*, 1: 394-95.   **136-37.** As soon . . . state. *Ford*, 34-36.   **137-38.** Behold me, *Congress*, 1: 144.   **138.** In the pleasure, *Ibid.*, 1: 445; an American, *Ibid.*, 1: 468.   **139.** It was impossible, *Ford*, 1: 89.   **139-40.** I traversed, *Ibid.*, 4: 213-14.   **140.** I have, *N. Y. Hist. Soc. Collection, 1878*, 207.   **141-42.** My dear Madam . . . none, *Ford*, 4: 311-24.   **142-44.** On arriving . . . America, *Congress*, 9: 403-05.   **144.** I have not, *Southern Bivouac*, N.S., 2: 427.   **144-45.** Dauphiné, *Congress*, 9: 320-21.   **145.** Here I am, *Ibid.*, 2: 131-32.   **145-46.** I am now, *Southern Bivouac*, N.S., 2: 427.   **146.** I think you, *Congress*, 2: 136.   **147-48.** In crossing . . . less, *Ibid.*, 333-40.   **148-49.** I scarcely, *Ford*, 4: 442-43.   **149.** I write you, *Ibid.*, 4: 388.   **150.** formed by, *Congress*, 9: 374.   **150-51.** The soil . . . tyranny, *Ibid.*, 9: 378-84.

CHAPTER IX

153. a canine appetite, *Ford*, 4: 366; the good model, *Congress*, 2: 131; besiege, *Ibid.*, 2: 253; **n.** The King, *Ford*, 4: 393.   **153-54.** If every advance, *Congress*, 2: 131.   **154.** I have, *Ibid.*, 2: 165.   **154-55.** And above all, *Ford*, 4: 426.   **155.** I rely, *Congress*, 2: 217; and we think, *Ibid.*, 2: 234; **n.** were it, *Ford*, 3: 195.   **155-56.** God forbid, *Ibid.*, 4: 467.   **157.** inviolate . . . compromise, *Ibid.*, 4: 475; I will add, *Ibid.*, 4: 476.   **158.** Let me add, *loc. cit.*   **158-59.** The second feature, *Ibid.*, 4: 477-78.   **159-60.** I own, *Ibid.*, 4: 479-80.   **160.** The constitution, *Plumer, Life*, 98; The mobs, *Ford*, 3: 269; I think, *Ibid.*, 4: 479-80.   **161.** unquestionably, *Ibid.*, 4: 89.   **161-62.** the American war, *Congress*, 2: 553-54.   **162.** A great political, *Ford*, 5: 79.   **163.** there is, *Congress*, 2: 375; I was, *Ford*, 1: 147-48; very much, *Randall*, 1: 513.   **163-64.** Wednesday, *Morris, Diary*, 1: 104, 113, 134, 220-21.   **165.** Possibly, *Ford*, 9: 505.   **166.** The Committee, *Letters of Lafayette and Jefferson*, 143-44; I was, *Ford*, 1: 145-46.   **167.** in moderating, *Ibid.*, 1: 146; Europe, *Monticello*, 19: 61; I am excessively, *Ford*, 5: 95-96.   **168.** And here, *Ibid.*, 1: 148-49.

CHAPTER X

169. to sink into, *Ford*, 1:149-50. **169-70.** Dear Sir, *Washington (Ford)*, 11:438. **170.** It was impossible, *Ford*, 5:139; It is not, *Ibid.*, 6:141. **171.** I am, *Ibid.*, 6:140-41. **172.** When the door, *Randolph*, 152. **173.** All whom, *Madison (Ford)*, 1:501; I consider, *Washington (Ford)*, 11:468; a universal, *Madison (Ford)*, 1:502; the danger, *Ford*, 5:148. **175.** I am only, *Ibid.*, 5:145; the noblest, *Randolph*, 139; a young gentleman, *Ford*, 1:150. **175.** the first chapter, *Vossler, Die amerikanischen Revolutionsideale*, 114n; The Gentlemen who, *Ford*, 5:136. **175-76.** Convinced, *Ibid.*, 5:147. **176.** useful truths, *Congress*, 4:427; venerable, *Ford*, 1:150; Ah! *Bernard, Retrospections*, 234; He went, *Ford*, 1:150-51. **177.** Behold me, *Ford*, 5:151-52. **177-78.** Here, *Ibid.*, 1:159-60. **178.** His most gracious . . . sword, *Maclay, Journal*, 10. **179.** Democracy, *Forman, Political Activities . . . Freneau*, 40; University, *Madison (Congress)*, 4:112. **180.** Jefferson, *Maclay, Journal*, 272; a Gentleman, *Washington (Bicentennial)*, 2:395-96. **181.** He has, *Walther, Gouverneur Morris*, 55; He was, *Ford*, 9:376. **181-82.** I think, *Ibid.*, 9:448-49. **183.** I had, *Ibid.*, 9:376; **n.** a bastard, *Wecter, The Saga*, 81. **184.** colossus . . . himself, *Ford*, 7:32. **184-85.** Take mankind . . . government, *Hamilton*, 1:408, 401; radically defective, *Dial*, 4:5. **186.** not only, *Ford*, 1:165; Hamilton, *Atlantic*, 30:707; **n.** I dislike, *Henry Adams, Letters*, 1:284. **187.** most perfect . . . existed, *Ford*, 1:165-66; **n.** her King, *Congress*, 5:513-14. **188.** I told . . . Caesar, *Ford*, 1:296; save us, *Ibid.*, 5:189; a dissolution, *Ibid.*, 1:163. **189.** The happiest, *Ibid.*, 5:157. **190.** I am, *Randolph*, 180; Where are you, *Ibid.*, 181; I have not, *Ibid.*, 182. **190-91.** I have written, *Ibid.*, 185-86. **191.** I hope, *Ibid.*, 186. **192.** dish is worth . . . person, *Harper's*, 70:535; abjured, *Schouler, Americans of 1776*, 100. **193.** I must beg, *Pol. Sci. Quar.*, 21:630-31; unparalleled prosperity, *Wecter, op. cit.*, 81. **194.** all the business, *Maclay, Journal*, 387. **196.** Democracy, *Adams*, 6:483-84. **196-97.** The salary, *Congress*, 3:215. **197.** I am, *Monticello*, 19:179. **198.** I never, *Ford*, 5:355; For my part, *Monticello*, 19:78. **200.** Get rid, *Forman, op. cit.*, 49f. **201.** Since the day, *Ibid.*, 46f.; unequivocally convinced, *Wandell and Minnegerode, Aaron Burr*, 1:159. **202.** national disunion, *Hamilton*, 7:10; free, unfettered, *Forman, op. cit.*, 54; How long, *Randall*, 2:73. **203.** with respect, *Madison (Hunt)*, 6:109; **n.** The confidence, *Ford*, 6:5-6. **204.** I would fain, *Washington (Ford)*, 12:174-75. **204-05.** How unfortunate, *loc. cit.* **205-09.** I was duped . . . corruption, *Ford*, 6:102-09. **209-11.** could not . . . retirement, *Ibid.*, 1:203-05. **211.** I did not, *Washington (Ford)*, 12:201-02. **212.** There was, *Ford*, 1:209; When I first, *Congress*, 3:527. **212-13.** exit . . . appeal, *Madison (Hunt)*, 6:129. **216.** I look, *Ford*, 5:274; I still hope, *Ibid.*, 6:377. **217.** In the struggle, *Ibid.*, 6:153-54. **217-18.** instead of, *Randolph*, 220. **218.** These representations, *Ford*, 6:164; He expressed

. . . public, *Ibid.*, 1:215. **218-19.** That as to, *loc. cit.*; I live, *Morison and Commager*, 1:241; to direct opinion, *Minnegerode, Jefferson*, 145. **221.** Consequently, *Ford*, 6:220; The Republic, *Ibid.*, 6:230-31; A perfect, *Ibid.*, 6:240. **222.** Upon her coming, *Ibid.*, 6:238; vast concourse, *Ibid.*, 6:260; We see, *Ibid.*, 6:434. **222-23.** Hamilton, *Ibid.*, 6:238-39. **223.** He is, *Conway, Omitted Chapters*, 190; If we preserve, *Ford*, 6:239. **224.** Let us explain, *Randall*, 2:155-56. **225.** I am doing, *Ford*, 6:323; Never, *Ibid.*, 6:338-39. **226.** most furious Jacobin . . . wish, *Ibid.*, 6:348-49; He will sink, *Ibid.*, 6:361; intermeddling, *Ibid.*, 6:368. **227.** The effect, *Madison (Hunt)*, 6:191; The President, *Ford*, 6:292-93; The publications, *Washington (Ford)*, 12:310. **228.** But I will not, *Ford*, 1:231; got . . . into, *Ibid.*, 1:254; For God's sake, *Ibid.*, 5:338. **229.** The motion, *Ibid.*, 6:291-92; I am then, *Ibid.*, 6:455-56; In this, *Randolph*, 189. **230.** I now take, *Ford*, 6:496; Let a conviction, *Washington (Ford)*, 12:402.

CHAPTER XI

231. The ascent, *Mass. Hist. Soc.*, 34. **232.** I return, *Ford*, 6:505; money-bound, *N.Y.P.L.*, 1:17; The whole commerce, *Ford*, 3:266-67. **233.** With the morals, *loc. cit.*; to give liberty, *Ibid.*, 5:66-67. **234.** we are a race, *Mass. Hist. Soc.*, 38-39; No body wishes, *Ford*, 5:377. **235.** degree of devastation, *Ibid.*, 7:509; Time, *Ibid.*, 6:520. **236.** intermeddling, *Ibid.*, 10:103; I have returned, *Ibid.*, 7:2. **237.** The little spice, *Ibid.*, 7:10; a warm zealot, *Ibid.*, 7:13. **238.** I read, *N.Y.P.L.*, 1:184. **239n.** I view, *Ford*, 8:80. **239-40.** Hamilton, *Ibid.*, 7:32-33. **240n.** disinclinations, *Washington (Ford)*, 12:220; grossest, *Ibid.*, 12:231. **241.** I intreat, *Madison (Congress)*, 2:80; Politics, *Ford*, 7:56. **241-42.** The main body, *Ibid.*, 7:75-76. **243.** From a very early, *Ibid.*, 7:82; Ambition, *Mass. Hist. Soc.*, 56. **244.** I pray you, *Ford*, 7:91-92; You are bound, *Madison (Hunt)*, 6:300; I protest, *Ford*, 7:93; I have, *Ibid.*, 7:94. **244-45.** it is the only, *Ibid.*, 7:98-99. **245.** Our latest, *Ibid.*, 7:95-97. **246.** Let us, *Ibid.*, 7:109. **247.** He spoke, *Sullivan, Familiar Letters*, 148; Gentlemen, *Washington Gazette*, Mar. 8, 1797. **248.** What other form, *Adams*, 9:107; lure, *Randall*, 2:337. **249.** I asked, *Adams*, 9:285; he never after, *Ford*, 1:273. **250.** our Eastern friend, *Ibid.*, 7:94. **252.** our wives, *Morison and Commager*, 267n; Were I to, *Ford*, 7:279. **253.** John Adams, *Henry Adams, Letters*, 1:338; That as to, *Ford*, 1:277; A boy of 15, *Ibid.*, 1:280. **254.** Mr. Adams, *Turner, Correspondence*, 1029; in every free, *Ford*, 7:264. **255.** I never, *Ibid.*, 5:175; the former, *Va. Mag. of Hist. and Biog.*, 12:257-58. **256.** Like Hessian flies, *Duyckinck, Cyclopedia of Amer. Lit.*, 1:344; United Irishmen, *Morison and Commager*, 1:272. **258.** Let us not, *Beard and Beard, Rise of Amer. Civilization*, 1:376; For my own part, *Ford*, 7:283. **261.** If this, *loc. cit.*; these and successive, *Ibid.*, 7:303. **262-63.** I am for, *Ibid.*, 7:327-29.

CHAPTER XII

264. Jefferson, *Va. Quar. Rev.*, 2:326. **267.** who looked, *Dict. of Amer. Biog.*, 1:431; We are sensible, *Culbreth, The Univ. of Va.*, 65; that lump, *Columbia Hist. Soc., Records*, 8:81-82. **267-68.** can be, *Bleyer, Main Currents*, 125. **268.** The American, *Ibid.*, 126; the majority, *Ibid.*, 127; every county, *Ford*, 7:439; The medicine, *Ibid.*, 7:440. **269.** open the eyes, *Ibid.*, 1:167; A group, *Adams*, 9:582; The campaign, *N. Y. Hist. Soc. Misc. Mss.* J; I never knew, *Woodfin*, 46. **270.** Sir, *Jones, America and French Culture*, 384; It does me . . . cause, *Linn*, 17. **270-71.** How does, *Ibid.*, 20-21. **271.** Let the first, *Ibid.*, 26; Will you, *Ibid.*, 33-34. **271-72.** That the charge, *Wortman*, 4; People, *Ibid.*, 34-35. **272-73.** Read, *Beckley*, p. 6. **273.** And Rehoboam, *I Kings*, 14:21-25. **273-74.** From the moment, *Congress*, 4:333. **274.** they . . . believe, *Ford*, 7:460; Thomas Jefferson, *Bryce, Amer. Commonwealth*, Chap. 53, n1. **275.** Every dissolute, *Henry Adams, History*, 1:80. **276.** A democracy, *Ibid.*, 1:85; those apostles, *Parrington, The Conn. Wits*, XXII; mad Democrats . . . misled, *Columbian Centinel*, Apr. 23, 1800; By their art, *Ibid.*, May 3. **277.** equivalent . . . precipice, *Ibid.*, May 7; crush the monster, *Ibid.*, May 10; Let us attend, *Ibid.*, May 28. **277-78.** I believe, *Ibid.*, Aug. 27. **278.** What security, *Va. Herald*, July 1, 1800; **n.** my opinion, *Ford*, 7:454. **279.** I believe, *Mass. Hist. Soc.*, 80; Behold you, *Corres. of Jefferson and du Pont de Nemours*, 29. **279-80.** Calumny, *McMaster, Hist. of the . . . U. S.*, 2:512n. **281.** bankrupt . . . himself, *Wandell and Minnegerode, Aaron Burr*, 1:204-05; I admit, *Hamilton*, 6:419; Nor is it, *Ibid.*, 6:420. **282.** humiliation, *Adams*, 9:578; Well . . . dispositions, *Ford*, 9:296-97. **283.** Sir . . . course, *Ibid.*, 9:297; Many attempts, *Ibid.*, 7:491. **284.** he must not, *Penn. Mag.*, 25:72; I long, *Mass. Hist. Soc.*, 85; The scene, *Randall*, 2:600. **286.** Yesterday expired, *Columbian Centinel*, Mar. 4, 1801.

CHAPTER XIII

287. a pacific revolution, *De Witt, Jefferson*, 2. **287-88.** As the storm, *Ford*, 8:22; The times, *Congress*, 4:376; The storm . . . countries, *Ford*, 8:7-8; you must depend, *S. Adams, Works*, 4:409. **289-90.** "Jefferson and Liberty," *pph. ed. by Kirtland, 1784.* **290.** most of them small, *Washington (WPA Guide)*, 47; the best city, *Wharton, Salons*, 179. **291-93.** Inaugural, *Ford*, 8:2-6. **294.** I would advise, *Penn. Mag.*, 25:75. **294-95.** great stone . . . houses, *Caemmerer, Washington*, 41-43. **295.** In meditating the matter, *Ford*, 8:39. **296.** There is something, *Mass. Hist. Soc.*, 94. **297.** the Constitution, *N.Y.P.L.*, 2:84; **n.** who should dare, *Va. Gazette*, Dec. 11, 1802. **298.** I am sensible, *Monticello*, 10:255-56. **299.** The principle, *Monroe*, 3:273; My principles, *N.Y.P.L.*, 2:47; enemies' hands, *N.Y.P.L.*, 2:170;

n. I have never, *N. Y. Hist. Soc. Mss.* **300.** In this horrid drudgery, *Ford*, 9:51; political principle, *Ibid.*, 8:126; It was my destiny, *Ibid.*, 8:126-27; **n.** I can say, *Ibid.*, 8:307. **301.** Is Jonas Clark, *Gallatin*, 1:37; With respect, *Ibid.*, 1:54. **301-02.** He is said, *Ford*, 8:68. **302.** We have, *Dwight, Oration, pph. 1801*, 29; let neither, *Fuess, Daniel Webster*, 1:56; Carry me, *Ibid.*, 1:605. **303.** Come, come, *Bernard, Retrospections*, 240-41. **303-04.** My wish, *N.Y.P.L.*, 2:73. **304.** I laid it down, *Ford*, 9:270; But the task, *N.Y.P.L.*, 3:71. **306.** a social, *Hunt, Life of Madison*, 273; But as to, *Washington (WPA Guide)*, 307; Mrs. Madison, *loc. cit.* **307.** of a pure, *Ford*, 9:311; I shall love, *Ibid.*, 10:262; I have no pleasure, *N.Y.P.L.*, 2:283; So that, *Ford*, 9:70; call on me, *Ibid.*, 9:104. **307-08.** presented, *Ibid.*, 9:307. **308.** Debt, *Ibid.*, 10:190; if the public debt, *Ibid.*, 9:264. **309.** If we run, *Congress*, 7:16; I wish, *Ford*, 8:171. **310.** Would it not, *N.Y.P.L.*, 2:476. **311.** We have a perfect, *Ford*, 8:99; We have the same, *Ibid.*, 8:156-57; And shall we, *Ibid.*, 8:124. **312.** In proportion . . . know, *Ibid.*, 3:189-90; as many Germans . . . citizens, *Ibid.*, 5:67. **313.** I have ever, *Amer. Hist. Rev.*, 33:833; as we wish, *loc. cit.* **314.** natural and habitual enemy, *Ford*, 8:144. **315.** we must marry, *Ibid.*, 8:145. **315-16.** The session, *Ibid.*, 8:144-45. **316.** two continents, *Ibid.*, 8:145. **316-17.** I wish, *Corres. of Jefferson and du Pont de Nemours*, 47-48. **317.** taking immediate measures, *Ford*, 8:146; **n.** Nothing but, *Monticello*, 19:132. **318.** There is, *Gallatin*, 1:115; as soon as, *Henry Adams, History*, 2:2. **319-20.** whole . . . country, *Randall*, 3:58. **320.** From this day, *Dict. of Amer. Biog.*, 11:324. **320-21.** Well . . . again, *Monroe*, 4:15-16. **321n.** Were half, *N.Y.P.L.*, 2:479. **321-22.** I confess, *Ford*, 8:295. **322-23.** More general science . . . at all, *Melbourn, Life*, 70-71. **323.** I am, *Corres. of Jefferson and du Pont de Nemours*, 36; like the oil, *Republican Advocate*, Dec. 17, 1802. **325.** It is a proposition, *Morison and Commager*, 1:293; crafty chief judge, *Ford*, 10:271. **326.** The judges, *Ibid.*, 8:311; any of those creatures, *Morison and Commager*, 1:293; certainly, *Boudin, Government by Judiciary*, 1:252. **329.** Kind, *Republican Advocate*, Apr. 15, 1803. **329-30.** they . . . fill, *N.Y.P.L.*, 2:199. **330.** Indeed the abuses, *Congress*, 4:463; You know, *N.Y.P.L.*, 2:478; No experiment, *Ibid.*, 3:33-34. **330-31.** I have lent myself, *Ford*, 9:30. **331.** no man, *Madison (Hunt)*, 9:307; Why . . . found it, *Smith, First Forty Years*, 221-26. **332.** nobody, *Amer. Hist. Rev.*, 33:385; pêle mêle, *Ford*, 8:277; When brought, *Ibid.*, 8:276. **333.** not merely, *Ellet, Court Circles*, 66; virago, *Ford*, 8:291; We have told, *loc. cit.* **334.** He is, *Colman, Seventy-Five Years*, 79. **335.** blasphemous crony, *Washington (WPA Guide)*, 158; he was, *Quar. Rev.*, 68:24; a tall . . . chief, *Plumer, Life*, 242. **336.** It is rare, *Ford*, 8:125; I am obliged, *Ibid.*, 8:189. **337.** What doth avail, *Sewanee Rev.*, 18:295; I have only, *Ford*, 8:189. **338.** it is so much, *Bernard, Retrospections*, 237;

To you . . . States, *Smith, First Forty Years*, 221-26. **339.** he . . . could not, *Quar. Rev.*, 68:23; My dear Sir, *N.Y.P.L.*, 3:251. **340.** When I hear, *Ford*, 9:232; Yesterday, *Plumer, Life*, 245-46. **341.** no man, *N.Y.P.L.*, 3:108-09; Never, *Bruce, John Randolph*, 1:221. **342.** His conduct, *Ford*, 1:304; n. *loc. cit.* **343.** Others, *Congress*, 4:547; Where all, *loc. cit.*; Is it, *loc. cit.*, 344. I determined, *Ford*, 8:339; what farmer, *Ibid.*, 8:343. **345.** our own brethren, *Ibid.*, 8:344; Our wish, *Ibid.*, 8:347. **347.** there is not, *Ibid.*, 8:111. **348n.** The President, *Madison (Congress)*, 2:221. **349.** We have borne, *North Amer. Rev.*, 208:65; Believe me, *Ford*, 1:493; I would rather, *Ibid.*, 1:484; pampered aristocracy, *Congress*, 6:436. **350.** The English, *Ibid.*, 5:604; the land, *Mass. Hist. Soc.*, 332; No two nations, *Ford*, 10:305; No two countries, *Ibid.*, 8:449-50. **352.** In fine, *Sears, Jefferson*, 55; **353.** We are, *Ibid.*, 61. **354.** present paroxysm, *Ford*, 9:194; Our eyes, *N.Y.P.L.*, 3:495-96; I think one war, *Ford*, 8:201; You Infernal Villain, *Sears, op. cit.*, 103. **354-55.** The Embargo, *pph.*, pp. 8, 12. **355.** James Turner, *Plumer, Memorandum*, 603. **356.** I have since, *Ford*, 1:139; Your quotation, *Congress*, 6:213. **356-57.** My wish, *Ford*, 1:110-11. **357.** My determination, *Ibid.*, 9:50; yet two years, *Ibid.*, 9:10; My longings, *Ibid.*, 9:178; flagitiousness . . . atrocious lies, *Congress*, 5:362; Those moral principles, *Monticello*, 16:319. **358.** Within a few days, *Corres. of Jefferson and du Pont de Nemours*, 144. **359n.** We have to thank you, *Congress*, 9:476-78. **360.** Of you, *Ford*, 8:251.

CHAPTER XIV

361. I am, *Mass. Hist. Soc.*, 144. **362.** I have, *Monticello*, 19:256; My temperament, *Congress*, 6:575. **363-64.** There is, *and* The whole, *National Intelligencer*, Aug. 1, 1809. **364.** From breakfast, *Ford*, 9:294; devoured by correspondence, *loc. cit.* **364-65.** busy, *Century*, 114:477. **365.** In a couple, *Mag. of Hist.*, 249-50. **366.** For this, *Mass. Hist. Soc.*, 179; I shall, *Century*, 114:478. **367.** with sincere, *Corres. of Adams and Jefferson*, 32; miserable . . . friend, *Adams*, 10:11. **368.** A letter *and* I have, *Ford*, 9:333-34. **369.** Never mind, *Corres. of Adams and Jefferson*, 16; My friend, *Adams*, 10:58-59. **370.** I agree, *Ford*, 9:425; the most sublime, *Ibid.*, 8:21; That it is, *Adams*, 10:54-55; intolerant, *Ford*, 9:417-18; n. History, *Ibid.*, 9:436. **370-71.** It is, *Ibid.*, 9:412-14. **371.** I can, *Congress*, 7:281; Would you, *Adams*, 10:210. **371-72.** Would I, *Ibid.*, 10:222-23. **372.** Tried myself, *Ford*, 10:114; While you live, *Adams*, 10:363. **373.** conqueror . . . roses, *Ford*, 9:274; an atrocious, *Ibid.*, 9:329; But our lot, *loc. cit.*; The Attila, *Ibid.*, 9:461. **373-74.** I considered him, *Monticello*, 18:294. **374.** The penance, *Ford*, 10:95; thanks be, *Monticello*, 19:256. **375-76.** Those who, *Ford*, 3:268-69. **375n.** I feel much, *Ibid.*, 9:331; One might, *Century*, 114:481. **376.** Their property, *Ford*, 4:89. **376-77.** I had, *Congress*, 6:430-31. **377.** There is, *Ford*, 1:11n. **377-78.** You tell me, *Ibid.*, 10:8-10. **379.** Some men, *Ibid.*, 10:42-43; Nothing, *Congress*, 7:359. **379-80.** Is this . . . paradise, *Ford*, 10:218. **380.** to exercise, *Calendar . . . Jefferson*, Pt. 1, 16. **381.** everything, *Ticknor, Life*, 1:36; extraordinary . . . reason, *Mass. Hist. Soc.*, 38. **382.** our colored brethren, *Melbourn, Life*, 65; looks like, *Montlezun, Voyage*, 1:74; **n. 5,** No body, *Ford*, 5:377; no person, *Ibid.*, 9:246; **n. 6,** It is, *Melbourn, op. cit.*, 66; Hume, *Congress*, 7:356. **383.** my greatest . . . time, *Monticello*, 19:194. **384.** When we, *N.Y.P.L.*, 4:391-92; to consider, *Ford*, 10:160. **384-85.** The judiciary, *Ibid.*, 10:170-71. **385.** The great object, *Ibid.*, 9:189; It is *and* Let them, *Mag. of Hist.*, 21:255-56. **386.** Our country, *Ford*, 7:451-52. **387.** It is, *Congress*, 7:213-14. **387-88.** I see *and* And what, *Ford*, 10:354-55. **389.** I join you, *Ibid.*, 9:435-36; I wish, *Ibid.*, 10:84-85. **390.** I hope, *N.Y.P.L.*, 4:490; Every kindness, *Ford*, 10:19. **391.** The question, *Ibid.*, 10:277-79. **392.** a real Christian, *Ibid.*, 10:5; An eloquent, *Monticello*, 13:377-78. **393.** A more beautiful, *Ford*, 10:5; The sum, *Ibid.*, 10:69. The doctrines, *Ibid.*, 10:219-20; deliria . . . priests, *loc. cit.* **393-94.** No, *Ibid.*, 10:220. **394.** I write, *Ibid.*, 10:67-68; You press me, *Ibid.*, 10:289. **394-95.** You judge, *Ibid.*, 10:12; genus, *Ibid.*, 7:460; genuine, *Buffalo Hist. Soc., Pub.*, 7:28; mountebanks . . . skulk, *Ibid.*, 7:18; Religious freedom, *N.Y.P.L.*, 5:3; parent . . . practice, *Amer. Jewish Hist. Soc., 1911*, 12; To penetrate, *Ibid.*, 28. **395-96.** I am, *Ford*, 10:95. **396.** I have . . . life, *Monticello*, 19:211-13; Is it, *Ibid.*, 17:423n. **397.** do not, *Ford*, 10:96; A good system, *Barringer, Univ. of Va.*, 1:252-54. **398.** It was, *Tucker, Life of Jefferson*, 2:401. **399.** an elastic step . . . boy, *Harper's*, 26:833. **401.** the land . . . lines, *Mass. Hist. Soc.*, 332; We are, *Ibid.*, 1:334. **402.** anxious, *loc. cit.*; Hue and cry, *Ford*, 10:248; Holy Inquisition, *Randall*, 3:465; dreadfully . . . The venerable, *Barringer, op. cit.*, 1:258. **403.** It is, *Honeywell, Educational Work*, 287. **404.** if he lived, *Gray, Thomas Jefferson*, 17; Our means, *Ford*, 10:22; The first thing, *Gray, op. cit.*, 68. **406.** Among these, *Mass. Hist. Soc.*, 303; Yourself particularly, *Ford*, 10:375; How happens, *Letters of Adams and Jefferson*, 195-96; Do you, *Randolph*, 288. **407.** Honesty, *Monticello*, 19:241-42. **408.** On winter evenings, *Randolph*, 297; I retain, *Ford*, 10:6. **408-09.** I weaken, *Mass. Hist. Soc.*, 263. **409.** the Being, *Ford*, 10:70. **409-10.** I have lived, *Ibid.*, 10:125-27; **n.** I have seen, *Ibid.*, 10:113. **410.** My business, *Ibid.*, 10:145; the religion, *Mass. Hist. Soc.*, 303-04; I have, *Corres. of Jefferson* (ed. by Ford), 274; the chill, *Ford*, 10:274. **411.** At the age, *Ibid.*, 1:1; invincible repugnance, *Monticello*, 19:246; I am, *Mag. of Hist.*, 21:256; Mr. Jefferson, *Madison (Congress)*, 3:265. **411-12.** He is, *Ticknor, Life*, 1:348-49. **412.** As they approached, *Randolph*, 335. **412-13.** My friends . . . then, *Randall*, 3:504n; history, *Independent*, 55:26; thin . . . spirit, *Webster, Private Corres.*, 1:364-65; **n.** most unfit, *Ford*, 10:331; is a dangerous man, *Webster*, *loc. cit.* **414.** I must sell . . . burial, *Ford*, 10: 377; **n.** The expenses, *Madison (Hunt)*, 9: 262. **414-15.** But why, *Ford*, 10: 377-78. **415-16.** You kindly . . . life, *Ibid.*, 10: 374-75. **416.** the pure, *Randall*, 3: 537. **416-17.** I have, *loc. cit.* **417.** my friend . . . wives, *facsimile*. **418.** Respected Sir, *Ford*, 10: 390-92. **419.** Do not imagine . . . neighbor, *Randolph*, 368; He talked . . . difference, *Niles' Register*, Nov. 25, 1826, 198. **420.** George, *Randolph*, 368; A Death-Bed Adieu, *Ibid.*, 370; This is, *Ibid.*, 369; Ah! Doctor . . . will be, *Randall*, 3: 548. **421.** Thomas Jefferson, *Adams, Life*, 636. **422.** he lives, *Madison (Hunt)*, 9: 248.

Bibliography

Note: This is a selective bibliography. It makes no claim to completeness.

BIBLIOGRAPHIES OF JEFFERSON

Johnson, R. H., comp., "A Contribution to a Bibliography of Thomas Jefferson," in *Writings of Thomas Jefferson*, Monticello edition, Vol. 20

Tompkins, H. B., comp., *Bibliotheca Jeffersoniana: A List of Books Written by or Relating to Thomas Jefferson*, G. P. Putnam's Sons, New York, 1887

Wise, H. W., and Cronin, J. W., comps., *A Bibliography of Thomas Jefferson*, Riverford Publishing Co., Washington, 1935. Lists 1,248 numbers.

Woodward, F. E., comp., *Reference List of Works Relating to Thomas Jefferson*, Malden, Mass., 1906

Catalogue, President Jefferson's Library, printed by Gales & Seaton. Sold at auction by Nathaniel P. Poor, Washington, D.C., February 27, 1829

WRITINGS BY JEFFERSON

Letters Subsequent to the Revolution, copied by P. L. Ford from the original Jefferson manuscripts. A typescript in 5 vols., to be found in the Manuscript Room of the New York Public Library. Some of these letters are published in Ford's 10-volume collection of *Writings*, but most of them are unpublished.

Writings, ed. by P. L. Ford, 10 vols., G. P. Putnam's Sons, 1892-99. This is by far the best collection of Jefferson papers.

Writings, ed. by A. A. Lipscomb and A. E. Bergh, 20 vols., Thomas Jefferson Memorial Association of the U.S., Washington, D.C., 1905 (Monticello Edition)

Writings, ed. by H. A. Washington, 9 vols., Taylor & Maury, Philadelphia, 1853-54 (Congress Edition)

Calendar of the Correspondence of Thomas Jefferson, 3 vols., Department of State, Washington, D.C., 1894-1903. Part I: Letters from Jefferson. Part II: Letters to Jefferson. Part III: Supplementary.

The Best Letters of Thomas Jefferson, ed. by J. G. de R. Hamilton, Houghton Mifflin Company, Boston, 1926

"A Bundle of . . . Letters Now First Published," *Buffalo Historical Society Publications*, ed. by F. H. Severance, Vol. 7 (1904), pp. 1-32

Classified List of Manuscripts, Books, Correspondence, etc., of Thomas Jefferson Offered by Purchase to the U.S. by S. N. R., ed. by S. N.

Randolph, Government Printing Office, Washington, D.C., 1889.
5 pp.

The Commonplace Book of Thomas Jefferson: A Repertory of His Ideas On Government, ed. by G. Chinard, Johns Hopkins Press, Paris, 1926

The Complete Anas of Thomas Jefferson, ed. by F. B. Sawvell, Round Table Press, New York, 1903

"Correspondence between President Jefferson and Abraham Bishop, Collector of the Port of New Haven," *New Haven Colony History Society Papers*, Vol. I, pp. 143-46

Correspondence between Thomas Jefferson and Pierre Samuel du Pont de Nemours, 1798-1817, ed. by D. Malone, Houghton Mifflin Company, Boston, 1930

The Correspondence of Jefferson and du Pont de Nemours, ed. by G. Chinard, Johns Hopkins Press, Baltimore, 1931

Correspondence of John Adams and Thomas Jefferson, 1812-1826, ed. by P. Wilstach, Bobbs-Merrill Company, Indianapolis, 1925

"Correspondence of Thomas Jefferson, 1788-1826," Missouri Historical Society, *Glimpses of the Past*, 1936, Vol. 3, pp. 77-133

Democracy, by Thomas Jefferson, ed. by S. K. Padover, D. Appleton-Century Company, New York, 1939. Contains selections from Jefferson's writings on the subjects of democracy and government.

The Educational Work of Thomas Jefferson, ed. by R. J. Honeywell, Harvard University Press, Cambridge, Mass., 1931

Houdon in America: A Collection of Documents in the Jefferson Papers in the Library of Congress, ed. by G. Chinard, Johns Hopkins Press, Baltimore, 1930

The Jefferson Papers, Collections of the Massachusetts Historical Society, Ser. 7, Vol. I, 1900. Letters to and from Jefferson dealing mainly with private affairs.

"Jefferson to William Short on Mr. and Mrs. Merry, 1804," *American Historical Review*, Vol. 33 (1928), pp. 832-35

Jefferson's Germantown Letters Together with Other Papers Relating to His Stay in Germantown during the Month of November, 1793, ed. by C. F. Jenkins, W. J. Campbell, Philadelphia, 1906

"Jefferson's Letters on Kosciuszko, 1809-1818," *Magazine of History*, Extra No. 36, 1915

"Letters of Jefferson," *Virginia Magazine of History and Biography*, ed. by B. C. Steiner, Vol. 12 (1905), pp. 257-68. Letters from the collection of James McHenry, Secretary of War under Washington and Adams.

The Letters of Lafayette and Jefferson, ed. by G. Chinard, Johns Hopkins Press, Baltimore, 1929

"Letters of Thomas Jefferson," *Magazine of History*, Vol. 21 (1915), pp. 246-56. Contains 23 letters to attorneys and overseers, from 1805 to 1822.

Memoir, Correspondence and Miscellanies, from the Papers of Thomas Jefferson, ed. by T. J. Randolph, 4 vols., F. Carr & Company, Charlottesville, Va., 1829

"A Memorandum [on Patrick Henry]," *Historical Magazine*, August, 1867, pp. 90-96

"Niemcewicz en Amérique et sa correspondance inédite avec Jefferson (1797-1810)," ed. by W. M. Kozlowski, *Revue de litérature comparée*, Vol. VIII (1928), pp. 28-45

Notices, Letters, etc. Respecting the Library Manuscripts of Thomas Jefferson, typescript, Library of Congress, 1898

"The Papers of Charles Thomson, Secretary of the Continental Congress, 1765-1816," *New York Historical Society Collections*, Vol. 1 (1878), pp. 1-286. About 100 letters exchanged between Jefferson and Thomson.

"Some Family Letters of Thomas Jefferson now in Possession of His Great-great-grandson, Francis Eppes Shine, M.D.," *Scribner's Magazine*, Vol. 36 (1904), pp. 573-86

"Some Jefferson Letters," *Southern Bivouac, N.S. Vol. II (1886-87)*, pp. 425-36, 632-38, 752-59. An excellent collection of letters to William Short.

Trois amitiés françaises de Jefferson d'après sa correspondance inédite avec Madame de Bréhan, Madame de Tessé et Madame de Corny, ed. by G. Chinard, Société d'édition "Les Belles Lettres," Paris, 1927

Thomas Jefferson Correspondence, Printed from the Originals in the Collections of William K. Bixby, Boston, 1916. Printed by the Plimpton Press, Norwood, Mass. Mostly letters to Jefferson.

"Unpublished Correspondence between Thomas Jefferson and Some American Jews," ed. by Max J. Kohler, *American Jewish Historical Society, 1911*, pp. 11-30

"Unpublished Correspondence of Mme de Staël with Thomas Jefferson," ed. by Marie G. Kimball, *North American Review*, Vol. 208 (1918), pp. 62-71

"Unpublished Letters of Jefferson [from Originals in Virginia Historical Society]," *Virginia Magazine of History and Biography*, Vol. 8 (1900), pp. 113-25. Contains 12 letters to R. H. Lee and Archibald Stuart written between 1776 and 1818.

ON JEFFERSON: BOOKS

Adams, H. B., *Thomas Jefferson and the University of Virginia*, Government Printing Office, Washington, D.C., 1888

Cabell, N. F., ed., *Early History of the University of Virginia, as Contained in the Letters of Thomas Jefferson and Joseph C. Cabell*, J. W. Randolph, Richmond, 1856

Channing, E., *The Jeffersonian System, 1801-1811*, Harper & Bros., New York, 1906

Curtis, W. E., *The True Thomas Jefferson*, J. B. Lippincott & Company, Philadelphia, 1901

Ellis, E. S., *Thomas Jefferson: A Character Sketch*. The University Association, Milwaukee, 1898

Ford, W. C., *Thomas Jefferson and James Thompson Callender, 1798-1802*, Historical Printing Club, Brooklyn, New York, 1897

Gray, F. C., *Thomas Jefferson in 1814, Being an Account of a Visit to Monticello*, ed. by H. S. Rowe and T. J. Coolidge, The Club of Odd Volumes, Boston, 1924

Lichtenstein, G., *Thomas Jefferson as War Governor*, William Byrd Press, Richmond, Virginia, 1925

Minnigerode, Meade, *Jefferson, Friend of France, 1793: The Career of Edmond Charles Genet*, G. P. Putnam's Sons, New York, 1928

Parton, James, *Life of Thomas Jefferson, Third President of the United States*, Houghton Mifflin Company, Boston, 1874

Pierson, H. W., *Jefferson at Monticello: The Private Life of Thomas Jefferson, from Entirely New Materials*, C. Scribner, New York, 1862

Randall, H. S., *The Life of Thomas Jefferson*, 3 vols., J. B. Lippincott & Company, Philadelphia, 1871. This is perhaps the best of the older Jefferson biographies.

Randolph, Sarah Nicholas, *The Domestic Life of Thomas Jefferson, Compiled from Family Letters and Reminiscences by His Great-Grand-Daughter*, Harper & Bros., New York, 1871. Contains a wealth of materials dealing with private and family matters.

Rayner, B. L., *Sketches of the Life, Writings and Opinions of Thomas Jefferson, with Selections*, Lilly, Wait, Colman & Holden, New York, 1832. This is based upon Mrs. Randolph's book.

Sears, L. M., *Jefferson and the Embargo*, Duke University Press, 1927. Perhaps the best study on the subject.

Tucker, George, *The Life of Thomas Jefferson, Third President of the United States; with Parts of His Correspondence Never Before Published*, 2 vols., Carey, Lea & Blanchard, Philadelphia, 1837. This is one of the earliest biographies of Jefferson.

Wiltse, C. M., *The Jeffersonian Tradition in American Democracy*, University of North Carolina Press, Chapel Hill, 1935

Witt, C. H. de, *Jefferson and the American Democracy*, trans. by R. S. Church, Longmans, Green, London, 1862. This work first appeared in the *Revue des deux mondes*, 1857-1860, and is unfriendly to Jefferson.

Woolery, W. K., *The Relation of Thomas Jefferson to American Foreign Policy, 1783-1793*, Johns Hopkins Press, Baltimore, 1927

ON JEFFERSON: PAMPHLETS

Alsop, Richard, *The Political Greenhouse for the Year 1798: Addressed to the Readers of the Connecticut Courant, January 1st, 1799*, Hartford, 1799. A 24-page pamphlet in verse.

Beckley, John James, *Address to the People of the United States: with an Epitome and Vindication of the Public Life and Character of Thomas Jefferson*, Philadelphia, 1800. 31 pp.

Clinton, De Witt [Grotius], *A Vindication of Thomas Jefferson against the Charges Contained in a Pamphlet Entitled "Serious Considerations," etc.*, New York, 1800. 47 pp.

Colvin, John B., *Republican Economy; or, Evidences of the Superiority of the Present Administration over That of John Adams, 1802.* 10 pp.

Danvers, Jno Thiery, *A Picture of a Republican Magistrate of the New School; Being a Full Length Likeness of His Excellency Thomas Jefferson, President of the United States, to Which is Added a Short Criticism of the Characters and Pretensions of Mr. Madison, Mr. Clinton and Mr. Pinckney*, New York, 1808. 96 pp. A virulent anti-Jefferson pamphlet.

Daveiss, Joseph Hamilton, *A View of the President's Conduct Concerning the Conspiracy of 1806*, Frankfort, Kentucky, 1807. 64 pp.

Dickins, Asbury, *The Claims of Thomas Jefferson to the Presidency Examined at the Bar of Christianity*, Philadelphia, 1800. 54 pp.

[Evans, Thomas] "Tacitus," *A Series of Letters Addressed to Thomas Jefferson, Esq., President of the United States, Concerning His Official Conduct and Principles: with an Appendix of Important Documents and Illustrations*, Philadelphia, 1802. 127 pp. and 46 pp. of appendix. An attack on Jefferson.

Grymes, Philip, [*Letter to Gabriel Jones*], July 20, 1803

[Hamilton, Alexander] "Lucius Crassus," *The Examination of the President's Message at the Opening of Congress, December 7, 1801*, New York Evening Post, 1802. 127 pp.

Julap, Giles, *The Glosser: A Poem*, March, 1802. 72 pp. "A squib against Jefferson."

[Linn, Rev. William], *Serious Considerations on the Election of a President; Addressed to the Citizens of the United States*, New York, 1800. 36 pp. Accuses Jefferson of atheism.

[Mason, Rev. John Mitchell], *The Voice of Warning, to Christians on the Ensuing Election of a President of the United States*, New York, September 30, 1800. 40 pp.

Mitchell, S. L., *A Discourse on the Character and Services of Thomas Jefferson, More Especially as a Promoter of Natural and Physical Sciences . . . October 11, 1826*, New York, 1826. 67 pp.

[Payne, Robert Treat], *Song of Jefferson and Liberty*. First sung at Wallingford, Connecticut, March 11, 1801. 14 stanzas.

[Smith, William L.] "Phocion," *The Federalist: Containing Some Strictures upon a Pamphlet Entitled "The Pretensions of Thomas Jefferson to the Presidency Examined,"* Philadelphia, November, 1796.

—— *The Pretensions of Thomas Jefferson to the Presidency Examined: and the Charges against John Adams Refuted*, Philadelphia, 1796. 2 parts: 64 and 42 pp.

Wirt, William, *A Discourse on the Lives and Characters of Thomas Jefferson and John Adams, October 18, 1826*, Washington, 1826. 69 pp.

[Wortman, Tunis] "Timoleon," *A Solemn Address, to the Christians and Patriots upon the Approaching Election of a President of the United States, in Answer to a Pamphlet, Entitled, "Serious Considerations,"* etc., New York, 1800. 36 pp.

—— *A Vindication of the Conduct of Thomas Jefferson Whilst Governor of the State of Virginia*, Richmond, April 12, 1800. 7 pp.

ON JEFFERSON: MAGAZINE ARTICLES

Anderson, D. R., "Jefferson and the Virginia Constitution," *American Historical Review*, Vol. XXI (1916), pp. 750-54

Bigelow, J., "Jefferson's Financial Diary," *Harper's Magazine*, Vol. LXX (1855), pp. 534-42. A splendid itemized account, based upon manuscript data.

Bowers, C. G., "Jefferson, Master Politician," *Virginia Quarterly Review*, Vol. II (1926), pp. 321-33

Brigham, J., "A Forgotten Chapter in the Life of Jefferson," *Green Bag*, Vol. XII (1900), pp. 441-49

Chinard, G., "Jefferson and the Physiocrats," *California University Chronicle*, Vol. XXXIII (1931), pp. 18-31

—— "Thomas Jefferson as a Classical Scholar," *American Scholar*, Vol. I (1932), pp. 133-43

Cooke, J. E., "Jefferson as a Lover," *Appleton's Journal*, Vol. XII (1874), pp. 230-32. Nothing to get excited about.

—— "Thomas Jefferson," *Southern Literary Messenger*, Vol. XXX (1860), pp. 321-41

—— "The Writer of the Declaration: A Familiar Sketch," *Harper's Magazine*, Vol. LIII (1876), pp. 211-16

Dodd, W. E., "Napoleon Breaks Jefferson," *American Mercury*, Vol. V (1925), pp. 303-13

Fisher, G. P., "Jefferson and the Social Compact Theory," *Yale Review*, Vol. II (1894), pp. 403-17. Dull and pedantic stuff.

Foley, J. P., "Outdoor Life of the Presidents; No. 2, Thomas Jefferson," *Outing*, Vol. XIII (1899), pp. 250-59

Ford, P. L., "The French Revolution and Jefferson," *Nation*, Vol. LXI (1895), p. 61

—— "Jefferson in Undress," *Scribner's Magazine*, Vol. XII (1892), pp. 509-16

—— "Jefferson's Notes on Virginia," *Nation*, Vol. LVIII (1894), pp. 80-81, 98-99

Ford, W. C., "Jefferson and the Newspapers," *Columbia University Historical Society Records*, Vol. VIII (1905), pp. 78-111

Fuller, M. W., "Jefferson and Hamilton," *Dial*, Vol. IV (1883), pp. 4-6

Gould, W. D., "The Religious Opinions of Thomas Jefferson," *Mississippi Valley Historical Review*, Vol. XX (1933), pp. 191-208

Guernsey, A. H., "Thomas Jefferson and His Family," *Harper's Magazine*, Vol. XLIII (1871), pp. 366-80

Hale, E. E., "With Jefferson Manuscripts," *Book News*, Vol. XIV (1895), pp. 65-67

Hamilton, J. G. de R., "Ripened Years: II, Thomas Jefferson: Time Treated Him Kindly," *Century Magazine*, Vol. CXIV (1927), pp. 476-85

Hardy, S. E. M., "Some Virginia Lawyers of the Past and Present," *Green Bag*, Vol. X (1898), pp. 57-68

Haworth, P. L., "Thomas Jefferson—Poet," *Bookman*, Vol. XXXI (1910), pp. 647-50

—— "Jefferson Family," *Tyler's Quarterly Historical and Genealogical Magazine*, Vol. VI (1925), pp. 199-201, 264-69

Kean, R. G. H., "Thomas Jefferson as a Legislator," *Virginia Law Journal*, December, 1887

Kimball, Marie, "A Playmate of Thomas Jefferson," *North American Review*, Vol. CCXIII (1921), pp. 145-56. An account of the relation between Jefferson and his granddaughter Ella Randolph.

McAdie, A., "Thomas Jefferson at Home," *American Antiquarian Society Proceedings*, N.S. Vol. XL (1931), pp. 27-46

Malone, D., "Polly Jefferson and Her Father," *Virginia Quarterly Review*, Vol. VII (1931), pp. 81-95

Mellen, G. F., "Thomas Jefferson and Higher Education," *New England Magazine*, N.S. Vol. XXVI (1902), pp. 607-16

Merriam, C. E., "Jeffersonian Democracy," in his *A History of American Political Theories*, 1906, pp. 143-75. An excellent brief account.

Merriam, J. M., "Jefferson's Use of the Executive Patronage," *American Historical Association Papers*, Vol. II (1887), pp. 47-52. A good study.

Morgan, J. M., "How President Jefferson Was Informed of Burr's Conspiracy," *Pennsylvania Magazine of History and Biography*, Vol. XXVII (1903), pp. 56-59

—— "Notes Relating to Some of the Students Who Attended the College of William and Mary, 1753-1770," *William and Mary Quarterly*, January, 1921, p. 34

Parmelee, M. P., "Jefferson and His Political Philosophy," *Arena*, Vol. XVIII (1897), pp. 505-16

Powell, B. E., "Jefferson and the Consular Service," *Political Science Quarterly*, Vol. XXI (1906), pp. 626-38. A valuable contribution to a little known subject.

—— *Quarterly Review*, Vol. LXVIII (1841), pp. 20-57. An excellent review article based on A. J. Foster's *Notes on the United States*, London, 1841.

Shippen, Mrs. R. L., "Inauguration of President Thomas Jefferson," *Pennsylvania Magazine of History and Biography*, Vol. XXV (1901), pp. 71-76

Thompson, D. P., "A Talk with Jefferson," *Harper's Magazine*, Vol. XXVI (1863), pp. 833-35

Warren, C., "Why Jefferson Abandoned the Presidential Speech to Congress," *Massachusetts Historical Society Proceedings*, Vol. LVII (1923-24), pp. 123-72

Wayland, J. W., "The Poetical Tastes of Thomas Jefferson," *Sewanee Review*, Vol. XVIII (1910), pp. 283-99

Wilstach, P., "Jefferson's Little Mountain," *National Geographic Magazine*, Vol. LV (1929), pp. 481-503

Wiltse, C. M., "Jeffersonian Democracy: A Dual Tradition," *American Political Science Review*, Vol. XXVIII (1934), pp. 838-51

GENERAL

Adams, Henry, *History of the United States*, Charles Scribner's Sons, New York, 1889-91. Vols. I & II: "The First Administration of Jefferson, 1801-05"; Vols. III & IV: "The Second Administration of Jefferson."

Adams, John, *The Works of John Adams*, ed. by C. F. Adams, 10 vols., Little, Brown and Company, Boston, 1850-56. Vols. 9 and 10 deal with "General Correspondence" and contain the letters exchanged with Jefferson.

Ambler, C. H., *Sectionalism in Virginia from 1776 to 1861*, University of Chicago Press, Chicago, 1910

Barringer, P. B., *University of Virginia: Its History, Influence, Equipment and Characteristics*, 2 vols., Lewis Publishing Company, New York, 1904

Becker, Carl, *The Declaration of Independence: A Study in the History of Political Ideas*, Harcourt, Brace and Company, New York, 1922

Bemis, S. F., *A Diplomatic History of the United States*, Henry Holt and Company, New York, 1936

Bernard, J., "Recollections of President Jefferson," in his *Retrospections of America, 1797-1811*, Harper & Bros., New York, 1887

Boudin, L. B., *Government by Judiciary*, 2 vols., William Godwin, Inc., New York, 1932

Bruce, W. C., *John Randolph of Roanoke, 1773-1833*, 2 vols., G. P. Putnam's Sons, New York, 1922

Caemmerer, H. P., *Washington the National Capital*, Government Printing Office, Washington, D.C., 1932

Charlton, T. U. P., *The Life of Major General James Jackson*, G. F. Randolph & Company, Augusta, Georgia, 1809

Chastellux, F. J., marquis de, *Travels in North America in 1780, 1781, 1782*, trans. by J. Kent, White, Gallaher & White, New York, 1827

Colman, Edna M., *Seventy-Five Years of White House Gossip: From Washington to Lincoln*, Doubleday, Page & Company, New York, 1925

Conway, John J., *Footprints of Famous Americans in Paris*, John Lane Company, London, 1912

Conway, M. D., *Omitted Chapters of History Disclosed in the Life and Papers of Edmund Randolph, Governor of Virginia*, G. P. Putnam, New York, 1801

Culbreth, D. M. R., *The University of Virginia: Memories of Her Student-Life and Professors*, Neales Publishing Company, New York, 1908

Davis, John, *Travels of Four Years and a Half in the United States of America during 1798, 1799, 1800, 1801, and 1802*, London, 1803. Sold by T. Ostell and H. Caritat.

Dodd, W. E., "Virginia Takes the Road to Revolution," in Carl Becker, J. M. Clark, and W. E. Dodd, *The Spirit of 1776*, The Robert Brookings Graduate School of Economics and Government, Washington, D.C., 1927, pp. 101-35

—— "Thomas Jefferson," in his *Statesmen of the Old South*, Macmillan Company, New York, 1911

Dunbar, L. B., *A Study of the "Monarchical" Tendencies in the United States from 1776 to 1801*, University of Illinois Press, Urbana, 1922, University of Illinois Studies (No. X)

Eckenrode, H. J., *The Revolution in Virginia*, Houghton Mifflin Company, Boston, 1916

Ellicott, Mrs. Mary, *Colonial Days in Virginia: A Souvenir of the Sesquicentennial (Yorktown, October 19, 1931)*, Braid & Hutton, Savannah, Georgia, 1931

Fay, B., *The Revolutionary Spirit in France and America*, Harcourt, Brace and Company, New York, 1927

Forman, S. E., *The Political Activities of Philip Freneau*, Johns Hopkins Press, Baltimore, 1902 (Johns Hopkins University Studies, Ser. 20, Nos. 9-10)

Fox, D. R., *The Decline of Aristocracy in the Politics of New York*, Columbia University Press, New York, 1919

Fuess, C. M., *Daniel Webster*, 2 vols., Little, Brown and Company, Boston, 1930

Gallatin, Albert, *The Writings of Albert Gallatin*, ed. by Henry Adams, J. B. Lippincott & Company, Philadelphia, 1879. Vol. I: Letters from 1788 to 1816.

Gay, S. H., *James Madison*, Houghton Mifflin Company, Boston, 1884

Guinness, R. B., "The Purpose of the Lewis and Clark Expedition," *Mississippi Valley Historical Review*, Vol. XX (1933), pp. 99-100

Hazen, C. D., "Thomas Jefferson in France," in his *Contemporary American Opinion of the French Revolution*, Johns Hopkins Press, Baltimore, 1897, pp. 1-53 (Johns Hopkins University Studies in Historical and Political Science, Extra Vol. 16)

Hunt, G., *The Life of James Madison*, Doubleday, Page & Company, New York, 1902

Jenkinson, I., *Aaron Burr: His Personal and Political Relations with Thomas Jefferson and Alexander Hamilton*, M. Cullaton & Company, Richmond, Indiana, 1902

Jennings, Paul, *A Colored Man's Reminiscences of James Madison*, G. C. Beadle, Brooklyn, 1865. Jennings was Madison's body servant and slave.

Jervey, Theodore D., *Robert Y. Hayne and His Times*, Macmillan Company, New York, 1909. Hayne was U.S. Senator from South Carolina.

Johnson, A., and Corwin, E. S., *The Age of Jefferson and Marshall*, Yale University Press, New Haven, 1921 (Chronicles of America Series)

Jones, H. M., *America and French Culture, 1750-1845*, University of North Carolina Press, Chapel Hill, 1927

La Rochefoucault Liancourt, Duc de, *Travels through the United States of North America . . . in the Years 1795, 1796, and 1797*, 2 vols., R. Phillips, London, 1799. Pp. 69-84 in Vol. 2 are devoted to Jefferson.

Lerner, M., "John Marshall and the Campaign of History," *Columbia Law Review*, Vol. XXXIX (1939), No. 3

Levasseur, A., *Lafayette in America in 1824 and 1825*, 2 vols., Carey & Lea, Philadelphia, 1829

Maclay, William, *Journal of William Maclay, United States Senator from Pennsylvania, 1789-1791*, ed. by Edgar S. Maclay, D. Appleton & Company, New York, 1890

McMaster, J. B., *A History of the People of the United States*, Vols. I-III, D. Appleton & Company, New York, 1885

MacNaul, W. C., *The Jefferson-Lemen Compact*, University of Chicago Press, Chicago, 1915

Madison, James, *Letters and Other Writings of James Madison . . . Published by Order of Congress*, 4 vols., J. B. Lippincott & Company, Philadelphia, 1865

—— *The Writings of James Madison*, ed. by Gaillard Hunt, 9 vols., G. P. Putnam's Sons, New York, 1910

Matthews, A., "Thomas Paine and the Declaration of Independence," *Massachusetts Historical Society Proceedings*, Vol. XLIII (1910), pp. 241-53. Refutes the claim of the Paine authorship.

Mehaffey, J. C., "Early History of the White House," *Military Engineer*, May-June, 1928

Melbourn, Julius, *Life and Opinions of Julius Melbourn*, ed. by J. B. Hammond, Hall & Dickson, Syracuse, 1847

Mesick, J. L., *The English Traveller in America, 1785-1835*, Columbia University Press, New York, 1922

Miller, E. J., "The Virginia Committee of Correspondence," *William and Mary Quarterly*, Vol. XXII (1914), pp. 93-113

Monroe, James, *The Writings of James Monroe*, ed. by S. M. Hamilton, 7 vols., G. P. Putnam's Sons, 1898-1903

Montlezun, Baron de, *Voyage fait dans les années 1816 et 1817, de New York à la Nouvelle Orléans, et de l'Orénoque au Mississippi*, 2 vols., Gide fils, Paris, 1818

Morgan, George, *The Life of James Monroe*, Small, Maynard & Company, Boston, 1921

Morison, S. E., *The Life and Letters of Harrison Gray Otis, Federalist, 1765-1848*, 2 vols., Houghton Mifflin Company, Boston, 1913

Mott, R. J., "Sources of Jefferson's Ecclesiastical Views," *Church History*, Vol. III (1934), pp. 267-84

Old South Leaflets, Boston: No. 127: *The Ordinance of 1784*; No. 128: *The Cession of Louisiana.*

Parrington, V. L., *Main Currents in American Thought*, 2 vols. Harcourt, Brace and Company, New York, 1927; Vol. 1

—— ed., *The Connecticut Wits*, Harcourt, Brace and Company, New York, 1926.

Philips, Edith, *Louis Hue Girardin and Nicholas Gouin Dufief and Their Relations with Jefferson*, Johns Hopkins Press, Paris, 1926 (Johns Hopkins Studies in Romance Literatures and Languages, Extra Vol. 3). This is based upon Jefferson letters in the Library of Congress.

Plumer, William Jr., *Life of William Plumer*, ed. by A. P. Peabody, Boston, Phillips, Sampson & Co., 1857

Rhodes, T. L., *The Story of Monticello, as Told by Thomas L. Rhodes, (40 Years Superintendent of Monticello) to Frank B. Lord*, American Publishing Company, Washington, D.C., 1928

Rowland, Kate Mason, *The Life of George Mason, 1725-1792*, 2 vols., G. P. Putnam's Sons, New York, 1892

Schouler, J., *Americans of 1776*, New York, Dodd, Mead and Company, 1906

—— "The Authorship of the Monroe Doctrine," American Historical Association, *Annual Report*, Vol. I (1905), pp. 125-31

—— *History of the United States of America under the Constitution*, 3 vols., W. H. Morrison, Washington, D.C., 1894; Vol. II. This is one of the few pro-Jefferson academic histories.

Sherrill, C. H., *French Memories of Eighteenth-Century America*, New York, Charles Scribner's Sons, 1915

Smith, Mrs. Samuel H., *The First Forty Years of Washington Society*, Charles Scribner's Sons, New York, 1906

Stanwood, E., *History of Presidential Elections*, J. R. Osgood & Co., Boston, 1884

Stevens, J. A., *Albert Gallatin*, Houghton Mifflin Company, Boston, 1890

Stockton, F. R., "The Later Years of Monticello," *Century Magazine*, Vol. XXIV (1887), pp. 654-58

Sullivan, William, *Familiar Letters on Public Characters, and Public Events, from the Peace of 1783 to the Peace of 1815*, Russel, Odiorne, and Metcalf, Boston, 1834. An all-out criticism of Jefferson.

Ticknor, George, *Life, Letters and Journals of George Ticknor*, ed. by G. S. Hillard, 2 vols., J. H. Osgood and Company, Boston, 1876. Vol. I contains some excellent materials on Jefferson.

Trent, W. P., "Thomas Jefferson," in his *Southern Statesmen of the Old Regime*, T. Y. Crowell & Company, New York, 1897, pp. 49-86

Trumbull, John, *Autobiography, Reminiscences and Letters*, B. L. Hamlen, New Haven, 1841. Tells of a visit to Monticello.

Turner, F. J., *Correspondence of the French Ministers to the United States, 1791-1797*, American Historical Association, *Annual Report*, 1903, Vol. II.

Tyler, M. C., *Patrick Henry*, Houghton Mifflin Company, Boston, 1887

Van der Weyde, W. M., *Who Wrote the Declaration of Independence?* Thomas Paine Historical Association, New York, 1911. A short publication full of nonsense. The author claims that Tom Paine wrote the Declaration.

Vossler, O., *Die amerikanischen Revolutionsideale in ihrem Verhältnis zu den Europäischen; Untersucht an Thomas Jefferson, Historische Zeitschrift*, Beiheft 17, 1929

Walther, Daniel, *Gouverneur Morris, Witness of Two Revolutions*, Funk & Wagnalls Company, New York, 1934

Wandell, S. H., *Aaron Burr in Literature; Books, Pamphlets, Periodicals, and Miscellany Relating to Aaron Burr and His Leading Political Contemporaries*, K. Paul Trench, Trübner Co., London, 1936

—— and Minnigerode, Meade, *Aaron Burr: A Biography Written, in Large Part, from Original and Hitherto Unused Material*, 2 vols., G. Putnam's Sons, New York, 1927. This is unrestrainedly hostile to Jefferson.

Washington, George, *The Writings of George Washington*, ed. by W. C. Ford, 14 vols., G. P. Putnam's Sons, New York, 1889-93

Washington, City and Capital, Government Printing Office, Washington, D.C., 1937 (W.P.A. American Guide Series)

Webster, Daniel, "Memorandum of Mr. Jefferson's Conversations [1824]" in *The Private Correspondence of Daniel Webster*, Little, Brown and Company, Boston, 1857, pp. 364-73

Weld, Isaac, *Travels through the States of North America, and the Provinces of Upper and Lower Canada during . . . 1795, 1796, 1797*, J. Stockdale, London, 1807. Vol. I, pp. 193-209, deals with Jefferson.

Wertenbaker, T. J., *Patrician and Plebeian in Virginia, or the Origin and Development of the Social Classes of the Old Dominion*, privately printed, Charlottesville, Va., 1910

Wharton, A. H., *Salons Colonial and Republican*, J. B. Lippincott & Company, Philadelphia, 1900. Pages 175-89 have some stuff on Jefferson.

Wirt, William, *Sketches of the Life and Character of Patrick Henry*, 10th ed., S. Andrus & Son, Hartford, 1849. A well-known book of little value; it was severely criticized by Jefferson.

Woodfin, M. H., "Contemporary Opinion in Virginia of Thomas Jefferson," in *Essays in Honor of William E. Dodd*, University of Chicago Press, Chicago, 1935, pp. 30-83

Woods, E., *Albemarle County in Virginia*, Michie Co., Charlottesville, Va., 1901

CONTEMPORARY NEWSPAPERS

Columbian Centinel and Massachusetts Federalist, Boston, 1800. Published Wednesdays and Fridays. 4-page issue.

Niles' Weekly Register, Baltimore, 1826

The Norfolk (Va.) *Herald*, January-December, 1800. Published Thursdays, Saturdays, and Tuesdays.

Republican Advocate (Frederick, Md.), December 1802-November, 1805, This was a Jefferson party paper.

Virginia Herald (Fredericksburg, Va.), January 1799-December 1800. Published Tuesdays and Fridays. 4-page issue. This was an anti-Jefferson paper.

The Washington Gazette, June 1796-December 1797. Published Saturdays and Wednesdays. 4-page issue.

Index

Adams, Abigail (Mrs. John), 126;
  Adams to, 246, 248; T. J. to,
  135, 290, 300n, 326, 372, 409
Adams, Henry, 186, 253, 275
Adams, John, 42, 44, 46, 52, 53,
  61-62, 84, 115, 121, 124, 139,
  149, 167, 178, 183n, 186-87, 196-
  99, 213, 240, 257-60, 265, 274-
  75, 277, 280, 290, 303, 326, 344,
  367-72, 383, 406, 418, 421-22;
  President, 243-63, 269, 278, 281-
  85, 291, 299-301, 322-24, 331-32;
  on T. J., 51, 132n, 367, 421; to
  T. J., 367-72; T. J. on, 254; T. J.
  to, 6, 167, 232, 241, 368-72
Adams, John Quincy, 267, 313
Adams, Samuel, 44, 288, 343; T. J.
  to, 295
Adet, P. A., 224n, 249n
Aesop, 155
Africa, 234, 382n
Agriculture, 110, 133-34, 142, 147-
  49, 160, 232-36, 293, 365-66,
  375-77, 379-80
Albemarle County, Va., 4-5, 38, 43,
  89n, 100-01, 359, 398
Alexander I, Czar, 383
Alexandria, Va., 175, 246
Alien Act (1798), 257
Alsop, Richard, 252
Ambler, Jacquelin, 20
American: Citizen, 336; *Minerva*,
  239, 267
American Revolution (1776-81), 86-
  104, 161, 223n, 257, 419; treaty
  of peace (1783), 112, 115
Ames, Fisher, 178, 276
Amsterdam, 149-50
Anderson, Robert, *From Slavery to
  Affluence*, 172n
Annapolis, Md., 43, 116-18, 124
Architecture, T. J. and, 26, 143-45,
  365, 399

Aristocracy, T. J. attacks, 71-72
Aristotle, 128n
Arkansas, 314
Arnold, Gen. Benedict, 93-94, 99
Assembly of Notables, France, 152
Assumption Bill (1790), 188-89, 193,
  205
Aurora (Philadelphia), 195, 336
Austin, Benjamin, 267; T. J. to,
  377-78
Austria, 390

Bache, Benjamin Franklin, 195, 227
Bacon, Edward, 111
Bacon, Sir Francis, 107, 181, 188,
  383
Baltimore, Md., 113-15, 294, 305,
  326, 328, 416
Bancroft, Edward, T. J. to, 233
Banister, Col. John, 100
Bankhead, Anne, 405
Banneker, Benjamin, 234; T. J. to,
  382n
Barbé-Marbois, Marquis de, 107,
  320; T. J. to, 119-20
Barlow, Joel, 208
Barnave, Joseph, 166
Barnes, J. (consul), to T. J., 352
Barron, Commodore James, 348-49
Bayard, James A., Hamilton to, 281
Beccaria, Cesare de, 17n
Beckley, John James, 272-73
Bellini, Professor, T. J. to, 137-38
Belinda. *See* Burwell, Rebecca.
Berlin, 155
Bernard, John, T. J. to, 25
Bill of Rights, 157-58, 161, 178,
  207, 259, 261, 264
Bishop, Samuel, 301-02
Blättermann, George, 402
Blair, John, 17
Bland, John, 42
Bland, Col. Theodorick, 98

449

Bloodworth, Timothy, 266
Bonnycastle, Charles, 402
Boston, Mass., 36 (Tea Party), 121, 267, 276, 285, 288, 295, 353, 406, 416n
Boston Gazette, 336
Bowdoin, James, 126
Bowers, Claude, quoted, 264
Bradford, Samuel F., 267
Bradford, William, Madison to, 32
Brazil, 390
Bréhan, Mme de, T. J. to, 162
Bryant, William Cullen, 354-55
Buffon, Count George Louis Leclerc de, 125
Burgoyne, Gen. John, 89n
Burke, Edmund, 41
Burr, Aaron, 199, 241, 243, 269, 279-85, 291, 327, 341-42, 345-47
Burwell (servant), 417
Burwell, Lewis, 16, 19
Burwell, Rebecca (Belinda), 16, 19-21, 28

Cabell, Joseph C., T. J. to, 23, 397, 403
Cabot, George, 179
Caesar, Julius, 188
Callender, James Thomson, 256, 260, 269, 278-79, 326-27
Calvin, John, 371, 393-94
Camden, Battle of, 92
Camm, Rev. John, 12
Campan, Mme de, 219
Canada, 353
Canning, George, 353-54, 390-01
Carey, Mathew, T. J. to, 394
Carr, Dabney, 34; wife of, 111
Carr, Peter, T. J. to, 15, 396
Carroll, Charles, 368n, 418
Cartwright, John, T. J. to, 379, 382n
Cary, Archibald, 34n, 112
Cathalan, S., T. J. to, 373-74
Catherine II, of Russia, 125, 219
Cervantes, Miguel de, 14, 120, 190, 393
Champion de Cicé, Jean-Marie, abp., to T. J., 165-66
Charleston, S. C., 278

Charlottesville, Va., 5, 95-97, 365n, 374, 398-403, 412
Chase, Justice Samuel, 260, 326-28
Chastellux, Marquis F. J. de, 106-07; T. J. to, 112-13
Château Thierry, 151
Chesapeake, attacked, 348-49
Chesterfield, Lord, quoted, 31
China, 133, 386
Chinard, Gilbert, 17n, 35
Christianity. *See* Religion.
Church, Mrs. Catherine, T. J. to, 229, 296
Cicero, 14, 166
Clark, Gen. George Rogers, T. J. to, 89-90
Clark, Jonas, 301
Clay, Henry, 82-83
Cleopatra, 383
Clinton, De Witt, 272
Clinton, George, 199, 213, 266, 341
Clymer, George, 368n
Cobbett, William, 267
Coinage, T. J. reforms, 117
Coke, Sir Edward, 18, 19, 397
Cologne, Germany, 150
Colorado, 314
Columbian Centinel, 276-78, 285
Columbus, Christopher, 383
Committee of Correspondence, 34-35
Condorcet, Antoine-Nicolas de, 219
Connecticut, 53, 80n, 252, 285n, 301-03, 305, 344
Constitution, U. S., 152, 154, 178-79, 325-26; Hamilton and the, 210; T. J. and the, 156-61, 175, 202, 206-07, 211, 225, 249, 261, 277-78, 291, 297, 302, 318, 323, 325-26, 378-79, 384, 386-88
Cooper, Thomas, 256, 260, 269, 326, 402; T. J. to, 17-18, 330
Cornwallis, Lord Charles, 94-95, 99, 104
Cosway, Maria Cecilia, 140-42, 410
Cosway, Richard, 140
Coutts, Rev. Mr., 29
Crawford, William H., T. J. to, 409n
Currie, James, T. J. to, 129

Dakota, North and South, 314
Dalrymple, Sir John, 35

Dandridge, Nathan, 9
Danton, Georges Jacques, 251
Dauphiné, France, 144-45
Dawson, Rev. Thomas, 11
Dearborn, Gen. Henry, 304-05
Declaration of Independence, 39, 45, 52-64, 234, 264, 277-78, 367-68, 374, 416, 418, 420-21; ref. to, 13, 17, 75, 77, 84, 126, 139, 153, 192, 285, 362, 374, 416
DeKalb, Gen. John, 91
Delaware, 63, 80n, 245, 285n, 344, 368n
Democracy, 257, 302; Adams and, 196, 248, 253; Hamilton and, 178, 184-86, 194; T. J. and, 66-67, 75, 97-98, 109, 154-55, 159-60, 175-79, 184-86, 192, 212, 215-16, 254, 258, 261-65, 268, 274-76, 284, 287-88, 304, 311, 325-33, 344, 369, 385, 397, 412, 414-15
Democratic party, 199. See also Republican party.
Dennie, Joseph, 268, 276
Despotism, 77, 155, 159, 261, 312, 326, 391
Dickinson, John, 45-46, 52, 64; T. J. to, 288, 299, 357
Dictatorship, T. J. on, 98
Digges, Dudley, 34n
Diplomats, T. J. and, 192-93, 313
Douglas, Rev. William, 7
Dryden, John, 14, 336
Duane, William, 269
Dugnani, Count, T. J. to, 362, 374
Dunbar, William, T. J. to, 317n
Dunglison, Dr. Robley, 402, 420
Dunmore, John Murray, Earl of, 35, 38, 50, 359n
Du Pont de Nemours, Pierre Samuel, 256, 279; T. J. to, 300, 316-17, 336, 358
Dupont, Adrien, 166
Dwight, Theodore, 302
Dwight, Timothy, 252, 302

Eaton, Gen. William, 346
Education, 74-76, 109, 160, 395-403
Ellery, William, 368n
Embargo, 310; Act (1807), 352-58, 366, 376

England, 13, 36, 38, 48-53, 60n, 219-20, 222-23, 227, 251, 319, 347-53, 373-74, 390-91; T. J. in, 139-40, 168; T. J. on, 39-41, 45-49, 58-60, 66-67, 159-60, 187, 206, 215, 242, 277, 308-09, 315-16, 321, 349-50, 354, 368, 375, 377, 391, 401. See also American Revolution.
Eppes, Francis, 131, 417; T. J. to, 407; wife of, 113
Eppes, John W., T. J. to, 269, 385, 411; wife of, see Jefferson, Mary.
Estates General, France, 162-65
Euclid, 368
Europe, 49, 219, 250, 348, 352, 357; T. J. on, 39, 108, 110, 122, 133-38, 142, 154-55, 158, 160, 163, 167, 175, 207, 216, 249, 263, 269, 311-13, 354, 373, 376, 390-91, 412

Farmer's Weekly Museum, 268
Fauquier, Francis, 11, 13-14, 16, 85
Federalists, 192, 194, 198, 213, 226, 237, 239-40, 243, 251, 254-58, 261-62, 264, 267, 270, 275-78, 279, 280-85, 291-92, 297, 299-302, 322-23, 327-30, 340-41, 343, 345, 349
Fenno, John, 195-97, 201, 202n, 208
Fenno, John Ward, 268
Fielding, Henry, 14
Florence, Italy, 148
Florida, 220, 314-15, 317-19, 353
Floyd, William, 368n
Fosset, Joe, 417
Foster, Sir Augustus, 305-06; on T. J., 334-35, 339
France, 52, 66, 78, 87, 104, 122, 174-77, 206, 214, 215, 219-27, 249, 251, 253, 255, 315-21, 338n, 347, 350-51, 353, 368, 374, 390; T. J. in, 122-47, 152-67; T. J. on, 159-60, 168, 315-16
Franklin, Benjamin, 46, 53, 61-63, 66, 118, 121, 123, 124, 128, 131-32, 176, 240, 254, 296, 383
Franks, Maj. David, 114
Fredericksburg, Va., 43, 72, 278

Freedom of the press, 157, 165, 207, 293, 329-31, 345; of religion, *see* Religious freedom.

French Revolution, 152-54, 161-67, 174-75, 177, 214-15, 219-20, 237, 250-51, 253, 257, 263, 308, 329n

Freneau, Philip Morin, 196-98, 200-02, 205, 207-08, 227-28, 269

Fry, Joshua, 4

Galileo, Galilei, 78

Gallatin, Albert, 256, 266, 283, 304, 306-10, 352-53; T. J. to, 300-01, 308-10, 318

Garretson, Rev. Mr., 270

Gaspee burned, 33

Gates, Gen. Horatio, 88-89, 92

Gazette of the United States, 195-96, 201, 202n, 268

General Advertiser, Phila., 195

Genet, Edmond Charles, 219-28, 251

Genoa, 148-49

George III, 18, 33, 35, 37, 39-40, 43, 46-49, 56-58, 139, 153, 179, 333

Georgia, 58n, 80n, 213n, 243, 265, 266, 285n, 290, 395

Germans, 312

Germany, T. J. in, 150-51

Gerry, Elbridge, 368n; T. J. to, 262-63

Gibbon, Edward, 145, 191

Gilmer, Francis Walker, 401

Goethe, Johann Wolfgang, 362

Goodrich, Elizur, 301-02

Graham, Rev. Richard, 12

Granger, Gideon, 303-05; T. J. to, 386

Grasse, Admiral François Joseph de, 104

Gray, Francis Calley, 404

Great Britain. *See* England.

Greene, Gen. Nathanael, 89

Grégoire, Abbé Baptiste-Henri, T. J. to, 382n

Grignon, Baron de, 125

Grimm, Baron Frédéric de, 125

Grotius, Hugo, 224

Hall, David, T. J. to, 311

Hamilton, Alexander, 178-79, 183-89, 192-228 *passim*, 231, 238-41, 248, 250, 255, 258, 265, 276, 280-81, 285, 306, 310, 327; death of, 327, 342-43; wife of, 184

Harrison, Benjamin, 34n, 42, 46

Hartley, David, T. J. to, 154

Harvey, John, T. J. to, 8-9

Haswell, Anthony, 259-60

Hatch, Rev. Mr., 419

Hawkins, Benjamin, T. J. to, 154

Hay, George, 260

Helvetius, Claude Adrien, 35

Hemings, John, 417

Henry, Patrick, 9-10, 18, 24, 34, 36-38, 41-42, 45-46, 69, 82, 84, 88, 89n, 97, 192, 198, 265; T. J. on, 10, 18

Hertz, Emanuel, quoted, 253-54n

Holland, 313; T. J. in, 149-50

Holy Alliance, 390

Homer, 7, 18, 111n, 336

Hone, Philip, 416n

Hopkinson, Francis, T. J. to, 101, 254-55

Horace, 372

Houdetôt, Elizabeth, Mme d', 125

Houdon, Jean Antoine, 180

Howe, Gen. William, 48

Humboldt, Alexander von, 331; T. J. to, 370n

Hume, David, 382

Immigration, 105, 311-12, 321

Indians, 5-6, 12, 89, 108-09, 155, 314

Industrialization, T. J. on, 134, 140, 142-43, 365, 375-80

Iowa, 314

Irish, 256

Irving, Washington, 306

Italy, 352; T. J. in, 144, 147-49

Italians, 105, 312, 399

Jackson, Gen. Andrew, 346, 374, 413n

Jackson, James, 266-67

Jarvis, William, 126

Jay, John, 179, 251; Treaty of (1794), 238-39, 251; T. J. to, 134, 376

Jefferson, Jane Randolph (Mrs. Peter), 3-8; death of, 50

Jefferson, Lucy, 110, 112, 129

Jefferson, Mary (Maria, Polly; Mrs. John W. Eppes), 112, 130-31, 190-91, 284, 407; death of, 342, 420n

Jefferson, Martha. *See* Randolph, Martha Jefferson.

Jefferson, Martha Wayles Skelton (Mrs. Thomas), 21, 28-31, 65-66, 89n, 166; death of, 110-11, 420n

Jefferson, Peter, 3-8, 16, 21, 39, 47, 68, 266, 406; death of, 9

Jefferson, Randolph, 8n

Jefferson, Thomas, chronology of: ancestry and parentage, 3-6; education, 7-14; at Williamsburg, 9-21; first love, 19-20; lawyer, 23-25; builds Monticello, 26-27; marriage, 28-30; member of the Virginia House of Burgesses, 32-38; member of the Committee of Correspondence, 34-35; member of the Second Continental Congress, 43-46, 50-65; writes the Declaration of Independence, 51-62; member of the Virginia General Assembly, 68-83; revises the Virginia code, 72-74; Governor of Virginia, 85-103; at Monticello, 104-06; loses his wife, 110-11; appointed to peace conference, but unable to sail, 112-15; member of the Annapolis Congress, 116-17; Plenipotentiary and Minister to France, 121-67; falls in love, 140-42; Secretary of State, 169-230; at Monticello, 231-42; nominated for the Presidency, 243-45; Vice-President, 245-85; President, 287-358 (re-election, 341-42); at Monticello, 361-420; creates the University of Virginia, 397-403; sinks into debt, 403-05; saved from bankruptcy, 414-17; makes his will, 417; last illness and death, 419-20; inscription on his tombstone, 421-22

Jefferson, Thomas, Governor of Virginia, 85-103; difficulties in wartime, 88-95; nearly captured by the British, 95-97; opposes dictatorship, 97-98; his impeachment attempted, 98-99; his vindication, 100-01

Jefferson, Thomas, Plenipotentiary and Minister, 121-67; consular duties of, 132-34; critical opinions of France, 135-38; visit to England, 139-40; travel in Europe, 142-51; advises French revolutionists, 153-54; observes the French Revolution, 161-67

Jefferson, Thomas, Secretary of State, 169-230; creates consular service, 192-93; Cabinet conflict on the French Revolution, 214-17; wishes to retire, 217-18; the Genet affair, 219-27; resigns, 229-30

Jefferson, Thomas, Vice-President, 243-85; relations with President Adams, 248-50, 283; Alien and Sedition acts, 257-60; draws up the Kentucky Resolution, 261-62; candidate for the Presidency, 262-85

Jefferson, Thomas, President, 287-360; inaugurated, 290-94; the problem of officeholders, 299-302, 304; Cabinet, 304-07; financial policies, 308-10; foreign policy, 311-12; Louisiana Purchase, 313-22; conflict with the judiciary, 322-28; hostility of the Federalist press, 329-31; introduces democratic manners into the President's House, 331-34; dinner parties, 337-41; re-elected, 341-42; Burr's intrigue, 345-47; trouble with Napoleon and the British, 347-51; the Embargo, 352-58; refuses a third term, 355-57; retires, 358-60

Jefferson, Thomas: abilities and character, 14-17, 47, 51, 86, 88, 102, 106-07, 265-66, 296-97, 361-65; books and reading, 7, 14, 17-18, 25, 27, 35-36, 128, 238, 336-37, 404, 409-12, 418; children, 30,

66, 106, 110, 112, 118-20, 129-31, 189-91; grandchildren, 405n, 406-08; great-grandchildren, 406; correspondence, 237, 379-84, 409, and *passim*; farming, 231-36, 365-66, 404; income and expenses, 25, 124, 174, 190-91, 232, 341, 404-05, 414-16; opinions on, 22, 44, 51, 86, 101-02, 106-07, 132n, 180, 281, 331, 413, 421-22; personal appearance, 10, 15, 44, 106, 180-81, 247, 290, 296, 333-35, 339, 363, 381, 398-99, 413; political attitudes of, 18, 31-39, 47-48, 66-68, 71-72, 177-79, 238-40, 243, *see also* Democracy; retirement from political life longed for, 48, 101-05, 169, 208-09, 228-29, 236-38, 241, 357

Jefferson, Thomas, writings of: *Anas*, 209; *Autobiography*, 411; *Commonplace Book*, 17-18; Declaration of Independence, 51-62; *Memoranda* (on travels), 144; *Notes on Virginia*, 107-08; *A Summary View of the Rights of British America*, 38-39

"Jefferson and Liberty," 279-80, 289-90

Jews, 82, 395

Job, Book of, quoted, 273

John Bull, 421-22

Jones, Rev. Emanuel, 11

Jones, John Paul, 126, 383

Jones, Gen. Joseph, 86

Jones, Dr. Walter, T. J. to, 298

Jouett, Capt. John, 95-96

Judah, Samuel, T. J. to, 410

Judiciary, T. J. and the, 322-28, 384-87

Kames, Henry Horne, Lord, 35-36

Kansas, 314

Key, Thomas Hewitt, 402

Kentucky, 213n, 262, 285n

Kentucky Resolution, 261-62

Kercheval, Samuel, T. J. to, 309

King, Rufus, 239, 313, 343

Knox, Gen. Henry, 179, 223

Lafayette, Marquis de, 89, 104, 124-26, 132, 152-53, 163-66, 383, 412-13; Madison to, 331, 414n; T. J. to, 108, 146, 177, 389

La Meth, Alexandre, 166

Langdon, John, T. J. to, 187n

Languedoc, 145, 149

Lawyers and their ways, T. J. on, 23-24, 73-74, 117-18

Lee, Arthur, 16

Lee, Charles, 49

Lee, Francis L., 34, 36-37

Lee, Gen. Henry, 196

Lee, Henry, 419

Lee, Richard Bland, 188

Lee, Richard Henry, 34, 36-37, 42, 46, 51-52, 63-64; T. J. to, 105n

Lee, Thomas L., 72-73

Leonardo da Vinci, 148

Le Sage, Alain René, 14, 120

Letombe (consul), T. J. to, 254

Lewis, Warner, 16

Lexington, Battle of, 43

Library of Congress, 404

Library, public, 74

Lincoln, Abraham, 63n, 252n, 265-66, 275, 291, 304n

Lincoln, Levi, 304-05

Linn, William, 270-71

Livingston, Robert R., 52-53, 266, 313, 317-21; T. J. to, 115, 315

Locke, John, 35, 55, 181, 188, 383

Lomax, John Tayloe, 402

London, Eng., 143, 155, 313, 348; T. J. in, 139-40

Long, George, 402

Louis XVI, 66, 87, 122, 135, 152-53, 162-65, 179, 219-21

Louisiana, 220, 314; Territory, 310, 314-22, 344

Luzerne, Chevalier de la, 126

Lyon, Matthew, 258-60

Lyon, France, 144, 162

McGregory, Uriah, T. J. to, 273-74

McKean, Sally (Señora Yrujo), 333-34

McKean, Thomas, 266, 279, 368n

Maclay, Senator William, 178, 180, 194

McLeod, Captain, 96-97
Macon, Nathaniel, T. J. to, 339
Madison, Dolly (Mrs. James), 306, 333, 358-59
Madison, James, 8n, 31-32, 70, 73-74, 79-80, 86, 101, 112, 154, 156, 172-74, 179, 191, 196-99, 201, 203, 212-13, 226, 239, 241, 248-49, 261-62, 266, 269, 276, 304-06, 324-26, 332-33, 340, 342, 348n, 358-59, 372, 383, 390, 398, 412, 414n, 417, 422; T. J. to, 20n, 114, 153n, 157, 223, 225-29, 237, 239, 244-46, 267, 373, 414-15; on T. J., 101-02, 203, 331, 411, 414, 422; to T. J., 88, 226-27, 414n
Madison, Rev. James, T. J. to, 136-37
Madrid, 155
Maine, 265, 305
Malthus, Thomas Robert, 321n
Marbois. See Barbé-Marbois.
Marbury vs. Madison, 324-25
Marie Antoinette, 219
Marmontel, Jean François, 14, 125-26
Marseille, France, 146, 149, 373
Marsh, Amos, T. J. to, 297
Marshall, John, 258, 284, 291, 322-25, 346, 386
Martin, James, T. J. to, 356
Marx, Joseph, T. J. to, 395
Maryland, 44, 80n, 213n, 283, 285n, 305, 326, 368n
Mason, George, 37, 70, 72-73, 156n; T. J. to, 216
Mason, John Mitchell, 271n
Massachusetts, 34n, 36-37, 53, 80n, 159, 194, 243-44, 267, 285n, 305, 343-44, 367, 368n, 421
Maury, Rev. Mr., 7
Mazzei, Philip, T. J. to, 105n, 241-42
Melbourn, Julius, 381-82
Merry, Anthony, 332-34, 338n, 346; wife of, 332-34
Michelangelo, 148
Michigan, 322

Milton, John, 14, 55, 336
Minnesota, 314
Missouri, 314
Monarchy, desire for, 175, 177-78, 181, 186-87, 196, 200, 207-08, 210, 212, 218
Monroe, James, 86, 102, 116, 241, 266, 299, 316, 318-21, 365, 383, 392, 398, 412; T. J. to, 122, 124, 127, 134-35, 222-23, 225, 243, 283, 298, 333, 350, 357, 390-91; to T. J., 299; Madison to, 348n
Monroe Doctrine, 316, 390-92
Montana, 314
Montesquieu, Charles de Secondat, Baron de, 14, 17n, 159, 288, 382
Monticello, 26-27, 29-31, 35, 95-97, 104-06, 112, 115, 169-72, 174, 191, 231, 237-38, 246, 269, 278-79, 307, 342, 358-59, 361, 363, 369, 372, 380-83, 398-99, 403-05, 412, 414-15, 421
Montlezun, Baron de, 382-83
Montmorin, Armand Marc, Comte de, 166-67
Moor, Jeremiah, T. J. to, 278n
Moore, Thomas, 295, 334
Morris, Gouverneur, 163-64, 178-79, 185, 226n, 281, 290
Motta, Rabbi De La, T. J. to, 395
Mounier, Jean-Joseph, 166
Muhlenberg, Frederic A. C., 213n
Muhlenberg, Gen. John Peter Gabriel, 89
Murray, William (Minister), 313
Music, T. J. and, 105

Napoleon I, 161n, 250, 308, 313-21, 347, 350-51, 354, 357, 372-74, 383
National Assembly, France, 165-66
National Gazette, 197, 200-01, 227-28
National Intelligencer, 363
Nebraska, 314
Necker, Mme Jacques, 125
Negroes, T. J. on, 233-34, 406
Nelson, Gen. Thomas, 84-85, 89, 93, 99

New England, 121, 256, 259-60, 268, 270, 274, 301, 304-05, 352, 354, 358, 406
New Hampshire, 80n, 160, 268, 285n, 305, 335
New Haven, Conn., 301-02
New Jersey, 80n, 285n, 342
New Orleans, 314-19, 346, 353, 374
Newton, Sir Isaac, 14, 78, 108, 181, 188, 368, 383
New York City, 167, 171-74, 199, 239, 270, 276, 320n, 348, 353, 416; T. J. in, 176-91
New York Daily Advertiser, 337
New York State, 48, 53, 80n, 95, 194, 241, 266, 285n, 342, 352, 368n; T. J. in, 198-99
Nicholas, George, 98-100, 261
Nicholas, Robert Carter, 24-25, 34n, 37
Nicholas, Thomas, 260
Nicholas, Wilson Cary, 405
Nicholson, Joseph H., 283; T. J. to, 327
Niles, Nathaniel, T. J. to, 288
Nîmes, France, 145
Norfolk, Va., 50, 353; T. J. in, 168-69
North, Frederick, Lord, 46
North Carolina, 50, 80n, 90-91, 199, 213n, 246, 266, 268, 285n, 355-56

Ohio, 343-44
Oklahoma, 314
Ossian, 11, 14, 106-07, 336

Padover, Saul K., 153n, 221n, 319n
Page, John, 84-85; T. J. to, 19-20, 26-27, 139-40, 342-43; to T. J., 20
Paine, Robert Treat, 368n
Paine, Thomas, 49-50, 184, 208, 268, 297n, 335-37
Paris, 122, 127, 169, 176, 313, 319; T. J. in, 108, 122-38, 140-44, 152-68, 410, 413; T. J. on, 146
Paris Moniteur, 242
Parker, C., T. J. to, 299n
Parr, Samuel, T. J. to, 401
Parton, James, 186
Partridge, Bellamy, 25n

Patterson, Robert, 259
Pendleton, Edmund, 24, 33, 34n, 42, 65, 71-74, 343
Pennsylvania, 48, 53, 63, 80n, 180, 245-46, 256, 285n, 305, 368n
Peter the Great, Czar, 149
Peters, Richard, 328
Philadelphia, 42-43, 66, 88, 123, 140, 152, 154, 156, 188, 191, 197, 202, 214, 218-22, 226n, 231, 235-37, 245-46, 254, 268, 274, 279, 405, 416; made national capital, 50; T. J. in, 44-46, 50-65, 113-15, 175-76, 191-230, 418
Pichon, Louis, and wife, 333
Pinckney, Charles C., 266, 343; T. J. to, 408-09
Pinckney, Thomas, 243, 280
Pitt, William (Lord Chatham), 13, 42
Pitt, William, the younger, 168
Plato, 14, 166, 298, 370
Plumer, William, 160, 335, 338, 340, 355
Poe, Edgar Allan, 403
Poland, 158-59
Political Observatory, 336
Political parties, T. J. on, 254-55
Pope, Alexander, 6, 14, 111n, 336
Portfolio, 276
Portugal, 313
Poussin, Nicolas, 383
Prescott, William H., Ticknor to, 411-12
Press, freedom of the. *See* Freedom.
Preston, Rev. William, 12
Price, Dr. Richard, T. J. to, 161-62
Priestley, Joseph, 256; T. J. to 287-88, 322, 370
Pringle, H. F., 25n
Prussia, 76, 150, 313, 390

Quakers, 233, 371, 392

Raleigh, Sir Walter, 383
Ramsay, Dr. David, T. J. to, 155
Randolph, Edmund, 156n, 180, 221, 223; Madison to, 101-02
Randolph, Isham, 4
Randolph, John, 174, 327, 341; T. J. to, 47-48, 349

Randolph, Martha Jefferson (Mrs. Thomas M.), 30, 48, 111-13, 118-22, 124, 129-30, 149, 172, 174, 189-90, 217-18, 229, 284, 366, 405-06, 419-20

Randoph, Peter, 9

Randolph, Peyton, 17, 24, 34n, 38, 41-44

Randolph, Thomas Jefferson, 23, 374, 379, 405-06, 412, 417, 420; T. J. to, 16-17, 340, 404, 415-16

Randolph, Thomas Mann, 174, 366, 405; T. J. to, 198, 229, 243

Randolph, William, 4

Raphael, 383

Reed, Walter, 403

Religion, T. J. and, 15, 77, 270-74, 370-71, 392-95

Religious freedom, T. J. on, 76-82, 157, 165, 207, 263, 274, 293, 395, 421

Republican Advocate, 323, 329

Republican (Democratic) party, 200, 213, 218, 228n, 237-38, 240-41, 243-46, 249, 254-55, 258, 264, 268, 279-85, 305, 327, 340, 342n, 343, 358, 361, 375n

Republicanism. *See* Democracy.

Revolution, T. J. on, 56, 155-56, 159-61, 217, 287, 308

Rhode Island, 80n, 285n, 368n

Richmond, Va., 145n, 175, 260, 299, 346, 365, 400, 416n; T. J. in, 86-95, 100

Ritchie, Thomas, T. J. to, 384-85

Rittenhouse, David, 208

Robespierre, Maximilien, 226n, 251

Roane, Spencer, T. J. to, 385

Robinson, Rev. Thomas, 12

Rochefoucault, Duc de La, 164

Rome, Italy, 145, 148

Roosevelt, Franklin D., 322

Rubens, Peter Paul, 383

Rush, Dr. Benjamin, 367, 368n, 410; T. J. to, 274, 364

Rush, Dr. Richard, T. J. to, 350

Russia, 219, 224, 386, 390   [216

Rutledge, Edward, 52; T. J. to, 155,

Sackville, Thomas, quoted, 337

San Ildefonso, Treaty of (1777), 314

Sandburg, Carl, quoted, 304n

Say, Jean Baptiste, T. J. to, 376-77

Schuyler, Gen. Philip, 184

Sedition Act (1798), 258-61, 323, 326

Shadwell, 3, 5, 9, 19, 26, 32, 172

Shakespeare, William, 6, 14, 140, 226, 336

Shays, Daniel (Rebellion), 159n

Sherman, Roger, 53

Shippen, Thomas Lee, 269

Short, William, T. J. to, 144, 146, 175, 216, 300, 311, 313, 357, 410

Slavery, 27; T. J. and, 67, 109, 172, 232-35, 412

Slodtz, M. S., 145

Small, Professor William, 12-14, 16-17

Smith, Professor (math.), 13

Smith, Rev. Cotton Mather, 273

Smith, Margaret Bayard, 363-64

Smith, Robert, 304-05

Smith, Samuel, 305

Smith, William (Minister), 313

Smith, William Laughton, 242

Smith, Col. William S., T. J. to, 155-56

Smollett, Tobias G., 14

Solon, 298

South America, 316, 388-92, 412

Southard, Samuel L., 421

South Carolina, 58n, 63, 80n, 155, 213n, 219, 266, 278-79, 285n, 343

Spain, 52, 76, 219, 314-16, 388-90

Spectator, 6

Staël, Mme de, 181; T. J. to, 349

States' rights, 261, 386-88

Sterne, Laurence, 14

Steuben, Gen. Frederick William von, 89, 93, 100

Stevens, Gen. Edward, T. J. to, 92

Stewart, Dugald, T. J. to, 401-02

Swift, Jonathan, 6

Tacitus, 368, 372

Taft, William Howard, 25n

Talleyrand, Charles Maurice de, 316, 318-20

Tammany Society, 199

Tariff, 378

Tarleton, Col. Sir Banastre, 95-97

Tasso, Torquato, 336

Taxation, 309, 341, 344
Taylor, John, 266; T. J. to, 356
Tennessee, 285n
Ternant, J. B. de, 219, 221
Tessé, Mme de, T. J. to, 145
Thacher, George, T. J. to, 394-95
Thompson, D. P., 399
Thomson, Charles, T. J. to, 393, 408
Thompson, J. W., and Padover, S. K., 319n
Thucydides, 368
Ticknor, George, 231, 380-81, 401, 411-12; T. J. to, 374, 395-96
Titian, 148
Toleration, T. J. on, 77-79
Toulouse, 149
Trenton True American, 336-37
Tripoli, 139, 351
Trist, Mrs. Elizabeth, T. J. to, 135, 238
Tucker, George, 402
Tucker, St. George, 86
Turgot, A. R. J., Baron de, 383
Turkey, 159
Turner, F. J., quoted, 250n
Turner, James, 355
Tyler, John, T. J. to, 330
Tyranny, 185, 289; T. J. on, 39, 49, 88, 109, 175-76, 232, 258, 261, 312

Utley, Dr. Vine, T. J. to, 409-10

Varnum, Gen. Joseph Bradley, 335
Vattel, Emmeric de, 224
Venice, 148
Vergennes, Charles Gravier, Count de, 132
Vermont, 258, 259, 285n, 323, 356
Vermont Gazette, 259
Versailles, 143-46, 152, 155, 162, 164, 165, 170, 176
Vespucius, Americus, 383
Vienna, 155
Villebrun, Chevalier de, 115
Virgil, 7
Virginia, 5-6, 8, 10, 13, 19, 20, 22, 24, 31, 37-38, 41-43, 50, 51, 53, 64-68, 76, 80n, 82, 83, 107-08, 129-30, 156, 188-89, 191, 199,

201, 205, 213n, 233, 236, 246, 260, 262, 270, 272, 276, 278, 279, 285n, 297n, 305, 326, 359, 399, 402, 412, 421; in the Revolution, 87-101; House of Burgesses and Assembly, 18, 32, 34-38, 68-86, 100-01, 116-18, 397-99
Virginia Gazette, 297n; *Herald*, 278
Virginia, University of, 365n, 382, 397-403, 417, 419, 421
Volney, Constantin François, Count de, T. J. to, 127n
Voltaire, 35, 137, 154, 383

War, T. J. on, 110; prisoners of, 89
Warden, D. B., T. J. to, 354
Washington, George, 38, 42, 49-50, 86-95, 104, 113-14, 118, 121, 132n, 152, 156n, 163, 167-78, 180-84, 191, 195, 203-13, 215, 218-30, 235, 238, 240, 242, 244, 247-50, 254, 258, 279, 304, 308, 331-32, 344, 355-56, 362, 383; T. J. on, 181-83
Washington, D.C., 43, 63n, 279, 284-85, 290, 295, 331-32, 334-35, 338-39, 374, 380, 383, 387, 404, 418; made national capital, 189; T. J. in, 279-359; 365
Washington Advertiser, 363
Washington Federalist, 285
Waterhouse, Dr. Benjamin, T. J. to, 393-94
Wayles, John, 28, 31
Weatherbourne, Henry, 4
Webster, Daniel, 302, 413
Webster, Ebenezer, quoted, 302
Webster, Noah, 239, 267-68
Weightman, Gen. Roger, T. J. to, 418
White, Alexander, 188
Whitney, Eli, 255
Whitworth, Lord, 319
Wilkinson, Gen. James, 346
William and Mary College, 4, 8, 74, 107n; T. J. at, 11-17
Williamsburg, Va., 6, 8-11, 14, 16-17, 22, 25, 28-29, 35-36, 38, 40-41, 43-44, 68, 74
Wilmington, Del., 43

Wilson, James, 35, 52
Wilson, Woodrow, 63, 403
Wirt, William, 260
Wolcott, Oliver, 179, 290
Wortman, Tunis, 271-72
Wyoming, 314
Wythe, George, 12-14, 16-17, 21-22, 24, 37, 52, 69-70, 72, 79, 154, 156n, 404n; T. J. to, 76, 148-49

Xenophon, 166

Yorktown, Va. (Cornwallis), 104
Yrujo, Marquis de, 333-34, 346; wife of, 333-34